WORKPLACE JUSTICE

Social Movements, Protest, and Contention

Series Editor: Bert Klandermans, Free University, Amsterdam

Associate Editors: Ron R. Aminzade, University of Minnesota
David S. Meyer, University of California, Irvine
Verta A. Taylor, University of California, Santa Barbara

WORKPLACE JUSTICE

Organizing Multi-Identity Movements

Sharon Kurtz

Social Movements, Protest, and Contention
Volume 15

University of Minnesota Press
Minneapolis • London

The University of Minnesota Press gratefully acknowledges permission to
reprint the following poetry in this book. Lines from "Heroines," from
The Fact of a Doorframe: Poems Selected and New, 1950–1984, by Adrienne Rich.
Copyright 1984 by Adrienne Rich. Copyright 1975, 1978 by W. W. Norton
and Company, Inc. Copyright 1981 by Adrienne Rich. Used by permission
of the author and W. W. Norton and Company, Inc. Excerpts from
Sister Outsider, by Audre Lorde, copyright 1984; reprinted by permission
of Crossing Press, Santa Cruz, California.

Published by the University of Minnesota Press
111 Third Avenue South, Suite 290
Minneapolis, MN 55401-2520
http://www.upress.umn.edu

Library of Congress Cataloging-in-Publication Data

Kurtz, Sharon
    Workplace justice : organizing multi-identity movements / Sharon
Kurtz.
        p.   cm. — (Social movements, protest, and contention ; v. 15)
    Includes bibliographical references and index.
    ISBN 0-8166-3314-2 (hardcover : alk. paper) — ISBN 0-8166-3315-0
(pbk. : alk. paper)
    1. Columbia University—Employees—Labor unions—Organizing.
2. Universities and colleges—Employees—Labor unions—Organizing—
New York (State)—New York. 3. Clerks—Labor unions—Organizing—
New York (State)—New York. 4. Group identity—Political aspects—
United States. I. Title. II. Series.
LD1226.5 .K87 2002
331.88'11'3781209747—dc21   2002006425

Printed in the United States of America on acid-free paper

The University of Minnesota is an equal-opportunity educator and employer.

12 11 10 09 08 07 06 05 04 03 02   10 9 8 7 6 5 4 3 2 1

To my daughter
Zoe Tong

Let us suppose that it is true that a . . . political movement with any hope of being heard and making change requires that a group speak in a single voice. . . . How, from the multiplicity of voices, will a single one be shaped?

—Elizabeth Spelman

If each of us chooses solely on the basis of color or race, then we are doomed. If each of us chooses to pretend that race and gender and class don't exist, or that somehow being American and being a part of this experiment in democracy exempts us from paying attention to those very real categories, or at least the reality that they manifest, then we are also doomed.

—John Edgar Wideman

Contents

Acknowledgments

It was many years before I understood the magnitude of the gifts appreciated in these pages at the beginning of books.

I begin with my thanks to the one thousand women and men of the Columbia clerical local for allowing me inside their union campaign for the year of their struggle. They represent the best spirit of the labor movement. For their openness, their willingness to explain their world as they saw it, for their insights and critique and sometimes their friendship, I am greatly indebted. My special thanks to Julie Kushner, Maida Rosenstein, June Benjamin, Mathew Jackson, Barbara O'Farrell, Raquel Perez, and John Stobo.

A community of life friends has been my company throughout this journey. Drawing on rich experience in labor, community, women's, and other progressive activism, each has generously offered me her thinking, wisdom, and challenges on issues of movements, diversity, and coalition work. Each has offered tireless support. My deep thanks to Erica Bronstein, Laura Foner, Cheryl Gooding, Julie Rosen, and Charlotte Ryan. Thanks, too, to Abby Rabinovitz, Mary Lenihan, and Tim Bornstein, other life friends who have sustained me with their thoughtfulness, insights, wisdom, and strategies for managing committed, creative, demanding work. Jo Shapiro has shared with me her skill and friendship and has come as close to saving my life as anyone has yet had to do. Together, they form an extended family without whom I would not have been able to carry out this project.

At Boston College, Bill Gamson, Eve Spangler, and Charlie Derber have created an engaged, supportive space for allowing the insights and challenges of social movement activism and sociological theory to interrogate and strengthen one another. Their individual work on movements, class, and labor and their enthusiastic belief in the importance of this project and the issues with which it grapples were critical in making the work possible for me. Julie Rosen, Charlotte Ryan, Cassie Schwerner, and Bill Hoynes were my touchstones—intellectually, politically, and personally—as I grappled with the issues of this project. David Meyer generously offered extensive, incisive critique of an earlier version of this work, as well as unflagging personal and professional support over the following years. Each of their work, along with that of my friends and colleagues David Croteau, Leslie Salzinger, and Pat Reeve (a historian), reminds me of the intellectual and political potential of good sociology and has helped me sharpen my own. Thanks also to Nancy Whittier, Ruth Milkman, and an anonymous reviewer of *Gender and Society* for invaluable critiques of earlier versions of my work.

At Suffolk University, thanks especially to my colleagues Alexandra Todd, Jim Ptacek, Carolyn Boyes-Watson, John Holley, Lori Rosenberg, and Janice Fama for their sociological insights, for critique of my work, for the inspiration of their own engaged scholarship, for picking up whatever tasks necessary to clear my writing space, and for their friendship and tireless encouragement. Thanks as well to Dean Michael Ronayne and the College of Arts and Science for the protected time of a faculty research grant.

Cynthia Peters became my critical writing companion over the last months of this project with her crucial editorial help, research support, political discourse, and insightful comments. She also generously offered extensive personal support, flexibility, optimism, and humor and in the process has become a greatly valued new friend. I appreciate Carrie Mullen at the University of Minnesota Press for her editorial support and boundless patience. Thanks to Julie Rosen, Tim McAndrew, and Tracy Rich, who have offered critical technical support. Thanks also to Cheryl Gooding for research support and intensive reading of chapter 7.

Many veteran labor activists generously offered me help in the early phase of this project with shaping the questions of this study and finding my way to the Columbia case: Erica Bronstein, Harneen Chernow, Marc Fromm, Cheryl Gooding, Eileen Haggerty, Carol Knox, Leslie Lomassen, Pat Reeve, Susan Winning, and Ferd Wulkin. Thanks also to Karen Jeffreys, an exceptionally talented organizer, for her enthusiasm and insights in the early stages of this project.

No single mother writes a book (or easily survives) without a community of what Patricia Hill Collins calls "other-mothers." Cheryl Gooding, Julie Rosen, Ada Velazquez, Sue Robertson, Erica Bronstein, Mary Lenihan, and Maria Tardanico have cared deeply for my daughter over the years of this project. My own mother, Alice Kurtz, has sustained both of us with continuous encouragement and support throughout the process.

Finally, I am grateful to my daughter, Zoe Tong. She has withstood the weekends and nights, year after year, of what as a toddler she used to call "mama work." Her spirit, boldness, incisive observations and probing questions, growing sense of justice, her humor, silliness, and irrepressible laugh inspire me (most of the time). Her journey and our journey together through school, community, and larger politics daily deepens my understanding of the complex realities of multi-identity politics.

For all these gifts, my cup runneth over.

Introduction

Posing the Dilemma

They collect at the corner, until they're about 15 and in their stride. "2-4-6-8. Columbia discriminates!" "Sovern, in your ivory tower, we're gonna fight you with union power!" "What do we want? A contract! When do we want it? Now!" they roar. "Mo' money, mo' money, mo' money mo'." Pauline commands the center of the picket circle. Purpose pumps through her veins, her voice, her stride. Whole body's staccato movements underscore the intensity of the demands, the mission. Mavis stands in front of the apartment building, calling up to a higher level, an updated version of the balladeer. It is not a love song she sings.

Police cars line the street, their flashing lights helping to mark the occasion. Passersby come to the corner, some in their fur jackets, others in their running outfits. They are prepared to be angry, yet more often than not this gives way to curiosity, even a smile. This crowd, especially the core of African American women, is singing, moving, serious and celebrating all at the same time. Even after it's done, no one wants to stop. "We'll be back, Mike, we'll be back," they chant in a frenzy. Three protesters embrace, knowing their harmony carried the mission, today not in the church hall but on the posh streets of New York City. Starting to cross the street, Robin turns back, raises her hands as megaphone and bellows, "Stop all discrimination at Columbia University!"

—Author's field notes, November 1991

Like the Columbia clerical union members protesting outside the home of then university president Michael Sovern, the excluded continue to struggle for justice. Over the past four decades, "the permanent excluded losers" have made important demands for institutional and cultural change (Lani Guinier, quoted in Puga 1993). "Diversity" challenges, as they have come to be known, continue to confront us everywhere. As the ongoing wars over affirmative action, gay and lesbian marriage, sexual harassment, living-wage campaigns, bilingual education, and multicultural curriculum illustrate, identity-based justice movements continue to be powerful actors structuring the social and political landscape.

Yet social movements have themselves been the object of such identity-based challenges, as well. Identity movements are collective efforts for justice by groups defined by particular social locations: gender, race, ethnicity, class, sexual orientation, age, disability, and so on. Powerfully, painfully, and persistently, such excluded groups have long criticized social movements that fail to recognize the full complexity of oppression. Today the labor movement wrestles with becoming fundamentally inclusive of workers of color and women workers as one of its survival tasks. In the 1980s and 1990s, the environmental racism movement challenged mainstream environmental organizations to recognize and prioritize the disproportionate environmental assault faced by poor communities and communities of color (Bullard 1993; E. Taylor 1996). Battered women's organizations have brought forth an astounding service infrastructure and changes in consciousness over the past decades (still with miles to go). Yet these organizations also confront the cries of unmet needs of battered Latinas and Asian Americans, immigrants, lesbians, women with disabilities, and prostitutes (Poore 1995). Many feminist organizations that are predominantly white professional class in their membership, while claiming to speak for "women," continue to advance the agenda of the most privileged of womankind. Gay and lesbian AIDS activists have at times experienced their erasure in a sanitized—that is, de-gayed—AIDS movement (Boehmer 2000). At the same time, charges of class and race privilege continue to confront gay and lesbian organizations. Diversity challenges—challenges to injustice—thus confront social justice movements no less than they do any other social site.

Critics call these identity-based challenges to social change movements the "politics of victimhood" played out to an absurd end. Some describe this as the "relentless proliferation of small differences," yet I suggest these criticisms are best understood as the recurrent problem of single-identity politics.[1] As powerfully as social movements have been buoyed by identity politics, they have also suffered from their undertow. In the name of unity and in the effort to defeat injustice, social movements have most often developed a "lowest-common-denominator" politics in which organizing occurs around the common injustice that everyone is said to share. This single-identity framework has excluded many and left their experiences of oppression on the margin.

The problem is that—our fictions, our myths (Hall 1991) to the contrary—oppression does not come in single and universal categories. Elizabeth Spelman (1988) points out that underneath good intentions gone astray is a failure to fully understand that there is no such thing as gender, race, class, or any other category of injustice "in the general." The womanhood, for example, of a Latina or African Caribbean domestic is something different from the womanhood of her white employer.

Intersectionality theory, on which this book builds, argues that there are multiple systems of domination that define one another.[2] Each one is shaped by and shapes the others. This is true at the institutional level (race- and sex-segregated labor markets) and at the cultural level (the stereotypes by which Asian American women versus men are viewed), as well as at the individual level. No single one of them—not class, gender, race, or sexuality—is primary or universal in the quest for liberation. Rather, the conditions that social movements challenge are shaped by the interaction of these many systems of domination.[3]

Not getting this, or not being able to put this concept into action, has been a problem of both liberation theory and practice. The traditional common-denominator approach to unity is rooted in dominant American color-blind ideals.[4] It is also based, in part, on the fear that diversity will weaken a movement organization. Sometimes unintentionally, and sometimes quite intentionally, a race- and gender-blind politics has sacrificed the concerns of those groups who are less powerful to those who are more. The former's demands for justice have been labeled secondary and divisive. Movements then themselves become the agents of injustice. These are the "dangers of an incomplete vision" (Lorde 1984, 135).

This potent dual-sided history of identity politics—great mobilizing power on one side, and dangers of exclusion or fracture on the other—poses a central dilemma for social movements. How does a movement draw on the mobilizing power of identity politics and achieve the unity necessary for victory? How does a movement achieve the unity necessary for victory and also address the multiple systems of inequality that shape the injustices the movement opposes? These are the questions at the heart of the larger Left today, as well. This unity/diversity quandary will be at the center of this study.

Rather than abandoning identity politics, I argue that we need to create a multi-identity politics that takes on multiple social injustices. This approach suggests the need for unity and alliances not only between movements but within them as well. Rather than finding unity by turning a blind eye toward people's "differences,"[5] multi-identity politics call for coalition "based on recognition of all the member's issues" and the systems of injustice that have shaped them (Gooding 1997b, 9). The unavoidable task, then, of each movement is to build internal coalitions. Coalition politics, as Bernice Johnson Reagon (1992) points out, are intrinsically conflictual. There is no magic trick that banishes the risks of multi-injustice politics. However, as we continue to witness, neither will the just claims of excluded groups simply be banished. Above all, we cannot make significant gains in our social change work until we consistently address multiple interlocking systems of oppression.

Labor

No movement is a more compelling, quintessential example of the limitations of single-identity politics than the U.S. labor movement. The 1995 election of new national leadership was heralded by many as a "watershed" for American labor. With unions then representing only 14.5 percent of American workers (down from the 35 percent all-time high in 1954),[6] the "New Voice" leadership embarked on a battle for the resurgence, if not the survival, of the American labor movement. Labor confronts a staggering range of capitalist assaults: globalization, deindustrialization, capital flight, privatization, deregulation, stacked labor laws, gutted occupational health and safety enforcement, use of contingent workers, and coercive workplace participation programs. Labor must also confront the consequences of its own earlier exclusionary politics. It is no secret that racism and sexism were part of the foundation of a good deal of the labor movement. Sometimes this was intentional as defense of skilled white male labor market privilege; sometimes it was an unintentional consequence of labor's strategy for opposing big capital and building a unified mass movement. Regardless, these exclusions have had profound negative social and economic consequences for the lives of women of all races and men and women of color in this country. Exclusions have also narrowed and weakened the labor movement itself. Labor's challenge today is to move beyond single-identity politics and to effectively address the multiple injustices that shape the conditions U.S. workers face.

When given the opportunity, women of all races and men and women of color have been avid, militant union supporters and activists and have benefited from union-won wages, conditions, job protection, and power on the job (Aronowitz 1992; Bronfenbrenner 1991; Foner 1978, 1980, 1981; Moody 1988).

Yet the task remains of creating a labor movement that matches the U.S. workforce in membership, leadership, agenda, and vision. As the editors of a special "Building on Diversity" issue of *Labor Research Review* argued:

> We don't have to tell you that the future of the labor movement lies in the millions of women and people of color who increasingly are embracing unionism or who constitute the unorganized workforce in the U.S. Nor do we have to tell you that unions committed to internal organizing as well as organizing new members need to develop leaders and organizers who reflect the faces and cultures of these workers. You know all this—the question is how. (Oppenheim 1991, vi)

Enter the Columbia Clerical Union

In March 1992, the one thousand clerical workers at Columbia University celebrated the end of a tenacious, inspirational ten-month campaign for justice in their workplace, also one of the nation's preeminent academic institutions. The union local, a few of whom we glimpsed in the opening narrative of this introduction, was two-thirds African American and Latina/o and three-fourths women.[7] Their struggle provides an opportunity to explore the challenge of multi-injustice politics.

The very existence of the clerical union at Columbia is a major labor victory of the 1980s, and one that was significantly built on multi-injustice politics. It is with great enthusiasm that the organizing and contract victories of sister clerical unions at Yale and Harvard have been heralded by many in the labor and women's movements eager to see struggles moving beyond past exclusionary politics. Clerical and administrative work, employing almost a third of all working women, has remained largely unorganized, particularly in the private sector.[8] Unlike the Yale and Harvard clerical unions, the Columbia local was substantially multiracial at the time of organizing, which makes it a particularly interesting and important case for analyzing the intersection of various forms of inequality.

The Columbia local has been a trailblazer in integrating race, gender, and class politics. Since its beginning as a part of District 65 of the United Auto Workers (and today UAW Local 2110),[9] the clerical local has confronted conditions of institutional racism and sexism in the workplace, as posed by the conditions of segregated labor markets. Organizers knew that to bring meaningful change to Columbia's clericals, their union would have to challenge the devaluation of clerical work (in money and respect), the differential treatment of workers of color, as well as the full range of worker injustices. The first contract brought much-needed relief through wage and benefit improvement, provisions against sexual harassment and personal work, and increased job security, health and safety, and worker voice. The early campaigns also won an equity fund to address a long history of racial inequities, affirmative action monitoring, and a pioneering child care subsidy program. The Columbia clerical workers' union has long been characterized by strong women's leadership, although in 1991 at the top, still white women's leadership. It is a union that has drawn particular strengths from its largely female, largely black and Hispanic membership.

During the 1991–92 academic year, the Columbia clerical local undertook a whirlwind of one- and three-day strikes and other embarrass-and-disrupt actions. Their chants "Mo' Money," "Contract Now," and "Beep, Beep, Columbia's Cheap" reverberated throughout the campus. As part of a campaign to reach Columbia's board of directors, they surprised New Yorkers at Macy's and posh Manhattan corporate offices. Occurring in hard economic and union times, the contract campaign raised wage demands and issues of basic trade union seniority rights in case of layoffs, which disproportionately threatened workers of color. The clerical union also identified de facto gender-based health care inequity, an average race-based wage gap of $1,100 between workers of color and white workers. The need for reclassification of long devalued clerical jobs was pivotal to bringing economic justice to these one thousand women and men. Against a well-resourced, fiercely antiunion employer, Columbia clericals won many of their demands. They developed new activists and leaders. Through all of this, the union also avoided schism and maintained unity. These are accomplishments to celebrate . . . and to study.

What might others in the labor movement—and other movements— learn from the Columbia clerical campaign? If, as Elizabeth Spelman, Patricia Hill Collins, Audre Lorde, and others point out, no single system of injustice stands alone, how did the intersections of race, class, and gender injustice emerge in the 1991–92 contract campaign? And how did the Columbia clerical workers respond to these injustices?

Making Identity

It is helpful to consider the challenge of integrating race, gender, and class politics as a question of identity. Collective identity, as sociologists call it, is a movement's answer to the question "Who are we?" It is not innate, automatically determined by a movement's membership. Nor, as some activists argue, is it automatically shaped by demands. Identity is neither permanent nor fixed. Rather, identity is socially produced, what we call a social construction. And as a social construction, it is a matter in which movements can intervene. How do they do that? And to what end?

Collective identity, I argue, is constituted in a range of *identity practices*. These include a movement's *demands, framing and ideology, culture, leadership, organizational structure,* and *support resources.* Identity practices are a collection of individual movement behaviors that accumulate to construct a movement's self-definition.[10] The array of identity practices suggests a variety of ways in which movements can forge themselves as vehicles of multi-injustice politics. The range also allows for movements to be multi-identity in some dimensions, and single in others, as is generally the case.[11] Clearly, structural and cultural conditions critically shape a movement's identity practices, as do the practices of opponents and other agents, as well.

To speak of identity is not to suggest that identity is the only or principal task of social movements, or that it should be. It is one of many threads in the fabric any social movement weaves. It is a stream that is visible at some points, underground at others—but always there (Gooding 1999). It is part of the mix with developing strategy, mobilizing members, amassing sufficient resources, handling internal conflicts, eluding social control efforts, working successfully to frame media coverage.

What kind of identity practices helped the Columbia local weave together race, gender, and union justice politics? District 65 fought consistently for *demands* that addressed not only class but race and gender injustice in the workplace. "*Each and every time* the union's negotiated a contract," emphasized Doris, "we have had issues of race discrimination on the table. We have been way out there on this issue." The strong female *leadership* was striking to most members and inspired many. Increasingly the local was developing leaders of color, although in 1992 not yet at the highest level. The union's *culture,* particularly in all-member events, drew heavily from the cultures of the union's largely black and Hispanic membership. *Organizationally,* the union developed *structures and processes* to enhance the participation of its largely female membership. Each of these practices, however taken for granted, contributed in important ways to the mobilization.

Yet objectively confronting institutional racism and sexism in contract demands does not necessarily translate into how a movement speaks of itself or how members think of it and feel connected to it. *Framing,* it appears, has great weight in the overall identity that participants or observers create. The clerical campaign primarily framed its issues in single—union—terms as part of its strategy of building unity out of the great diversity of its workforce. Mostly, race and gender inequalities were folded in as part of a long contract list of issues. For the most part, the language of a traditional trade union contract campaign dominated in the leaflets and above all in the daily sound track of union events. The explicit framing around discrimination in the demonstration that we glimpsed at the opening of this introduction occurred primarily in public events like this one or in writings aimed at wider public support. In these, issues of racial "discrimination" were more often articulated and analyzed than gender injustice. The *outside resources* the union pursued were labor, elected politicians, and campus allies including faculty, students, and other campus unions. These resources primarily defined this as a Columbia union struggle. The union did not much pursue, nor was it much the recipient of, offers of support from race- or gender-based community organizations. As I will later argue, these practices, especially framing, were significant in many fewer workers perceiving their campaign as a vehicle of race and gender justice than the leaders' deep commitments and the union's demands would have suggested.

Thus District 65 successfully wove together its multi-justice campaign with a combination of single- and multi-identity practices. Contrary to what I thought when I started this study, identities are rarely just single or just multiple. Just as we need to move beyond either/or notions of gender or race, race or class, so too can we see movements as a mix of both single and multi-identity politics, as created by different practices. And as different Columbia members came from different social circumstances with different ideologies, interests, and priorities, this variation can serve mobilization well.

The union's mix of multi- and single-identity politics can be described as a "do it with demands, but don't talk too much about it" approach to diversity issues. Over the years, District 65 had developed its organizing wisdom for fighting injustice and maintaining unity in the context of the conditions at Columbia. It was both a strategic and ideological choice. The predominant single-identity—union—framing spoke to the union's critical need to create a sense of commonality out of a large, diverse, high-turnover workforce that was relatively new to unions. "There's a limit. We can't go too far with any one issue. We risk losing everyone else," emphasized one leader. "It's in our demands that we put our weight behind fighting important issues of discrimination by race and gender," said another leader. Yet she also pointed out that there were also issues of inequities "on the basis of seniority, on the basis of what department you work for," and other factors as well. Ideologically, many union activists, as many Americans more broadly, advocate for a color- and gender-blind approach to balancing diversity and unity. They deeply feel that the union should be a vehicle for everyone with no regard to race or gender. "Color/gender blind is inclusive and democratic," said one union leader.

District 65's strategy, like that of most movements, needs to be understood contextually as a product of "options under pressure."[12] The union's practices allowed the organization to do persistently what most unions fear: tackle difference—that is, inequality within its membership and between itself (mostly female) and the maintenance union (mostly male)—and still maintain unity. These differences in conditions are built into the structure of race, gender, and class segregated labor markets (both external to Columbia and within the university). The result is that workers face great variation in wages, conditions, job security, advancement, autonomy, and respect (Edwards 1979). Although these differences can be critical obstacles to unity, the Columbia clericals' efforts have been able to inspire solidarity.

To glimpse some of the range of practices clerical unions have used to work for all kinds of justice, I will briefly examine the Yale and Harvard campaigns that, under very different structural and historical conditions, have tackled gender and race, as well as class domination, in the workplace. The mostly white Harvard clericals spoke of a "women's organizing culture." It served as a secondary theme supporting their primary themes of self-representation and democracy at work. Yale's 1984 first contract campaign developed connections with women's, civil rights, and labor movements. Under differing conditions (most important, the Harvard and Yale cases were first campaigns and were overwhelmingly white), each of these unions shaped practices that successfully—and differently—moved beyond lowest-common-denominator politics. As in the Columbia campaign, each package of identity practices had its strengths and weaknesses.

Movement identity is created by participants as well. It is a complex interactive process among a movement and its members. Members bring a range of ideologies, experiences, and political histories to their process of making meaning of the struggle. How did Columbia clericals read their movement? In what ways had race and gender been "politically meaningful" in the campaign (Bookman and Morgen 1988, 12)? District 65 succeeded in forging a union identity out of a diverse, new-to-unions workforce of 1,000 clericals. Many of those who had never participated in collective action came to feel "empowered" as part of a collectivity, which they felt had taken on Goliath.

Theirs was a "union" identity that was clearly racialized and gendered, although not centrally defining of the campaign. There were, as we would expect, Columbia unionists who spoke proudly of the union's commitment to fighting for racial justice. They praised District 65 as being "what unions should be." Others spoke with inspiration about the union's strong women's leadership. "There's some pretty mighty women out there," was a frequent sentiment. There were members who appreciated the union as a site of cross-race encounters in often segregated lives and workplaces. Across race and gender, these elements of the campaign tied some activists to their movement and enhanced their activism. The race and gender justice components of the campaign featured large in how these workers thought about their campaign. They had come to see, as District 65 president David Livingston had described after their 1985 union victory, "the struggle at Columbia . . . as a combination of labor struggle and struggle for women's rights and the civil rights of minorities" (*Distributive 65 Worker,* December 1985, 1–2).

Yet surprisingly, in my conversations with members, such a view was in the minority. For a significant number of workers, the refrains of "We Shall Overcome"—or, in nineties terms, "No Justice, No Peace"—were more faint than I had imagined having read Livingston's quote and having heard others like it. For the majority, the rounds of "Union Maids" were virtually inaudible.[13] Across race, many clericals, including self-declared feminists, rejected the notion of their union as a vehicle of "change for working women."

This was true despite the fact that the union fought passionately over key demands that confronted structural race and gender inequality in the workplace. It was true despite the union's 75 percent female and 64 percent African American, Hispanic, and Asian membership, and despite union leadership that was highly committed to progressive gender, race, and class politics. And it was true across race and gender for many participants who considered themselves committed activists in movements for racial justice and/or explicit feminists. For them, too, this was a hard-won victory, but they predominantly defined it as "just a union" fight.

Unraveling the how and why and so what of this seeming contradiction will be at the center of this book's story. How is it that a social movement so diverse in membership and that deeply valued and fought for race and gender justice was so widely experienced as "just a union" fight? Workers, of course, made their own judgments about the nature of the Columbia clerical struggle. Naming one's struggles is certainly one of the critical rights of self-determination of any group. Yet these questions take us on a sobering journey into the complexities and the depth of challenge of creating multi-injustice politics. District 65 had succeeded in creating an organization that felt comfortable enough to a range of workers, but members were qualified in speaking of their campaign as a vehicle for challenging racism and were even more unlikely to see it as a vehicle of challenging sexism. What the movement had objectively done, and what its leaders had intended in challenging racism and sexism, was not necessarily so experienced on the individual level.

The answers to the puzzle are found in several places. Many workers see workplace racism as intransigent and the limited options available for dealing with it ineffectual. Although they appreciated the union as a means of survival, many workers spoke in a very qualified way about their campaign as a vehicle of race justice. This is as much a comment about the nature of contemporary racism as it is a comment on the union. Yet to the degree that any identity other than "union" emerged in response to my interview questions, it was much more frequently race than gender. As part of a long tradition of black women's activism, many members saw their efforts as part of what women do on behalf of uplift in black communities. Many white women's experience as "other" to the black and Hispanic female majority in the union greatly occluded gender politics. The intersection of race and gender in this workplace in the context of the union's not emphasizing comparable worth made gender politics an unlikely campaign identity. It is not surprising that "sisterhood" was not the "anvil" that many women at Columbia have used "to forge [their] political identities."[14]

The invisibility of institutional sexism and the stigma associated with feminism were also significant in the low significance of gender politics in members' definitions of the struggle. The union's practices, especially its framing, discouraged such a definition. "I've never heard it in that light," "It's never been put that way," noted many women, vigorously rejecting the notion of their campaign as connected to "change for working women." Except for the sense that the predominant female membership and the vulnerability of single moms had brought forth a stronger attack on the union by the administration, institutional sexism remained invisible. As is the norm in America, and as a color- and gender-blind ideology suggests, matters of race(ism) and even more so sex(ism) were little discussed in the meetings.[15] There were discussions of "bringing up" the wages of workers in the bottom grades—workers who were primarily black and Hispanic. There were conversations about the difficulties of single mothers carrying out a long strike. Otherwise, silence largely prevailed. As hard as District 65 has pushed to bring race and gender justice, participants' reflections reveal the many challenges of creating a movement for all kinds of justice.

The constraints within which the movement operated were critical, particularly the fragile support from the mostly male maintenance union, which made the clerical union approach gender framing with great caution. The union's stretched resources in the face of a fierce antiunion employer were important. "Columbia bombarded us," activists summed up. "We never had a time that we could sit back. . . . What we can talk about has so much to do with time and resource constraints." The historical moment, including the Crown Heights conflict and the Hill/Thomas sexual harassment hearings, accentuated the dangers of explicit identity politics.[16] The latter painfully illustrated the long history of oppositional gender and race politics and showed little hope of a multijustice vision.

Collective identities come with consequences: positive and negative. The Columbia clericals' multi-in-deeds, mostly single-in-words approach successfully achieved a union identity out of a disparate workforce. It also won advances against class, race, and gender injustice. Contrary to fears of multi-injustice politics, the union achieved solidarity, minimizing potential conflicts inside the union and outside with critical supporters. These are formidable accomplishments.

Yet the data suggest that avoiding the risks of schism may not be the only concern in crafting multi-identity politics. In some areas the union's approach may have incurred resource losses by *not* making identity politics more explicit. We will hear evidence of lost potential internal resources: a kind of undermobilization of those for whom more explicit race or gender politics resonated. Although a minority, there were those who mourned the union's not pursuing (and I would add not being offered) support from race-based community organizations. There was a small but noticeable cluster of women of all races who, when I asked about the union as a means of "change for working women," or "the union as connected to women's movement activism," said with regret that they had never heard that before, but relished the idea, and said they'd be attracted to it. These workers' values were similar to the values of those whose activism had been enhanced by the union's commitments to social justice—only these members needed to see more of those connections. In a campaign that had to work hard to get and keep members involved, this is not insignificant. I will also consider lost potential external support resources from outside black, Hispanic, and women's groups. These resources are critical in a prolonged, tough fight such as District 65's.

The Columbia campaign provides an important model of unionism committed to the many dimensions of workplace justice. The case also makes clear that the business of identity politics is complex. The strategic moment, historical and structural conditions, ideology, resources, and the (sometimes correct) fear of fracture all enter into the swirl to shape the identity that a movement forms at any particular time. The identity created by a movement at one moment may be viewed by participants in light of the identity it created in a different period. There are moments when more explicit identity is possible and advisable, and moments when it is not. Different activists will be drawn to varying elements of a struggle and its collective identity. Shaping identity is a matter of great complexity and fluidity. At different times the choices will come with different consequences.

The Debate on the Left

Today labor scarcely stands alone facing the diversity/unity challenge of identity politics. Many other movements grapple with the same challenge, and it is at the heart of the strategic moment of the U.S. Left. From different ideological locations, progressives have challenged the wisdom and viability of identity politics as the basis of a Left movement. A procession of identity-based movements came to prominence in the sixties and beyond, each inspired by the civil rights movement and using what became a master frame of rights, injustice, and identity (Snow and Benford 1992). How, ask Left strategists in a post–Cold War era of many disconnected movements, does the U.S. Left shape a winning majoritarian strategy? Pointing to the Right's ability to capture the notion of "universality" and "common good," many fervently argue that the Left must turn away from the politics of identity and toward the politics of commonality. While a unifying sense of a larger progressive agenda exists in millions' hopes and politics, it has little organizational presence, and even less influence on U.S. domestic and foreign policy. This constitutes a very real and critical agenda.

Central, of course, is what exactly is meant by identity politics. As sociologist Todd Gitlin notes, there is a "spectrum of meanings" associated with identity politics.[17] One location in that spectrum is defined by cultural identity politics, featuring a movement's desire for "recognition," "affirmation," and the opportunity to "express" its "distinctness" (Gitlin 1997, 155–56). Cultural politics, as Gitlin argues (1995), have been particularly influential at universities, and in academic discourses of cultural studies, poststructuralism, and some women's studies.[18] Yet "recognition" struggles do not represent the entirety of identity politics, as evidenced by the environmental racism movement, comparable worth movement, and movement for gay and lesbian marriage, parental, and other family rights. Affirmation may indeed be a goal, but it is not the only goal, as these material struggles for justice illustrate. It is thus critical to understand that these movements are not merely organizing around "difference." Rather, they are organizing in opposition to *domination*, not only culturally but institutionally, as well as in health care, schools, workplaces, and government policy.

At the center of great political and intellectual debate, "identity politics" is a term with many conflicting meanings. Some see identity politics as a cultural approach of "new" social movements (such as the representation of women or gays in film) in contrast to the material politics of "old" class-based social movements (such as union demands for wages or better health benefits). In contrast, I argue that identity politics can be both material and cultural politics in response to perceived issues of any particular social location. The Columbia case is especially interesting because it stands at the intersection of what have falsely been called "new" (gender- and race-based) and "old" (class-based) movements.[19]

Those who question cultural identity politics are concerned about the Left's declining attention to class. It is "the issue that barely dares whisper its name," argues Gitlin, a leading advocate of commonality politics (1997, 153). Social movement theorist Stanley Aronowitz makes the same point in his book *The Politics of Identity* (1992). He argues that vibrant race- and gender-based movements, while valid, have diverted attention away from class-based issues. As indicators of inequality keep rising, Gitlin, Aronowitz, and others are quite right to be concerned about class inequality and to question U.S. political culture's silence regarding class. Unlike the first half of the twentieth century, when class identity politics commanded the U.S. political landscape,[20] the diminished condition of much of the U.S. labor movement has also contributed to this silence. Aronowitz and Gitlin are also correct to criticize many race- and gender-based movements, which have often relegated class to a secondary issue or dropped it out altogether.

Yet, as intersectional theory argues, it is critical to recall that there is no class problem—such as growing inequality and the lack of livable wages, affordable housing, health care, and child care (Gitlin 1997, 162)—that is unshaped by issues of race and gender. Gitlin uses the term "politics of equality" to refer to struggles against class injustice (154). Yet these are not necessarily oppositional to "identity politics" using a broader definition. What are the identity politics of a public school funding battle waged by a poor or working-class community of color, or the battle by Asian women garment workers against fashion designer Jessica McClintock for unpaid back wages, if not "politics of equality"?[21] Gitlin, as well as other critics, also underrecognizes the presence of class issues in many race and gender struggles, thus missing the very opportunity for confronting class injustice that he himself prioritizes. If we see identity politics as efforts for justice and equality (as well as recognition and cultural representation) by groups experiencing ongoing domination, and if we cease to see class justice existing separately from race and gender justice, then the gap between identity politics and politics of equality begins to close.

Critics who take issue with identity politics would more accurately be described as contesting *single*-identity politics: fragmented politics that don't capture complicated, overlapping, fluid identities; incorrect assumptions about the supposedly monolithic experience of a specific identity; the invisibility of class; and the unlinking of class and race, leading to increased benefits primarily to the most class privileged people of color.[22]

Gitlin's central question is "How can people organized around their differences from others coalesce with those others toward common ends?" (1997, 155). If we again clarify that people are organizing not around "difference" per se but around "different conditions of domination," then this concern is quite correct. His own answer, in fact, reads quite similarly to what I call a multi-identity politics, which includes at its core the idea of each movement as an internal coalition.

> There is no magic bullet. But surely common ground on class issues can be found across race lines—or, better, common ground can be *made*, for it is not lying around in a state of nature, to be stumbled upon like nuggets fallen from a rainbow. It has to be created by organizers who are self-conscious about the urgency of forging cross-identity links, committed to the difficult work of overcoming group rancor and forming alliances. (158)

Activist and writer John Anner grapples with similar issues in *Beyond Identity Politics* (1996). Rather than jettisoning identity politics (perhaps his book would have been better titled "Beyond *Single*-Identity Politics"), Anner suggests the path for the Left is in looking to "community and labor organizing revitalized by identity politics, and a new politics of identity that strives for identification with other communities of interest and especially with the poor and working class" (12). He adds, "A reinvigorated social justice Movement with a capital 'm' will have to develop mechanisms of reconnecting identity politics with class issues, putting matters of economic justice on the front burner while showing how a racist, sexist power structure—now somewhat more integrated—works to deny most people the basics of life" (11). In this, the labor movement has a particularly critical role to play. Labor educators José La Luz and Paula Finn argue:

> Labor unions remain the only large multiracial, multiethnic democratic institutions in our society. In a nation as racked by racism and sexism, and diminished by the poverty of its efforts toward a meaningful, robust democracy, the union movement holds a crucial responsibility to become a bastion for propagating inclusion and democracy. The institutions of

labor are the only institutions in our society adequate to the task of bringing about this sort of change. In order to accomplish this, unions themselves must more fully practice their commitment to these principles.
(1998, 171)

For labor, as for most social movements, these are critical issues to success, if not survival. "Identity organizing—or creating democratic voice
within unions for the various identities within the union—is critically important to long-term organization and movement building for labor," argues
Cheryl Gooding, longtime labor activist and educator. "To build long-term
commitment to the union and the labor movement, people have to see
themselves reflected in the institution's priorities and practices. It is not
only ideological, but pragmatic. This is a 'must do,' a core issue for labor.
Integrating identity strategies can be a critical part of a 'winning strategy'"
(Gooding 1999). There are in fact many promising signs. Increased clerical
and service organizing victories, struggles of immigrant garment and service
workers, growing women's leadership at the local level, the development of
gay and lesbian labor organizations, and labor campaigns over child care,
sexual harassment, and domestic partnership are just some of the many important developments.

Progressives inside the labor movement and out look to labor to function as it has at other historical moments, as a vehicle for widespread social
change. "To articulate a social vision, identity issues are essential. Labor
needs to be speaking not just to current membership, to those workers at
that time, but speaking to the widest population," argues Gooding. Labor
thus creates a popular definition of itself as a fighter for the widest spectrum
of working people, and as a vehicle for the widest spectrum of social justice.

This Project: What It Is, How It Came to Be

For thirteen months between April 1991 and May 1992, I was a participant-
observer of the Columbia clerical union contract campaign. As a past Boston
hospital rank-and-file organizer with a history with District 65, UAW, I was
seen as a friend of the union. I was generously welcomed into this movement and given access that few would be afforded. For the months of highest mobilization, I lived in New York. In periods of less activity, I traveled
back and forth between New York and Boston, being present in New York
around key campaign events. For many months when the struggle heated
up, I became a full-time member of the Columbia clerical union struggle.

The joys were great, but the activist-researcher role presented many
contradictions and discomforts. The union assigned me the task of working

with the faculty and graduate student support committee while I was present to do my research. This work provided me a legitimate reason to be present at all levels of union events while remaining a peripheral player. I was introduced at a few union meetings as someone who had worked with District 65 in Boston and who would be "helping out" in the office while I did research for a book I was writing. I explained who I was and what I was up to as I hung out with people or interviewed them individually. I developed my own guidelines about what specific tasks I was and was not able to do for the union without compromising my research role. Most important to me was not to take a speaking part in any meetings, that is, not to be seen as (and not to be) someone moving any agenda forward in the union strategy debates. This only occasionally came to explicit conversation when I was directly asked to do something I felt was inappropriate—like arguing the union leadership's position on some strategic issue—and declined. The rest of the time, people may have noticed and just thought I was less a good organizer than they had hoped for. Working in the union office made it impossible for me to directly research the diverse work site cultures created by workers in different parts of the university, and how those cultures interacted with the union campaign (di Leonardo 1985, Feldberg 1987b, Sacks 1988a). My location in the union did, however, allow me an overview of the contract campaign and access to the full range of union events.

Many hours of work together meant that I was able to become friends with some of the wonderful women and men who made this union and this struggle. As with other political activism, the friendships forged in movement struggle have a special quality. Each is a special gift.

Instrumentally, the trust that comes from months of intense work together, late-night missions, and confidences shared in the heat of struggle has contributed to validity. Yet I remain a (knowledgeable) outsider, who undoubtedly at points just didn't "get it."

At first, it seemed that the questions about weaving together the progressive race, gender, and union politics that animate this study were central to the union, as well. Over time, though, as the campaign heated up, it became clear that our priorities and our understanding of these questions differed substantially. Whereas it was my primary research question, it was not an open problem with which the union was struggling. For union leaders, as the campaign unfolded, these questions often seemed to have little to do with the union's pressing priorities and strategic debates. They were also outside many participants' definition of their own situation: race and gender were seldom used categories in members' conversations. In the appendix, I ponder the many issues of "engaged" or "activist scholarship" that challenged me and the union leaders I worked with most throughout this study.

Over the months, at less frantic points in the struggle, I conducted a series of semistructured interviews focusing on workers' experience of the workplace, the strike, and the interlocking role of race and gender in both of these. In this labor campaign, class issues are woven through anything said about race and gender, and at times class issues are highlighted in the book. Because I felt that for many unions, the challenge of multi-injustice politics clustered around race and gender, and less so around class, the former were the object of detailed examination.[23]

The sample of union members was diverse by race, gender, class, educational background, university work area, and level of movement participation. The forty-three unionists from this campaign whom I interviewed (72 percent female, 61 percent of color)[24] were close to being race and gender representative of the union membership, with the exception of Hispanic men, who were underrepresented.[25] The sample also included a range of levels of activism: top union leaders, staff, elected rank-and-file leaders, activists from the strike and negotiating committees, workers who struck but were otherwise inactive, and strikebreakers. The sample was weighted to activists at varying levels (75 percent), as they were the ones to whom I had greater access. This seemed reasonable, as they had more experience of the movement as a basis of discussion. I made a point of including activists from opposing sides of the union's key strategy debates, including those who were labeled "dissidents." They are part of the sample, although not disproportionately so.

The interviews most often took place after work or at lunchtime. The average was one hour, with a range from thirty minutes to three and one-half hours. The vast majority were individual interviews, but two were done in pairs and one in a small group. Key leaders were kind enough to be interviewed three or four times each. Unless members objected (and very few did), the interviews were tape-recorded and subsequently transcribed.

I promised confidentiality to all respondents. This was an issue for some workers, a nonissue for others, and some would have been happier to have their making of history noted. This range of reactions yielded a sad dilemma, which I've felt the need to resolve in the direction of protecting those for whom confidentiality was important. Consequently the names here are pseudonyms, and where important, I have taken the liberty of changing other identifying features while leaving the overall impression of the union member. The few exceptions to anonymity are my descriptions of public actions of top union leaders. Quotes published in other accounts that have used real names have been repeated here. I have, for the historical record, listed the names of the key leaders of the campaign.

I also compiled a collection of the documents of the campaign, which I analyzed. These often provided a useful, differing perspective from fieldwork and interview data (see appendix). The union provided me access to documents from earlier campaigns and extensive video coverage of the 1985 strike period.[26]

From Where Do I Speak? Locating Myself in the Telling

Marxism, feminism, and other social theories have taught us well the power of social location in shaping knowledge. This is not to deny the role of ideology or inquiry, nor is it to subscribe to the belief that people's ideas are inevitably determined by their location. But position does matter.

My telling of this gender, race, and class story is shaped by my being a white female professional.[27] Part of what makes the Columbia case particularly interesting and important are the challenges posed by a multiracial, largely female membership. It is critical to acknowledge my experience of these events as a white activist academic in a union struggle that is predominantly African American and Latina/o working class.

My interest in the Columbia clerical workers emerged out of my years as a rank-and-file union organizer in Boston-area hospitals during the busing era.[28] Unlike New York, the hospital industry in Boston is still today largely unorganized. This is a very significant industry to the city and state economy, and especially to women workers and/or workers of color. In the 1970s and into the 1980s, organizing campaigns developed in more than a dozen area hospitals, including those with prominent national and international reputations.[29]

Especially given the historical moment of the busing conflict, questions of race politics and class politics predominated. Organizing in the communities, a high level of racist violence in the neighborhoods and schools, a screaming debate in the papers, courts, city council, and the Left all swirled around our unionization efforts. It is an extreme understatement to say that these and other conditions (the Harvard Medical empire's vast resources, the role of union-busting firms, antiunion labor board rulings, inadequate union commitment and resources) created obstacles for these union struggles. Yet such a statement leaves unexamined the challenge of integrating race, class, and gender politics.

Inside the hospitals, the highly internally segmented organization of labor by race, gender, and class (and class fractions within the working class) continued to structure major issues for, and obstacles to, collective action

(Edwards 1979). At Massachusetts General, the city's largest hospital, where I worked as a clinic secretary, competing solidarity challenges were omnipresent. While the organizing committee aimed at "one big union" for 5,000 workers, a core of registered nurses and tradesmen began separate organizing campaigns.[30] These efforts were fueled by a positive sense of their own specific work issues and professional and trade identities. However, each group was almost exclusively white, and their desire for separate unions was, as they frequently articulated, also motivated by wanting to avoid being in a union with "those people," meaning the rest of the service workers. Even within what the labor board would consider one "service unit" of 3,000 workers, class and race differentials in conditions, politics, and identity were substantial.

It was a many-year campaign involving hundreds of workers in the majority of departments. Like many organizing campaigns, it was the site of precious cross-race, class, and gender friendships, risks and bravery, and inspiring personal and political changes. Yet the competing solidarity claims based on race, class (fraction), and gender were a preeminent factor in the failure of the various organizing efforts.[31] There was no lack of trying. Rank-and-file union leaders and progressives spent hour upon hour over the campaign's many years strategizing about how a union campaign committed to racial justice and class unity should speak and act.

Later, studying social movements such as the civil rights movement and the history of Local 1199 hospital organizing victories in New York City and Charleston, South Carolina, gave me a glimpse of the concept of identity politics and its power. When and how does the power of identity politics get invoked? What structural conditions and what movement practices does it require? Years of community and labor organizing in the 1970s and 1980s that were unable to move beyond a small committed core made perfectly clear that the lessons I as a young person had drawn about mass mobilization from the movement explosions of the 1960s were simplistic and inadequate. There was a whole lot more than good ideology and good practice involved in moving people from "objective oppression" to participation in a fight to overturn it.

Like the politics of the historical period, my relationship to identity politics became increasingly acute and complex. I had come of age with the television images of fire hoses and Bull Connor's white tank in Birmingham in 1963 (Morris 1984). I'd become an activist in the context of the antiwar, Black Power, and working-class community organizing efforts of the 1960s and 1970s. One year of sexism in academia, however, did more than fifteen years of consciously chosen work and organizing in sex-segregated occupations to make gender politics equally salient for me with race and class. The powerful lessons taught by the writings of many feminists of color opened my eyes to the layers of exclusion and injury that single-identity social movements have practiced.

Much of the activist labor power and leadership of these hospital campaigns had come from white college-educated leftists from professional-managerial class backgrounds. As David Croteau has carefully and insightfully examined, such cross-class social movement meetings are fraught with cultural conflict (Croteau 1995). Even when working hard to develop working-class leadership, and to avoid substitutionism, white professional-managerial activists came with a culture that was race, class, gender, and (Left) politics specific.[32] Despite conscious efforts to the contrary, we college-educated white progressives unintendingly imprinted our culture on the union drive. It often did not resonate with, and sometimes was in direct conflict with, the white, African American, and Caribbean working-class cultures of many union members.

The Columbia story I had originally expected to tell is not the one I am telling. The hospital workers' "Union Power, Soul Power" and the Farmworkers' "Viva la Huelga" were two powerful union efforts waged on the basis of race-class identity politics in a historical period of massive mobilization and social upheaval. In Boston, the successful unionization of Boston University's clerical workers into District 65 engaged with and transformed gender and class identities of many workers.[33] Years ago as I examined identity-based labor mobilizations, I thought about that part of what had been lacking in the efforts I'd participated in, and marveled at the engine identity politics had provided for these movements, although under very different material conditions. These Local 1199 and United Farm Worker strikes occurred in periods of mass mobilizations of the 1960s and 1970s, and in very different political and economic conditions than those providing the context of the Boston hospital organizing. Yet at the outset of the thinking for this study, I must admit, I hoped to find a silver bullet, "plant grow" for social movements. I sought the case that dramatically established the power of identity politics in a labor context. Such stories are a Weberian ideal type and would decidedly have utility. I will offer glimpses of stories that are much less clear but nonetheless illuminate the role of identity politics in social movement strategy. No one will be surprised that I have no magic wand to offer. Simple stories rarely exist. Life, political life, and organizing are always more complicated. We do have much to learn from the Columbia and other university clericals who have taken the lead in creating unions for all kinds of justice.

What I hope to accomplish here is to bring attention to that which is usually unconscious. Every movement, however unconsciously, develops a collective identity. We'll look at exactly how those identities are developed, and consider their consequences. What is at stake is not only unity versus schism, as conventional organizer wisdom suggests, but resources and level of mobilization as well. Contrary to lowest-common-denominator wisdom, risks to social movement victories are thus associated not only with explicit identity politics but with their absence.

Reading What Follows: How the Book Is Organized

Like many case studies, this book is an attempt to address multiple audiences and multiple agendas. Many readers will primarily be interested in close discussions of the case; others primarily in the broader questions of social movement theory. My hope is that readers will find individual sections useful even if they are not read in the context of the whole book.

The first part of the book fills out the larger context for this study of the Columbia campaign. Chapter 1 summarizes the basic story of the Columbia clerical union struggle—the conditions the union faced, and the union's inspirational fight. Chapter 2 examines the single-identity problem. Drawing on intersectionality theory—a type of race, class, gender, and sexuality theory—I review the problem of identity politics and make a case for multi-identity politics. Chapter 3 examines labor's long-standing single-identity problem and recurrent identity-based resistance efforts by workers of color and women workers. Together, these stories of labor and identity politics provide the historical context for the Columbia clerical mobilization. Chapter 4 draws on social movement theory to concretize what we mean by collective identity. I introduce the concept of *identity practices,* by which movements create collective identity. The range of identity practices affords a number of options for how movements, in differing conditions, can develop multi-injustice politics. I also consider the structural conditions that impinge on their use.

In these "theoretical" chapters, I have tried to maintain the perspective of "theory in service": using theory only as it helps to illuminate the discussions, with additional comments left to the endnotes. Theory often has a way of taking on a life of its own, as theorists often "understand themselves as developing theory more about than for the movements" (Epstein 1990, 39).

In chapter 5, I begin to analyze the 1991–92 Columbia contract campaign, looking specifically at the identity practices this movement used to challenge institutional racism and sexism in the labor market. Chapter 6 considers the meanings that members made of their campaign. How did they read the union's identity practices? In what ways did race and gender hold meaning in their struggle? We will hear of the union's successes and a number of obstacles, including the union's practice and the intransigent nature of racism, to members more fully seeing the union as a vehicle for race and gender change. Chapter 7 briefly reviews the identity practices of other clerical union movements at Yale and Harvard. Although these movements faced very different conditions than Columbia's, they do help us see a range of ways unions can make gender and race politics significant in their campaigns.

Chapter 8 will examine the underlying strategic dilemmas that challenge movements dealing with multi-injustice politics. I will evaluate potential benefits and risks of differing approaches. Contrary to popular thinking on the dangers of explicit identity politics, I will argue that Columbia, Yale, and Harvard evidenced impressive solidarity. Further, I argue that movements may also pay a price for *not* giving expression to a full range of identity politics. Limitations in developing a multi-injustice politics may cost a movement in lost internal and external resources (undermobilization), in progress made against systemic injustice. They also cost the larger Left desperately needed, well-rooted connections between movements. Chapter 9 considers the implications of such social movement practice for the labor movement and the larger Left, as each struggles to extend its influence.

As several Columbia clerical workers pointed out, the history they make rarely counts. This is a case that affirms the promise of multi-injustice politics and reveals the ongoing challenges in such work. At the least, I hope this study honors their efforts. They have been highly committed trailblazers and consistently pushed further than most unions in fighting for progressive race, gender, and class politics. At most, I hope this book offers some tools in all our continuing efforts at fighting for all kinds of justice.

1

"Mo' Money": Columbia Clericals on Strike

We came together one thousand strong and we took them on. We're tiny—nothing compared to Columbia—and we waged war, and we stuck to it, and we won. I'm proud to be part of this union. It's a feeling of accomplishment. We did something here.

—Doris

I wanted to fight really hard for this union, because I'm not going to be here forever, but other people will be. People after me . . . it's been good to go out and really believe in a cause and rally around it, really put your heart into it. I don't think we get a lot of chances to do that nowadays.

—Calvin

The nightly news coverage of the New Hampshire 1992 presidential primary may have brought us images of a beaten industrial working class. Yet the Columbia clericals, for those who were listening, told a different story of a vibrant labor movement that was very much alive and fighting. It was in their demonstrations and their membership meetings, many hundreds strong, that the power and spirit of this union movement was most present. Whether in front of Macy's Department Store, the posh midtown offices of a Columbia trustee, or on campus for international journalism awards, the one thousand clericals of Columbia University waged their battle for health care, job security, livable wages, and equity. With a membership that was two-thirds people of color, and three-fourths women, the union fought workplace gender- and race-based equities. In a recessionary period of high unemployment, the local also experimented with innovative "in-and-out" strike tactics for an economically vulnerable workforce and won important gains.

The presence of District 65 at Columbia, along with sister clerical and technical unions at Yale and Harvard, embodied important union victories of the 1980s. Clerical work is done by about a quarter of all employed women and represents the "largest single occupation for women."[1] Clerical workers were long viewed as "unorganizable" by virtue of women's "temperament" and family obligations. The higher status and "nice" conditions of the occupation compared to blue-collar jobs, as well as the notion of women as working only until marriage, led to the view that clericals were not "real workers."[2] With few exceptions, clerical workers were long ignored by the labor movement,[3] though public-sector clericals were unionized in the 1960s and 1970s following the passage of collective bargaining rights for public employees (D. Bell 1985). Over the last two decades, more unions and working women's organizations have made inroads in unionizing clerical workers.[4]

University organizing has been a bright spot, with significant clerical union victories at both public and private institutions in the 1980s and 1990s. The monetary benefits for women have been striking: "In 1990, clerical workers represented by unions earned 34 percent more than did nonrepresented workers."[5] Yet despite the growing importance of clerical workers in the economy, both in numbers and as located in a growth sector, private-sector clericals remain a vast unorganized workforce and a central challenge for the revitalization of labor.

In this chapter, we will travel the arduous journey of Columbia's clerical workers during their 1991–1992 contract struggle. Their union has always walked a difficult road, and we will begin by reviewing the organizing that brought this union into being. We will glimpse the day-to-day lives of Columbia clericals in their offices and the kinds of experiences that fueled their campaign. Many in this country remain skeptical about the need of clerical workers to be unionized, but the stories here offer convincing evidence to the contrary. Having set the stage, we will follow their movement, the opposition they faced, and the creative strategies they fashioned to surmount it over one tough year.

Describing his union experience, James Johnson, an early Columbia clerical activist, said, "It really bothers me the way history books don't tell stories like this one, of people who fought the battles of everyday life. Our accomplishments should be counted for something." In this chapter, I aim to recount the events of this campaign. In later chapters, I will look at what this struggle can teach us about race- and gender-based identity politics; but first, some background.

The Unionization Marathon: Columbia Clerical Union Beginnings

In September 1980, Julie Kushner of District 65 met with a committee of ten Columbia clericals who had launched a new union drive by collecting two hundred union cards. Together they embarked on a prolonged, often bitter campaign to unionize Columbia University's clerical workforce.[6] District 65, based in New York, had prioritized white-collar organizing, including universities, legal services, social services, adult education, museums, and day care centers. District 65 had long been recognized as a leading progressive union. Said Jean, a union veteran at Columbia, District 65 "is the best of unions. It represents what unions should be. I'm proud to be part of it."

Although District 65 is no longer a distinct entity, it played an important role in labor organizing during the last half of the twentieth century. Beginning in the 1930s as a union of Jewish dry goods workers, Local 65 later came to organize low-wage black and Puerto Rican workers, many of them women. It fought not only for better wages but for a chance to break the race barrier between stock and front office positions. Having survived the McCarthy era with other Left unions such as Local 1199 (drugstore workers), in the 1950s it was reintegrated into the RWDSU (Retail, Wholesale, Department Store Union) (Fink and Greenberg 1989, 26). The union had a close relationship with Local 1199, offering critical support of its groundbreaking organizing efforts among the city's largely black and Hispanic hospital workers during the late 1950s and 1960s. In the 1970s, union president David Livingston hired several women organizers and began the effort to unionize white-collar workers.[7]

In early 1979, District 65 affiliated with the United Auto Workers (UAW) in an agreement that brought UAW support to the fiscally troubled District 65 but allowed 65 to maintain substantial autonomy.[8] Over the years, District 65 has actively worked on a wide range of other progressive causes, such as civil rights, divestment, the freeze, health care reform, and women's issues.

Columbia clerical workers did not win their first contract until 1985, a decade after they had started organizing.[9] A prior clerical organizing campaign had ended in defeat in 1976, even though neighboring clerical workers at Barnard, Teachers College, and Union Theological Seminary had found success. Other sectors of the Columbia workforce had previously achieved union status. Maintenance and security workers had unionized with the

Transit Workers' Union (TWU Local 241) in the 1940s. Cashiers and cafeteria and library workers on the main campus, as well as workers at Columbia Presbyterian Hospital, had unionized with the Drug, Hospital, and Health Care Employees union (Local 1199) in the early 1970s after an arduous campaign.[10]

Julie Kushner's analysis of the campus and the prior organizing defeat set a clear strategy. Clericals worked in forty-two buildings, yet six of these contained the majority of workers. The first campaign had done well in a number of academic department offices but had not taken root in the large offices. It was here that many long-term employees and the majority of people of color worked. It was here that the next campaign would be made or broken.

Kushner also prioritized expanding the organizing committee. The original committee of ten was young, white, and single. It was expanded to a committee of twenty-five people who would be more representative of the workforce, which by the election had become approximately half workers of color. A second tier of supporters who could attend some meetings, and a third tier, a network of one hundred contacts who could carry out union tasks during the workday, were set up to carry out the work of reaching all members. Lunchtime sessions to talk with workers about the union were critical in reaching a workforce with pressing demands of families, school, and other after-work commitments.

The conditions at Columbia facilitated recruiting. Salaries were low. As labor scholar Richard Hurd notes, clerical salaries, especially at prestigious universities, often stay below market wages. Ivy League institutions have hoped to substitute their prestige for decent pay, which the Harvard clerical drive countered with its slogan "We can't eat prestige."[11] Faculty supporters noted a $2,000 gap in the hiring minimums between Columbia clericals and their unionized counterparts at Barnard.[12] Clerical wages dramatically trailed those of long-unionized, mostly male maintenance workers.

Favoritism, promotional difficulties, and a lack of voice were also focal points of union activism. As one white worker of seventeen years described,

> The pay raises weren't coming through and the people who knew somebody were getting the promotions. Your work load increased because that's what they expected of you. . . . I hate to sound biased, but the men all seemed to get the promotions and the ladies were bypassed. And when you applied for something, they sort of told you, "Well, ahem, maybe you were getting a little old," or "maybe a woman couldn't handle it." Then I realized I need someone to talk for me. And then I sought out the union. (Gold and Goldfarb 1986)

The lack of protection in case of a dispute with a supervisor and the lack of job security also provided momentum to the union drive.[13] "I saw so many injustices to other employees," recalled one activist, a single African American mother. "Before we received our contract an employee could be fired at any time. And because I'm the head of a household, having job security is very important to me, because I cannot afford to lose my job" (Gold and Goldfarb 1986).

Although favoritism seemed to be an important part of the landscape for many workers, it was significantly shaped by racism. James described the situation at the time of organizing the union in the early to mid-1980s:

> When you get there, they steer you toward something you didn't come or apply for.... They're always steering minority people to "available" job areas. These jobs were high demand, high intensity, high traffic, high supervision areas. Eighty to 90 percent [in these jobs] are minorities.... Most technical jobs... [good] computer jobs were white, not minorities.... The business school and a few other areas were meat grinders.... Smaller academic departments were white. No one thought this was an accident.

Katherine, a young white activist from that time, concurred:

> There was definitely a difference in the kind of work people did. You could see it in the controller's office. Black and Latina workers, well it was like sweatshop conditions. They worked all squished together, under heavy surveillance. Where we worked [in an academic department], conditions were much better. It was a difference in the kind of work, too, a lot of repetitive filling out of forms, almost assembly line work, versus individual work with professors.

These differences in working conditions are part of a segregation of labor found both internally in specific workplaces and externally in larger labor markets. Internally, many large service sector workplaces such as hospitals and universities are characterized by many finely graded layers in the hierarchy, each with different pay, conditions, and methods of labor control, which can make organizing difficult (Edwards 1979). Externally, Columbia's workers were part of a larger race-, sex-, and class-segregated labor market. *Closed Labor Markets*, a 1985 study, documented that black and Latino workers were "tightly segmented in a narrow range of industries in the city's private sector" and "virtually excluded from 130 out of 193 industries in the city's private sector" (Stafford 1985, viii–ix). "Black females," the study noted, "are more concentrated than any other group in the study."

They were disproportionately employed at banks and health and social services, all of which offered little chance for advancement.[14]

The depth and breadth of workplace complaints offered plenty of ground for the union to till and helped the organizing committee overcome skepticism about unions in a clerical workplace. "To me," recalled one of the first stewards, a young Asian woman, "unions were for people who work in factories, and since I worked in a perfectly nice sort of white collar job, I could never really see the need for one. It was a long process, I remember, going from being very passive about it and not interested, to now ending up being a steward" (Gold and Goldfarb 1986).

The union also benefited from activists whose political work in other settings helped them get involved in workplace organizing. Jean, a white, divorced, single mother of three, who had been very active in the New York community control/school strike, became involved in the union, not out of her own grievances, but from a sense of injustice about her coworkers' situation.[15]

> Because I got a salary increase that I thought I deserved, my coworkers didn't get one [though they deserved it as well]. I felt terrible about it. I got involved in the union because I have two daughters, and two granddaughters. Anything I can do now is going to help them ultimately.

"When I was at college, anytime something happened with black students, we'd all get involved," said Robert, a leading African American union activist. "I felt this was a way to do something about what I believed in.... I just showed up at the next meeting, and just kept coming for the next 5 or 6 years." Progress was steady, and by March 1981, with a majority of union cards, they filed for election with the National Labor Relations Board (NLRB).

Waiting, Waiting, Waiting

The union's greatest challenge became how to sustain worker involvement for the next four and a half years until the first contract was signed. The issue of legally defining who would be included in the bargaining unit (the potential union), other legal maneuvers by the university, and the labor board's backlog dragged the case on and on.[16] Unaffectionately referring to this period as "Death Valley Days," members wince as they remember how they "just fought to stay alive in everybody's consciousness."

Finally, in April 1983, two years after filing for an election, the labor board resolved the bargaining unit issues in the union's favor and set an election date. In the "balloon days" of April, pro-union balloons abounded; a flurry of activity filled the campus up to election day, May 4, 1983 (Hurd 1989a, 36). The union won 468 to 442. Columbia, however, contested the results by challenging 97 ballots.[17] Again, union supporters waited. As demanded by the delay and the high turnover rate, activists kept organizing.

In January 1984 the university unilaterally cut back health care (including 150 percent increases in deductibles).[18] A petition signed by 630 workers (more than the number of pro-union election votes) demanded the university reverse its position. "We wanted to make it clear we weren't just the majority, but the *overwhelming* majority," said Kushner.[19] In April the administration also reduced clericals' maternity benefits. A second petition with even more support was sent to Mayor Koch, Governor Cuomo, and Senator Moynihan, asking them to press the NLRB to speed up the process.

During this time, "there was a community of faculty and students who supported us. That had a huge impact," said Katherine. "Even the holdouts who identified with the faculty and students had to decide *which* faculty and *which* students to identify with." The union marked the first anniversary of its election, with a "very large and very angry" rally, said local organizer Maida Rosenstein (Hurd 1989a, 37). In late May, the labor board ruled in support of the union against the university's objections. Again, the university appealed.

Dramatic developments during the 1984–1985 school year moved the union toward militant action. The ten-week strike by the sister clerical and technical union at Yale captured national attention and inspired Columbia's clericals. "The Yale strike was a huge boost...what a tremendous thing," recalls one leader. "And it lasted a long time, so we could keep talking about it," noted Sally Otos, an early union officer (38).

Frustrated with their own situation, and inspired by Yale, Columbia clericals took a strike vote and set a February 4 deadline. The union was confident that the university feared a repeat of Yale. It worked. Finally, on January 30, 1985, the university entered into an interim agreement with the union: if the labor board ruled in the union's favor, the university would not pursue further appeals. They would accept it and negotiate. In February, the labor board ruled in the union's favor. Columbia clericals were finally an officially certified union. Kushner recalled with deep satisfaction, "We partied...that night, we took over the Amsterdam Cafe. There must have been two hundred people who came. Everybody was there. That was a really big victory party. And a week later, we had an official campus party. It was so exciting."

In spring 1985, the twenty-two-day occupation by the Columbia Coalition for a Free South Africa (CCFSA) pushed the campus into a crisis that grabbed national and international attention.[20] Demanding that Columbia divest itself of holdings in South African businesses, the action drew support from many directions, including Harlem residents and organizations. Although not officially endorsing the action, District 65 leaders and members were very supportive of the student effort—including bringing food, sitting in during lunch hours, and providing legal and tactical support. Together, the Yale strike and the Columbia divestment occupation had made the repertoire of campus disruption clearly available for the Columbia clericals to draw on.

"They Never Thought Clericals Would Ever Strike"

By September 1985, the union, frustrated with seven months of contract negotiations, set a strike deadline of October 17. Strike plans were made, including a network of picket captains, and faculty, student, and labor movement supporters. Coming directly from all-night negotiations, the committee entered to make its report to a "packed-to-the-rafters" union meeting. "Energy in the room was electric," said Katherine. When the committee, in accord with the recommendation of a federal mediator, recommended to "stop the clock" for twenty-four hours, the membership overwhelmingly called for immediate strike action. Ilene beamed as she recalled,

> We kind of had control, took our fate in our own hands. The negotiating committee said it recommended to go back to work and not strike. With one voice, this huge "NO" came out. It was amazing . . . one of the most amazing experiences of my life. And then we went over to chant and taunt. It was a real example of workers' power. We were commanding them [the organizing committee]; they weren't commanding us. It was so empowering.

Having agonized over the question of how ready members were to strike, the negotiating committee were thrilled at the members' display of determination. So taken off guard was the university that the picketers hit the pavement chanting, "Hey, Mike, we're on strike," just as President Sovern reported to university trustees that the strike had been averted.

The following five days were filled with hard work, but an ecstatic high for many members. A huge strike committee (more than seventy-five picket captains) coordinated spirited picket lines with music, song, and dance. Faculty and student supporters moved 450 classes off campus. Labor movement support brought an array of trade unionists to Columbia and disrupted campus deliveries. On the following Monday, the committee was able to bring in a settlement to the jubilant membership.

Many of the activists of the 1991–1992 campaign begin their chronicle of union activity with this 1985 strike. "When I saw all there was to this, that they had organized and kept together," says Luke, a union activist, "I took notice. I was impressed, and said, 'Let me pay more attention to this group.' That's how I started getting involved with the union." Janet remembers, "On the picket line, when we were striking, there was such a togetherness, everybody was just so family oriented. And we just bonded together, and it gave us strength. And from that day on, I just said, 'Hey, this is good. This is great.'"

Contract Win

The first contract victory in 1985 brought major achievements in wages, health insurance, and other benefits. A $125,000 "special adjustment fund" to deal with decades of racism and favoritism and an affirmative action monitoring committee were established.[21] A grievance procedure, sexual harassment and personal work protections, Martin Luther King holiday, and other changes were instituted. Workers now had a collective voice. Jean exuberantly notes, "We were out on strike for three and a half . . . days, which is a miracle in terms of a first contract. I couldn't believe that we could settle such a beautiful contract in such a short time. But our strike was strong" (Gold and Goldfarb 1986).

"Afterwards we felt marvelous," Ilene recalls. "It was good to see these women had the guts to say, 'We won't accept this.' We did this. We accomplished something." Jean, too, remembers,

> It was just the most incredible, wonderful experience. It is something that is irreplaceable and would never be forgotten. It's a sense of community that we don't have in this country in any other way. I think the sense of power had a lot to do with it, that we were taking control of our lives. We were making sacrifices, and were to gain something worthwhile. We weren't alone. The experience of wielding power is not easily reversed.

Averting a strike three years later in 1988, Columbia agreed to further wage and step increases, and to raising the bottom grades. The contract also meant health and safety and tuition benefit improvements. Perhaps dearest in the hearts of the union was winning an innovative child care fund: $40,000 was allocated to help defray members' child care costs.[22] Positioning the union for future battles, the contract included an agreement to undertake a reclassification process in which all one thousand jobs of the clerical unit would systematically be evaluated for their work duties and pay.

Working out the arrangements of this classification process became a matter of minibargaining between the university and the union over the next three years. Yet for the vast majority of the union members, who were neither on the reclassification committee nor stewards engaged in the daily work of carrying out the contract, the union movement largely disappeared in the interim years. Francine, a longtime activist, put it succinctly, "We have two modes—crisis or sleep. We have to figure out some way to move beyond that, to make the union an ongoing presence in between contracts." Union leaders take issue, noting that the crisis never let up. "We were never in a period that wasn't in struggle. Columbia bombarded us." Staff, officers, and stewards were in constant motion trying to make the university live up to the contract, handling the steady flow of warnings and grievances, and signing up newly hired employees. And the members, leaders point out, are hard to get to meetings in between contract times. While leaders worked tirelessly, as Francine pointed out, for most members, in between contract struggles, the union assumed its other identity: largely a service agency, an insurance policy, rather than a social movement. Then, as in the 1991 strike, especially with the high turnover, each contract campaign required a good deal of mobilization from the ground floor.

Who Are the Columbia Clerical Workers, and What Are Their Grievances? Some Stories from the Office Floor

In department offices from English to physics, architecture to anthropology, in career services, financial aid, the registrar's office, professional schools of business, law, and social work, the one thousand clerical workers made Columbia University run for students and faculty. The women and men who do this work come to Columbia from a variety of circumstances. There's a single black mother in her twenties, from a working-class background, struggling to support her child, not being able to make ends meet; a thirty-something white department secretary, brought up in a professional family, educated in an elite institution, and married to an academic. There is a Latina clerical who worked her way through Columbia as an undergraduate; a thirty-year-old white secretary from an avid many-generation professional family who's pursuing a nonlucrative career in the arts and is going into her second decade on the margin, perilously close to homelessness; an Asian American woman from a professional-class background for whom Columbia is a preprofessional interlude between undergraduate and graduate education. There's a white single mother who has a few years of college education, and whose family has always worked in working-class service jobs and been union activists. She lives from paycheck to paycheck. And there's a non-college-educated African American man from a poor working-class background for whom Columbia is a relatively stable way to support his family.

Within these trajectories, the job holds different meanings to different individuals. For some, it is a reliable, interesting, or at least tolerable place to make money to support oneself while pursuing passions, and hopefully futures, in theater, writing, music, and the arts. For other clericals, it is a painfully inadequate income for supporting kids, but the best one is likely to get in a race- and sex-segregated labor market. Some workers consider it a job that will allow the development of new computer or other technical skills, and hence a ticket to a better spot in the labor market. It is a job that through pay and tuition waivers allows an undergraduate education, or graduate training for sought-after professional careers. For some, it is the starting place to climb the managerial ladder.

In many ways, Columbia clerical workers enjoy their jobs: their relationships with coworkers, the skills their jobs enable them to develop and use, being in a university setting, working with students or faculty, and the tuition waivers to take classes.

Yet the university, Columbia clericals tell us, was often not such a nice employer. The same injustices that fueled the original clerical organizing at Columbia were at the heart of this contract campaign. The union found that gains made at the bargaining table were often wiped out in daily management practices between contracts. Central administration, the union argued, had made little effort to overturn department managers' decisions and enforce the union contract. Said one exasperated steward, "There is little management review at Columbia. Management just runs around roughshod. It's like Teddy Roosevelt or something." Grievances were rarely resolved except through arbitration.

Here's a quick look at the conditions the District 65 clericals confronted in their 1991–1992 contract struggle.

No Seniority Protection against Layoffs

Despite the centrality of this issue to trade unionism, and despite previous contracts, Columbia's management practices had countered seniority in the event of layoff. Although layoffs had previously been rare, sixty layoffs occurred in the three years prior to 1991 contract negotiations. The union noted, "Using loopholes to avoid recall, Columbia has placed only 10 of these workers in vacant positions, while hiring almost 200 new workers."

Because black workers as a group had longer seniority, this issue had an important racial dimension. Consider the following cases:

> [A] Grade 9, a black woman, . . . was laid off from the Office of Student Financial Services after 29 years on the job. Another grade 9 in the same office with less than a year seniority, but a different title was retained. The difference in the two jobs: one worker processed regular work study students, the other worker processed special job corps students. This member was out of work for an entire year. The union grieved, but settled the case in order to get her back to work. She was placed in a grade 8 job, forced to take a pay cut amounting to several thousands of dollars. . . .
>
> [A] Grade 8, a black woman, 7 year worker. . . was laid off right before Christmas. She applied for many jobs in her grade and was wrongfully denied the positions. With two kids to take care of, unemployment running out, this member was forced to accept a grade 6 position. After 7 years at Columbia this worker was offered only $18,519—the minimum for the grade 6 job. She took $4,565 pay cut.[23]

Low Wages: Classic Comparable Worth Pay Inequities

"I'm just one paycheck away from homelessness," said Carmella, a Latina office assistant who is a single mother. Columbia constituted a quintessential comparable worth case. The wage structure illustrated the consequences of long-term devaluation of clerical skills, and long-term unionization by mostly male maintenance workers. In 1991 the starting salary for the highest-paid clerical union position ($21,367 for a grade 9 program coordinator or research assistant) was *less* than the starting salary for the lowest-level maintenance classification ($21,500 for a light cleaner), represented by the maintenance workers union (TWU Local 241).[24] This wage pattern had persisted after six years of union-won improvements for clericals. These numbers tell much of the difficult daily realities for Columbia's clericals, many of whom are single mothers.

"They [the administration] abuse the fact we're young, ambitious, and willing to be nonprofit slaves," said Allison, a young white woman, "because we think that somehow this'll be a step up in our career. But it's not really, and I feel I'm being taken advantage of."

In addition, clerical workers noted many salary inconsistencies among themselves, which they saw as the result of any of a variety of factors: different departmental power and resources, favoritism, not rewarding seniority, and discrimination. All of these issues had led the union in 1988 to fight for a classification process that it hoped would lead to a rational reevaluation of all one thousand clerical jobs. By the time of the contract effort, labor and management had agreed on a new point factor job evaluation plan and a job questionnaire.[25]

Columbia didn't much reward seniority, often hiring new workers at higher pay than long-term workers. Lucia, a Latina starting her third year at Columbia, recounts, "I was given the position at the $18,000 minimum. One year later, they hired someone new. She's an office assistant at $20,800 . . . she knew people." For those workers, disproportionately African American and Latina/o, for whom a Columbia job is more than a one- or two-year stepping-stone, being "taken advantage of" can calcify into long-term discrimination.

Race-based Wage Discrimination

By 1991, workers of color comprised 63.1 percent of the clerical workforce. Blacks were 34.7 percent (28.3 percent women and 6.3 percent men), Hispanics 23.7 percent (15.8 percent women and 7.9 percent men), Asians 4.8 percent (3.3 percent women and 1.5 percent men), and whites 36.9 percent (27.1 percent women and 9.8 percent men).[26] District 65 won important improvements in its first two contracts, including an equity fund to make up for past discrimination and representation on the university's affirmative action committee. However, members continued to report differential practices in hiring, pay, and promotion. Going into the campaign, the union argued that a $1,100 average pay gap existed between workers of color and white workers: $21,985 versus $23,085 per year.[27] District 65 pointed to hiring patterns as an important source. Workers of color continued to be disproportionately located in the lower grades. "For employees hired since July 1, 1990," the union argued, "minority starting salaries averaged $1,400 lower than the starting salaries for white employees," as white employees were much more likely to be started at salaries above the grade minimum.[28]

Health Care Inequity

Whereas members of other unions had up to five free health plans to choose from, District 65 members had none. District 65 members paid up to $1,500 a year for health plans that other unions had for free. This was an even more acute problem for clericals, given their very low pay (the lack of comparable worth) and their high number of single-parent families.[29]

The university, meanwhile, hoped to use the District 65 contract to set a new health care pattern for all its employees, including faculty and managers, and thus pushed for health care givebacks, such as raised deductibles.

Work/Family Policy

The child care plan was a source of pride and financial support for clerical workers. Yet the $40,000 fund was used by just under a quarter of the District 65 members. The union asked for substantial increases in the fund to $700 per member with eligible children for a total increase of approximately $120,000. The university offered to increase the fund by $2,500. Caring for sick kids presented a continuing problem for many District 65 members, many of whom were single moms. Workers longed for a reliable leave policy for parents of sick children. Antonietta recounts how such a problem had brought her into union activism:

> I started getting involved with the union because my son fell on his head and had to have stitches. And I called my supervisor and I told him, "Look, I'm not coming in because my son fell." He called me back and said, "You don't have any sick days, so we are gonna have to dock you for it." It was like a month before my anniversary, so I was gonna get fifteen or so sick days. He called me to tell me that even though I had twenty vacation days. So I got very upset. Why can't you use my vacation time? "Oh, we can't do that, because you have to let us know ahead of time." So I said, "Okay, fine, the next time my son decides to fall and break his forehead, I will let you know ahead of time. How's that?"

Health and Safety

Despite public perceptions of white-collar work as safe and clean, Columbia clericals faced a range of health and safety concerns. Increasing use of computers had come with eyestrain, repetitive motion injury, printer noise, and other ergonomic issues, as well as special concerns for pregnant women. Columbia's old physical plant meant problems of ventilation, air quality, asbestos removal, temperature, and overcrowding. Workers in several areas complained that renovations were often undertaken without warning, adequate preparation, or worker input. A union health and safety committee tackled these issues but reported consistent problems in arranging worker input and in bringing quick resolution to urgent situations.

Respect and Consideration

Owing to the combined effects of class, race, and gender in the workplace, union members found they were frequently treated disrespectfully and excluded from decision making. Columbia is an institution that worships at the altar of professionalism, and clericals often don't count. One organizer sums up the members' experience: "They weren't given much respect." "Peons," "little people," "drones," or "cogs in the machine" is how many described faculty members' and students' view of clericals. "The faculty treated them like servants, and the students who come from fairly affluent backgrounds treated them like they were just their servants, too."

Eric Foner of Columbia's history department, and a leading faculty supporter, described this phenomenon. "Clerical workers, in a sense, the better they do their job, the more invisible they are . . . I think the whole effect of the . . . [1985] strike, itself, was to make people just think about these workers as human beings, fellow workers on the campus, rather than just invisible, anonymous people" (Gold and Goldfarb 1986).

Yet clerical worker devaluation is a problem with great staying power. "They come to ask me to do some work for them," says Kate, a young white woman from a professional-class background. "Often, they do not even say hello. If they do, they do not see *me,* or recognize *me, the person.*" Lucia, a working-class Latina, recounts a revealing incident:

> The administrator comes in with cake. I'm there, and she says, "I don't have anyone to sing happy birthday with." She goes and rounds up other people. They all come in, and they sing. Then they divide up the cake, give it all out—a plate to everyone in the room. At the very end, when there's not even a piece left, she offers me a plate of crumbs. I say, "No." She's embarrassed. She wants me to get her off the hook. She says, "Oh, take it to your daughter." I say, "No. She wouldn't like it."

Maxine, an African American steward, was particularly disturbed about management's comments during a grievance process over a worker's using lunchtime for therapy appointments. "I said, 'You people just don't care about your employees.' The immediate supervisor said she didn't have to care about the employees. 'We give you a check and we get your service in return. That's all we have to do.' I had that saying above my bulletin board in the office."

The personal disrespect that Columbia clericals experienced is widely shared by others in the occupation. As labor activist and scholar Susan Eaton notes, the role of support staff is "literally to 'support' the person to whom they are assigned. Their work becomes incorporated into 'his' work in nearly all cases" (1996, 9). Clerical work is easily devalued in part because it has a lot in common with "predominantly female caretaking work," and also because "the specific nature of [clerical work] is not well understood."

> Many faculty members, especially if they have never performed clerical work, think it is simpler than it actually is. The myriad number of steps

required to type, edit, correct, format, proof, print, duplicate, collate, staple and distribute any single document, even with computer technology, are not often part of their consciousness. (10)

At Harvard, clericals responded to this invisibility by plastering copy machines and file cabinets with stickers reading "Harvard Works Because We Do" (10). The invisibility and devaluation of what clerical workers do is a significant factor underlying wages, conditions, and the lack of respect.

Contract Demands: A Difficult Translation

As any union member or staff person knows well, the world of workplace injustices is dramatically pared down to a series of specific contract demands. After surveying the members, leaders assess possibilities, develop strategy, and help members set priorities. The key union demands in this contract included the following:

- Seniority layoff protection
- Health insurance parity
- Wage increases: across-the-board increases, raising grade minimums, step increases for service of midrange and long-term workers, upgrading the bottom grades (81 percent of color)
- Union codetermination in the final phase of the job reclassification process
- Improved health and safety protections
- Increased child care subsidies

These demands made for a hard fight.

"Wherever You Are, Columbia, We'll Be There": A Brief Chronology of the 1991–1992 Contract Campaign

It started orderly and slowly enough. In spring 1991, the union elected a negotiating committee from different areas of the campus and prepared its proposal. After surveying members on potential contract issues, leaders whittled the panorama of injustices into a bargaining package. On the underpopulated playing field of a summertime campus, the negotiations inched on. It was a frustrating, ritualized choreography of minimoves, with all parties knowing well that the big moves would come only in the tension of the closing hours before a fall strike deadline. For New York City and the nation, that August, other events commanded attention. Crown Heights erupted in riots following the death of a seven-year-old African American boy hit by a car driven by a Hasidic driver, and the stabbing death of a visiting Hasidic student from Australia who was killed by blacks in retaliation.

As fall approached, the union's contract machine cranked up. Leaflets, petitions, and lots of union activity greeted returning students and faculty. Members crammed into lunchtime mass meetings, held in two shifts, to hear the negotiating committee's report and to arm the committee with a strike authorization vote. The union called area meetings in every corner of the campus, providing workers with a manageable setting for asking questions and getting answers about the potential strike. Workers on East Campus held a bake sale to raise money for the hardship fund.

Meanwhile the union built its organization for the campaign. While the twenty-six-member negotiating committee continued to strategize and negotiate, picket captains were also recruited for each area of the campus to provide grassroots coordination of the strike. With some regularity, these two groups met to consider strategy and make plans for the campaign. The next level of leadership consisted of union officers (Vivian Hill, Marlene Mansfield, Barbara O'Farrell, John Stobo, and Booker Washington) elected members who were already in place. Two active members, June Benjamin and Ivan Zatz-Diaz (later replaced by Fred Johnson), were hired by District 65 for the strike period and went on leave from the university. These worker leaders joined union staff—organizer Mathew Jackson, general organizer Maida Rosenstein, and vice president Julie Kushner—in making up the leadership of the strike. Rosenstein, who had originally been a Columbia clerical worker, and Kushner, the original organizer, were widely seen as "the leadership" and provided the strategic, tactical, and logistical direction of the union.[30]

The union also reached out to supportive faculty who signed a letter calling on the administration to negotiate. The student support committee tabled daily on the main campus walkway and held a forum to prepare students for life in a strike zone.

The union debated an all-out strike. The leadership lobbied the membership to accept a series of limited, escalating events. They believed that "playing smart" was the right approach during those tough economic times. And so the union adopted an innovative "in-and-out" strike strategy—a series of limited strikes declared at short notice that would disrupt normal life at the university but would not require low-wage workers to carry the financial burdens of a long strike. This multiple-events strategy would also help the union to bring many novice members into a state of combat readiness. By holding back, the leadership argued, more members would be ready to go out on strike when—and if—the union called for an open-ended strike.

Mounds of picket signs were made. Negotiations continued. Tension mounted.

On (and Off) Strike

"Strike One" came on a sunny Thursday, October 10, 1991. Picket lines and blue police barricades clogged the front entrances of the campus, where the morning crowd poured out of the subway and off the buses. Chants of "Contract now" and "Mo' money," tambourines, and whistles filled the air. Members filed into the meeting hall and further debated the strategy. A lunchtime rally showed an outpouring of support from other unions and elected officials. Afternoon pickets at all campus entrances capped the day of union muscle flexing.

Understanding the element of surprise as a strength of its strategy, the union kept the university community—including, unfortunately, union members—awaiting the next quick move. Rumors flew; chaos abounded. "It's Wednesday, right?" "Tomorrow we'll walk right after lunch, right?" Although powerfully illustrating the impossibility of a thousand people having a secret plan, the union mobilized hundreds of workers for "Strike Two" on Friday, October 18. The day was filled with more passionate arguments about strategy, and more testimonials of support from other unions. A tremendously high-spirited midtown demonstration at the offices of university trustee John Zuccotti yielded the first agreement in the local's history with a Columbia trustee to meet with the union.

Having accepted the argument for guerrilla warfare strategy, many members advocated for an all-out effort to "embarrass and disrupt." With the chant "Wherever you are, Columbia, we'll be there," union members set out to make good on their words. The Friday night union team in Central Park politely and helpfully greeted the business school alums making their way into the elegant dinner party in the park. Guests appreciated the directions and the program . . . oops, a strike flyer. Another day on Park Avenue, a clerical duo, union leaflets in hand, guided the well-dressed elderly women coming to tea, sandwiches, and literary discussion with the chair of Columbia's English department. There was a thornier welcome at the Roosevelt Hotel, site of the business school's fall fund-raiser. The transport-a-demo carload of District 65 members suddenly jumped out of a taxi to greet the donors with picket signs and flyers, much to the chagrin of the hotel's handcuff-flashing, fist-wielding director of security.

The union seized the occasion of the well-publicized Cabot Awards in international journalism to keep the pressure on. A "C-O-N-T-R-A-C-T--N-O-W!" human billboard and accompanying leafletters greeted the award recipient journalists and their entourage as they made their way up the Low Library stairs.[31] That night as the black ties and evening gowns entered the awards ceremony, a demonstration of two hundred members and supporters chanted ferociously. They were decked out for Halloween, with a few dozen wearing brightly colored Mike Sovern masks. Unusual for this campaign, the protest was covered by *Newsday.*[32]

Strike strategy continued to be avidly debated. Union leaders found this "in-and-out" strategy to be at least equally challenging, if not more difficult, than the traditional long strike. "Even though we've only struck a total of five days," said one leader in late November, "it's like we've been on strike for months. The organizational tasks are immense. It's exhausting. We have to keep organizing, and reorganizing. It's also hard for people to keep making the transition back and forth between realities," she said, referring to the militant collective power of life on the picket lines and then the more individualized daily tensions of life back in the offices. "It was torture to go back in," said one member. "Everyone acted like you were a fool, and you were coming back in with your tail between your legs." Yet the strategy helped to avoid the kind of polarization that comes with long strikes. A number of union members who had not previously honored the strike were moved to support the union.

Debating Discrimination

As the semester progressed with no resolution in sight, each side fortified its position. The *Columbia Daily Spectator* reported that President Sovern challenged the union's claims of race and gender discrimination as mere efforts to "invoke sympathy," as evidenced by the union's lack of litigation on these issues.[33] These claims, while not much visible in literature to union members, had been quite noticeable in literature given to faculty and to the public (see chapter 5).

Union officers quickly wrote a letter to Sovern reasserting race "discrimination in hiring and salary," and the administration's "refusal to provide equal pay and benefits to a group of 80% women workers."[34] The letter was signed by ninety-one members, and poster-sized versions plastered many offices.

Senior Vice President Joseph Mullinix responded with an open letter to the Columbia community. He defended the pay gap between clerical and maintenance workers by arguing that the latter possess "highly specialized skills, or who perform other duties which command a higher salary in the marketplace." While acknowledging a gap in average salaries of white workers and workers of color, he critiqued the lack of statistical control for other variables and argued that "whites are more than twice as likely as African Americans to have attained a bachelors or graduate degree."[35]

"Ugly" was the response of many members. The union countered that the university's "on record position is that support staff jobs do not require degrees and that educational background is not a major factor in determining the grade level of support staff."[36] UAW president Owen Bieber wrote a "Dear Michael" letter to Sovern, saying that Mullinix's comments "smack[ed] of the very kind of 'African-Americans are inferior and/or underqualified' prejudice that I assume from our shared experience on the Board of the NAACP Legal Defense and Education Fund you find as abhorrent as I."[37] Leading members of the Women's Faculty Caucus also wrote a letter to their membership challenging Sovern's disregard of specialized skills of clericals, as well as the university's acceptance of labor market devaluation of clerical work.[38]

Cross-Union Solidarity

In a groundbreaking event, District 65 formed a Columbia union council with other campus unions: TWU (maintenance and security workers) and Local 1199 (other support staff). The council pulled off a powerful display of interunion solidarity as the unionists readied the university community for the upcoming third strike.

> Bright 65 and 1199 hats, TWU signs, buttons, and banners offered a preview of precedent-setting solidarity to come. . . . A mass of union members filled Columbia's central plaza. A circle too big to fit on the plaza became two, three circles twirling around. Drums, whistles, percussion sticks, and chants pulsated through the crowd. It was much too loud, it was later reported, for the contemplation of Rousseau, Adam Smith, French verbs, or factor analysis. At Dodge Hall security was taken off guard, trying too late to hold its perimeter. The door creaked open, first one slithered, then hundreds pushed through. A call of "Shut it down, shut it down" broke out. The trench coats with the walkie-talkies nervously patrolled the lobby's edge. In the end, the union did not hold what they had unexpectedly taken: the visibility of the union power was enough for this day.[39]

The administration faced fires on another front. The department chairs made quite a stir in a letter trouncing the university's arts and science budget-cutting plans, which was covered on the front page of the *New York Times*.[40] Given the import of the financial crisis to the contract campaign, faculty and student allies' rejection of the administration's "equal pain sharing" strategy was important to the union. Faculty allies challenged the administration about the origin and depth of the fiscal crisis.[41] Some also criticized the university's stance toward the union, as it disproportionately placed the burden of the financial crisis on the backs of the most vulnerable members of the community. Although sides were never polarized in the way they might have been during an extended strike, the university's effort to play off the union's demands on the one side, against faculty program demands and student financial aid demands, on the other, largely failed.

The Three-Day Strike

A flurry of phone banking, picket captains meetings, logistical preparations, and a children's picket on Veteran's Day (a public school holiday, but a Columbia workday) escalated the tension in the days before the third strike. The usual intense all-night negotiating session to hold off the impending strike yielded some results. Controversy raged at the November 13 union meeting. Members lined up at the floor microphones and for hours debated the path to victory. By noon, the university had taken back its agreement, and hopes for a settlement had stalled.

The union was out on strike. Members of Local 1199 joined in solidarity strike. Lucia recalls, "It was very moving. . . . I've never been active before. It was very emotional. Seeing everybody together. . . I almost wanted to cry, because I could feel the power." Within a short time, a wild, militant demonstration was tearing through the Upper West Side, in and out of university buildings, bringing the message of the strike. "All these months of waiting, negotiating, being patient," said Simone. "For once, we had them scared. They think, 'Oh, these nice clerical workers and secretaries.' We made them think on that one again." To avoid crossing the strike, 450 classes moved off campus, as arranged by faculty and graduate student supporters.[42] They were relocated up and down the neighborhood in pizza shops, church halls, jazz clubs, neighboring colleges, frat houses, and professors' and supporters' apartments.

Buoyed by the previous day's militant march, and this strike's first and rare *Times* coverage (with the hook of Columbia students learning Greek verbs in a Greek restaurant), union supporters picketed entrances.[43] Teams of strikers turned up the heat to persuade strikebreakers. As part of the union's strategy to take the strike to the university trustees' businesses, clericals descended on Macy's Department Store.[44] A high-spirited, loud demonstration grabbed the lunchtime shoppers' attention.

As the three-day strike ended, the union faced a decision: an all-out strike or a disciplined return in formation? Monday called the question. As part of democracy, Columbia style, strategy debates reached the boiling point. For many, the symbolic meaning of a no-contract return to work was clear: "We're giving up." "It's unethical, wimpy." "We're throwing away our power." "If we go back in now, we'll never come back out again. Never!" Luke countered, "Where's the defeat? We said we'd go out for three days and we did. We did exactly what we said we'd do." The leadership argued for "fighting smart," for not being pushed out onto the picket lines just before the Thanksgiving and Christmas holidays. Hours of intense disagreement yielded a decision to return to work, in part to "support the leadership."

Debating Democracy

The return to work also yielded many disheartened, weary members who wondered if they had not bowed to leadership at a time when they should have gone with the opposition. "The masses are who should control this," said Ilene, a longtime activist who revels in the grassroots-based "glory days" of 1985. She believed that the leadership alienated a lot of people. "You have to have certain basic respect for the members. The members need to be involved, they need more meetings, more control. You can't have all generals, you need soldiers to fight the war. In the end, [the leadership] didn't trust the members."

Martin, a union leader, strongly disagreed. "As leadership, we're responsible to get as much out of the people as possible, to get as much out of the university as possible. We're going to take people further than they're ready to go. We've got strong leadership who knows what the membership is capable of and new techniques that are being recommended." The leadership found many of the outspoken dissenters to be adventurous. "I heard members arguing, 'I'm ready to go on strike,' recalled one local leader, and we'd try to respond, 'Not everyone is as strong as you are. Not everyone can afford to stay out for the duration. We need a strategy for the *whole* group.'" The strength of the opposition was never measured. In the end, most members endorsed the leadership's strategy. Some were convinced of the merits of the argument, some deferred to the leadership's experience and judgment, and some just gave up. Yet neither issue was ever fully put to rest in the campaign. The strategy debate raged on, and at a much reduced volume, the critique of the union's decision-making process continued to be heard, as well.

The issue of strike strategy, for many, was crossed with the issue of democratic process. How much should a social movement organization in combat rely on its leadership? How much, or little, democratic input can it afford? As labor educator and diversity trainer Erica Bronstein put it,

"There's an inherent tension in leadership between setting out and fighting for a successful strategy, on the one side, and facilitating a good democratic process, on the other. Especially when you're fighting a war, it's even more difficult. The army does not function as a democratic organization." A union on strike is indeed at war, but unlike the army, people can leave—or disengage—without penalties.

While the mass membership meetings were filled with a great number of rank and filers passionately arguing strategy, some members raised criticisms about just how democratic that process really was. "They'll call us in about something," Mavis, a negotiating committee leader, reported some members had said of the large meetings. "But it's complicated stuff, and we need more time to think about all of the options before the decision gets made." She suggested holding meetings the day or night before important votes so that people could thoroughly discuss the strategic options before making a decision the next day. Jasmine, a strike committee member, voiced a stronger critique. "I had a number of people who felt like the decisions had been made already by the top leaders and the negotiating committee. And these meeting were to report, not to ask *whether*." "Browbeating, is what I'd call it," said Allison, another strike committee activist. "[Top leaders] let the conversation go on and on until people agree or give up. They equate support of the leadership's position with support of the union. Opposition is equated with union busting. That silences people who disagree."

The Struggle That Would Not End: Playing Hardball

In December, the university renewed its counterattack, cutting off the automatic payroll deduction of union dues. By sabotaging the union's income, the university sought to split membership from leadership and pressure the latter to settle . . . for anything. The union understood this to be a major union-busting initiative, and now a fight for survival. District 65 began the arduous effort to hand collect dues from its one thousand members by setting up a system of credit union accounts.

District 65 also pursued the support of elected New York politicians, particularly focusing on the discrimination issue. The fiftieth annual DuPont–Columbia University Awards in broadcast journalism on January 30, 1992, offered the union another high-visibility opportunity to embarrass the university and bring its case to the public.

Negotiations continued, with the union calling in heavier hitters: UAW regional director Phil Wheeler was brought in to high-level negotiations. Wheeler's addition to the union team, along with UAW president Owen Bieber's letter to Michael Sovern chastising the university for the Mullinix letter, made clear that the university was confronting not only District 65 but the resources of the United Auto Workers as well. Bieber's letter, union activists felt, also raised the university's concern about the discrimination charges becoming a topic of wider public discourse.

Finally, in February the union saw real motion on the university's part. The administration ceded on the union's health care demand. For the first time, low-paid District 65 members would have access to free health care plans. It was a tremendous cause for celebration, and taken as a sign that the strategy was working. It was something for union members to hold onto as they hunkered down for the rest of the fight. Yet the strong display of cross-union solidarity by Local 1199 had hardened the university's resolve to end 65's right to sympathy strike. To the surprise of some union leaders, this became an important principle of democratic rights for union members who were willing to cede a number of material issues. "Sympathy strikes are so rare," said one local leader. After 1199's support, "People understood the importance of the principle much more personally."

Meanwhile other fights heated up on campus. In February, students organized to save "need-blind admission" and "full-coverage" financial aid, policies that were critical to student class and race diversity. During a faculty senate meeting debating the financial aid plan, student protesters occupied an adjacent part of the administration building. A campus budget crisis forum organized by graduate students and faculty included the union, as well as other campus groups. A delicate alliance was built between the students and the union. Further campus disruption loomed.

Victory at Last: "We Did It!"

With graduation and the first anniversary of the campaign visible on the horizon, union leadership began organizing the final effort to bring in a contract. In early March, Columbia informed the union of its intent to declare an impasse and implement its last best offer if a contract agreement hadn't been finalized by March 12.[45] Union members voted to set the deadline for an all-out strike. This was despite some lingering anger about earlier strategy decisions, on one side, and some continuing fear about a long strike, on the other. The threat of a disrupted commencement was enough to force Columbia to settle. On March 23, 1992, the membership voted to accept the new contract.

The union party was one serious celebration!

Particularly in the context of an economic recession, a health care crisis, a dwindling labor movement, and a fierce antiunion opponent, the Columbia clericals saw the contract as a wonderful victory. All the clericals' sacrifices—membership meetings, negotiations, planning sessions, strike committee meetings, phone banking, picketing, leafleting, collecting dues, and striking—had paid off.

Perhaps most dear to them were the health care gains. "A lot more children, and a lot more parents," reveled Judy, "are going to be seeing the doctor now." They increased the pay of the lowest-paid workers, who were majority black and Latina/o. They improved seniority protection against layoffs, won an across-the-board raise, and secured a reclassification process. This was an important step, which could set the foundation for an eventual effort for comparable worth (although this issue was never defined as such). There were important new health and safety protections, and an increase in the child care subsidy to $50,000. In the economic and labor climate, it was a marked success.

Making Meaning

What meaning do we make of these events? Union members themselves would underscore their gains in health care, in a climate in which merely holding on to past benefits was often considered beyond reach. They would speak of their innovative in-and-out strategy, and the tremendous controversy it stirred. From opposite locations, union leaders and some members would speak of the conflicts and stresses inherent in a democratic organization in the midst of battle. It is an important debate about what constitutes real democracy, and how that is combined with the demands of social movement struggle.

Many Columbia workers were first-time activists who had increasingly been drawn into the movement over the months. They found it to be a powerful, transforming experience. Jennifer summed up her experience: "It was new to be able to take action with other people. I've never done that before." "I'll do whatever it takes for me and my family to move ahead," said Suzanne, another activist. "I feel it was a fight for future generations. . . . I used to be a shy person. I learned to get up and speak. I'm a lot more confident. There's nothing that can stop me. Now, I say, Suzanne, you can really make a difference." Above all, participants would tell the story of their tenacious, agonizingly prolonged battle against a well-resourced, prestigious institution: a victory against Goliath.

All of these stories are important and worth telling. But they are not the story I will tell. Rather, I will direct our attention to how Columbia clericals integrated gender and race issues with a traditional class-based approach in their union campaign. We have seen that the movement addressed itself to significant conditions of gender, race, and class injustice. How did the union weave these together? What were the challenges to social movement unity of such multi-injustice politics? Had race and gender politics been politically meaningful to union members? How did this struggle link up with larger social movements? In short, what kind of collective identity did the union fashion?

Before we can begin to address these questions, we need some preparation. In the next three chapters, I will look at the problem of single-identity politics, labor's history of this problem, and the practices by which a movement creates its identity. With these tools, in chapter 5, I will return full force to the Columbia case to explore how the Columbia clericals brought race and gender into their campaign.

2

The Single-Identity Problem

*Masses of people are re-evaluating who they are, where they are in society,
and what society owes them—and challenging the structures that exist. . . . The exciting thing about the Civil Rights Movement is the extent
to which it gave participants a glaring analysis of who and where they
were in society. You began to see all sorts of things from that. People who
were Spanish-speaking in the Civil Rights Movement, who had been
white, when they got back, turned Brown. . . . The movement for students'
rights, the women's movement, the gay movement, all offer the same possibility. Nobody will rest because everybody will check out what their position is.*

—Bernice Johnson Reagon

*In a curious twist of fate, we find ourselves marginal to the movements for
women's liberation and black liberation irrespective of our victimization
under the dual discriminations of racism and sexism. A similar exclusion
or secondary status typifies our role within class movements. . . . The process
of dominant society. . . insidiously pervades even the movements for race,
gender, and class liberation.*

—Deborah King

Identity politics, as these two quotes suggest, hold tremendous power for
injustice struggles: great mobilizing power and great power to replicate the
injustices of the larger society. These two sides of identity politics represent
the uses and misuses of identity politics.[1] As the Columbia clerical union

works to integrate race, class, and gender justice, what is helpful to understand about these dynamics of identity-based movements? Negotiating the dual sides of identity politics, we will see, is a recurrent challenge of social movements. "It is," as sociologist Eve Spangler puts it, "a problem with a history":[2] the single-identity problem.

History provides dramatic evidence of the mobilizing power of identity-based politics. The civil rights movement produced an earthquake on the U.S. landscape: social, political, cultural, ideological, and psychological. The following decades witnessed a procession of powerful actors speaking for dominated groups: African Americans, women, Native Americans, welfare recipients, Puerto Ricans, Chicanos, Asian Americans, black feminists, gays, lesbians, and bisexuals, the elderly, disabled, and many others.[3] Posing fundamental material and cultural challenges to U.S. society, identity-based movements have waged war at every institutional site: schools, workplaces, churches, health care, courts and police, news and entertainment media, and others. Furthermore, each movement has sought recognition as a distinct, unique (although internally diverse), self-defining social group and has demanded recognition of a unique history of injustice and resistance, and of a unique culture, which has not dissolved into the supposed great American melting pot.

These movements are also about the work of redefining long stigmatized or devalued identities. "Black is beautiful," "gay pride," "the personal is political" ring in our ears. Whether through fighting for legal or economic reform, consciousness-raising groups, development of new language, changing dress and hairstyle, creating or reclaiming of cultural practices, these movements have revalued stigmatized identities. Gloria Anzaldúa, Chicana lesbian, writer, and cultural theorist, speaks of being "haunted by voices and images that violated us, bearing the pains of the past, we are slowly acquiring the tools to change the disabling images and memories, to replace them with self-affirming ones. . . . To make face is to have face—dignity and self-respect" (Anzaldúa 1990, xxvii).

These changes are often described as "empowerment." They are. Yet they also reflect changes in collective identity. "Identity," says social theorist Stuart Hall, "is a narrative of the self; it's the story we tell about the self in order to know who we are" (1991, 16). Identity is a political process. It happens over time and is not stable or fixed "once and for all." Identity "goes on changing and part of what is changing is not the nucleus of the 'real you' inside, it is history that's changing. History changes your conception of yourself" (15–16). Identity is "political," as it emerges in the context of systems of oppression and as a part of the process of opposing oppression, struggling for a new ordering of the relations of power. Change in individual consciousness, then, is not solely or primarily a process of individual self-reflection but most often occurs in the setting of a group that analyzes and reposes "personal problems" in the context of larger social and economic injustice. Such personal transformation in consciousness continues to be both a consequence and a source of identity politics mobilization.

Today the continuing challenges of identity-based movements shape the terrain of a good deal of political discourse. We debate affirmative action, bilingual education, multicultural curriculum, sexual harassment, hate speech, date rape. Should we have marriage, health insurance, and adoption rights for lesbian and gay families? Within public policy debates, within social movements, themselves, and within social theory, the reverberations of challenges posed by identity-based movements of the past decades continue to be felt.

Although identity politics have fueled so many important movement mobilizations, there is an underside. Social movements themselves have often become yet another site of injustice. Powerfully, painfully, and insistently, race, class, gender, and sexuality theory has brought us lessons of the distortions of single-identity social movements. Most movements have falsely claimed singular identities, driving a steamroller over diversity, and contributing to the oppression of some segments of their own membership base. This is what Stuart Hall refers to as the "one identity to each movement" fiction (17), or what the scholar Deborah King terms "monism."[4] It is a repeated, painful failure of social movements to come to terms with multiple, simultaneous domination. From the long-standing race and gender exclusion of the labor movement, to traditional environmental groups' ignoring of toxic dangers faced by communities of color (Bullard 1993), to the silencing of lesbians in the breast cancer movement (Boehmer 2000), to the marginalization of poor women's concerns within the abortion rights movement (Fried 1990), to the subordination of women in black nationalism (Combahee 1982), progressive movements have long been marked by the injuries of single-identity politics (D. King 1990). Identity, these theorists show us, is a powerful foundation on which to build resistance, but it also provides the basis for continuing oppression, however unwitting.

How would the Columbia clerical movement orient itself in a context clearly shaped by multiple, interdefining systems of inequality? One thousand Columbia clericals worked in an occupation long defined and devalued by its white femaleness and increasingly its of color femaleness (see Davies 1979; Blum 1991; Glenn and Feldberg 1995; Sacks 1988a). The wages and lack of respect and control of clerical workers can only be understood fully as the product of class, gender, and race oppression. These problems are highlighted by contrast with faculty and managers, and, in terms of pay, with the maintenance workers at Columbia. Within the membership, race is critical to confronting differences in pay, work area, layoffs, and, many workers would argue, promotion. For most movements, the assertion of additional, conflicting identities and justice claims by groups within their membership can hold great danger. With the possibility of conflict or schism, the raising of identities—except for the one approved category of injustice— is seen as deadly terrain to be avoided, or at least, navigated with great care.

To answer this question, we will examine the critique of single-identity movements offered by intersectional theory. Particularly over the past decades, race, class, gender, and sexuality theorists, mostly African American women, as well as Latinas, Native and Asian American women, many lesbians, and some white and/or male allies have used intersectionality to carefully examine identity politics.[5] In response to invisibilization, exclusion, and distortion, their work explodes the long dominant idea of single-oppression movements and theory. They expose the error of either/or approaches to injustice: gender or race, race or class, race or sexuality. And they propose thinking about identity as an "intersection" of systems of domination—a point where our various locations within race, class, gender, sexuality, and power relations come together and help define who we are as political actors.[6] This alternative approach to identity is particularly helpful in allowing us to understand the challenge confronting Columbia clericals. How can they integrate gender and race politics into traditional unionism? As this theory suggests, how can they not?

A Critique of Single-Identity Movements

Exclusion and marginalization from race only, or gender only, or class only freedom movements is not new. As Audre Lorde put it,

> Those of us who stand outside that power often identify one way in which we are different, and we assume that to be the primary cause of all oppression, forgetting other distortions around difference, some of which we ourselves may be practicing. . . . There is a pretense to a homogeneity of experience covered by the word *sisterhood* that does not in fact exist.[7]

Black women have long recognized and theorized about the multiple-oppression context of their lives (Collins 1990; Giddings 1985; hooks 1981; Combahee 1982; Hull, Scott, and Smith 1982; Smith 1993). Let's take a brief look at some of the ways black women's experience and political issues have been excluded over time by various single-identity movements.

Despite its origins in the abolition movement, the nineteenth-century movement for women's suffrage was largely an organizational vehicle of white, privileged women.[8] The racist and classist abuses (ideas and practices) of the suffragettes have been well documented (Davis 1983; Giddings 1985; hooks 1981; King 1990; et al.). For decades many white women (and male supporters) framed their demand for the vote in terms of "insur[ing] immediate and durable white supremacy" (Amott and Matthaei 1991, 124). White suffragettes denied black women membership in "their" organizations on "the grounds of expediency," that is, to avoid alienating white southern support (Davis 1983; hooks 1981; King 1990). Through autonomous organizations and networks, black women mobilized not only for suffrage but against lynching and segregation, providing support to young domestic workers just migrating from the South, and other conditions pressing their communities (Terborg-Penn 1985). As historian Paula Giddings recounts, even after the passage of women's suffrage, the (white) Woman's Party refused to concern itself with the flagrant denial of black women's voting rights (1985, 166–69). Speaking of white suffragettes, these women at whom "human excrement / is flung," feminist poet and theorist Adrienne Rich asks, "how can I give you / all your due / . . . recognizing / as well / that it is not enough?" (1984, 294–95).

Black women have also experienced marginality and subordination in race-based movements. In the civil rights movement, Ella Baker, Fannie Lou Hamer, Daisy Bates, Jo Ann Robinson, and other women assumed critical leadership roles, organizing the church and community based armies for justice. Yet in a world where Martin Luther King Jr., his lieutenants, and other ministers presided, women were often blocked, "channeled away from formal leadership positions and confined to the informal level of leadership." As what Belinda Robnett terms "bridge leaders," black women "contributed significantly to the extraordinary nature of the grassroots leadership within the civil rights movement."[9] The subordination of women in the Black Power and black nationalist movements was quite explicit (Combahee 1982; Giddings 1985; Taylor 1999, 13, citing Elaine Brown). The Combahee River Collective, a Boston black women's collective in the 1970s, describes black feminists' "feelings of craziness before becoming conscious of the concepts of sexual politics, patriarchal rule, and, most importantly, feminism. . . . we had no way of conceptualizing what was so apparent to us, what we knew was really happening."[10]

Thus those who are oppressed in multiple ways find themselves erased by single-injustice movements. "We are rarely recognized as a group separate and distinct from black men, or as a present part of the larger group 'women' in this culture," says bell hooks (1981, 7).

Feminism and antiracism have often treated race and gender justice as mutually exclusive, if not oppositional. Such "either/or" movement practices—either race or gender—"relegate the identity of women of color to a location that resists telling" (Crenshaw 1994, 94). Nowhere is this more sharply seen than in the Anita Hill/Clarence Thomas hearings. In fall 1991, highly contentious confirmation hearings for Judge Clarence Thomas, George Bush's nominee to the Supreme Court, were dominated by sexual harassment charges by law professor Anita Hill. Her charges stemmed from her work with Thomas at the Department of Education and ironically at the Equal Employment Opportunity Commission (EEOC) (see Morrison 1992). When to defend himself from the sexual harassment charges, Thomas invoked the history of lynching, it was meant to mark him, but not her, as African American. Black women's experience of slavery and its aftermath including lynching and the institutionalization of rape were thus (intended to be) erased. The sense of betrayal of "airing dirty linens in public" was most dramatically visible in the reactions of many African Americans to Hill's testimony of sexual harassment. Even if it were true, argued many African American men and women, Hill's testimony was a betrayal, and a setback to race progress symbolized by Thomas's nomination to the Supreme Court, despite Thomas's conservative stance on such issues as affirmative action and welfare (Crenshaw 1992; McKay 1992; Stansell 1992).

In an oppositional multi-injustice identity politics, active resistance of women of color has long taken a variety of personal, artistic, literary, academic, cultural, social welfare, and political forms. The explosion of scholarship and activism of feminists of color, which this chapter only briefly considers, is powerful testimony to this resistance. Some activists have continued to work within race-based movements, some in and with white-dominated women's organizations, in each case finding some allies in the process. With multiple experiences of exclusion, opposition, and invisibility in each of the single-issue movements, and to pursue an organizational agenda centered on their own priorities, other feminists of color have joined a long lineage to create a rich network of autonomous organizations.[11]

A Critique of Single-Identity Theory

In the Akron women's convention of 1852, a jeering male critic asked how women could expect to exercise the vote when they depended on men to get across puddles and out of carriages. Sojourner Truth's powerful "Ain't I a

Woman?" speech exposed this privileged white experience of American womanhood (Spelman 1988, 80). As a former plantation slave, Sojourner Truth "ploughed and planted, and gathered into barns. . . . And ain't I a woman?" she asked. "I have borne thirteen children and seen most all sold off to slavery. . . . And ain't I a woman?" (Davis 1983, 60–64). Sojourner Truth traveled the country in the mid- to late 1800s speaking on behalf of the abolitionist and women's rights movements. Following in her wake, many women of color, working-class women, and others have worked to ensure that theory and scholarship are based on a multiplicity of experiences. As María Lugones put it:

> When I do not see plurality stressed in the very structure of a theory, I know that I will have to do lots of acrobatics—of the contortionist and the walk-on-the-tightrope kind—to have this theory speak to me without allowing the theory to distort me in my complexity.[12]

Just as feminists have shown the poverty of theory based on white male experiences, so too have many feminist theories been derived largely from the experience of white middle-class women. When Asian American women, Latinas, African American and Native American women, and white working-class women's experience has been erased, distorted, marginalized, or "otherized," theory is distorted and impoverished.

For example, under the work of race, class, and gender theorists, notions about the sex segregation of the labor market have yielded to much greater complexity. As progressive economists Teresa Amott and Julie Matthaei (1991) and others (Collins 1990; Dill 1987, 1988) have shown, when economists note the "surge" of women into the paid labor force, they are usually talking about white middle-class women, and ignoring the women of color and poor women who for generations have worked for wages, often as domestics in others' "private" space. Taking into account this experience of women of color has also substantially challenged the idea of a neat public/private split along gender lines—an idea that has figured large in analyses of patriarchy and the sexual division of labor (Collins 1990).

Work on sex segregation of the labor market without attention to racial segregation left us ill equipped to respond to the reality that the floor of white women's possibilities has often substantially constituted the ceiling for many women of color.[13] As opportunities opened for white middle-class women and they escaped from clerical work to which they had axiomatically been assigned up to the 1970s, clerical work has become a significant occupation for many women of color. In New York City, at the time of the

Columbia campaign, clerical work also constituted an important labor market possibility for African American men (Stafford 1985, xi–xiv). Further, women of color experienced segmented labor markets not only in terms of their own earning potential but also in having less potential male earnings to rely on given black men's long exclusion from trades and public protection jobs such as firefighting (Baca Zinn 1990; King 1990). (See chapter 3.) Popular celebrations of women's entry into professions are well tempered not only by questions of ghettoization and resegregation (Reskin and Roos 1990) but also by the concentration of black women into the public sector, highly vulnerable in antitax periods and times of budget cutbacks such as ours in which the social safety net has been unraveled (Higginbotham 1997). These differences in material conditions also create substantial obstacles for cross-race and cross-class women's solidarity. Understanding these dynamics of race- *and* sex-segregated labor markets is critical to understanding the Columbia clericals' situation.

Otherwise astute theoretical work that uses institutional racism as its starting place has at times been guilty of not taking patriarchy into account (Baron 1971, 1985; Carmichael and Hamilton 1969). The raging debates around William Julius Wilson's (1978) work—"Is it class or is it race?"—never figured gender oppression into the equation. This is amazing in light of the history of female-bashing made famous by U.S. Senator Moynihan's blame-the-black-matriarch approach (1965), an approach that has poisonously pervaded the welfare discourse (Baca Zinn 1990). Male/female relations are significant in Wilson's *The Truly Disadvantaged,* where he argues that the decline in black marriage is the product of structural economic changes driving black men out of the workforce rather than a problem of morals. Yet Wilson's analysis accepts the dominant view of female-headed households as "dysfunctional" by definition and fails to critique sexism and "consider economic or social reorganization that directly empowers and supports...single Black mothers" (Crenshaw 1989, 165). Critical legal scholar Kimberlé Crenshaw goes on to argue that the route to "a more complete theoretical and political agenda for the Black underclass" is "only through placing [black women] at the center of the analysis [so] that their needs and the needs of their families will be directly addressed."[14]

Distorted theory, needless to say, often leads to misguided social policy and social movement strategy. How else might we approach this?

Intersectionality: Beyond Single-Identity Politics

With this consistent record of problems, what is to be done with identity politics? In quickly reviewing the ways single-identity politics have limited and distorted movement practice and theoretical work, I have used an intersectionality approach. What conception of identity and identity politics is found here?

This large and rich network of theorizing and activism certainly does not constitute a single perspective. As sociologists Maxine Baca Zinn and Bonnie Thornton Dill point out, "Feminisms created by women of color exhibit a plurality of intellectual and political positions" (1996, 326). "Intersectionality," or as Baca Zinn and Dill term it, "multiracial feminism," is an "evolving intellectual and political perspective" with "a set of analytic premises."[15] While there are differences among its advocates, I find it useful to examine the core "analytic premises" of most of those developing an intersectional approach. Looking at the work of a core group of writers such as Patricia Hill Collins, Kimberlé Crenshaw, Bonnie Thorton Dill, bell hooks, Deborah King, Audre Lorde, Barbara Smith, Maxine Baca Zinn, and others, we can identify a core of ideas shared by most scholars advancing the intersectional approach. What does this perspective suggest for how to move beyond single-identity failings? How might it help us understand the challenge of the Columbia clerical movement?

Let's review intersectionality's core ideas about identity and identity politics.

1. *These are structurally located identities, "positioned within unjust power relations":* race, gender, class, and sexuality.[16] These are "differently situated social groups" with "varying degrees of advantage and power" (Baca Zinn and Dill 1996, 323). Each of these identities is understood to have been socially produced rather than biologically determined. "Race," say sociologists Becky Thompson and Sangeeta Tyagi, "is about *everything*—historical, political, personal—and race is about *nothing*—a construct, an invention that has changed dramatically over time and historical circumstance" (Thompson and Tyagi 1996, ix). "There is a continuous temptation to think of race as an *essence,* as something fixed, concrete and objective. . . . And there is also the opposite temptation: to see it as a mere illusion."[17] While each of these categories of inequality is a social creation, which has changed across time and place and specific group, each one has institutional and cultural and personal components that powerfully shape all apsects of our lives.[18]

In contrast to many social theories of difference and practices of "diversity management" by employers, political parties, and social service agencies, intersectionality analyzes structures of social inequality. Rather than examining *difference,* this perspective analyzes *domination.* This is a theory of *power relations:* these group identities are "shared locations" in these systems of power relations.[19] We must retain categories such as oppression, exploitation, and white supremacy, argues Nancy Hartsock, "rather than talk only about a sanitized 'difference'" (Hartsock 1996, 266). "Conceptualizing these systems of oppression as difference," argues Collins, "obfuscates the power relations and material inequalities that constitute oppression."[20]

2. *This is a nonadditive conception of identities that sees systems of domination as interdefining one another.* The dominant single-identity perspective is additive: race plus gender plus class. It is what philosopher Elizabeth Spelman critiques as the "pop-bead" model: "One's gender identity is not related to one's racial and class identity as the parts of pop-bead necklaces are related, separable and insertable in other 'strands' with different racial and class 'parts'" (Spelman 1988, 15). Rather, this intersectional approach argues each system of injustice defines and is defined by the others, leaving us with what Collins calls a "matrix of domination" (1990, 1998). Rather than talking about women "in the general," this approach suggests that there is no gender out of context of race and class (Spelman 1988). This is true not only for those in dominated groups but also for those in the dominating positions: My womanhood was as much defined by my whiteness and professional class position as was the womanhood of Columbia clericals whom I interviewed defined by their class and race locations.[21]

The alternative is the notion of many genders—each being differently constituted by race, class, and sexuality. Similarly, we can speak of many working classes.[22] Thus the notion of "multiple" inequalities "refers not only to several, simultaneous oppressions but to the multiplicative relationships among them" (King 1990, 270).

The multiple systems of domination thus correct the "either/or" approach of single identities, replacing it, Collins suggests, with a "both/and" approach: both race and gender, both class and race, and so forth.[23] Collins suggests we conceptualize a "matrix of domination" in which systems (or axes) of domination shape one another at different levels of social analysis (Collins 1990, 1996, 1998).

3. *Intersectionality occurs at various levels of institutional, cultural, and individual analysis, and in the dynamics among them.*[24] The structural level of analysis focuses on institutions such as workplace and economy, education, church, government, medicine, and so on. Structurally, intersectionality is visible in citywide or employer-specific sex- and race-segregated labor markets. The paltry wages for which most clericals still work and the Columbia

clericals' racially differentiated experience of layoffs are two examples. The cultural level includes ideologies that explain and justify oppression, and the ways in which different locations are symbolically represented.[25] On a cultural level, intersectionality analyzes stereotypes or "controlling images" through which dominated groups are viewed (Collins 1990). For example, some clericals reported images of the "minority single mother" to be a factor in their evaluations for raises or promotions.[26] Regarding individuals, intersectionality theory analyzes self-definitions, identity, consciousness, or interpersonal interactions—such as different views by Columbia clericals on unions, feminism, or the salience of race and gender identity in the workplace. However invisibly, each system of domination constructs the others.

4. We cannot assume any automatic, unitary, generic identity for any location. "Individuals do not fit neatly into unidimensional, self-identical categories" (Martin and Mohanty 1986, 204–5). Each location, and thus any identity, is in fact constituted by multiple systems of oppression, as well as individual history and ideological stance.[27] Collins describes African American women as having a "shared (though not uniform) location in hierarchical power relations in the United States. The existence of group interests means neither that all individuals within the group have the same experiences nor that they interpret them in the same way" (1998, 224). Whether, and on what basis, Columbia workers—black, Latino/a, Asian, white women and men—will see themselves as a collectivity becomes an open question. They will, as we would expect, differ substantially in whether and how they see gender inequality working with racial and class inequality in shaping their union struggle at Columbia.

5. Ideological understandings of any location vary enormously.[28] Although some critics assume identity politics to consist of nationalist or separatist ideology, identity-based movements can and do differ greatly in their ideologies. In the 1960s, integrationist civil rights organizations and nationalist Black Power organizations differed in their ideologies over the assessments of the nature of racism and their strategies for combating it.[29] The ideology of a labor campaign challenging racism is similarly an open question, which the Columbia clericals answered with an "antidiscrimination" approach.

In considering the question "On what basis do third world women form any constituency?" Chandra Mohanty argues for more overt attention to ideology. "After all, there is no logical and necessary connection between being 'female' and becoming 'feminist'" (1991, 6–7). She adds, "It is not color or sex which constructs the ground for these struggles. Rather, it is the way we think about race, class, and gender—the political links we chose to make among and between struggles."[30] Different reactions of clericals to their union's female leadership, to affirmative action, to the notion of "color blindness," to Al Sharpton's role in the Crown Heights conflict all well illustrate the role of ideology in constructing identity.

6. *Identities or locations are not only sites of oppression but also sites of resistance, and places where people go about the business of making life.* "I am not only a casualty, I am also a warrior," proclaimed Audre Lorde (1984, 41). This resistance often reshapes the nature of the oppression itself. Resistance "is not always [or only] identifiable through organized movements," cautions Mohanty. It is also "encoded...in the minute, day-to-day practices and struggles."[31] "From acts of quiet dignity...to involvement in revolt and rebellion," women and men in conditions of injustice wage resistance often using the constraints of their position as a springboard to resistance (Baca Zinn and Dill 1996, 328). The realities of women's second-shift responsibilities led the clericals at Columbia to replace much of the traditional after-work meeting format with lunch meetings in two shifts. These have greatly facilitated overall participation for men and women, both those with children and without. Yet Mohanty reminds us to make no assumption of resistance. She "challenge[s] the notion 'I am, therefore I resist!' ... the idea that simply being a woman, or being poor or black or Latino, is sufficient ground to assume a politicized oppositional identity" (1991, 33).

7. *Intersectionality rejects gender, class, or race primacy.* Much critical social theory identifies a single social relation—be it class (capitalism), gender (patriarchy), or race(ism)—in whose overthrow is rooted universal liberation. Many feminist theorists, particularly radical feminists, have argued that patriarchy is primary both in historical origins and as the pattern for domination off of which all others are copied. Meanwhile, Marxists recognize gender and race as critical matters of domination ("the woman question," "the race question") but consider them secondary to class exploitation. The idea, long used by much of the labor movement, that labor market racism and sexism are "secondary" significantly explains the nonunionized state of many clerical and service jobs today, and the diminished state of the labor movement. District 65's success partly hinged on finding ways to integrate gender and race inequality into their organizing issues.

However, intersectionality theory does not privilege any particular system of domination, nor does it consider them identical or parallel systems[32] or equally salient in structuring experience in any particular circumstance.[33] As we will hear, across race and gender, many Columbia clericals found institutional racism to be much more defining of their experience in the workplace and their union campaign than institutional sexism.

8. All individuals simultaneously occupy positions as oppressed and oppressor (Collins 1990, 1996; Lorde 1984). There are "few pure victims or oppressors," argues Collins (1996, 214). While "not denying that specific groups experience oppression more harshly than others," Collins, Lorde, and others note that individual social groups occupy positions of "privilege and penalty" (Collins 1996, 215, 218). "Intersecting forms of domination produce locations of both oppression and opportunity" (Baca Zinn and Dill 1996, 327). A group of white Columbia clerical workers face issues of class domination, but they may also have experienced "unacknowledged benefits" of whiteness (327): greater likelihood of starting salaries over the grade maximum, less likelihood of layoffs, or less experience of everyday racism. Straight women of color may encounter these and other experiences of racism but are insulated from institutional heterosexism (such as benefit policies) or individual heterosexist attitudes of coworkers or supervisors. Intersectionality thus highlights the "both/and position of simultaneously being oppressed and oppressor" (Collins 1996, 215). This structures much of the challenge of multi-identity politics and also provides significant potential for alliance building.

9. In a world of "one identity to a movement," the lived experience for those on the downside of multiple systems of oppression is fragmentation, erasure, partial denials, marginalization, and conflict. The title of Hull, Scott, and Smith's groundbreaking collection—*All the Women Are White, All the Blacks Are Men, But Some of Us Are Brave*—well captured black women's experience of exclusion. As Audre Lorde eloquently describes it, "I find I am constantly being encouraged to pluck out some one aspect of myself and present this as the meaningful whole, eclipsing or denying the other parts of self... [rather than] allowing power from particular sources of my living to flow back and forth freely through all my different selves, without the restrictions of externally imposed definition" (1984, 120–21).

10. Organizationally, intersectionality suggests the need for autonomous identity-based organization and the need for coalition across identity groups. Autonomous organization is needed for consolidation, articulation, support, and control. Activist, historian, and musician Bernice Johnson Reagon sees a need for a separate space in which a group develops its identity, articulates its agenda, and gathers strength. This serves as a "nurturing space where you... take the time to try to construct within yourself and within your community who you would be if you were running society.... Of course the problem with the experiment is that there ain't nobody in there but folk like you, which by implication means you wouldn't know what to do if you were running it with all the other people who are out there in the world" (1992, 505).

Thus, Reagon argues, coalition is critical, yet with the understanding of its difficulty, and fragility. She adds, "I feel as if I'm gonna keel over any minute and die. That is often what if feels like if you're *really* doing coalition work.... [It] is some of the most dangerous work you can do" (503, 506). Yet it is, Reagon suggests, the only way to "stay alive" (504). While creating barriers, the intersectional nature of oppression also begins to suggest a path for developing the coalitions needed for profound social change.

In the labor movement, as we will see in chapter 3, men and women of color, women of all races, and gays and lesbians have often created separate organizational spaces (committees or caucuses or separate organizations) for developing their own agendas, strategies, and strength for the ongoing coalition work as part of their unions.

Beyond Single-Identity Politics

Intersectionality theory lays bare the failings of single-identity politics. The breadth and depth of this critique poses obvious and fundamental questions. Given the persistent problems we have examined,[34] are identity politics the right way to go, the right strategy for progressive social movements? Does the use of identity as categories of resistance unintendingly give more power to the very categories of domination this resistance hopes to eradicate? Is the "logic of identity" necessarily "a logic of boundary defining that produces excluded, subordinate others"?[35] Can there be a nonessentialized identity politics? Can identity politics be reworked consistent with a multiinjustice understanding? Or should identity politics just be abandoned?

Although the undertow of identity politics is formidable and undeniable, the flood of responses to *This Bridge Called My Back, Some of Us Are Brave, Black Feminist Thought,* and the work of Audre Lorde, Toni Morrison, Alice Walker, and others is testimony to the powerful, positive vehicle of resistance that a more complex intersectional identity politics has constituted for many women of color, as for other groups. As social theorist Steven Seidman argues, "Identity constructions are not disciplining and regulatory only in a self-limiting and oppressive way; they are also personally, socially, and politically enabling" (1996, 391). Political scientist Nancy Hartsock similarly writes that despite the difficulties, identity politics have "been an important resource for social change" (1996, 265). How do we not lose this mobilizing power, and at the same time deal with the recurring underside?

I am reminded of Stuart Hall's words. Arguing that identity is histori-cally constructed, and that there is no such thing as a stable, unified subject, Hall says, "There is no way" people of the world "can act, can speak, can create, can come in from the margins and talk, can begin to reflect on their own experience unless they come from some *place*" (1991, 18). He argues for coming to "a new conception of our identities," which "has not lost hold of the place and the ground from which we can speak, yet it is no longer contained within that place as an essence (20). "While there are cer-tain conceptual and theoretical ways in which you can try to do without identity, I'm not yet convinced that you can. I think we have to try to reconceptualize what identities might mean in this more diverse and plural-ized situation" (15). This reconceptualization, I argue, allows us to rework essentialism but allows us to draw on identity to foment resistance.

Kimberlé Williams Crenshaw, African American critical legal scholar, argues similarly that "at this point in history, a strong case can be made that the most critical resistance strategy for disempowered groups is to occupy and defend a politics of social location rather than to vacate and destroy it" (1994, 112–13). For dealing with the failings of single-identity politics, she adds,

> Does that mean we cannot talk about identity? Or instead that any dis-course about identity has to acknowledge how our identities are con-structed through the intersection of multiple dimensions? A beginning re-sponse to these questions requires that we first recognize that the organized identity groups in which we find ourselves are in fact coalitions, or at least potential coalitions waiting to be formed. (114)

Crenshaw offers the example of women's marginalization in antiracist efforts. This recognition "does not require that we give up attempts to or-ganize as communities of color. Rather, intersectionality provides a basis for reconceptualizing race as a coalition between men and women of color [and] . . . may provide the means for dealing with other marginalizations as well. . . . Race can also be a coalition of straight and gay people of color." Crenshaw concludes, "With identity thus reconceptualized [as potential coalitions], it may be easier to understand the need for, and to summon the courage to challenge, groups that are . . . in one sense 'home' to us . . . and

[to] negotiate the means by which these differences will find expression in constructing group politics" (114–15).

I, too, am unwilling to abandon identity politics as a critical mobilizing source of oppositional politics. Rather than a "single voice," which Spelman pondered how any movement would construct, we need to aim for the many voices of a chorus—which, like Crenshaw's coalition, is "waiting to be formed." To the degree to which a theoretical approach can provide the "bases and supports for coalitions," and serve as a "resource for the development of new and more inclusive social movements," intersectional theory offers an important foundation (Hartsock 1996, 256–57).

How well did the Columbia clerical union do at creating its "potential" coalition? How well did it build on the intersection of race, class, and gender politics? Our analysis of the Columbia case will be helped by two additional stops. First, within labor, identity politics is a problem with a long history. To fully understand the Columbia clerical challenge of integrating class, race, and gender justice, we need to review labor's history of identity politics. It is, we will see, a quintessential example of the exclusionary nature of a single-injustice movement and the mobilizing power of identity-based movements by those so excluded.

Second, we need to consider how any movement creates identity. How could a movement mindful of this critique go about creating a multi-injustice identity? How is it—through what practices—do movements usually create single- or multi-identity politics? For this, in chapter 4, we will turn to social movement theory, which will provide us additional conceptual tools.

3

Labor and Identity Politics:
Historical and Contemporary Experiences

Labor's revitalization as an enduring political force will depend on its ability to organize, unify, and inspire its traditional constituents, as well as groups which will form the majority of tomorrow's union members: women, people of color, immigrants, gays and lesbians. Labor has histori-cally asked women workers, workers of color, gay and lesbian workers to join organized labor on the basis of their identities as workers only—a solidarity based on denial of sexism, racism and heterosexism as addi-tional oppressions that also must be addressed. But solidarity based on de-nial has not worked; it has made the house of labor feel like less of a home for many of us, and has weakened the labor movement.

—Cheryl Gooding

"LABOR'S BACK!" declares the bumper sticker. Hopefully. The 1995 elec-tion of new national leadership—"A New Voice for American Workers"—has been widely celebrated as a (potential) turning point for the labor move-ment. Under the leadership of John Sweeney, Richard Trumpka, and Linda Chavez-Thompson, the AFL-CIO committed itself to a full-throttle effort at rejuvenation and transformation. The New Voice program aimed to "build a new and progressive political movement of working people," "construct a labor movement that can change workers' lives," and "lead a democratic movement that speaks for all American workers" (Brecher and Costello 1998, 29). As the 1996 mission statement of the AFL-CIO put it, labor's task is "to bring economic justice to the workplace and social justice to our nation" (Moberg 1997, 25).

The task of renewal is no small one. Labor faces a staggering set of conditions: globalization of capital, antilabor trade agreements, increasing contingent workforce, increasing diversity of the U.S. workforce, increasing inequality in the United States, new technology, and stacked labor law, among others. Unionization rates have long been in a "free fall" from their 1950s high of just over a third of U.S. workers to 13.9 percent of U.S. workers overall, and 9.4 percent of private-sector workers in 1999 (Bureau of Labor Force Statistics). Internally, many unions face challenges to move beyond being an "insurance company and law firm," and become thoroughly democratic and activist organizations (Fletcher 1998, 17). Unions often confront public perceptions of labor as a selfish special interest and an irrelevant actor—a relic of a previous industrialized society, and a weakling no longer able to significantly influence social, political, and economic events.

As unionists attempt to revitalize the existing movement and organize millions of new members, labor's response to "diversity," as it is often called, including race and gender segregation in the labor market and the workplace, is critical. The labor movement's long, often shameful history of single-identity politics plays no small part in the diminished state labor finds itself in today. Luckily, the revitalization builds off of vibrant organizing and unionism—of which the Columbia clericals are a part—that has embraced a social justice philosophy and made labor a vehicle for all kinds of justice.

The stakes are high. "Labor unions remain the only large multiracial, multiethnic democratic institutions in our society," argue labor educators José La Luz and Paula Finn (1998, 171). "[A] strong and vibrant labor movement," adds labor educator Gregory Mantsios, "is critical to a democracy and to the well-being of its populace" (1998, xviii). Like their predecessors, labor leaders before the great industrial unionization campaigns of the 1930s and 1940s, new AFL-CIO leaders "face a similar challenge: encourage dramatic change or see their own organizations plunge toward extinction" (Brecher and Costello 1998, 27).

The new leadership committed itself to build a widened mass movement, saying, "The Federation must be the fulcrum of a vibrant social movement" (32). This means increased activism, increased attention to unorganized workers, and wider coalition.

After six years of new leadership, the movement has shown some important changes in its commitment to, and success in, new organizing and in its influence on national politics. As news commentators during the extended postelection counting of the 2000 presidential election pointed out, while labor's support of Gore had not brought victory, the resources labor brought to the contest significantly impacted the closeness of the race. Yet, as still declining union density suggests, the battle for resurgence has not yet turned the corner.

Labor's continuing effort to broaden from a narrow economic agenda advanced by many unions to a broader social justice vision includes making connections to larger communities beyond the workplace. Trade unionism must "speak to the totality of problems facing our members and the working class as a whole," as labor leader Bill Fletcher Jr. argues. "It must be the haven of the dispossessed. It must be the haven for Chicanos fighting for land and political power. It must be a home for Asian immigrants working in the new sweatshops" (1992, 11–12). To address the totality of problems that workers face, labor organizations must bring multi-identity politics to their mobilization efforts.

Aspects of Labor's Varied History of Identity Politics

An African American Columbia union activist, Calvin, told me that his friends often asked him why he was "wasting his time" in the Columbia organizing effort. For many African Americans, labor's virulent, even violent, history of discrimination is a good reason for distance from organized labor. Yet as Calvin told his friends, he saw the union at Columbia as an important vehicle for social change—one that could speak directly to the needs of women and people of color. "Look at who is in this room," he said in a strike authorization debate. He argued that the large female and minority membership made this an important social justice struggle.

Both Calvin and his friends are correct. A brief look at labor history shows that unions have often used identity politics to elevate white male workers at the expense of people of color, as well as women. However, as labor sociologist Ruth Milkman argues, much of this exclusion was practiced by craft unions, which represented only one of four important waves of union organizing. Each wave, she suggests, emerged in particular conditions and had a unique logic, and consequently distinct practices.[1] Attempts to create gender- and race-blind (single) labor identity politics, as the CIO did in its focus on industrial workers in the 1930s and 1940s, brought great benefits to many previously unorganized women and/or people of color. Yet ultimately these efforts excluded the vast majority of women and/or workers of color, who, given sex and race segregation in the labor market, worked outside the core industries, which were the strategic base of these drives.

There is also, however, a powerful history of multi-identity politics being put to progressive use in unions and other worker movements, giving working women and people of color a critical vehicle of resistance. Probably least well known are these powerful stories of identity-based resistance, in which the labor movement has given African Americans, Chicanos, Puerto Ricans, Asians, and other male and female workers of color, as well as white women workers, an effective forum for fighting labor market injustice. Sometimes this has occurred through official union campaigns, sometimes through organizations marginal to, or outside of, the labor movement.

In this chapter, we will look briefly at the many ways identity politics have played out in labor's history, giving special attention to Local 1199's hospital workers' organizing in the 1960s as an example of a mostly positive use of multi-injustice politics. This is not meant to be a comprehensive review of labor history, but a brief look at significant trends in labor's experience of identity politics. The challenges confronting the Columbia clerical campaign, and the multi-identity challenges central to labor movement revitalization, need to be understood in the context of this varied history of labor's experience of identity politics. What does such multi-identity unionism look like? How does labor do this? What traditions does labor have to draw on—or to avoid at all costs—in trying to meet this challenge?

Many would argue that traditionally social unionists have used a strong single-identity-based appeal: class. Despite decades of raging disagreements over the ultimate social vision and the route to it, progressive trade unionists mobilized around a vision of the labor movement as a pivotal vehicle for social justice for the working class—if not the transformation of the entire society. Inverting dominant ideology, labor activists affirmed the individual and collective value of members of the working class as the true producers of value, and as critical agents of social change. The labor movement affirmed and drew strength from working-class values and cultures, as well as contributing to their shaping.

Yet labor's use of identity politics was never only class based. As intersectionality theory argues, class identity does not exist in isolation from other identities and oppressions. "Class never appears in its pure form," concurs social movement theorist Stanley Aronowitz. "It is always alloyed, short of what might be called the rare instances of 'epochal' transformations, with other identities, discourses, movements" (1992, 72). While framing itself as a single unitary identity, the working-class identity as used and developed by the labor movement was in reality very ethnic, race, and gender specific. According to labor historian Mike Davis, the "U.S. labor movement of the late nineteenth century . . . failed to generate a working-class 'culture' that could overcome ethno-religious alignments outside the workplace"

(1986, 41). Aronowitz adds: "I want to argue that America has never produced the conditions that would foster class identification as a category with effects on everyday existence.... Even the class-oriented left felt obliged to work through other identities—including race identities—because they believed these were...primary among those they sought to reach."[2]

Race, Gender, and Class in Early Organizing

Most often, to the labor movement, the "working class" has meant the most privileged sectors of the class: white, skilled craftsmen or industrial workers. Craft unionism of the late nineteenth and early twentieth century excluded women and/or people of color, seeing them as a threat to wages that tight control by organized skilled laborers could wrestle from bosses.[3]

But organized labor was not always defined by its racist and sexist practices. The Knights of Labor, for example, which reached its peak membership (between 700,000 and 1 million) in 1886, was founded on the principle that no male worker should be excluded on the basis of color, race, or national origin.[4] Women were not eligible for membership until 1881, but by 1886 the Knights had established a department of women's work. At its height, the Knights included 113 all-women assemblies (including black and white women), from housekeepers to farmers to factory workers (Baxandall et al. 1976, 119). Across the South, Knights of Labor assemblies were often half black. The Knights actively recruited unskilled laborers, and the trade union sector with the Knights of Labor (such as the cigar makers, bricklayers and carpenters) lowered the barriers of entry for people of color (Foner 1974, 49). The Knights also built bridges between the labor movement and the early women's movement as well as the movement against racial injustice.[5] Ida B. Wells, black activist and journalist, said of a Knights meeting she attended in 1887, "It was the first assembly of the sort in this town where color was not the criterion to recognition as ladies and gentlemen" (Foner 1974, 57). Although the Knights could not maintain themselves as a diverse working people's organization, they represented an important model of cross-race solidarity.[6]

The American Federation of Labor gained prominence in the late nineteenth century, with Samuel Gompers at the head, echoing many of the Knights' original progressive goals. But Gompers's goal of taking in the "whole laboring element of this country, no matter of what calling," was short-lived, with the AFL accepting segregation and exclusion among its locals (64, 67–69, 75). White ethnic communities, though rooted in different subcultures and often in competition with one another, often shared a key element: a white racial identity and racist practices. Labor historian Herbert

Hill argues that "race and racism were crucial factors in determining the characteristics of organized labor as a social institution" (1987, 35). Under the "anti-coolie" slogan, Chinese workers were driven from cigar, boot, shoe, and other trades. Identity politics have often been at the center of labor-supported state policies. Arguing for the passage of the Chinese Exclusion Act of 1882, Gompers said, "Maintenance of the nation depended upon maintenance of racial purity" (43). These exclusionary laws sentenced Chinese workers and their families to generations of "split-family life," with men working in the United States, and women and children remaining in China until sons or "paper sons" had come of working age.[7] A serious economic depression during the late 1890s strengthened skilled white craftsmen's determination to exclude workers of color. Some AFL union constitutions delineated separate locals for unskilled black workers, with clear constitutional prohibition of transfer or mobility into apprenticeship or more skilled positions.

Yet the AFL's white, male, craft-based exclusionary practices during this period tell only part of labor's story. Assuming a variety of organizational forms, efforts by African American, Latino/a, Asian workers, and women workers of all races have drawn strength from identity politics to mount important challenges to racist and sexist exclusion and discrimination stemming from both the workplace and the AFL. In 1881, for example, black washerwomen, domestics, and cooks in Atlanta struck for living wages and greater autonomy. Their efforts reflected the "labor consciousness of Black women and left little doubt about how serious Black women were about improving their wages and work conditions" (Harley 1998, 46). Outside traditional labor organizing practices, black women established their own organizations to deal with the needs of black working women, who were most often domestics. Scholar Roslyn Terborg-Penn describes the creation in 1897 of the White Rose Industrial Association, which worked alongside the White Rose Working Girls' Home to protect domestic workers who had recently migrated to New York City from the South (1985, 142). The organization provided housing, academic and vocational education, and programs in race pride. Similar work was undertaken in the early 1900s by the Association for the Protection of Negro Women (and other organizations) in many cities (142–44).

Sexism, as well as racism, was useful to white male unionists in their attempt to consolidate power and respond to the assaults of industrialization. Women who were in the paid workforce were considered by unions to be a "threat to the labor movement"—"weak," "vulnerable," "passive," and "unorganizable." Union support of the family wage—a wage large enough for men (but not women) to support their families—boosted white male income and eroded women's (whether single or married and supporting children). By the twentieth century, the balance in labor's position between protection of working-class families from the assaults of capitalism and protection of white male labor privilege from female competition had shifted to the latter (May 1985, 7–11). Said Gompers, "It is the so-called competition of the unorganized defenseless women workers, the girl and the wife, that often tends to reduce the wages of the father and the husband" (9). Two solutions were possible. Either unions organized women and waged a cross-gender fight for equal pay, or they removed the weak link. The labor movement "brotherhood" chose the latter, which maintained not only white male labor market privilege but patriarchal relations in the home and wider society (Hartmann 1979, 217–19).

Unions denied crafts training to young white women (women of color were largely confined to domestic or agricultural work), who learned under the only conditions they could: often as strikebreakers or in nonunion shops (Balser 1987; Hartmann 1979, 1981). Although sex (and race) segregation of labor certainly predated AFL exclusionary efforts, Milkman points out that the AFL's exclusion came in a critical period of "economic expansion and major occupational shifts," thus having a significant impact on the "consolidation of the sexual division of paid work" (1980, 98). This "multifaceted hostility of AFL unions towards women workers" (118) included outright exclusion, refusal to charter women's locals, high initiation and fees, or lowered fees as the justification of second-class union citizenship (Kessler-Harris 1985a, 116).

Despite hostility from official unions, women participated in dramatic organizing drives, such as the 1909 "Uprising of the 20,000." Mostly Jewish women, these New York City shirtwaist workers walked out to protest falling wages, long hours, and an unfair system of fines subcontractors levied against the workers. Twenty-year-old Clara Lemlich, an immigrant garment worker, exemplified her union's militance when she called out at a prestrike mass meeting, "I have listened to all the speakers, and I have no further patience for talk. I am one who feels and suffers from the things pictured. I move we go on a general strike!" (Amott and Matthaei 1991, 116). The "girl's local" of the International Ladies Garment Workers Union (ILGWU Local 25) grew substantially from these 1909–1912 organizing strikes (Kessler-Harris 1985a, 126). Their struggle received important support from middle-class feminists, including, later on, a woman professor from Barnard who helped the union extend its basic trade union education to a full liberal arts program.[8] The union translated its militance, energy, and "women's culture" into extensive educational, social, and health care programs, which were enthusiastically embraced by the membership (Feldberg 1987b). But men firmly occupied leadership of the union, and when the women leaders of Local 25 developed a plan to increase union democracy, the male leadership interpreted their "proposal as an attempt of Communist women to gain control of the union," and dismantled the local.[9]

While women carved out limited space in the labor movement, male union leaders pushed for protectionist legislation, which limited the hours, type of work, and other conditions of women's labor. Seeing (white) women as needing "special protection" was an extension of both the logic of the garment union's paternalism and the exclusivity of the AFL unions. Although unions opposed such government interference in labor-management struggle, protective legislation was an acceptable exception, given women's "vulnerability," and provided a way to contain women's labor market competition (May 1985, 10). "We cannot drive the females out of the trade," Cigarmakers Union president Strasser is quoted by Hartmann as saying, "but we can restrict their daily quota of labor through factory laws" (1979, 226). Many women workers and progressives supported this legislation as the most viable way to improve the abusive conditions confronting women workers (Kessler-Harris 1985b). The pervasive ideology of the period made such appeals to women's special status seem natural and inevitable. Yet other feminists opposed this female difference framing, arguing instead for an equality-based policy. The special-protection framing, while winning short-term gains in some conditions of women's labor, had substantial long-term consequences in solidifying sex-segregated occupations and at best second-class union membership.

"Special protection" did not, of course, apply to women of color, who were not the targets of white male paternalism. Nor did the revered "family wage"—even with its sexist connotations—fall within their grasp, as the wages of black males did not approach those of their white counterparts. With women of color so largely confined to domestic work and excluded from other occupations as the result of racism and sexism in the labor market, the vast majority of this early history of "women's" experience in the organized labor movement is a history of white women (King 1990, 288).

But outside "the house of labor," black women were not idle in their collective action. In the 1920s and 1930s, domestic workers formed several short-lived unions. As Dill's 1988 study of domestic workers explores, over the decades black domestic workers developed survival networks critical for social activities, support, information sharing, and strategizing about how to deal with individual employers and how to chart a career path in domestic work. As King points out, "Into the first quarter of this century, organized labor's approach to economic disadvantage held little promise for blacks or women, and thus no promise for black women" (1990, 286). The relatively smaller numbers of African American and Caribbean women who had escaped domestic work for industrial employment had little place in unions.

> In 1929, the ILGWU, representing 45,000 white dress-makers, did launch a special effort to unionize the 4,000 black women working in New York City dress shops. At this time, black women earned from eight to twelve dollars a week, while union workers received from twenty-six to forty-four dollars a week. (Terborg-Penn 1985, 151)

Elsewhere in the African American labor movement, resistance sometimes took the form of black unions, like the Brotherhood of Sleeping Car Porters, led by labor and civil rights activist A. Philip Randolph. With 15,000 black porters working in its sleeping cars, the Pullman Company was the largest employer of black workers in the United States. In 1925 Randolph founded the Brotherhood, but it did not gain entry into the AFL until 1936 and did not win its first contract until 1937 (Yates 1998, 113–14). In some periods, Randolph combated racism from within "the house of labor," and at other times he founded extraunion black labor formations such as the Negro American Labor Congress.[10]

CIO's Nondiscriminatory Unionism: Advances and Limitations

With the rise of the Congress of Industrial Organizations (CIO) in the 1930s to respond to new mass production industries, hundreds of thousands of blacks and women won union representation.[11] This organizing was for the most part a case of *nonuse*[12] of race- and gender-based identity politics: the CIO organized on the basis of the "inclusionary logic of industrial unionism."[13] The transforming migration of black Americans out of the South as cotton declined and into the industrial centers of the North, especially as a consequence of war, closed immigration, and growing industrial expansion, brought many African Americans, especially men, into industrial unions (McAdam 1982; Baron 1971). While cotton declined in the South, tobacco continued to be an important crop and source of employment for black women. During a 1937 strike of the tobacco workers in Richmond, Virginia, five hundred "white garment ladies" from the ILGWU joined the black women on the picket line. "The police were furious," says historian Philip Foner, and they raged about "*white* women out here parading for n..."[14]

The CIO formally opposed discrimination, sometimes out of strategic necessity, sometimes out of principle, viewing it as an employer effort to undermine class solidarity. The record of actual practice was uneven. Some CIO unions were able to enforce antidiscrimination rules on the shop floor. For example, the United Packinghouse Workers Association (UPWA), as labor educator and economist Michael Yates recounts, fought for equal pay and open access to the highest-paying jobs for (mostly) men of all races. At Swift, the union monitored hiring and successfully grieved company discrimination in 1950 (Yates 1998, 113). African American workers, mostly male, in CIO unions benefited from wage, benefit, and grievance protections of the unions. This period was marked by the entry of black workers into many industrial jobs and unions. In many industries, however, internal job segregation with differential pay, health risks, and conditions continued. The maintenance of separate department seniority lists maintained racial exclusion, for example, in the steelworkers and autoworkers unions (111). Mike Davis points to the wave of "hate strikes" between March and June 1943—100,000 "man days" lost—in opposition to the upgrading of black workers (1986, 81).

Many women clearly benefited from the CIO's efforts, but its focus on the pivotal mass production industries such as auto, steel, and rubber meant that women, who mostly worked in sex-segregated occupations, remained peripheral (Milkman 1993c). Though the CIO organized women tobacco and textile workers across the South, mostly female Mexican American pecan workers in Texas, and black women laundry workers in Chicago, among many others, there were still only about 800,000 women unionists in 1940, out of 11 million women in the workforce (Foner 1980, 319–33).

A major boost to women's CIO membership came as World War II Rosies entered mass production industries, but this was short-lived. This period also opened the door for black women to come into mass production jobs, and with them, CIO union membership, although internal job segregation and pay differentials often persisted. Through the efforts of women union leaders, "some unions, notably the United Automobile Workers, did make special efforts to aid their female members. Many unions sought to provide child care and other community services for women workers, and several negotiated contracts providing for maternity leave without loss of seniority for their female members. By the end of the war most unions had endorsed the idea of "the rate for the job," or "equal pay for equal work" (Milkman 1980, 130). Women who came into the labor movement during this time gained the benefits of trade unionism and left behind an important legacy of "gender-conscious protest."[15] Yet most were laid off at the end of the war, and few unions stepped forward to protect women's employment (Foner 1980, 389–93).

After the AFL-CIO merger in 1955, the federation failed to intervene in the continuing notorious race-based exclusionary practices of the building trades, railway unions, and other skilled crafts. Women were de facto excluded because of patriarchal notions of women's work and union-supported protectionist laws that kept women out of higher-paying industrial jobs. In the 1970s, the affirmative action programs, which were governmentally ordered in response to African American resistance to continuing exclusion from the skilled work in a variety of industries, were also met by widespread union opposition to what unions termed "reverse racism." Long after black workers had become a sizable percentage, if not majorities, in many unions, union staff and leadership positions continued to be virtually all-white provinces (Hill 1987, 33).

Black Resistance

In the late 1960s and 1970s, African American trade unionists formed caucuses or extraunion formations (or, as castigated by the labor movement, "dual unions") to undertake the struggle in a number of unions. A caucus of Bethlehem Steel workers at Sparrows Point (Maryland) brought an important affirmative action suit. United Community Construction Workers (Boston) fought for desegregation of construction. The Dodge Revolutionary Union Movement (DRUM) and its spin-offs (in Detroit) and the United Black Brothers of Mahwah (in New Jersey) fought racism in the auto plants and UAW. On the national level, the Coalition of Black Trade Unionists was formed in the early 1970s.[16]

These struggles by the African American community against racist exclusion have most often centered on access to higher-paying trades or public protection jobs for men of color. In solidarity, and as family members lacking indirect access to the wages of better-paying male jobs, many black women supported these efforts. African American women also participated in the black caucuses and organizations of the 1970s. The second convention of the Coalition of Black Trade Unionists in 1972, for example, was attended by 1,141 delegates, of whom 35 to 40 percent were women (Foner 1978, 92).

Public-sector and service sector organizing began in the 1950s and 1960s with blue-collar sanitation and highway workers and came to include teachers, service workers, clericals, and professionals, as well. Public-sector employment skyrocketed during the Kennedy and Johnson admin-istrations as part of the "Great Society" programs.[17] Although this latest wave, like the CIO, organized on the basis of occupation, not race and gender identity, it has significantly transformed the gender and race demo-graphics of U.S. union membership (Milkman 1990, 100). Women and workers of color were recruited not as the result of conscious identity-based targeting "but as a by-product of their recruitment of particular categories of workers who seemed ripe for unionization" (100). As a result of public-sector strikes and political pressure on a state-by-state basis, the right to or-ganize was won (Bell 1985, 283). This brought forth dramatic increases in public-sector unionization: public-sector union density more than tripled between the late fifties and late seventies (Juravich and Bronfenbrenner 1998, 262).

These public-sector organizing campaigns have at times embodied re-sistance identity politics, with some having an integral relation to the civil rights movement.

> Organizing black government-workers also led to breakthroughs in tradi-tionally non-unionized areas of the country, most notably the south. Here, black sanitation- and highway-workers receiving low wages and no job security or rights, asked public unions to organize and represent them. "Dignity" was a common theme in these drives, and links to the civil rights movement were more than rhetorical—civil rights activists were often pro-union activists as well. The civil rights movement defined social enfranchisement as an end; public-sector jobs and public-sector unions became part of the means. It was hardly coincidental that when Martin Luther King, Jr., was killed in 1968, he was visiting Memphis to support striking AFSCME sanitation-workers. (Bell 1985, 285)

Fierce groundbreaking private-sector and nonprofit organizing strug-gles were also significantly propelled by class and race identity politics. Highly visible cases include Chicano and immigrant farmworkers (United Farm Workers), black and Puerto Rican hospital workers (1199, the Na-tional Union of Hospital and Health Care Employees), and Chicana gar-ment workers (Amalgamated Clothing Workers of America) (Foner 1978, 1980, 1981). Public and service sector unions have embraced issues of par-ticular concern to working women in groundbreaking comparable worth campaigns, and efforts around child care, family leave, and sexual harassment (Bell 1985; Milkman 1993c). This unionization has been especially significant for black women, who disproportionately work in the public sector (Amott and Matthaei 1991; Higginbotham 1997). These unions have also been the site of significant leadership development of women of all races, although often confined to the local level.

Summary

These varied traditions of labor's identity politics are all visible today. The exclusionary use of race-based identity politics continues in some unions. It is these practices that loom largest in defining images of labor and identity politics and point many progressive labor activists to argue avidly for a race (and gender) blind trade unionism. Despite decades of struggle that have included affirmative action and mandated apprentice programs, African Americans continue to be largely locked out of the building trades. This is evidenced in the continuing pickets and arrests as construction workers of color vie for their share of the jobs (see Kadetsky 1992). Periodically, the smoldering tensions regarding court-ordered affirmative action programs in police, fire, and school departments burst into flame.

As we have also seen, however, this is not labor's only history of identity politics. There is another significant thread—as best seen in Knights of Labor, CIO organizing, and public-sector organizing—that has worked for nondiscriminatory class politics. These have brought tremendous gains of union membership to millions of women workers and workers of color and their communities. Yet given the "nonuse" of explicit race or gender identities, race and sex discrimination often continued inside union workplaces and unions themselves. Also, the continuing race and sex segregation of labor and domestic work often meant most workers of color and/or women workers remained outside of the labor movement when it pursued a strategy of organizing core industries.

Finally, there is also an often underappreciated history of identity-based struggles of white women and women and men of color to the oppressive conditions of their labor—as seen in the uprising of the 20,000 women garment workers in New York City in the early 1900s, to the Sleeping Car Porters Union, to the washerwomen's, farmworkers', and sanitation workers' organizing, and more. Sometimes these took the form of workers' associations outside of unions; other times they were conducted in the name of, and with the resources of, organized labor. As we will review shortly, such efforts continue today in immigrant garment and service worker organizing, clerical organizing, and more.

Each of these three traditions of labor's identity politics very much provides the context for Columbia clericals—as well as the larger labor movement—as they try to create a truly inclusive unionism and fight for full workplace justice. These traditions provide critical lessons of what unions can draw upon in weaving together class, race, and gender politics. Because less is known of these identity-based resistance struggles, and because they constitute an important part of labor's experience with identity politics, it is useful to consider such a case in depth.

"Union Power, Soul Power": The Role of Class, Race, and Gender in Local 1199

In the late 1950s and the 1960s, Local 1199 organized thousands of hospital workers in campaigns that were projects of both the labor and civil rights movements. The union was no stranger to work in the civil rights movement: Local 1199 had supported the Montgomery boycott and had become a friend of Martin Luther King Jr., who called 1199 "my favorite union" (Foner 1980, 426). These hospital campaigns, first in New York City and later in Charleston, South Carolina, are interesting case studies in organizing that integrated race, class, and gender politics, although the latter was rarely made explicit. In 1959 Local 1199, Retail Drug Employees, began organizing the workers in New York City's voluntary hospitals—as opposed to for-profit or public hospitals.[18]

Voluntary hospital workers—90 percent black and Puerto Rican— were among "the most needy and neglected group of workers in New York City."[19] These included housekeeping and kitchen workers, porters, nurse's aides, and orderlies. Wages of a porter at Montifore and other hospitals were less than half that of porters at unionized drugstores: $36 for forty-four hours versus $72 with benefits for forty hours (Foner 1980, 425). The first six months of organizing secured a union contract for workers at Montifore, but intransigent hospital administration at seven other hospitals led to a strike of more than 3,500 workers, largely women, in May 1959 (428). The strike rallied widespread support of black and Puerto Rican leaders, including NAACP leader Thurgood Marshall and congressman Adam Clayton Powell behind "la cruzada," as New York's *El Diario* termed the campaign (428–30). The strike was also quite successful in mobilizing New York trade unionists, particularly Central Labor Council president Van Arsdale. "Union chiefs who long ago retired their marching shoes in favor of taxicabs or Cadillacs," commented the *New York Times,* "have taken their place on the picket line beside the Negro and Puerto Rican strikers" (430). A forty-six-day strike brought a grievance mechanism, arbitration, wage increases, overtime pay, but no direct union recognition, which the union saw as requiring further struggle.

In 1962 further strikes at Beth-El and Manhattan Eye, Ear, and Throat Hospitals brought further even greater mobilization of black and Puerto

Rican communities. Labor historian Philip Foner, from whose account of these events I largely draw, describes the Committee for Justice for Hospital Workers. With a membership of 235, it included many notable veteran civil rights activists. A letter for the committee was signed by author James Baldwin, labor and civil rights leader A. Philip Randolph, and Joseph Monserrat, national director of the Migration Division of the Puerto Rican Department of Labor. It argued:

> As leaders of the Negro and Puerto Rican communities, we believe that the hospital strikes symbolize in most dramatic form the second-class citizenship status and sweatshop wages of all minority group workers in our society. The hospitals' refusal to agree to such a simple request as a secret ballot election and the elementary right of union representation ... constitutes nothing less than a determination to perpetuate involuntary servitude among the minority group workers at the bottom of the economic ladder.[20]

The intervention of Governor Rockefeller to support passage of collective bargaining rights for workers in voluntary hospitals brought an end to the sixty-two-day strike. Before a year was up, thousands of hospital workers celebrated these new legal rights. By 1965 Local 1199 had grown to 30,000 workers, and by 1968 they celebrated their milestone win of a minimum of $100 weekly salary for 21,000 New York hospital workers.[21] Shortly before his death in March 1968, King addressed an 1199 rally: "You have provided concrete and visible proof that when black and white workers unite in a democratic organization like Local 1199, they can move mountains."[22]

Under the slogan "Union Power, Soul Power," Local 1199 tried to move mountains in Charleston, South Carolina. In early 1969 a group of black women hospital workers in Charleston contacted Local 1199, which had recently formed a National Organizing Committee, under the honorary chair of Coretta Scott King. The situation exploded after the firing of twelve leaders of four hundred workers of the Medical College Hospital of the University of South Carolina. These nurse's aides, orderlies, and kitchen and laundry workers had tried unsuccessfully to organize on their own. Charleston, Foner describes, was "one of the few large Southern cities that had not been touched by the civil rights movement. It had also been largely bypassed by the upsurge in trade unionism since the 1930s" (1980, 440). The campaign confronted more than their employer. "We had to fight the whole power structure of Charleston and of South Carolina. We were up against Governor McNair, Mendel Rivers, and Strom Thurmond," said Mrs. Brown, a union activist (Baxandall et al. 1976, 361). The Carolinas, in the 1960s, had the lowest unionization rate in the United States (Fink and Greenberg 1989, 129–30). Governor McNair also declared his resolute opposition to public-sector unionism (Foner 1980, 441).

As had other community-wide civil rights campaigns that preceded it, the Charleston effort used "mass meetings, daily marches, evening rallies in churches and union halls, boycotts of stores and schools . . . daily confrontations and mass arrests" (441). By the end of the first week, a hundred arrests had occurred; by several weeks later, the governor had sent in 600 state troopers and National Guard. A Mother's Day march drew 10,000 supporters. Arrests continued. The support, however, was not without its conflicts. There were local black leaders who wanted to avoid the confrontation that came with SCLC campaigns, and a "violent fringe" who broke discipline by taking more militant action.[23]

Framed as a joint labor–civil rights issue, the campaign was made a national issue. The campaign was supported by a range of other civil rights organizations and black officials. Coretta Scott King came to Charleston to speak and lead demonstrations and was active throughout. A full-page *New York Times* ad with Coretta Scott King's picture ran with the statement "If my husband were alive today he would be in Charleston, South Carolina."[24] The story made national news for weeks. Unions from across the country sent money and declared support. Especially strong was support from Walter Reuther, president of United Auto Workers. Substantial support came from liberal politicians, black and white. A group of twenty-five congresspeople asked Nixon to appoint a special mediator to resolve the situation (Fink and Greenberg 1989, 146).

It was King who named the gender reality of this organizing. She noted how impressed she was by "the emergence of black women leaders . . . following in the footsteps of Harriet Tubman and Sojourner Truth—of Rosa Parks and Daisy Bates and Fannie Lou Hamer. And they will be a source of great pride to the black people and to the entire labor movement" (Foner 1980, 442). Strike leader Mary Ann Moultrie similarly declared to the 1969 AFL-CIO convention delegates:

> We 400 hospital workers—almost all of us women, and all of us black— were compelled to go on strike so that we could win the right to be treated as human beings. In this struggle we had to take on more than just the managements of two hospitals.
>
> We had to fight the entire power structure of the state of South Carolina. . . . We had to face 1,200 National Guardsmen armed with tanks, and bayonets, and hundreds of state troopers. All because 400 black women

dared to stand up and say we just were not going to let anybody turn us around. . . .

A year ago, nobody ever heard of us. We were forgotten women, second-class citizens. We worked as nurse's aides. We cleaned the floors. We prepared the food in the hospitals. And if it had not been for the union, we would still be forgotten people.

We have demonstrated to the city of Charleston, to the state of South Carolina, and to the people all over America that we can and we will over-come. And nobody, just nobody, is going to turn us around.[25]

Increasing arrests and daily actions, increasing national support for the strikers, along with increasing federal intervention eventually brought a compromise settlement.[26] This included pay increases, a grievance procedure, a system of union dues deduction through credit union accounts, and reinstatement of fired workers. It did not win official union recognition. One activist proclaimed, "We built a winning combination of 1199 union power and SCLC soul power. 1199B is here to stay in Charleston" (Baxandall et al. 1976, 361). The union had hoped that the settlement would function as a "foot in the door," as it had in its New York City campaign. "At the time of settlement," labor historians Leon Fink and Brian Greenberg argue, "many of the second-level 1199 and SCLC staff left [Charleston] convinced that the foundation for a successful union local had indeed been laid" (1989, 155). The hospital administration, however, reneged on its part of the agreement. With the sudden removal of the vast support resources of 1199 and SCLC, the local workers' organization was unable to sustain itself and collapsed.[27]

Despite this collapse, many local black leaders described the hospital strike as a transforming event in the community, "like a revolution," yielding increased political power for Charleston's blacks. For 1199 nationally, the campaign brought substantial new organizing outside of New York, as the union had gained "credibility" and "strengthened its image as a 'civil rights union'" (Foner 1980, 444; Fink and Greenberg 1989, 158). "Particularly for black urban workers," argue Fink and Greenberg, "the 'union power, soul power' crusade broke down barriers separating labor organizing from the community-based militancy of the era."[28]

Although captured in the elegant words of Coretta Scott King and Charleston leader Mary Ann Moultrie, the gendered nature of the struggle was little acknowledged. As District 1199's president Leon Davis later came to note of labor more broadly, "There is not sufficient appreciation or understanding among the leaders of organized labor" of the role of women in the workforce. He went on to "attribute the lack of success in organizing workers to our inability to adjust to this challenge. . . . Our attitude towards women is too often the same as management's" (Foner 1980, 455).

The Underside of Identity Politics in 1199

Whereas Davis identified the union's shortcomings in understanding the role of women in the workforce, he did not apply any similar understanding to the structure of male power in the upper echelons of union leadership, over which he long presided. The legacy of 1199's white male leadership, its centralized constitution, and the top leaders' private meetings and shared history in Left organizations (the Communist Party in particular) created enormous obstacles to any nonwhite or nonmale or nonleftist aspiring to leadership in the union (Fink and Greenberg 1989, 211). With Leon Davis, 1199's president for the previous half century, approaching retirement, the union could no longer delay its "day of reckoning" (211). While the rhetoric and many of the practices of 1199's progressive white male leadership boosted democracy in the union and affirmed the idea that the leadership should come from the rank and file, in fact, the challenge of sharing decision-making power across race, gender, and class remained.

Thus the race and class identity politics of 1199, which so greatly propelled grassroots mobilizing in the 1960s, were not always evident in the union's structure or decision-making process. Labor scholars Fink and Greenberg argue that while "celebrated as the heroic best hopes for the future and patronized as unformed intellects, younger black leaders held the prestige of union office without commensurate, decision-making responsibility" (214). When African American Doris Turner emerged as heir apparent to Leon Davis for New York's 1199, no structure was created for her difficult transition. Instead Davis expected her to learn by osmosis, a paternalistic "Watch me and you'll understand" approach that assumed Turner would unquestioningly adopt Davis's political vision and mission (213). In fact, according to labor historian Joshua Freeman, Turner's concerns were "more parochial, aimed at preserving a hard-won personal and institutional power base" (1984, 381). Assessing Turner to lack the competence to assume leadership, the old guard dragged out the process of passing on real authority. Turner's supporters felt that the old leadership would "do anything to undermine her" (Fink and Greenberg 1989, 219).

When the old guard did turn over leadership of New York 1199 to Turner and national 1199 to Henry Nichols, an African American union leader from Philadelphia, the union plummeted into a severe, bitter, extended conflict. It became "triangulated internal warfare" among New York City 1199, national 1199, and its parent union, RWDSU (219). Significantly crossed into the conflict was the issue of the planned merger of 1199 and the Service Employees International Union (SEIU).

The conflict was often race framed, as well. Turner supporters saw the old guard's (and their supporters') criticism of Turner as racist. Some opponents felt Turner's inexperience and mistakes were forgiven by 1199 members because of their strong identification with her. She was, as Gloria Steinem called her, "a kind of walking personification of 1199" (Foner 1980, 454). As one Turner loyalist put it, "We believe in her. She's a fighter who grew up with her people" (Fink and Greenberg 1989, 221). And she was an African American female leader in a union whose previous leadership had not reflected its membership in race or gender terms. Using what Cornel West calls "racial reasoning," many workers may have admired Turner less for her leadership abilities and more for her "rise from a dead-end job to the top of the largest unit in the union" (Freeman 1984, 381). Turner gave increased prominence to race-based practices within the union (what Fink and Greenberg called a "combination of black nationalism, business unionism, and an ethnic/political club house" [1989, 220]).

The conflict "splintered the leadership and the membership" and resulted in loyalty tests and mass staff departures (Hudson and Caress 1991, 70). At times the conflict became violent, including a letter bombing and death threats (Fink and Greenberg 1989, 211). This complex, multifront conflict, continuing over much of the 1980s, left the organization incapacitated in contract battles with the hospitals and other employers. The union became incapable of competently carrying out its most basic organizational tasks.

Identity politics at 1199 had propelled the union toward tremendous power and gains for its membership but also undercut democratic process and the ability to work across race, class, and gender lines, and eventually the union's ability to execute fundamental tasks. Successful union campaigns, such as support of Jesse Jackson's 1988 New York campaign, the home care workers' organizing and contract campaign, the 1988–1989 hospital contract campaign, and the election of executive vice president Dennis Rivera to union presidency in 1989 all helped to move the union out of the crisis.

Yet the crisis left lingering lessons. "A union that recognized... togetherness as the only winning strategy and soul power as a crucial complement to economic organization had come apart in racial animosity and mistrust" (Fink and Greenberg 1989, 223). The 1980s leadership struggle remains a sobering reminder of the potential dangers—the underside—of identity politics that had so successfully built the union in an earlier period.[29]

Identity-Based Resistance Today

Recent labor battles in the 1980s and 1990s underscore the importance and challenges of integrating a multi-identity politics into the work of organizing. In New York City in 1982, for example, a contract struggle of Sportswear Local 23-25 of the International Ladies' Garment Workers' Union (ILGWU), made up mostly of Chinese immigrant women, put 20,000 garment workers on strike. Their massive and ultimately successful effort exposed the lie of the false but widely held belief that immigrant workers are "passive, vulnerable workers with little capacity for militancy and minimal interest in unionism" (Milkman 1993b, 282). In the period before the strike, union activists learned to take into account the ways that class, gender, and ethnicity would affect their organizing. Katie Quan, Local 23-25 activist, says that when she worked with mostly men restaurant workers, she found they came to meetings on time. "Of course, you'd have to hold the meeting where they wanted it, and at the times they wanted to meet. I had meetings at my house at one o'clock in the morning because that's when all the waiters get off work" (289). But organizing women had a different set of challenges. Women workers drifted into meetings an hour or two late depending on their kids' nap schedules. They brought their children with them and so didn't want to come out in bad weather or when colds and flus were circulating. "And when we finally managed to have a meeting," says Katie Quan, "it was hard to keep it focused. They'd talk in one sentence about [the organizing effort] and then, in the same sentence, they'd start talking about their kids, about changing diapers and all that stuff" (289). Quan noted that these workers brought strong class consciousness to their unions. In this Local's struggle, class allegiance outweighed ethnic allegiance, with workers understanding that management represented interests other than their own. This left many Chinese factory owners pitted against their workers. On the other hand, the fact that the strike was being debated in Chinese newspapers and was the talk of the town in Chinese neighborhoods meant that the work of these immigrant women garment workers had entered into a public forum, giving them a strong ethnic base of attention and solidarity.

Being attentive to the multiple identities of the garment workers meant a successful strike—one that not only preserved union benefits for the garment workers but provided evidence to the union of the importance of these immigrant women workers. Thus, in the aftermath of the strike, the garment workers won a child care center in Chinatown—a benefit the union had previously considered but had not followed through on (290). The community looked on the union with more respect and began to "turn to the union as spokesperson for the garment workers and began to include the union in all kinds of community coalitions" (294). Women rose in the ranks of the union leadership, and the newly formed Chinese Committee of the Coalition of Labor Union Women became a training ground for Chinese women workers.

Working for Inclusion

Many organizations have avidly worked to develop women's leadership in the labor movement. Thousands of women in unions or union drives have attended women's trade union summer schools. Building on a tradition going back decades,[30] these schools have been organized by university and other externally based labor educators, as well as some unions themselves.[31] Centered in female trade union leadership, the Coalition of Labor Union Women (CLUW) has moved many women's issues onto labor's agenda and has sought to strengthen women's participation in unions by nurturing more democratic union procedures and by increasing their role in leadership positions (Balser 1987, 162). In some regions, like New York City, CLUW has particularly been a vehicle for African American women (Harriford 1989). Leadership of women has emerged especially at local levels of public and service sector unions.[32] Women's committees within unions have also been important in creating what labor educator Ruth Needleman calls "independent space" for the development of a women's culture and agenda and strength to push for it (1998b, 161). The "New Voice" labor leadership elected in 1995 brought Linda Chavez-Thompson, a Latina woman, to the top level of the AFL-CIO in a newly created position of executive vice president, and changes in the executive council also brought more women to the top level. However, Needleman argues that women are still not represented in top leadership positions. Instead, they are "more like invited guests than homeowners in the house of labor, carefully selected and screened, welcomed in small numbers and shown to their appropriate place."[33]

Race-based caucuses also continue to organize and exert their influence within unions. As with developing women's leadership, Needleman describes the tensions in this relationship:

> The creative tensions between the official voice of labor and the newer voices of women and people of color play out at the annual meetings of the AFL-CIO organizations set up to foster inclusion and address sexism

and racism. These organizations, the Coalition of Labor Union Women (CLUW), the A. Philip Randolph Institute (APRI), the Labor Council for Latin American Advancement (LCLAA) and the Asian Pacific American Labor Alliance (APALA) have official AFL-CIO status and, to a degree, are expected to promote AFL-CIO policies and priorities. At the same time their meetings provide significant independent space for activists to network and organize for their own positions. (163)

The increased concentration of national black union leadership has led to increased, though still inadequate, influence of the Coalition of Black Trade Unionists (CBTU), argues African American studies scholar Manning Marable (1997). When CBTU and other groups were not consulted in the candidate selection for the 1995 election, CBTU "drew up eleven demands calling for more minorities and women as delegates, executive council members and staffers" (Brecher and Costello 1998, 38). The new position of executive vice president occupied by Linda Chavez-Thompson and the expansion of the Executive Council from thirty-five to fifty-four members with a decision to reserve at least ten seats for people of color were positive steps[34] ... with many more to be taken (La Luz and Finn 1998, 187). William Burrus of the Postal Workers and a CBTU leader remarks on remaining issues of tokenism. "You can't hold them [top AFL-CIO leadership] accountable until they're forced to recognize the political strength of groups like women, African Americans, and Latinos" (Brecher and Costello 1998, 38). Labor activists May Chen and Kent Wong call for the "move from rhetoric into action ... to embrace the diversity, foster the inclusion, and build the movement for social justice that is long overdue.... We must transform not only the leadership, but also the very culture and identity of the labor movement" (1998, 201). Labor educator Cheryl Gooding makes a similar argument.

> To welcome all workers into the house of labor, and to build unity among all, unions must become multicultural organizations: sharing power with, and accepting leadership from, the people who have historically been marginalized by unions; building organizational cultures and practices that reflect labor's increasingly diverse base. (1997a, 62)

"The struggle for diversity and inclusion within the AFL-CIO," Chen and Wong remind us, "is not only a principled and moral fight, it is a battle very much in the self-interest of the labor movement" (201). This, then, is a significant part of the effort at labor's revitalization—an effort of which the Columbia clerical union was very much a part.

Conclusion

The labor movement clearly has a long and mixed history of identity politics. Single-identity politics have indeed been at the core of exclusionary, discriminatory practices protecting the job rights of the most privileged, who have been seen as *the* working class. While these are the images that define most people's notions of labor's identity politics, it is important to recall that this is not the only story. CIO unions, attempting to organize without regard to race and gender, have brought great benefits to working men and women of color, as well as white women, but were not always able successfully to counter discrimination. They also often left the lion's share of such workers out of unions' efforts, as they did not work in the strategic core industries. Men of color, women of color, and white women have also used multi-injustice politics to fight inspirational battles against class, race, and gender oppression in the workplace.

Unions' inability to deal consistently with a full range of workplace injustices has contributed to a weakened labor movement. Yet in the multifaceted history of the labor movement—from the black domestics' highly developed survival networks, to the 1909 and 1982 uprisings of the 20,000, to the Columbia clerical's insistence that we "look around the room" and see the many women and people of color who are experiencing workplace injustice because of those identities as they interdefine their class identity—we see strong evidence of the mobilizing potential that multi-identity politics bring to labor.

How would a union campaign build such a multi-injustice movement? Before we look at how the Columbia clerical union took up the task, we need to ask how *any* movement builds an identity, be it single or multi. For this, we turn to the next chapter.

4

What's in a Name? Making Movement Identity

How does a movement develop a sense of "we"? Collective identity is a group's self-definition. It is a movement's answer to the question "who are we?" A key task of social movement theory, argues sociologist Alberto Melucci, is "to clarify how collective actors come to define themselves as a unity" (1989, 217). By approaching identity as a process, a task, an accomplishment, social movement theory can offer movements tools for analysis and intervention. Where in their practice, exactly, have movements created single identities? How might they create a multi-identity movement? How do movements create any identity at all?

Collective identity is not automatically determined by a movement's membership. Nor, as some activists argue, is it automatically shaped by demands. Identity is neither permanent nor fixed. Rather, identity is socially produced, what we call a social construction. And as a social construction, it is a matter in which movements can intervene. How do they do that? And to what end?

In this chapter, I will develop the concept of *identity practices,* by which movements shape identity. It is a tool for analyzing just *how* movements do this. The concept of identity practices allows activists and scholars to look at the arenas in which, and the extent to which, movements create single versus multi-identities.[1] These practices are constrained by a range of material and cultural conditions, I will argue, and have important mobilizing consequences, as well.

Collective Identity As a Question

As any organizer well knows, neither the existence of oppression, no matter how severe, nor the availability of social movement organizations guarantees mobilization. Studying collective identity helps us with the puzzle of how people translate conditions of injustice into the basis for resistance. "What," asks social psychologist Bert Klandermans, "makes people define their situation in such a way that participation in a social movement seems appropriate[?]"[2] "Collective identities that people deploy to make public claims" need to be seen as "an accomplishment of a set of collective actors that derives from their common interests, experiences, and solidarity," argues sociologist Verta Taylor (1999, 25). On what basis do collectivities mobilize? How do preexisting structural locations such as gender, race, class, or sexuality become "politically meaningful" in that process? (Bookman and Morgen 1988, 12). And at Columbia, *which* identities would become meaningful, and in which ways?

Melucci argues that identity must be understood not as a thing but as a process. It is a process of meaning making that is collective and that occurs in social interaction, and in social networks. As we will see in the Columbia case, this is a process occurring on multiple interacting levels: individual, collective (social movement or movement organization), and broader political discourse.[3] "How is it that individuals' sense of who they are becomes engaged with a definition shared by coparticipants in some effort at social change" (W. Gamson 1992a, 55)? Rather than being done once and for all, identity is an ongoing process subject to reworking in the context of changing historical events and conditions, ideology, movement membership,[4] social control efforts, countermovements, and other factors. Identity building, as social movement activism more generally, however, is not unconstrained. It is partly shaped by concrete structural and cultural conditions, which are both opportunities and constraints for prospective social movements.

Such collective identity, then, is both a "source" and a "product" of mobilization.[5] As Klandermans describes a movement's process of making meaning more broadly, "On the one hand, the social construction of meaning precedes collective action and determines its direction; on the other, collective action in its turn determines the process of meaning construction" (1992, 82). Thus collective identity both helps to create and is created by social movements.

As we have already begun to see, there are consequences to identity construction. The construction of multi- versus single identity has significant effects on the kinds of justice sought and (sometimes) won. The kinds of identities developed can affect the connection potential members feel to a movement, and (along with other factors) the likelihood of their participation. Sociologists Debra Friedman and Doug McAdam note that movement "identities function as powerful selective incentives motivating participation.... One of the most powerful motivations of individual action is the desire to confirm through behavior a cherished identity.... This grants the social movement a powerful incentive to help compel participation."[6] We will hear such testimony of some Columbia clericals, whose union activism drew on their sense of being social justice advocates. There were some black women whose union activism built on their identities as race women. We also will hear from those women of all races who suggest that an explicit women's identity in the campaign would have helped to inspire their participation.

Studying collective identity construction, then, is a piece of examining the process of how actors make meaning of their own social location, how they use, transform, and are constrained by their material and cultural context, and with what consequences. Before I specifically take up each of these issues—including a detailed presentation of identity practices—it is helpful to briefly sketch out some context.

Drawing on Social Movement Theory

Recent thinking about collective identity represents a welcomed integration of three theoretical approaches to social movements: resource mobilization theory, social constructionism (framing), and new social movement theory.[7] A brief look at these perspectives is helpful for understanding social movements and the role that identity plays in their development. Resource mobilization theory emerged in the United States in response to the civil rights, antiwar, and other movements of the 1960s, 1970s, and 1980s, and in response to earlier theories, which saw movements as expressive, pathological "symptoms of strain" caused by breakdown in the social structure.[8] In contrast, resource mobilization saw social movements as rational "politics by other means" of those excluded from traditional electoral politics.[9] This suggested that analyzing social movements meant evaluating structural conditions ("opportunity" and "constraint") faced by "challengers," and the "resources" that these groups were able to mobilize to meet their goals.[10] Such resources include not only money but mass base, informal networks and formal organizational infrastructure, communication networks, leaders, legal resources, access to media, and cultural resources.

Questions of how grievances and collectivities were socially defined originally had little place in the theory, since the theory saw grievances as omnipresent and took collective actors as its beginning point.[11] Such cultural or ideological dimensions entered resource mobilization theory through important case studies of the civil rights and women's movements.[12]

Political process theory, developed as an important sharpening of resource mobilization theory,[13] has increased understanding of "the broader
social processes and political circumstances that affected the ability of challengers to lodge claims effectively" (Meyer 1999, 82). These include such factors as migration, urbanization, industrialization, splits among political elite,
splits between political and economic elite, changes in level of repression,
changes in judicial or regulatory climate, changes in international pressures
on a particular state, all of which can be important in "reducing the power
discrepancy between insurgent groups and their opponents" and creating
greater "political leverage" (McAdam 1982, 43).

Yet as social movement theorist David Meyer argues, political "opportunities do not *cause* protest; once we acknowledge this, our attention rightly
turns to the factors that contribute to successful mobilization when opportunities are available" (1999, 84). For this, work on framing and identity—
as advanced by the second, social constructionist perspective—has been
critical.[14] Social problems, this perspective reminds us, are not objective
matters. Rather, they are the subject of ongoing processes by which people
interpret and define their situation.[15] Framing considers how movements
define grievances and solutions to these grievances so as to be in line with
individual members' beliefs and values, to inspire collective action, and to
resonate with the larger political culture. Movements face many challenges
in their efforts to define social conditions in a way that inspires mobilization.
Authorities, countermovements, media, and other social actors all enter a
contest for meaning, a contest to which movements often bring the fewest
resources to bear. I will return to a longer discussion of framing a little later
in the chapter when I present the concept of identity practices.[16]

It is European new social movement theory, the third perspective, that
has centrally put identity issues before us. Grappling with the flourishing of
peace, women's, and environmental movements in a world in which activism
had, by history and Marxist theory, long been defined by class-based politics, European social movement theorists placed great significance on the
question of collective identity. As "the structure of capitalism and social
control have taken new forms," so too did the theory see social movement
resistance as taking new forms and occurring on new sites (Epstein 1990,
45). One of the important changes of contemporary society has been increased
individuation, Melucci argues. "The main actors within the system are no
longer groups defined by class consciousness, religious affiliation or ethnicity,
but—potentially at least—*individuals who strive to individuate themselves
by participating in, and giving meaning to, various forms of social action.*"[17]

This theoretical approach highlights "the politics of personal transformation" and sees them as a product of collective action (Taylor and Whittier
1992, 109). In mobilizing non-class-based collectivities, in transforming
individual experience, in developing alternative culture, in making cultural
as well as material demands, these movements were seen by new social movement theory as creating new identities.[18]

New social movement theory then opened a much-needed door to looking at identity and a range of cultural questions in social movement process.
Yet we need to watch out for misleading paths. First, the theory's central division of "old" (class-based/material) and "new" (for example, gender-based/
cultural) movements is historically inaccurate. Women and/or people of
color, for example, have a long history of resistance and struggle. Slave
rebellions, black women's clubs, the antilynching movement, Garveyism,
the suffragette movement, Women's Trade Union League, and Brotherhood
of Sleeping Car Porters well illustrate. The mobilization of these groups is
not "new." Second, it is also at complete odds with the analysis of multi-
identity politics: class does not (and never did) exist in isolation from gender
and race.

Third, this old/new split thus obscures the exact challenge of the Columbia clericals and many other contemporary labor movements.[19] One of
the things that makes the Columbia case interesting to Left strategists and
social movement theorists is that it undertakes to integrate "identity issues"
in a so-called old social movement (labor).[20] Certainly many race-, gender-,
and sexuality-based identity movements are about making material demands on the state and corporations, as well as cultural change. Pay equity,
housing discrimination, affirmative action, public school funding, and gay/
lesbian marriage and parenting rights are, as sociologist Eve Spangler puts
it, "as material as it gets."[21]

It is also critical to understand what new social movement theory
means—and does not mean—by identity. I have discussed identities located in systems of domination: race, gender, class, sexuality. This context,
which is critical to intersectional theory, is not a necessary or important
condition of identity formation for new social movement theory. New social movement theory sees movements as responding to the social changes
of late modern society that have made the "quest for individual identity a
central pursuit of modern life."[22] To those movements resisting domination
by class, race, gender, and sexuality, such a perspective is a disturbing erasure of oppression. For new social movement theory, while structures of inequality *may* be the basis of a movement identity, alternative community,
culture, and values may just as well.

Although identity is an important task of all social movements, I find it important to distinguish identities located in, and responding to, enduring systems of social inequality from other movement identities.[23] I shall reserve the term "identity politics" for this first category of structurally located identities. The concept of identity practices, however, can be used in analyzing any movement.

Sidestepping the limitations that I have discussed, many social theorists have integrated new social movement theory's insights with those of the political process perspective. By the millennium's turn, consensus in social movement theory has seen identity as one of three interacting elements key to social movement emergence, development, and success: (1) "political opportunities and constraints," (2) "internal movement organization, tactics and strategies," and (3) "the construction of interpretive frames and collective identities" (Taylor and Whittier 1998, 623).

Identity Practices

The notion of identity as a process poses obvious questions. What is that process? What are its components? How could someone best observe the process of identity construction? How is this process impeded or facilitated by structural and cultural conditions? What are the consequences, such as in mobilization, victories, changed consciousness?

Identity practices, the central analytic tool of this study, are an inductively derived concept. It emerged out of my fieldwork dilemma of trying to observe collective identity at Columbia. This was a movement whose publications, especially those addressed to outside audiences, were sometimes very explicit about gender and race justice (see chapter 5). Yet these categories did not much appear to be part of the daily lived reality of the campaign. Just what identities was this movement developing? This puzzle drove me to look at a range of the campaign's daily practices. Other social movement analysts—Paul Lichterman in studying grassroots environmental groups, and Taylor and Whittier in studying women's movement culture—have similarly directed us to pay attention to concrete practices.[24]

Collective identity, in my experience, is generally not the object of direct and conscious attention by progressive groups.[25] Yet it is something that movements always do de facto. Collective identity, I argue, is not only a matter of ideology and demands (as some movements understand it), or solely culture (as do others). Rather, collective identity is constituted in a range of *identity practices: demands, framing and ideology, culture, organizational structure and process, leadership and organizational power, and outside resources.* These practices are a collection of specific social movement organization behaviors, each seemingly small, but which aggregate, and together construct a movement's collective self-definition.[26] This set includes both cultural and material elements, usually intermingled. However silently or unconsciously, this process of identity construction occurs among groups differently located in social systems of inequality, each situated with differing interests, power, and resources.

Although I discuss these as six distinct practices to enhance clarity, the boundaries between them are not always clean, and the practices are mutually interacting. It is important to note that identity construction is only one dimension of a movement's agenda in each practice.[27] For example, while a movement's demands help to construct collective identity, a movement has many other concerns in how it formulates its demands, such issues as winnability and long- versus short-term goals.

Identity practices are part of the action of any social movement organization, but in briefly describing these six practices, I will highlight issues related to multi-injustice politics. I will briefly sketch out each of the practices and will leave a fuller elaboration to take place as I use the practices to analyze the Columbia case in the next chapter.

Demands and Program Formulation

The demands a movement makes indicate the conditions of injustice—both material and cultural—a group seeks to change. Recall that multiple systems of domination shape different experiences of injustice for different groups within a movement. Do the movement's demands, around which a mobilization occurs, address important issues of material or cultural domination for all identity groups within the membership, or only for specific identity groups? What priority does a movement assign to these goals? For example, does a union include domestic partnership—gay and lesbian family benefits—in its health care demands? Would the Columbia clericals' contract demands seek to address the difference in average wages of white workers and workers of color, or the problems of parents—usually mothers—who need sick leave for sick kids?

Framing and Ideology

Media and movement media sociologists remind us that events in the world do not speak for themselves. Rather, meanings are constructed in a political contest among participants of vastly differing resources: movements, countermovements, authorities, other sponsors, and the media. Frames are interpretive devices that movements (and other social actors) employ to define contested issues and events. When teachers threaten to strike and shut down a major urban school system, do they define the issue as union rights and worker respect? Or is the conflict about quality education for poor urban children, mostly of color? Or both? What does the movement tell us about the questions "What is the issue? Who is responsible? What is the solution?"[28]

What identities does such a definition imply? How is the struggle itself named or defined in official campaign literature, or in approaching the media? What about speeches, comments in meetings, signs, chants, and songs at demonstrations? How resonant is the frame with larger cultural themes, particularly those of specific identity communities? Is the struggle at Columbia a routine contract campaign and/or a fight for social justice? If so, what kind? Is it an issue of race injustice, gender injustice, class injustice, or all? Frames are important in defining social and political conditions as unjust and changeable through collective action. (Potential) activists need to "believe that protest is both necessary and potentially effective" (Meyer 1999, 84). Increasingly, movements are trying consciously, strategically, and effectively to intervene in these framing battles.

The framing process is permeated by ideology, which is a deeper level of analysis.[29] Frames "are more flexible and situationally influenced constructs than formal ideological systems and more easily and rapidly communicated to target groups, adapted to change and extended to blend with other frames" (Tarrow 1992, 190). While an ideology such as conservatism or socialism or feminism applies to a broad range of different issues, movement organizations differ in the degree to which they collectively hold a unified ideology, apply it to all their efforts, and strategically choose to articulate it.

What ideology—deep analysis—if any, does the movement offer for the situation its members confront? Is the analysis specific and narrow or more systemically defined? Is there one system of injustice involved or many? What vision of transformation and social justice does the movement offer? How does this resonate with the world views or collective history of struggle of differing groups of (potential) members?

Culture

In whose image is a movement culture created? Is it resonant with, or is it in conflict with, the larger culture(s) of particular identity communities within a movement? This could include values, norms, music, social events, language, food, dress, holidays celebrated, religious practices, rituals. Longtime community organizer Linda Stout highlights language as an invisible factor that makes a movement feel home to some, alien to others (1996, 117–25). Taylor and Whittier note the significance of ritual as "a cultural mechanism through which challenging groups express emotions that arise

from subordination, redefine dominant feeling, and . . . express group solidarity" (1995, 176–78). Thus, through ritual, "collective actors express emotions—that is, the enthusiasm, pride, anger, hatred, fear and sorrow—that
mobilize and sustain conflict."[30] Also, another identity process is "the politicization of everyday life through the use of symbols and everyday actions to
resist and restructure existing systems of domination" (Taylor and Whittier
1995, 173). What rituals, symbols, or everyday actions would emerge as
part of the resistance in these clerical movements? In what ways and to
what extent did the Columbia clerical union culture reflect the preexisting
cultures of its highly diverse membership not only by race, gender, class,
and age but also by parenting status, student status, personal interests, politics, religion, or life focus? As we will see at Columbia, there may be different cultural spaces within a movement: any of these cultural practices can
be differently present in formal and informal cultural sites of an organization.
To which members did the union culture feel like a comfortable enough
home?

Organizational Structure and Process

Through what organizational structures and practices does the movement
group conduct its affairs? Stout alerts us that "logistics of organizing . . .
how and where meetings are held . . . who makes decisions, how members'
participation is maintained" are part of the "invisible walls" or barriers that
members of oppressed identity groups "slam into" (1996, 17). When, where,
and in what format do meetings occur? Are these arrangements congruent
with material realities of members lives, or do they exclude a particular subgroup of the members?

Forms of organization have often been identified as gender specific[31]
or gender and race specific (Robnett 1996; Sacks 1988a, 1988b). Would
these be visible in the clerical unions at Columbia, Harvard, and Yale? By
what mechanisms does a group undertake its work? How are tasks divided?
What is the process of decision making? Is it hierarchical or egalitarian,
voting, and/or consensus based? What ideals about how members relate
to one another and to their opponents does a movement emphasize in
deeds or speech?[32] Whose participation do these practices encourage or
discourage?

Has the movement organization or members of the organization created "free spaces"[33]—identity-based caucuses, networks, summer schools,
and conferences? For example, does a union have a black, Latino, or Asian
caucus? A gay and lesbian caucus? What functions and power do these for-

mations have? What conditions might account for the emergence of such a caucus at Yale, and its absence at Columbia? How has the movement organization, as a whole, dealt with these formations?

Leadership

How is power organized in the movement group? Who holds organizational power and through what mechanisms did they come to hold power? Is power representative of the various identity communities who make up the movement organization? Or does the leadership represent the demographics of an earlier time in a movement's history? What definition of leadership is operating, and is that reflective of a particular identity community within the organization?[34] What conscious efforts, what structured programs if any, does the movement make to develop new leadership, particularly of those who have historically been excluded?[35] What degree of power is exercised by those in second or third leadership tiers in an organization?

Leadership, as we will see in the Columbia case, is significant in shaping many of the other identity practices. The demands, framing, and efforts to secure outside support resources are especially in the domain of leaders' decisions.

Outside Resources

Central to resource mobilization theory is the idea that the resources a movement mobilizes, both internally and externally, are critical to its success. Such resources additionally give messages—implied or explicitly stated—about whom this struggle is for. They help us to define who is the "we" of any struggle: Who are the individuals and organizations that the movement group contacts for support, or who make initiative to the movement? Do these include representatives of other identity struggles? What kinds of support do they offer? How visible are they to participants? Did they help frame the struggle? At Columbia, what resources did the movement use? To what extent did they augment campus labor allies with identified race- and gender-based organizations or leaders? What impact would this have on mobilization?

Each of these identity practices may be carried out consonant with single- or multi-identity politics, and in a multitude of ways. Contrary to a "yes/ no," "all-or-nothing" perspective, these practices suggest collective identity is a question of "in what ways?" and "to what extent?" Yet the data in these clerical cases suggest there may be a tip-over point at which a critical mass of identity practices has been reached, so that participants would speak of a struggle as an identity-based mobilization.[36] Framing appears to be a particularly significant practice in how activists define their movement.

These identity practices were derived inductively in the course of fieldwork and analysis. They do, however, find substantial correspondence in the categories others have developed in analyzing feminist and multicultural organizations about which I later became aware.[37] Sociologist Patricia Yancey Martin's work on feminist organizations similarly recognizes a broad range of organizational dimensions, by which a group can engage in oppositional gender politics. Feminism, Martin notes, is not limited to organizations that espouse explicitly feminist ideology or adopt a collectivist organizational structure. Identity practices also encompass several conceptual tools that other social movement analysts have suggested for approaching identity or cultural processes of social movements, more broadly. Yet I do not intend for "identity practices" to be read as an attempt at a totalizing concept that hopes to supplant or encompass many other conceptual tools of social movement analysis. Rather, I see identity practices as a useful collection of dimensions, a tool that can be used in conjunction with other conceptual tools for describing social movement culture and identity.

Identity practices will stand for now as a set of six that will guide our analysis of the Columbia and other labor cases. I say "for now" in the hope that others will find this a useful tool for analysis and practice. When it is applied to more cases, other identity practices may yet emerge.

Both Structural and Cultural

One of the strengths of identity practices as an analytic and organizing tool is that it draws together both cultural and material elements of oppositional politics. As I have argued earlier, it is unproductive to label social movements as either cultural (i.e., "identity movements") or material (i.e., "political movements"). Taylor and Whittier similarly critique "the binary oppositions in social movements theory... the distinction between expressive and instrumental politics, identity and strategic activism, cultural and structural change, and rational and emotional action" and call for "a more nuanced set of constructs that gets beyond these dichotomies" (1999, 5). The false characterization of identity politics as solely cultural (and expressive) is certainly one source of the eagerness by Gitlin and other Left strategists to dump identity politics as a Left strategy.[38]

Some movements do challenge only political or economic distribution, and some develop alternative culture that poses no challenge to anyone outside a closed community or sect. But few movements fall into these polarized categories. Most movements are located between the two poles, and the question is how they combine material and cultural elements. It is fruitful to speak of the relative emphasis of cultural and material challenges.[39] As sociologist Steven Buechler argues, "attempts to dichotomize movements as political or cultural obscure more than they reveal about the role of both aspects [and I would add how they interact] in all movements" (2000, 185). Exploring the nuances of how oppositional groups differently emphasize the material and cultural elements of their work is a far cry from declaring one strictly "identity" and one "political."

In identity practices, the cultural and material dimensions may be intertwined in any one practice. For example, many movements actively pursue both material and cultural demands. Confronting the racial inequities many Columbia workers of color report in promotion and evaluation, as we will hear them describe, is a material demand. However, as some of them argue, changing this problem requires confronting race, class, and gender specific notions of being a "good worker." Gay and lesbian demands around family rights are both material and cultural. Gathering support resources, another identity practice, brings material benefits such as money, labor power, and bodies to a picket line but also offers cultural resources: a definition of self, group, and mission. Organizational structure would seem to be quite straightforwardly material. As Martin has discussed, however, organizational features can be saturated with ideological meaning: probably no other element is seen as more singly defining of a feminist organization than its internal structure (1990).

Levels of Movement Identity

Other social movement theorists have developed categories for analyzing collective identity.[40] One that I have found particularly useful to the clerical cases we will consider is William A. Gamson's levels of collective identity formation (1992a, 1992b). Gamson suggests that collective identity occurs in three possible layers: organizational, movement, and social location.[41] Organizational refers to the specific movement organization: the Columbia clerical District 65 local, "the union." The specific organizational identity may be embedded in a larger social movement: labor, women's, black freedom, and so forth. Finally, either of the first two layers may be linked to an underlying social location: race, class, gender, sexuality, age, ethnicity, nationality, disability, et cetera. Most powerful, suggests Gamson, are movements in which collective identity is a single "amalgam" of all the levels:

SNCC (Student Non-violent Coordinating Committee), the civil rights movement, and Black America.

This concept will be helpful to our discussion. My own experience with the issue of collective identity in labor movement work is that it is an organizing component that activists don't think about much head-on. Fairly consistent practice in labor organizing, both initial unionization and contract struggles, is to build primary collective identity to the specific union organization. Traditionally, unions have fostered a labor movement consciousness. *If* there is development of a third-level identity, it is usually either to an occupational/economic sector (clerical workers, university workers, skilled trades) or to a class identity ("the" working class).

Columbia clericals, like most unionists, built identity principally at the organizational level: District 65 at Columbia or "the union." To the degree that a movement identity was built, it was to the labor movement, with a (generalized) movement for racial justice invoked in a minor way. The social location level was little invoked; to the degree it was invoked, it was workplace and occupation specific—Columbia University clerical workers. Women of color, working-class women, people of color, African Americans, Latinas, and women are some of the other potentials for this third level.

The construction of an identity is not only organizational but very much ideological. As identity practices suggest, at each level a collective identity involves an ideological position that offers an analysis of the problem the movement faces, implying solutions and potential allies. In the late 1960s, for example, civil rights and Black Power movement activists organized very different analyses of American racism and how to combat it. Union activists, leaders, and progressives of all sorts have argued for more than a century over business unionism, social unionism, social democracy, communism, and other ideologies.

In this campaign, when Columbia District 65/UAW claimed its labor movement identity, it saw itself in a lineage of progressive social unionists who have fought for worker democracy, against racism, sexism, capitalism, environmental risks, and U.S. intervention abroad, and for a range of other broad social change issues, as well. Yet when the Harvard Union of Clerical and Technical Workers (see chapter 7) differentiated itself from much of the labor movement, it is the tradition of fist-pounding, cigar-chomping, macho, sexist, racist, antiquated, possibly corrupt union leaders advocating narrow business unionism from whom they stood apart.[42] Will the real labor movement please stand up? This is in part an issue of ideology.

Claiming a larger movement identity can be an ideological and/or a strategic issue. As we will see, the assertion by Harvard's clerical workers' union leaders of HUCTW's "femaleness," but generally not its feminism, worked to avoid the negative associations with feminism as a movement and an ideology. Creating a movement's collective identity may tie a campaign to a controversial or troubled larger social movement.

Questions of ideology may also arise at the level of social location. "Black women," "women," "African Americans," "Latinas," "workers": with what ideology is the larger group being invoked? If we move beyond flash card appearances, what analysis is a movement associating with that category? Whose vision of a social location is a group invoking: African Americans as understood by Nation of Islam leader Louis Farrakhan or by socialist theologian Cornel West? Feminist communist activist and scholar Angela Davis or conservative Republican Supreme Court Justice Clarence Thomas? Anti-abortion women's groups and abortion rights groups both draw on "womanhood," but with different analyses. There is a similar contest among integrationism, Afrocentrism, or nationalism. At each level, the identity constructed is a matter of ideology.

Boundaries

Boundaries are often seen as a central element of shaping collective identities. Movement sociologists Verta Taylor and Nancy Whittier argue boundary construction and maintenance to be one of the core processes of identity construction.[43] Boundaries "establish differences between a challenging group and dominant groups" and may be social, cultural, institutional, geographic, and so forth (1995, 173). As Taylor and Whittier's study of lesbian feminism illustrates, many movement actions establish and enforce such boundaries.

Boundaries are part of the process of establishing "some shared characteristic"—marking a social location, a site at which a collective identity is constructed (1992, 110). Movements are not the only actors to construct boundaries; this is a significant part of the process of domination. As Stuart Hall writes of resistance efforts, "I cannot conceptualise a politics that has no 'frontier effects,' which doesn't involve symbolically staging the line between 'us' and 'them'" (1995, 66).

Yet this is part of the central problem of multi-identity politics: how do movements contend with multiple potential boundaries? These may at different times emerge as crisscrossing lines, overlapping circles, or concentric circles.

I would argue that movements differ in the salience and the permeability of their boundaries, and the rigor and invective with which the boundaries are drawn and maintained. They differ in the attitude they have to those across the boundary (a question of ideology). They also differ in who or what they define as the "them." In the civil rights movement, for example, segregation, not whites, was defined as the enemy, and in an ideology of nonviolent direct action, those on the other side of the boundary were prayed for.

Movements differ in the degree to which assertion of one identity has to make others feel excluded or turned into the enemy. This is the question that comes up with caucuses in union or other organizations. Does the formation of a black, Latino, women's, or gay and lesbian caucus for support, for articulating grievances and alternate strategy, necessarily make those in the dominant group feel excluded or attacked? Obviously, the answer depends in part on the caucus's practices and ideology, and on the manner in which an organization's leadership responds. Central to the Harvard clerical union's identity during its unionization and first contract campaign was the value of "treating everyone with kindness and respect," which very much included management, as well. The positive assertion of an identity—who we are—does not necessarily produce a negative reaction by and toward those who we are not. This is certainly the perspective with which many diversity consultants in corporate, nonprofit, and movement settings undertake their work.

Further, as Collins and other proponents of intersectional theory argue, the categories of "us" and "them" are quite complex—with some of us being some of them. As Hall argues:

> Part of us is already on the other side of the barricades, and part of the Other, even of the Enemy, is already inside us. Nevertheless, in the positional play of politics, the line sometimes has to be drawn. What I am trying to imagine is a politics which can recognise the arbitrariness of that cut. What would be the nature of a politics in which people know every commitment to be partly a fiction, but are still able to act? (1995, 66–67)

Multiple boundaries are unavoidable, as intersectionality argues and the histories we have reviewed illustrate. They exist. The solution, intersectional theorist Kimberlé Crenshaw has argued, is coalition. As itself an internal coalition, the task of each movement is to contend with multiple boundaries. How do movements do this? This is a central question we will be considering in the Columbia and other clerical union cases. It is here that multi-identity practices may be helpful.

But the movement's practices are not the only factor shaping success or failure in meeting this challenge.

Action by Other Social Agents

As in all other framing contests, a social movement is but one player. "It isn't," argue Friedman and McAdam, "just the SMO [social movement organization] that has a stake in defining the group's collective identity" (1992, 166). Employers or other authorities enter a social movement contest with their own strategies, with which a movement must interact.[44] These include (1) ongoing management strategies that compromise the structural conditions a movement faces and (2) social control strategies shaped for a specific campaign. The Columbia administration's change in personnel policy after the first strike to increase the number of women in low-level management, some union leaders argued, had deflected gender identity issues in the 1991–1992 campaign. The administration's memo for responding to the union's discrimination charges, on the other hand, turned out to be the single action of the campaign that most intensified racial identity. An employer could, as happened in Boston hospital organizing efforts, choose to emphasize race or gender or class fraction identities in hopes of fracturing a movement.

Media, countermovements, other movements, government, other interested individuals or groups—all have the capacity to influence the collective identity constructed. Events not directly related to a specific social movement may also be constructed by any of these social actors so as to shape a movement's collective identity formation. As in other framing contests, all players are not equally resourced so as to effect the outcome. "The survival chances of an SMO often rest on the outcome of just such contests for control of the group's image. Yet, in waging these contests, SMOs typically find themselves at a distinct disadvantage" (166).

Conditions Impeding and Facilitating Creation of Multi-identity Politics

The contest over movement identity occurs in specific conditions. The strategic choices movements face are significantly shaped by structural and cultural conditions. It is critical to note the role of structural factors in shaping the possibilities and wisdom of various identity practices in a labor case. Historical and contemporary cases suggest these factors include:

The existence and condition of a prominent active national movement. For example, as consistent with the notion of master framing (Snow and Benford 1992), there was a much greater likelihood of a race-based identity struggle by labor during the civil rights/Black Power era than at the present moment. The Right's "backlash" against feminism, for example, may discourage women from highlighting the gendered aspects of a campaign. When a larger movement is strong, it may offer resources, and its existence helps establish such an identity-based campaign for justice as legitimate. In a time of weakness or attack, association with an external movement may not be popular or helpful to a particular movement organization's campaign.

Proximity of other identity-based movements. David Meyer and Nancy Whittier's notion of social movement spillover—the multiple ways in which one movement may impact others[45]—may occur in a specific local setting. For example, the campus divestment movement and the organizing against racist violence at Columbia in the 1980s created much more space for clerical unionists to address issues of racism in the (university) workplace. Similarly, the Columbia divestment occupation and the Yale clerical strike impacted the Columbia clerical unionists' sense of the possibilities of disruptive tactics on campus. Thus the demands, framing, and tactics of the 1985 Columbia clerical movement can be seen, in part, as the spillover of other university-based movement struggles.

The length and size of struggle. Longer struggles provide more opportunity and necessity for increased resources, including those of explicitly identity-based groups. Larger struggles would similarly have more likelihood of attracting more explicitly identity-based external resources. Sometimes small struggles, however, can become a cause célèbre.

The composition of the (potential) membership. Movements with homogeneous or relatively homogeneous membership will have fewer diversity/unity issues to negotiate in constructing a collective identity. The all-black and almost all female composition of Charleston hospital workers facilitated the use of a race/class collective identity. That they framed this as race and class but not gender identity reminds us, though, that there is nothing automatic about the link between demographics and identity. The high concentration of white women clericals and technicals at Yale and Harvard facilitated their development of a (largely white) women's identity politics.

Structural conditions of domination within which a movement operates. The hiring practices that have created decidedly racially segregated departments in many hospitals, for example, make race-based identity claims more likely.[46] The same management practices that create myriad layers of differing pay and conditions make class-based identity harder to achieve in collective action (Edwards 1979). As I will discuss in the chapters that follow, the changing pattern of race and sex labor market segregation at Columbia, along with the union's practices, made the creation of gender justice politics in the campaign more unlikely. The predominate white femaleness of the

Yale and Harvard clerical workforce during their first contract efforts facilitated the creation of gender politics as part of these campaigns.

Level of identity conflict in a community. These can play either way. The racial conflicts in Crown Heights and the Anita Hill/Clarence Thomas hearings were high-profile, high-conflict events during the Columbia campaign. Although top union leaders suggest these events heightened rank-and-file leaders' commitment to the race and gender justice elements of their campaign, the silence about these issues in the meetings suggested discomfort with asserting identity issues in the workplace. In Boston hospital organizing in the 1970s, the inflamed busing conflict severely incapacitated multiracial class-based organizing.

Kind of issue or grievance involved. Incidents of violence or flagrant denial of justice are among the most likely to invoke identity politics, as well as mobilization. Consider the racist murder of fourteen-year-old Emmett Till in 1954, months before the Montgomery bus boycott,[47] or the court verdict setting free the police officers who had beaten Rodney King in Los Angeles in 1992. Chronic institutional and cultural racism or sexism, which are hard to prove, and which members perceive they have little ability to change, are not as likely to yield identity framings.

Risks of repression for invoking identity-based politics. As African American and Latina Columbia clericals repeatedly pointed out, charging discrimination in one's workplace is risky business. These risks are particularly significant for low-wage single moms who consider themselves "a paycheck away from homelessness." In other institutional sites, and with other identity struggles, the risks vary.[48]

At Columbia, a number of structural and cultural factors made race, gender, and class identity politics less likely. Institutional racism and sexism, as we will hear from clerical activists, are seen to be omnipresent, hard to prove, and hard to change. There were no vibrant national movements on these issues at the time; if anything, race and gender justice movements were under attack. The Right's PC (political correctness) attack on multiculturalism[49] and articles about the "backlash" against feminism[50] filled the popular media. New York City's Crown Heights conflict and the Hill/Thomas case could have worked either way but seemed mostly to inspire silence. While the struggle was torturously long for the participants, the in-and-out nature of the strategy made race and gender identity practices less likely than the continuous ten-week strike at Yale in 1984. The one-thousand-member size made this a struggle worth other social actors' investing their time and support resources. Whereas members may well have experienced repercussions for individual grievances about racial discrimination, a collective race-based politics would have carried fewer risks. More empirical work including more case studies will be needed to clarify the impact of these and other structural and cultural conditions on identity formations.

In the following chapters, I will deploy the notion of identity practices to analyze how the Columbia clericals integrated gender, race, and class politics both in opposing workplace injustice and in affirming diversity. How did these identity practices take shape in the Columbia clerical campaign? I will also draw in other labor campaigns—the clerical organizing campaigns at Yale and Harvard Universities. Although these campaigns occurred under significantly different conditions, my brief comparative discussions will help to clarify the range of identity practices that can be used by labor campaigns—as the product of strategic decisions by unions and other social movement activists in the context of specific structural and cultural conditions.

5

Identity Practices: Creating a Union for Class, Race, and Gender Justice

Civil rights, war and peace, . . . women's rights and issues of that kind. We've always regarded that as union business. It's not a special thing we do. It's the normal thing for our organization.
—David Livingston, president, District 65, 1985

As do most social movement organizations, the Columbia clerical union created a strong collective identity at the level of its specific organization: Columbia local, District 65. "We came together one thousand strong and we took them on." The "we" here was union. The battle was primarily over improving the pay and benefits package. Despite the diverse paths bringing them to the university, what these one thousand women and men did share was that they worked at Columbia as clericals. The union worked to transform this fact and their opposition to the conditions of that work into one shared "union" identity.

In a large, highly diverse workforce with high turnover and little previous knowledge of unions, that was a plenty tall order. "What's amazing and truly miraculous," said union leaders Jean and Doris, "is that people pull together to the degree they do. There are so many different stories of who people are and why they're here at Columbia."

Within that collective union identity, District 65 wove in its deep commitment to fighting all kinds of injustice and to creating the union as a home to all its diverse workforce. They had developed an organizing wisdom that did this through a combination of both single- and multi-identity practices.

Union leaders over the years had found that workers were remarkably willing to fight for principles of fairness and justice, if done in the right way. The right way drew on trusted leadership and a strong commitment to fighting discrimination. It drew on a high level of participation by, and servicing of, members that helped the union be seen by a range of workers as a comfortable-enough home. The right way meant pursuing multi-injustice politics primarily in deeds, and secondarily in words. This included presenting people with facts, emphasizing winnable demands, and avoiding unnecessary politicization.

District 65's operating wisdom emerged in part out of ideology, and in part as a strategic assessment of their opportunity structure and best strategic options. District 65 organizers were mindful of the complexity of the clerical union's membership, issues, and structuring factors. As Eva, a white union leader said,

> There's got to be a balance. . . . What the union is fighting can't just be in racial terms . . . there's going to be a variety of different kinds of inequities in people's experience. I mean it's not just race discrimination. It's not just gender discrimination. It's not just on the basis of seniority. It could also be on the basis of the department you work for, whatever. . . . So I feel like the forum that we fight in has to be geared toward dealing with the overall inequities.

"We need to appeal to the broadest group," argued Doris. Ted added, "You've got as many points of view as you have members. You've got to find a common denominator. By exerting appropriate leadership, you've got to try to pull more people in and try to raise that bottom line."

To do this, the clerical local emphasized "doing" multi-injustice politics and minimized talking about them. Demands were by far the primary vehicle for race and gender justice. "We've always tied this in to contract negotiations, not touchy-feely stuff . . . and not to demands that we can't win," said Eva. Other practices—leadership, organization, and culture—were also important in creating a multi-injustice politics. The union's framing was predominantly that of a traditional trade union contract struggle. "Discrimination" or race and gender "inequities" appeared in leaflets among the long list of items on the union's contract list. They most strongly emerged in high-visibility occasions directed at external audiences. Some leaflets for members discussed the race wage gap in depth; very few discussed the gender gap with the maintenance union. Inside the union, a traditional trade union sound track predominated. I found that race was little audible as a category in the daily life of the union, gender even less so. The external support resources that the union sought and used developed a labor movement identity.

Thus the clerical union developed a "do it but don't talk too much about it" approach to fighting racism and sexism and developing an inclusive union. This was a mix of both single- and multi-identity practices, largely folding race and gender justice efforts into regular "union business," as then District 65 president David Livingston suggested in the chapter epigraph. Many of the identity practices (demands, culture, organizational structure, and leadership) were significant in creating a multi-identity movement organization. Other practices (framing and support resources) mostly contributed to a single—union—definition of the struggle. Together they helped District 65 wage a multi-injustice fight. Yet having race and gender justice woven into the union's culture, structure, and demands, but often not explicit in its framing, had important implications for how union members thought—and didn't think—about their campaign. In chapter 6, I will explore how Columbia clericals perceived their contract struggle, but before we get to that, let's take a more in-depth look at the union's identity practices. To provide context to my discussion of the Columbia clerical workers' 1991–1992 identity practices, in each section I include some background on their identity practices during their organizing in the 1980s.

Identity Practices at Columbia

Demands

Columbia leaders have rightfully seen their union as a trailblazer in integrating race and gender justice into their demands. Leaders speak with deep pride and commitment. "We have *always*," emphasized Doris, had issues of "race discrimination on the table *each and every time.* We have been way out there on this issue."

District 65 well understood from the beginning that changing the conditions of clerical work at Columbia would demand nothing less than confrontation with institutional classism, sexism, and racism in the labor market. The union made such efforts integral to its demands, although not always explicitly so. In the first contract, the union made great strides in confronting the full range of issues based in class, race, and gender injustice: wages, benefits, job security, health and safety, sexual harassment, respect, and lack of voice.

The union's commitment to dealing with institutional racism was evidenced in the energy it put early on into assembling data that revealed race-based discrepancies in the university's pay policies. "After we were organized, and we got the data, we . . . felt it was our obligation to expose these issues. Pay equity became a buzzword in the press and the labor movement. For us, this translated into a race issue, as well," explained Nina. The first contract fought for and won what the university insisted be called a "special adjustment fund." The fund set aside $125,000 to deal with a history of institutional racism, salary irrationalities, and favoritism. Three-fourths of the recipients of special adjustments were black and Latina/o workers. Nina voiced the central question raised by one black activist before the first strike. "'Would a union that was half white be willing to go on strike for demands where the gains would disproportionately go to minority workers?' We hoped so, but we didn't know. We found the answer was yes."

The union also won representation on a university Affirmative Action Committee, which monitored promotions for upper grades. The union had hoped that its seat on the Affirmative Action Committee would serve as a vehicle for ongoing struggle over institutional racism, but it was disappointed. "There were just so many tasks to keeping the local going, and we'd have to keep refighting over every inch of ground with the university," said Carole. There were just not enough union resources to be truly effective on the committee.[1]

The discrepancies persisted. People of color were more often hired into lower grades and into "poorer" departments with smaller wage funds. The hiring system gave managers discretion over starting pay, often heavily rewarding educational backgrounds (despite the university's agreement that education should not be weighted heavily in classification matters). Differential success at obtaining promotions and a pay system that penalized long-term workers (disproportionately people of color) also contributed to the race wage gap.

Several 1991–1992 contract demands addressed these issues: "bringing up the bottom" two grades, creating several seniority pay steps for long-term workers, raising all grade minimums, and the reclassification demands.[2] Most of these demands spoke to all workers across race but would disproportionately have impacted senior workers and workers of color. They could thus close the "race wage gap" or at least prevent it from widening. The union's demand for seniority layoff protection (see chapter 1) responded to the increasing number of clerical layoffs without recall. With black women having longer tenure at Columbia, and disproportionately affected by the layoffs, the union's seniority layoff protection demand had race and gender implications.

There were other key components of the race wage gap. The problem in each grade of higher starting salaries for white workers was raised in the leaflets but was primarily addressed in demands in a backdoor way through reclassification. Also, the recurrent charge by many black and Hispanic workers of blocked access to promotions was not captured in these demands. Any contract proposal must, of course, reduce the field of all injustices down to winnable, strategic priorities. Yet it is essential to recognize that the wage discrimination faced by black and Hispanic workers in the bottom grades was only one component of a larger issue.

On the gender front, the first contracts made great strides. All of the wage, benefit, and union rights gains won in 1985 confronted the long-standing devaluation of clerical work. The contract also had protections against sexual harassment and personal work (such as fetching coffee and taking care of private correspondence). In the 1988 campaign, gender-based issues took on greater prominence—that is, at least in the written public materials. Comparable worth, which was then in fashion in public and some union discourse, was explicitly discussed at length in the union's publicity materials, along with issues of racial inequity and departmental inequalities. The successful demand for a reclassification process for the one thousand clerical jobs addressed these issues. The union formed a family committee, conducted a survey, and prepared membership support. Child care, largely framed as a family issue, was one of the union's key demands. After a hard fight, the union wrestled an innovative child care subsidy of $40,000 from the university in the last strike-averting hours of negotiations.

The union went into the 1991–1992 contract with quintessential comparable worth problems: the lowest maintenance starting salary was higher than the highest clerical starting salary. Sex- and race-segregated labor markets, clerical work devaluation, and the decades-longer history of male maintenance worker unionization account for this wage configuration. The classification process won in 1988 would give the union a chance to name invisible labor performed by many clerical workers. As Karen Sacks argues about hospital clerical workers in *Caring by the Hour,* management often demeans clerical work by considering it to be a collection of rote and repetitive tasks. This is despite the fact that management depends on their mostly female clericals to carry out "invisible mental planning and coordinating" that goes unrewarded because it is unnamed and unacknowledged (1998a, 129). At Columbia, reclassification sought to make visible clericals' real workload and was a demand that partially redressed the gendered nature of invisible work.

Skyrocketing health care costs and a low pay scale made health care parity a priority for many members. TWU members, three-fourths male, received free health care benefits for which clericals, three-fourths female, paid up to $1,250 annually.[3] For the low-wage clericals, especially the single moms, fighting for the TWU's five free health plans was a high priority, but the university was resolute on holding down health care costs. "We were," explained Nina, "fighting for women's health."

Child care demands again addressed family and particularly women's needs. The union hoped to greatly extend the child care subsidy won in 1988. They also proposed that workers be allowed to use their sick time for sick child or other sick family care. It was an issue that the union eventually conceded in an effort to prioritize their health care demands. Thus the 1991 demands continued the clericals' commitment to union politics that strategically challenged the many interlocking realities of class, race, and gender domination. The union had shaped these as winnable demands, but they were ones that would require a difficult fight.

Framing and Ideology

Overall, the union put forth its effort as a "campaign for a just contract." "Just" could refer to the myriad of issues identified in the demands. Challenging racism and sexism were thus woven in with the many inequities the union fought to improve. Race and gender (justice) were sometimes more explicit and prominent, often less. For District 65, this was a practice that enhanced its ability to create a "union" identity out of its very diverse workforce and that continued to bring forth solidarity across diversity.

Early Organizing: "Justice Now"

Very consciously, the union early on used words like "inequities" and "unfairness." These were understood by many workers of color to be about race but also referred to the myriad other injustices that Columbia workers encountered.

This strategy was shaped in part by the experience of an earlier unsuccessful campaign that "got the reputation of being sort of bra burner types . . . white goofy radicals or something," explained Carole, one of the initial organizing committee members. "So there was a definite carry-over, a wariness, you know you're going to have to prove where you're coming from. . . . And I don't think we had any [paid] minority organizers for several years." Nina recalled the remarks of an older woman during the initial organizing. She referred to the previous drive by saying, "I hope you're not one of those commie bra-burners." Nina laughed as she remembered replying, "Last time I looked, I was wearing a bra." As for the "commie" part of the label, Nina talked about the damaging effects of red-baiting in the labor movement.

"We talked about transfers given on an unfair basis," said an organizer from the 1980s campaign. "To black workers that was racial discrimination, to white workers, favoritism," said Nina. "It was easy to focus on race without saying that," she added. "We knew from the beginning, if we were really trying to change the system at Columbia, the biggest impact would be on the nonwhite workers' economic condition."

After the election, despite the university's legal challenges, the union felt more secure articulating issues of gender and race justice. The slogan "Justice Now" provided an umbrella framing for a range of justice issues. As the local negotiated its first contract, a large poster-sized petition signed by hundreds of union members which dotted the campus during the negotiations, named race and gender. "As a predominantly female workforce nearly half of whom are minorities, we have specific needs." These needs included affirmative action and child care, as well as equitable salaries, benefits, health and safety protections, and others.[4] A Left organization at the university also put out a leaflet explicitly talking about "job ghettos."

Dramatic events of the 1984–1985 school year made a context of increased gender- and race-specific framings. The strike by clerical workers at Yale University brought issues of comparable worth to media and public attention. Yale provided great inspiration and highlighted the issues of institutional sexism in the labor market. Similarly, in spring 1985, the divestment movement was an occasion of union leaders and members unofficially coming together with campus activists around antiracism issues. "Black people at Columbia took note of that," said James, an African American union leader. These events, like later organizing against campus racist violence, created a climate in which racism was explicitly named and opposed, facilitating the construction of antiracist politics within the union struggle itself.

When Columbia did go out on strike in October 1985, traditional union slogans vastly predominated in the strike signs and chants. The "Justice Now" framing, highly visible on signs and leaflets, worked well in tying together the traditional union "contract" frame with more explicit race and gender justice concerns. A few signs like "Affirmative Action," "Apartheid Must Go," "76% women: We gotta make a living," "Union Women United for Child Care," and "Comparable Worth" decorated with women's symbols were mixed in the sea of traditional District 65 "On Strike" signs. Explicit discussions of race injustice, for example in the demand for affirmative action, coexisted with more vague bureaucratic language of the "special adjustment fund," as the university insisted it be called.[5] The fight against race and gender discrimination was highlighted in the *Distributive Worker* (the

District 65 newspaper) and in a video *With One Voice,* both celebrating the first contract victory (Gold and Goldfarb 1986). These issues were strong priorities to the most active. In the year following the strike, the union newsletter carried articles on affirmative action, sexual harassment, International Women's Day, and South Africa, along with articles on grievances, health and safety, the contract, and other traditional union business.[6]

The 1991–1992 Campaign

As in most contract campaigns, the daily lived reality of the movement was framed in traditional union strike language. In the written framing, the "Justice Now" button of the 1985 strike had been updated to a "United for a Just Contract" button with Halloween colors and an owl for the season. In the leaflets, the language was of baseball: "Strike 1," "Strike 2," "Fair Play," and "Bases are Loaded." Overall, a contract laundry list of issues framed the leaflets: improved and equitable wages, seniority layoff protection, health care, and so on. On the picket lines, five or six hundred people usually chanted, "Contract... Now." In response to "What do you want?" the answer was almost always "A contract," and occasionally "Justice." Signs and slogans demanded "No Contract, No Work" and proclaimed "Beep, Beep, Columbia's Cheap." "Mo money, mo' money, mo' money, mo" was a very popular chant that made folks smile and resonated well with contemporary pop African American culture (noteworthy as a cultural practice).

Occasionally, "No Justice, No Peace," made an appearance. At a few high-profile events—like the demonstrations at the prestigious Cabot and DuPont Awards—the union gave race-based identity framing more prominent standing along with other union issues. The chants "2-4-6-8 Columbia Discriminates" and "Extra; extra; read all about it. Columbia's racist, no doubt about it" were used along with a dozen union standbys. Similarly, the call-and-response chant "Who's got the money? / Sovern's got the money / Who's got the limo? / Sovern's got the limo / And who's got the IRT? / WE'VE got the IRT" drew attention to income and class-privilege discrepancies. President Sovern's 5.4 percent pay increase, announced in 1991, the union often pointed out, amounted to more than $18,000 per year—around the size of many members' salaries.[7]

The sound track of daily life in the campaign was framed almost exclusively in single-union identity language. Predominantly in the nitty-gritty of negotiations and report-backs over the months, the demands were discussed in a raceless, genderless, and classless trade union language. This was the language of wages, seniority, step increases, classification, and other contract demands. All of this, of course, is also largely a matter of the traditional trade union script, the default frame: this is simply what strikers on picket lines and union members in contract meetings usually say.

Explicit conversations about racism and sexism were extremely rare. Nina pointed out how critical it is that those conversations happen in a context of trust. "The negotiating committee is the place we'd bring those conversations." This was the group that knew the issue, had a long history with the union, and a long history of working together. Nina added, "I recall this is where we had a conversation—a rather heated one—about the Anita Hill case." Doris, another leader, argued that "you can't have such conversations in meetings. People don't know each other... well enough. These are conversations for one-on-one meetings with members."

In other meetings—strike committee, building or area meetings, or membership-wide meetings—discussions were much more about "bringing up the bottom" and "the 3s and 4s" than dealing with "racial injustice" or "institutional racism." Ted used the race wage gap as an instructive example of how the local has built support for fighting racial discrimination without making a big deal of it. "Bringing up the 3s and the 4s," he pointed out, "that's a great illustration of a demand that seems neutral, but actually is about race.... You don't have to be necessarily overtly expounding antiracist talk to be doing the work of countering discrimination." He is right. To some extent, it seems that such language was coded, that is, understood to be about race. Yet as we will hear in chapter 6, such a lack of explicit race and especially gender framing appears to be significant in the meaning members made (and didn't make) of the struggle.

There were key leaflets that centrally gave an explicit race and gender justice frame to the Columbia clerical workers' struggle.[8] One of the most notable was the well-distributed pamphlet "Fair Play, Fair Pay," which greeted the returning campus in September.[9] This delineated race and comparable worth injustices in pay and noted the cases of four women, three black and one white, who had suffered egregious layoffs. The pamphlet presented the comparison of union starting wages: $21,500 to $48,000 for TWU versus $16,681 to $21,367 for District 65. These were dramatic facts. "Bases Are Loaded," a pre-three-day-strike pamphlet, carried a full-page article called "Facts about the Equity Gap: Does Columbia Discriminate?" that laid out the facts of the race wage gap.[10] Several others had short sections providing statistics on the race wage gap.

The fall 1991 mobilization period also included a critical union/management volley over the issue of race and gender discrimination, which generated more explicit and central multi-injustice framing. Again, as in the 1985 campaign,

University President Michael Sovern said that "there is nothing to" allegations made by District 65 claiming the University discriminates against minority and women employees.... If the University did discriminate against them, then the employees could take legal action instead of using the allegations as a bargaining tool, Sovern said. "The union is, of course, looking for ways to invoke sympathy."[11]

The union sharply responded with a poster-sized letter to Sovern signed by eighty-one members of the strike and negotiating committees. In it, the union challenged Sovern to "provide a satisfactory explanation for the $1,100 salary gap between minority and white workers" and reminded him that seeking a remedy in litigation would "take years to resolve and would exceed the cost of remedying the gap now." Further, the union said, "Your refusal to provide equal pay and benefits to a group of 80% women workers, who are forced to strike to shame you into fairness, is sexism."[12]

University senior vice president Joseph Mullinix's response, in an open letter to the Columbia community, attributed the race wage gap to whites being "more than twice as likely as African-Americans to have attained a bachelors or graduate degree."[13] Union members, especially African Americans, found the letter ugly. District 65 responded that the university had agreed in the reclassification process that education per se would not be weighted heavily as a criterion of job evaluation. The union also noted that the statistics cited here were not Columbia specific. It is interesting that it was Mullinix's attempt to dodge the discrimination charge that most gained member attention and most inspired the racial identity of the union campaign.

As for his dismissal of the sexism charge, Mullinix defended the university in terms of the labor market norms that have long structured and justified the lack of comparable worth. He claimed that those to whom clerical workers were being compared, namely, the mostly male maintenance workers, "have highly specialized skills or... perform other duties which command a higher salary in the marketplace."[14] The union never laid out a critical analysis of the university's marketplace defense. It was the (Graduate) Student Support Committee that did. Clerical workers, too, they retorted "possess 'highly specialized skills'" and exposed Mullinix's argument as: "Since the marketplace devalues work performed by women, it's okay for Columbia to do it too."[15] It was also the Women's Faculty Caucus that wrote against "following the law of the 'marketplace'... and oppose[d] such arguments, which historically, as today, have devalued women's work and rationalized paying women less than men."[16]

Unfortunately, this support letter addressed to women faculty colleagues around the Christmas break was largely unseen by the members.[17] The issue of sexism in the Mullinix letter was lost; the exchange was defined by most members as one solely about racism. Of all the many times interviewees turned to the Mullinix letter to make a point, none ever cited it as an example of sexism. As we will consider in chapter 8, comparable worth case studies suggest this is an important untapped source of mobilization useful for demands the union had already undertaken, and for setting the stage for an eventual comparable worth battle.

Many union leaflets did name the "race wage gap" and articulated gender differences in pay: "race and sex discrimination," "discriminatory practices," "Columbia's hiring and salary practices are unfair to all of us, but especially minority and senior workers."[18] Yet in the avalanche of flyers and letters, race- and especially gender-explicit messages did not have an overwhelming presence. Often these were found in a long list of contract issues: "fair and equitable wages, job security and seniority rights and parity in health benefits."[19] Frequently, issues of gender and race injustice were subsumed in the category of "unfair" or "pay inequities." Although several leaflets presented the stats of the "race wage gap," very few—mostly those for public audiences—presented the "gender gap." The unspecified term "discrimination" was used. Some workers, as we'll hear in chapter 6, read this to be about race, some about race and gender, and others understood "discrimination" to be about the full range of favoritism and injustice that Columbia workers encounter. While some leaflets explained the mechanisms that gave rise to a race wage gap, none really laid out a full analysis of comparable worth and the devaluation and invisibility of clerical work. For example, the article entitled "Facts about the Equity Gap: Does Columbia Discriminate?" speaks to the race wage gap, but not the gender.[20] Participants were much more likely to understand "discrimination" to be about race than gender. As we'll hear from members, the fight against sexism was not seen as being embodied in any contract demand. The dramatic facts of institutional sexism were not constructed to have any life in the movement off the written page. Indeed, so unclear was the framing that one faculty supporter wondered why there was no mention of comparable worth in the union literature and speculated (wrongly) that it must be because the issue had been successfully resolved.

Strikingly, the leaflets that used explicit language of race and particularly gender injustice were disproportionately for public consumption: faculty, students, trustees, New York City residents. In the leaflets distributed to all Columbia faculty, and in those given out to the public at the Cabot and

DuPont Awards, and in front of trustees' workplaces and Sovern's home, explicit statements about the race and gender composition of the workforce and the discrimination they suffered were much more central. At Macy's the "COUNT US OUT OF YOUR THANKSGIVING PARADE" leaflet centrally noted, "the people in our union are predominately women and minorities. Many of us are single parents. . . . we're tired of being treated as second-class citizens. We get paid less than workers in comparable (predominantly male) jobs."[21] "Columbia's Dirty Linens Aired at Last! Discrimination against 1,000 workers!" shouted the headline of a flyer given to those attending the prestigious DuPont Awards Ceremony. It explicitly laid out the statistics of the "gender gap,"[22] as did a "Dear Faculty" letter a few weeks later.[23]

This was no accident. President Sovern argued the union was just trotting these issues out for sympathy, or "playing the race card," to use a popular phrase these days. But the union knew well that these were real issues that defined this struggle as an important moral battle. It was rightfully prepared to garner outside support around these issues for leverage against the university. There was just much less sense that this would also matter *inside* the campaign—that it might enhance internal mobilization. "This [1991]" was a "different time" than the period after the Yale strike, Eva, another of the leaders, noted. "Comparable worth: that's not very popular these days." The union's sense of its "options under pressure" led them to see little internal mobilization advantage to such explicit framing, and a lot more risk of fracture.[24] With audiences outside of Columbia, there was a better trade-off between the moral ground gained and the risk of conflict.

The children's march (on a public school holiday, but not a work holiday) was certainly one of the union's strongest efforts at bringing to life the idea that this was a movement of working parents, and particularly working mothers. Gender's main appearance in discussions was the frequent reference to "single parents" by members in the debates over strategy: single parents couldn't afford the loss in pay that a lengthy strike would entail.

For maintaining TWU support, District 65 was particularly cautious around gender framing, especially regarding comparable worth issues. The few articulations of comparable worth in leaflets were met with criticism by some TWU leaders. As we will see, this important constraint on gender framing posed significantly different conditions from those encountered by Yale clericals, who received the fullest support from the blue-collar union.

We can see this in the discussion of the union's health care demands. The debate on health care was framed as "parity"—that is, parity between unions. Although Nina argued the contract was a fight for women's health (and she was right), written materials never reflected this. The local put out a full-page leaflet entitled "Columbia's Health Care Discrimination: Why Do Support Staff Pay More for the *Same* HMO Insurance?" The leaflet asked, "What's going on?" and explained the university's complex HMO formula.[25] It never mentioned or invoked gender in any way: single mothers or discrimination against women. Contrast this explanation with the statement by the Graduate Student Support Committee: "Health benefits and salary minimums are issues of discrimination by gender against the entire bargaining unit. The clerical workers are overwhelmingly women.... The health and wage policies reflect how women are valued as workers in the context of the university as a whole."[26]

Framing Classification

The framing of the classification demand is another good example of how gender- and race-based issues were often obscured in traditional trade union language. The classification study (initially won in 1988) was designed to bring rationality to the bargaining unit, and to address favoritism and departmental inequalities. It had also created the vehicle for reevaluating clerical job skills. In this contract, the local fought over pay raises, guarantees against pay drops, and power sharing in the implementation of the classification study. While the study was critical to dealing with labor market sexism in this quintessential female occupation, as top union leaders pointed out, classification was a tool for dealing with institutional racism, as well. This classification campaign could potentially address racial inequalities among individual employees, as well as in work areas with the greatest African American and Hispanic concentrations.

Economist Julianne Malveaux notes the compounding economic effects of institutional racism and sexism observable in comparable worth cases. She argues for the necessity of identifying "'black women's crowding,' which is defined as distinct from the 'women's crowding' that white women experience" (1985b, 54). In examining data from Washington State's comparable worth case, Malveaux notes,

> Where all women were overrepresented, but black women were underrepresented, workers were paid an average of 94% of what they should have been paid based on job evaluation estimates. But in jobs where black women were overrepresented (with their representation in a job category at 15% or more), workers were paid 76% of what they should have been paid. (54)

Malveaux points to benefits for the entire black community when comparable worth is implemented. For the large number of black female-headed households "the need for black women to earn equitable pay cannot be overstated" (54). For two-earner families, comparable worth "frequently makes the difference between black family poverty and black family survival." Black men, who are more likely to work as clericals, would directly benefit as well (54–55).

Unfortunately, the union's reclassification demand was never framed as addressing broad social injustice, specifically institutional racism and sexism. This, as we'll discuss in chapter 8, was largely the result of the union's effort to keep the peace with TWU, the maintenance union, which quickly took offense at comparable worth talk. Rather, classification remained a largely abstract, vague, bureaucratic process to respond to pay inconsistencies and the general undervaluing of jobs by a stingy administration. Clearly, classification is only the groundwork for a larger, eventual political battle for comparable worth. At Columbia, a full frontal assault on pay equity at this time didn't make sense. The union would be in a much better position after the reclassification process was complete. And comparable worth is not without its problems. There are also a number of swamps in which the gender, race, and class biases reside as persistent viruses in the project of achieving pay equity. Comparable worth campaigns have to negotiate a morass of technical issues that, as Acker notes, easily obscure the fundamental political nature of struggle (1989).

Classification never came alive as an issue of import to most members during this campaign. It remained more a matter for a few expert union representatives. Classification demands are not the hottest issue going. Explaining the long-term issues of comparable worth, and the gender and race equity lying underneath classification demands, may well have raised the commitment to these demands. At the least, such a linkage would have set the groundwork for an eventual, tough, head-on battle.

The union then had waged its war with a mix of union (single-identity) and class, race, and gender (multi-identity) framings. For public audiences, the latter were more prominent. For insiders, a trade union contract approach greatly predominated.

Culture

It's hard not to be struck by the vibrance of the union's mass membership and public events:

> Eight buses traveled flotilla style through the traffic. Members chanted, and clapped, and rocked so hard the bus felt like it was shaking. Marked by police barricades, boosted by a sound system, the singing and chant-

ing, and dancing and rocking continued. Chant leaders emerged from the crowd using gospel, rap, jazz, and spoof. It is much less a demo, more a happening. Folks coming down the street, usually so unwilling to take a leaflet, couldn't wait to take the paper out of our hands, craving as they were to figure out what's this about. Like someone who knows they host great parties, this local throws demos, carrying the mark of varying African American and Latino communities in New York City.[27]

At the large membership meetings, demonstrations, and parties, the chants, singing, and music strongly reflected a range of African American, African Caribbean, and Latino cultural traditions of the majority of the members. Steel drums propelled the high-energy demonstrations. In the chants of "No Justice, No Peace," and in the call and response there was an echo of other black community protests, and a deep resonance of the moral mission of much African American church culture, in which many of the members, especially women, were quite involved.

Interestingly, many white members' strongest memories of the 1985 picket lines centered on exactly such qualities. This union culture helped members feel that they were on a moral crusade, part of a community, and at the same time have a lot of fun. "We Are Family" played at the 1985 celebration. Many kids were in the room. In 1991 the song was no longer hot, but there was still the same feeling at membership-wide union events. On the Saturday that we made mountains of picket signs, a small contingent of children made signs that gave voice to the effects of Columbia's wages on working mothers' children. Although the number of families involved was small, the children's picket also reflected an important part of the spirit and agenda of the union.

Although I would not want to overdraw this, the union during the 1991–1992 contract campaign could be characterized as having two cultures. The informal one was apparent in the large events, where members dominated. In these, the diverse cultures of the various African American, Caribbean, and Latino communities of which members are a part set the tone. In contrast, a more dry, bureaucratic meeting style constituted the formal culture of the multitude of small or medium sized meetings that filled activists' calendars over the year.

Organizational Structure and Process

From the beginning, the union has explicitly shaped its organizational structure to meet the needs of its workforce—mostly female and increasingly of color. In the early 1980s, the organizing committee developed a multitiered structure that allowed most workers to participate from their desks, or come to occasional lunchtime meetings. A small core that met regularly in the after-work slot was disproportionately young, white, and college educated. They worked hard at recruiting members of color, but the early committee remained racially unrepresentative. "We always worked at it, it was always a problem finding minority people who wanted to be active in the union," said James, who was active early on. "The union was very persistent around this. There were always folks who were too busy. Minority folks who were involved, we gave others a window, made the union accessible to folks." A few African Americans and Latinos joined the core; the second and third tiers were increasingly multiracial. Eventually, a black organizer came onto the paid staff.

By 1991 the participatory structure of the union, which relied heavily on an engaged rank and file, drew twenty-six members into the negotiating committee, and a slightly larger number onto the strike committee. These activists bridged the gap between informal leadership in their departments, and the more formal leadership structure of the union. Committees met frequently for contract negotiations or to plan or execute strike-related activities. As events escalated, all-union mass meetings provided opportunities for members to debate strategy. Subcommittees worked on particular projects.

District 65's organizational structure did not include caucuses, a common feature of many other progressive unions. "We never had a caucus . . . and that seemed right, people never needed it," said one white leader. She continued, "Black workers saw the union as the way to deal with their issues, as an organization that could be theirs." As we'll hear in the interviews in the next chapter, many agreed. Yet other workers' responses are more complex than this interpretation of the lack of a caucus would suggest.

Leadership

Ted, a long-term District 65 leader, pointed to chief organizer Julie Kushner's conscious effort in 1985 to develop multiracial women's leadership in the early organizing. "She relied on every feminist empowerment technique in the books. Trying to get consensus, versus promoting factions . . . thinking about how people could be supported, encouraging women, pushing them to become leaders." It worked. Some women drew on leadership they had developed in the church, community, and civil rights, black liberation, and Left struggles of the 1960s and 1970s. Some followed labor movement activism in their own families. Many women found new strength and skills and became union activists and leaders.

Carole, another longtime leader, remembered that before the strike, members used to think they had to get "some burly guys here from the UAW" to do the picketing. But the strike helped them to realize their own power. "There's this famous story about a gray-haired woman from the registrar's office . . . who stood up to this truck and all of the guys realized that they could stop trucks, that they weren't going to get run over."

Although women were making their presence known on the picket line, they were less visible in the formal leadership in terms of stewards. During the first round of elections, Carole recalled being "appalled by the number of men who were elected." To help prepare more women for leadership roles, the local sent several women to a leadership program at Black Lake, the UAW education center. It provided powerful inspiration and affirmation of a women's and antisexist identity of the union. "If it wasn't for that, I doubt I would have been as interested," said Jean, another long-term leader of the local.

Again in 1991, the strong women's leadership was striking to most participants and inspired many. "It's not just Julie [Kushner] and Maida [Rosenstein, the two top union leaders]," said Janet, a white activist in her thirties. "There are a lot of women on the negotiating committee that are very much their own person, and I admire them for that. It's nice to see there's so many strong women that are also really decent people. It shows that strength in a woman does not mean she becomes less of a woman." As powerfully seen in the singing and chant leading at the demonstrations on the streets of the city, many African American women rank-and-file leaders drew on skills and a culture of women "do-ers" nurtured in black churches and other community groups (Ladner 1993). They organized in their buildings and strengthened the foundational networks of the union.

While women and men of color were strongly represented throughout the union structure in 1991–1992, the highest level—critical in actual strategic power—remained white female. It is this top level that shaped most of the other identity practices, yet the 1991–1992 campaign did see a marked increase in new leadership development of African American and Latino members, especially women.

Although interested and talented people were recruited for leadership during the contract campaign, there was little systematic development of concrete skills, strategic thinking, political background, and personal nurturance. New leaders, while greatly valued, largely felt their way and learned from doing. During the nonstrike periods, District 65 had sent a few new leaders to national UAW training programs, including the women's leadership programs. The contrast to the Harvard Union of Clerical and Technical Workers (see chapter 7) is striking. For HUCTW, such leadership development is seen as a very high priority, a core component of the union's work and a female "taking care of" style of organizing.

Outside Resources

For its first strike in 1985, District 65 at Columbia had mobilized great support from the New York labor movement and elected politicians. Columbia clericals decidedly felt the solidarity of New York labor with them on the picket lines and in their struggle more broadly. On campus, the union sought and received labor support and tremendous solidarity by faculty and students. All of these were critical to their success.

In 1991 the formation of a campus labor coalition and the sympathy strike by Local 1199 were groundbreaking events and provided crucial support. These developments served to shape a campus labor identity, as well as a labor movement collective identity (Gamson's level 2). Providing the music to one of the large, militant rallies, 1199's participation strengthened the struggles' multi-identity cultural practices.

Also, as part of the larger labor support at a one-day strike membership meeting, a District 65 vice president came to offer solidarity. An African American, he whipped up the crowd with his "This is not a plantation" speech. It was one of the rare explicit race framings of the issues by a person of color throughout the campaign.

The support of faculty, graduate students, and campus ministry was critical to the union and helped to construct a campus movement identity. "Faculty for a Fair Contract" issued a series of letters educating the university community about the union's issues and certifying their import for the entire community. They also undertook the huge task of mobilizing fellow faculty to move several hundred classes off campus. Faculty supporters incorporated the union's struggle into a post–Anita Hill sexual harassment vigil that the Women's Faculty Caucus sponsored. A coalition of student groups included the union in another post-Hill antiracism and -sexism demonstration. Unfortunately, these events were out of sight of most union members.

The union maintained contact with the Black Student Organization during the 1991–1992 contract campaign. Columbia clericals sent a few members to the meetings of the students protesting the cutbacks in financial aid (which would particularly impact students of color, and the school's racial and class diversity). Progressive students at this meeting pushed for working with the union. Other students were reluctant. In part, it appeared to be due to their class or antiunion politics. However, strategy discussions revealed that many students and faculty saw the union's demand in the most narrow economistic terms and had no sense of the union's commitment to broader social justice. Here the union's own framing of its struggle was also a factor.

Off campus, the union solicited support from other trade unionists and politicians, including New York congressman Rangel and assemblymen Frank Barbaro and Ed Sullivan. The latter two called the university and spoke of "investigat[ing] the possibility of holding official public hearings to investigate discrimination at Columbia."[28]

The union made some efforts toward the NAACP, which did not come to fruition. Otherwise the union did not substantially draw in support from a range of African American, Caribbean, Puerto Rican, Latino, and (black, Latino, white, and multiracial) women's organizations, leaders, or churches. Nor, it is important to note, did any of these make any initiatives to the union, although with the campaign's minimal publicity, they would have been hard pressed to know the struggle was occurring. Union leaders noted the lack of community support initiatives as well as the particular organizational conditions in these movements which made such alliances difficult. It is a striking contrast to the 1199 and Yale cases. It was a loss mourned by at least one Latina member, who beamed as she spoke in the interview about the possibility of black and Latino community ministers and leaders supporting the Columbia struggle.

One problem, of course, is that gathering resources and building alliances in the short run is resource consuming. District 65 had no extra staff resources. Members, of course, could participate in such work. Yet this too would require coordination by member leaders or staff. As Cheryl Gooding points out, this is an area in which locals need support from the state and national federations (1999).

Another problem is with *which* community groups and leaders, with *which* political perspectives, the union should develop support relations. Members represent a diverse range of political and ideological perspectives on questions of racial and sexual politics, as all else. As we'll discuss in chapter 8, these are tricky questions. Yet a movement that is mute on such questions— some of which may be controversial—needs to find its voice so that it can make a decision to take advantage of potential supporters, should they so desire.

As we also examine in chapter 8, in a tight contest, these additional resources can be determinative. They can also help to affirm elements of a group's identity, which can impact internal mobilization. Further, it seems that allies are more free to articulate identity specific justice claims. These relationships also help to create outside movements as a point of reference, thus starting to reshape what Gamson has described as the social movement level of collective identity (see chapter 4).

Practices of Other Agents

University

Throughout the case review, we've looked at the conditions that Columbia clericals faced in the university. It is important to remember that unlike a snowstorm, these conditions don't simply fall from the sky. Rather, they are the consequence of agents' actions—in this case, the university's routine labor market practices. Together, these labor market practices created a gender, race, and class hierarchy of segregated and varied work experiences at Columbia. This made one of the key obstacles District 65 worked to surmount in creating a unified social movement organization.

As another contestant in this social movement struggle, the university made strategic and tactical moves with which the movement interacted. The university's commitment to holding the line on the contract, especially on health care, put together with the union's commitment in the opposite direction, necessitated a long struggle. When put together with the constraints created by low wage conditions of Columbia clericals, this yielded the protracted in-and-out strategy that District 65 adopted. This extended campaign in turn heightened the union's challenge of maintaining solidarity across the differences of the clerical workforce—which it well survived.

The university had no interest in a gender- or race-specific framing, unless it wanted to attempt a divide-and-conquer strategy. To avoid repeating errors from the 1985 contract, the university integrated its negotiating committee to include African American women and men and white women. Negotiating committee members, especially African Americans, often commented to one another with sarcasm, anger, and disgust on what they perceived to be very conscious, very strategic tokenism or "window dressing." The absence of such negotiating committee members would also have disgusted union members and would likely have fueled oppositional race politics. So while receiving no accolades from the union, the university's organizational practices seem to have been successful enough.

In framing its counterproposals, the university avoided any race or gender explicitness. Only in response to the charges of race and gender discrimination (the Mullinix letter) did the university use race- and gender-specific framings, which had the unintended consequence of strengthening the race identity politics the letter had hoped to diffuse.[29] In another unintended consequence, the university's effort to control cross-union solidarity also had the opposite effect. As we will hear in the next chapter, as workers deeply appreciated Local 1199's solidarity, the university's move to curtail sympathy strikes only strengthened the labor movement identity and solidarity of the campaign. It also had the unintended effect of broadening the union's resources and the scope of the conflict by directly bringing in the UAW.

Media

Columbia clericals were noticeably locked out of the media. The minuscule coverage they received, as is most often the case in labor movement coverage, was largely framed in traditional trade union contract terms (see Ryan 1991). One *Newsday* article picked up the "discrimination" charge, citing the comparable worth and health care statistics.[30] A *Times* article, focusing on the strike relocation of classes to cafés, clubs, and churches, included the union charges and administration disclaimers of discrimination.[31]

Given New York City's level of union conflict, it may have been difficult to achieve coverage and effect an injustice framing. However, given the heightened media attention to race in the post–Crown Heights period in New York, more race-explicit framing and the use of black and Latino community support resources may well have been able to create more of a media opening for the campaign. Similarly, more explicit framing around the injustices experienced by women of color may have found an opening in the period of the Anita Hill/Clarence Thomas hearings.[32] Yet these were highly charged contexts that of course also carried the heightened concern of identity-based conflict.

Summary: How the War Was Waged

The Columbia local successfully waged its contract battle with a mix of single- and multi-identity practices. Together these created primarily a "union" collective identity at the level of their specific organization. These practices challenged many intersecting effects of class, race, and gender domination in this workplace. Many identity practices (demands, culture, organizational structure, and leadership) made race and (less so) gender politically significant to the struggle, but other union practices (framing, support resources) often deflected the salience of race and especially gender. Largely the union pursued a "do it, but don't talk too much about it" strategy of creating multi-identity politics.

In its demands, the union prioritized the many race- and gender-based justice issues, weaving them in with traditional class-based (union) issues.

In its framing, the union tended more toward single identity—union—politics. District 65's framing of wage discrepancies sometimes used race-specific, and more infrequently gender-specific, language. This explicit framing was especially directed to the university, faculty supporters, politicians, and the public. Internally, especially in everyday oral communication, the union more often used an economic inequity frame and spoke in a more generic, a-racial, a-gendered trade union language.

For the union, this collection of practices worked to bring in a hard-won victory. As in its previous efforts, the union succeeded in maintaining cross-race solidarity as it tackled workplace racial injustice—another important accomplishment. Throughout, there was no fracture, no overt conflict around issues of diversity, combating racism and sexism. Thus the Columbia clerical local went further and accomplished more than many unions with regard to integrating progressive race and gender politics into a trade union agenda. It is in just such campaigns that the labor movement's future is to be found.

Especially in a time when multicultural politics were under attack, just what did this component of the campaign mean to members? Collective identity, we recall, is constructed on both movement and individual levels. Did the race and gender practices have any effect on individuals' participation in the mobilization? They clearly did for some members. Yet the surprising answer is that the percentage of workers of color who have defined this as a struggle for racial justice is much smaller than we might have imagined. Nor, across race, did most women—even self-identified feminists—see this as a forum for fighting sexism.

As we will hear in the following chapter, race and gender, fighting racism and sexism, had much less political meaning to members than I would have imagined. Members' talk points to a range of reasons—legal, ideological, and the union's own practices—why they attach smaller meaning to race and gender in the campaign than a review of documents might have suggested. In what ways were race and gender politically significant to District 65 members during this campaign? Members' words suggest the depth of the challenge of making this—or any labor—movement a vehicle for race and gender justice.

Let's listen.

6

Making Meaning of the Strike: How Race and Gender Counted for the Participants

I think they [the university] view us as kind of bootstrap poor, disenfran-chised, primarily female, single-parent union, which is half of the problem with this whole struggle. 'Cause there is just such a lack of respect. So, I tell people it has been a good experience and it has been a good struggle. And the union is needed at this particular institution, because multiculturalism does not exist here... even though it is supposed to be a bastion of learning.

—Calvin

You don't think about bringing up incidents of racism. You don't think about those kinds of things. I think that's one of those taboos.

—Aiesha

In 1985, at the closing of the strike, David Livingston, then president of District 65, was asked, "What marks the Columbia campaign for history?" He answered that "the struggle at Columbia emerged as a combination of labor struggle and struggle for women's rights and the civil rights of mi-norities."[1] Part of what I wanted to know was whether and how members thought about their union in terms of the race and gender justice efforts within their campaign. Objectively, the Columbia union had consistently been a trailblazer in weaving efforts at race and gender justice into its union-ism. What *meaning* did this hold for the members? Movement identity, we recall, is made at both the individual and collective levels. It is a com-plex interactive process between movement and members, in the context of available cultural meanings and structural conditions. How did Columbia clerical workers perceive efforts at countering racism and sexism? What weight did they take on? Did they contribute to the mobilization?[2]

There were workers who could not have spoken more passionately about the union's role as an instrument of race justice, gender justice, or both. When I first came to Columbia, Jean, a white activist, filled me in on the union's history.

> I'm proud of our union. It's so understanding of what women need. I'm proud of the fact we researched numbers about racial discrimination and made affirmative action an important part of our demands. This helped minority workers feel they were an important part of this union. White workers were shocked. Nobody wanted to be part of racial discrimination. The fact that we brought it out and publicized it was very important.... The union performed a teaching function, saying something like this shouldn't exist.... District 65 is the best of unions. It represents what unions should be.

Doris, an African American activist, spoke emphatically about the "discrimination issues" in this struggle. "I'm proud of what we've done here. Race discrimination [has been] on the table *each and every time.* . . . These issues have always been a subject of our efforts." Jennifer, an Asian American member who called for the union to "keep pushing on the discrimination issue," gave the following assessment: "I think they're doing well. Problems that can't be addressed in one contract, they put it on the table and work on it. They're doing a good job. The fact that this is New York City adds a dimension—a multicultural dimension. It's an opportunity to put our ideas into practice for equality among races." For some, the union was greatly appreciated as having created a rare multiracial meeting ground in a segregated and sometimes racially charged society. Across race, there were union members who had deeply committed themselves to race-based demands to "bring up" the workers at the bottom of the pay scale. The union was also seen as a site of impressive women's leadership, which inspired many members. The union offered a forum for a diverse group of workers to improve their lot—across race, gender, and class lines.

This was just the beginning of the story. These responses about race and gender justice were in fact a minority. In part, this is as much a comment on the nature of workplace racism and sexism and legal remedies to counter them, the invisibility of institutional sexism, and the stereotypes of feminism as it is a comment about the union. But the union's identity practices, which emphasized a "do it but don't talk much about it" approach to race and gender justice (see chapter 5), also played a key role in members' tendency to downplay the race and gender politics of the campaign. Framing, this case suggests, is a particularly significant practice in shaping how most participants construct identity. In the context of very little union discussion of sex segregation of clerical work and the lack of comparable worth, it was not surprising that to the limited degree workers saw any collective identity beyond "union," race greatly prevailed over gender. As part of the tradition of black women's community activism, many participants saw themselves as fighting for family and survival, and hopefully community uplift. This, too, contributed to the salience of race over gender in collective identity. Thus the race/gender intersection in this workforce, the identities and ideologies workers brought into the campaign, and the dominant either/or single-identity approach to movement identity also shaped the meaning that members made of their contract campaign.

For all these reasons, most members were quite qualified in their perception of their campaign as a vehicle of race justice and were even less likely to consider it a vehicle of gender justice. Surprising to me, this was true of members who were committed to movements for racial justice, and of those who defined themselves as feminists, as well. In this chapter, I will explore how Columbia clerical workers self-identified, first and foremost, as union members and the complex ways in which they did or did not conceive of the union as a vehicle for race and gender change.

Experiencing Union Identity

When I asked workers what was important about this campaign, as we would expect, they appreciated the campaign in union terms. "We took them on." "We did it." "We hung together." The "we" was union, the Columbia clerical local—what Gamson calls an organization-specific identity. They celebrated their toughness, their perseverance, and the empowerment they had experienced as a group and as individuals. Jennifer captured the sense of collective power she had experienced.

> It was new to be able to take action with other people. I've never done that before. It's an experience you take with you to other situations. There is a sense of... solidarity that you never forget, something that you take with you. It could be your neighborhood, it could be anything. It's been quite an experience. Once you've taken that action and seen what you can do, it changes you.

Suzanne, whom we heard earlier in the book, reported her newly found confidence and sense that she could "really make a difference." This is just the kind of empowerment the union aims to create.

Creating a "union" identity in a clerical workplace such as Columbia University is a plenty big task. Some members, disproportionately workers of color, have a little knowledge or experience of union. "Otherwise," as one steward put it, "basically they say, 'What's a union?'" Except for the active, committed core, to most members the union is a service organization and a "law firm."[3]

Most approach the union with the mix of images of trade unionism available in the media—an antiquated holdover from an industrial-based society in the 1930s and 1940s, irrelevant in an "upscale," prestigious institution of higher education. Unions are "not necessary" for white-collar workers, said one member. He added, "You know, it's a blue-collar thing." "An anachronism," said another, "a dinosaur trying to apply thought patterns that worked for industrial situations." "I think of unions as a macho, male institution," said another. Some are skeptical about in whose interest a union operates. Is this another boss? An outsider coming between the employer and the employee? It is a collectivity with which one's fate is now tied up, as opposed to making one's own best way. Like most organizations, forging a collective identity requires confronting the skepticism, fatalism, and inefficacy that characterizes how so many Americans, especially those who are working class, approach electoral or grassroots politics (Croteau 1995).

And as we've heard earlier, Columbia clericals, some from diverse backgrounds, were on a multitude of trajectories in which the job and the strike held very different meanings. One of the fundamental challenges that the Columbia clerical union confronted was creating a collectivity out of such diversity.

And they did. The entire contract script from negotiating team elections and committee reports to strike votes, picket lines, strike days, and all-membership meetings certainly created a union identity. Allison said, "Suddenly I realize I am part of a union! Basically that happened to me, I mean [before now] I paid my dues and I didn't think about it." "It's a coming together of all the rank and file, and saying that you're a union, and you have a common interest, and you are together," said Calvin, an African American activist, adding, "It lessened the feelings of isolation." Jennifer said, "It's empowering as a process...it's empowering seeing what people coming together can accomplish."

It is important to note, though, that the union identity remained partial and ambivalent: a work in process. As we will hear in the upcoming pages, many members, even some of the most active, use the term "they" as opposed to "we" when referring to the union. Antonietta reported that as she went to update people in her building, "Over and over, I'd be telling people, 'You are the union.' I mean it was like a separate entity, even [for] some people who were completely supportive." Such a separation clearly is significant in "shap[ing] a sense of belonging" on the basis of any identity.[4]

Members, in response to my question about what was important to them about the struggle, celebrated specific contract gains—especially the health care win and the raises. A few spoke with satisfaction about how the administration had been unable to take away District 65's right to solidarity strike, which they perceived as an important labor principle. For these workers, the solidarity they had received from other unions, especially 1199, and the university's attack on it, helped to reinforce that the "we" here was the labor movement (what Gamson refers to as a level 2—movement level—identity).

Asking about Race and Gender

In this union, as in many social settings, talking about race and gender was tricky. They were little part of the sound track, not part of the regular conversation in the organization. Were they taken-for-granted categories, part of the background reality like sky and sun? As sociologist Bonnie Thorton Dill reminds us, "Most people view their lives as a whole and do not explain their daily experiences or world view in terms of the differential effects of their racial group, class position, or gender" (1987, 208). Ted, a Columbia leader, made the same point. "It's difficult to segregate these things into separate spheres. They all cut into one another." Also, individuals come with their own ideological predispositions on racial justice, feminism, social movements, and so forth, which were largely beyond the scope of this study to examine.[5]

Further, the failures of feminist movements and academics to shape their work consistent with an intersectional approach have often meant the imposition of a feminist or gender primary analysis on the struggles of black women, Latinas, other women of color, and working-class women (of all races).[6] Black historian Elsa Barkley Brown points out the recurrent problem in the definition of "women's issues and women's struggle" in a way that assumes the separability of women's struggle and race struggle. Such a defining of terms fails to consider that "women's issues may be race issues, and race issues may be women's issues" (1990, 174). Black women "community workers," "as contemporary representatives of a historical tradition of Black women making social change," argues sociologist Cheryl Gilkes "decide for themselves and their community the appropriate objects of their efforts and the . . . goals to be achieved" (1988, 54). It is the right and necessity of each group to define its own project, its own identities. With all of this in mind, as Dill argues, it is important to "study individual and group perceptions, descriptions, and conceptualizations of their lives so that we may understand the ways in which different women perceive the same and different sets of social structural constraints" (1987, 208).

This effort to understand movement identity on the individual level was challenging. I began with very open questions to allow union members to structure their answers in their own terms. This allowed me to see whether race, gender, and class were categories workers spontaneously used to describe or interpret their experience. In response to "What was important to you about this campaign?" only a few answered in any racialized or gendered terms. I then asked about what role race and gender had played in the campaign. What role had the "large number of minorities" and the "large number of women" at Columbia in the union played in shaping the union and this struggle? Eventually I asked whether members saw the union as a vehicle for dealing with race injustice and gender injustice. For the most part, race and especially gender were not frequently or easily used categories. Understanding race talk and gender talk of Columbia clericals, we will hear, also involves paying attention to silences.

Let's listen.

Race Talk, Race Silence

The union's racial composition was certainly well noted by the membership. In the interviews, workers of all races spoke of the union being "mostly minority," "mostly black and Hispanic." A few noted the large number of "single minority mothers." Some workers of color spoke appreciatively of the union as a site of cross-race encounters. Reginald described the growth that being part of a multiracial union had brought for him.

> It cuts the isolation and brings social maturity for us all. Having grown up in the South you would think . . . you just don't trust whites. This is something you just don't do. . . . I've grown, I've come out of my shell, in a sense, and this is pretty much due to the union. . . . I would have had the reaction that a lot of minorities have towards whites. And you come to understand that not *everybody* is prejudiced. . . . There are people out there who as a rule are straightforward, and fair, and will treat you accordingly.

It was more noticeably white workers, often unaccustomed to being in an integrated, and also predominantly black and Hispanic, setting, for whom the union's identity was much more consciously racialized. Janet had come from a segregated white background:

Really I never thought of the union in racial terms, the union mostly representing minorities until the meetings. I looked out across the faces, and
it's really stunning when you're there, you really realize how, in fact, the
union is predominantly people of color. Before that it wasn't something I
thought about. . . . Columbia is very segregated.

In a segregated workplace and society, several of the white folks interviewed appreciated the cross-race experiences they encountered in the union.[7]
These welcome, unusual happenings were eye-opening, growthful, and sometimes challenging for whites in different ways. Allison, for example, said her
experience in the union with a majority people of color offered a positive
contrast to the predominantly Scandinavian suburb she lived in. It was her
first experience "right in the center of a lot of activity of a minority group,"
and it inspired her to do "a lot of observing, and appreciating, and a lot of
listening."

Another white member, Lawrence, noted that being in the numerical
(and cultural) minority was a learning experience: "I wasn't unwelcomed. I
was a member, people listened to me. . . . It was something I never experienced before. Being a white man, I have certain privileges. I can't deny it.
This kind of put the shoe on the other foot." Janet appreciated that the
union provided her with her first opportunity to get to know African Americans "as people." She added, "I hope I don't sound racially prejudiced, it's
more the fear of the unknown, as opposed to racial prejudice."

A diverse union membership working together provided an important
opportunity to make the "unknown" more familiar and to develop cross-
race solidarity. Several union officers and activists suggested this was one
reason why the university had so opposed the union's time-off request for
membership meetings. "They *know*," said Martin, "the more people gather,
and exchange ideas, and work together, they. . . bring about a close relationship." All member gatherings are a way to deal with the isolation created by the internally segmented labor market.

For many workers of color, the multiracial, predominantly black and Hispanic nature of the workforce was, as we would expect, taken for granted.
The culture of the union, especially at informal events, was quite black centered. As Nina, a white union leader, pointed out in a conversation about
workers' perceptions of the union, "Much of this is taken for granted. It's
more just a regular part of who we are, what we do. We've created a whole
culture that brings it together." Longtime labor activist and scholar Susan
Eaton made the same point: "Identity and cultural issues can be critical. Yet
most of the time people don't think about them, they just act them out as

part of daily life in the union." While taken for granted, "when they're working, these practices can go a long way in helping people feel at home, connected to the union."[8]

In these ways, the union leadership's sense of accomplishment at having created a "sense of multiracial community" in a world in which "race [is] a continuing discomfort in our lives" is well supported by members' experience. Yet when talking about the union as a vehicle for fighting racism, the responses were more complex.

When I asked what in the contract had been important to her, Lana, an African American negotiating committee member, said, "Of course, the discrimination issues; I am really proud that we took that on." Jennifer, a new Asian activist, also answered, "Certainly the discrimination issue." What was curious, though, was how very few others spoke about the issue in celebrating their victory, especially given the difficulty of the fight. For most workers, the demands over narrowing "the race wage gap" did not significantly define the struggle. With few exceptions, what rare direct naming of racism there was, was mostly done by top white women leaders. Yet most workers of color interviewed powerfully experienced racism on the job.

Talking about Racial Discrimination

Of the twenty-six Columbia activists of color I interviewed, about 60 percent responded with one or more accounts of racist incidents; 40 percent reported no incident. Self-reports of racism are a difficult data source to evaluate. First, how do we evaluate the veracity of these reports? "You've got to evaluate it, it could be totally false," said one leader. "You've got to look into it carefully," many union activists of all races cautioned. University personnel data through federal government reports were unavailable because of regulations regarding public access. Because the number of grievances filed on issues of racism is quite low, this offered no supporting data. On the other side, as studies in sexual harassment and rape well illustrate, the lack of reports provides no reliable indication of the extent of a problem. As with sexual harassment, stories of racism at work are often not told, as people know they would rarely meet legalistic evidentiary requirements. Further, in my interviews, talking about racism with an only somewhat known white person isn't everybody's idea of a smart or worthwhile expenditure of energy. Often I would be told more stories, and important stories, late in the interviews, when trust was higher.

The recurrent pattern in the aggregate data from the union of the university's differential hiring rates into each grade and pay within these grades suggests a problem of racial inequity. I will make the not surprising call for further research, which was beyond the scope of this project, to systematically evaluate hiring, pay, promotion, and disciplinary practices in such a workplace. In the meantime, with consciousness of its limitations, I argue that these self-reports offer us insight into the ways workers of color perceive this workplace and union campaign.

Of those (60 percent) who reported racist incidents, two-thirds reported an incident of their own (or their own *and* a friend's or coworker's). The other third spoke only of friends' or coworkers' experiences. The leading types of incidents discussed were promotion/evaluation, and individual racism. Pay differences (as distinct from promotion), disciplinary differences, and tracking were all by far secondary. In each of these areas, there was a range in whether members talked about racism as an individual flaw or a systemic problem, as well.

Isabella related what happened when her supervisor instructed clerical workers to speak only English on the job. "I blew up. I don't need to speak Spanish to tell them what I think of management, and they know that . . . I got very upset." Elba added, "My baby-sitter, she doesn't speak English at all. How are they going to ask me, how would they *dare* to tell me that I cannot speak my main language on a personal phone call? If you do not want to hear my talking Spanish, you get away from my desk." Carmella, another Latina, reported a supervisor insisting she didn't "talk right," and wanting to tape-record her to prove it to her.

Lisa noted she was the only person in her large, otherwise white office who was asked, "What's that marijuana smell?" And as students of color in predominantly white universities often experience, "If something happens, like when the [Los Angeles] riots happened, they all come and ask me. They assume, I'm the spokesperson for all people of color." "One thing I have never really encountered was racism or prejudice in any other position I've ever held," said Aiesha, "but [here at Columbia], I think I got a first-hand view of what it's like to be discriminated against." She was sworn at by a white student from a privileged class background, who then tried to get her into trouble with her boss. Aiesha perceived this to be both a race and class assault.

Favoritism in promotions was the single biggest complaint. "They practice [discrimination] in my office, yes," explained Andrea. "All the upper promoted people are all white. I think something should be done. . . . You know in this day and age, we've had so many people die for the cause of equality—you're equal, yet you're not," she added. Martin, an African American leader, concurred, believing that racism explained "the hiring of outsiders in higher positions than people who were there much longer."

Gabriella, a new Latina activist, agreed: "In our area there is no Hispanic that has a higher position." Mavis bitterly explained the sense of despair that some people feel as a result of being part of an organization that seems "intent on keeping people down."

> Top administrators are very quick to say a lot of people don't try to pro-
> mote themselves. Well, that is a lie. That is a lie. People try very hard. I'm
> not the only one going from position to position, and finding out how
> hard it is to grow. People start to lose hope, and stop trying...

Gloria, an African American member, was skeptical of the role of the union in a university. She believed that people should "not be relying on an outside group," but be "empowered" and learn "to advocate for themselves." Gloria had been successful in doing this, and she didn't support the strike. To her coworkers, she was a "scab." Yet Gloria fervently agreed that people of color were passed over for promotions, especially working-class African American women who didn't have a college education. Referring to union studies that showed people of color disproportionately represented in the lowest ranks, she said, "I know that to be true, absolutely true. I've seen it. Black women have tried to move and advance and just have been locked in. They get consistently turned down. And the next thing you know a white male is brought in."

These racist practices around promotions are so commonly understood, says Gloria, that "in fact, it's like a running joke among those of us who know the administrators." Feagin and Sikes's study of middle-class blacks similarly describes the magnitude and persistence of barriers to employ-ment—what some refer to as the "concrete ceiling."[9]

Some members felt that these instances of racism were rooted in the fact that "there are some nasty people" in the world, as Luke said. "I mean... they are nasty against each other and they are both the same color. I don't know, I just try to ignore that, really." Martin argued:

> Racism is a *big* indictment. It's a word I'm not comfortable with. But
> again, and I think it would cause a lot of problems for anyone who would
> hear it... I don't think, I would say I *know* it doesn't exist *systematically*, I
> know it's not *structured*.
>
> And Columbia has a strong antidiscrimination policy, especially when
> it comes to race, sex, stuff like that. A very strong policy, strictly enforced.
> I know it's something that's not a matter of policy. You have people com-
> ing in with different ideas.... Sometimes it seeps into their decision mak-
> ing, and that's where it does the university a disservice, and it does the
> employees a disservice who are under that person.

Others believed there was a more institutional basis for the ways racism played out in interpersonal relations. Lily, who is Asian, offered her analysis:

> Management has their certain corporate mannerisms, their certain way they speak, they interact, communicate. That sort of formality that not all of us adhere to. It might be cultural. They [black workers] are perceived as being outside, or unable to join the group.... People who say they are not career oriented. They want to work to earn money, to provide food and clothing for their children....
>
> And that's fine, that is satisfactory. [But] the perception is that if you don't want to do that, then somehow you are not contributing enough. Or, even worse, you are lazy.... It is not overt, [it's] what they might call institutional racism....
>
> I think their [whites'] perception of black workers is wrong. Because they [whites] can't see themselves as having a distinct culture. Until they see themselves as having a distinct culture and distinct mannerism, separate from most, they won't recognize them.... And again, the perception is that they don't want to contribute. You are not doing enough.[10]

Lily's observations find support in sociologist Ivy Kennelly's study that found negative stereotypes of single mothers to characterize white employer's views of black women workers.[11]

Maxine believed that the pay gap was also rooted in systemic racism. "Of course we know they discriminate. When [Mullinix] says that blacks are less smart than whites, or less likely to go to college than whites, we know by that he discriminated. I believe that in other areas... you know, they do pay whites more than they pay blacks."

Analyzing the segregated nature of work areas was one of the points of disagreement in the interviews about institutional racism. Before unionization, segregated work areas, or "job ghettos," as some called them, were common. "You see it in the controller's office. Black and Latina workers... working under sweatshop conditions, squished together, under heavy surveillance. Where we worked [in academic departments], conditions were much better. [There] was a difference in the kind of work, a lot of repetitive filling out of forms, almost assembly line work," said Katherine, an early white activist.

While diminished over the intervening years, race-dominated areas were still noticeable. Members often remarked on how academic department offices were white. "Look at this university. Why am I the only person of color in this office?" asked Lisa. "It helps having that college education. I have two shots against me, being Hispanic, being a woman.... It's the caste system," and she added, "The lighter, the better." White workers, like Janet, also described the workplace as segregated. She noted, "The academic offices also seem to be sort of segregated," and added that "in my entire ten years," despite turnover, "there's only been one black in that entire time."

Luke, an African American leader, mostly downplayed the role of racism and argued against considering "Columbia, itself, racist." He eloquently described a key form of institutional racism that often played itself out in organizations unintentionally.

> It is a shame that people who run businesses and corporations are male, white, and they tend to want the same thing around them. I think that is true for everybody. If you are doing something, you just want to have your image around you. And I think that would be the same for a woman.... Unfortunately, until society moves away from that stereotyping, you will have some level of discrimination.

Luke argued that "most departments, I'm not going to say *all,* but most departments really go on your skills." He concluded, "Obviously there is discrimination, but put it in its proper perspective."

Luke and other activists suggested the dynamics that produce segregated offices, and lack of promotions, are much more complex than the charge institutional racism implies, due in large part to the preferences and actions of black workers themselves:

> So is the department wrong because they want to have all white people in their area? Or is it a black person applied for the job and was turned down? Maybe no one applied for the job because they heard it was an all-white department and I don't want to be there. So I don't know that enough to say that this department is being racist.... What is the type of work? What kind of opening? Maybe the good openings are filled.

Ted, a white union leader, believed that the prevailing attitude among professors and students was that "they want someone who looks like them to be there in their office." Ted suggested that this problem was exacerbated by a kind of "white flight." At the payroll department in Hogan Hall, he said, the clericals were "almost all female, and they're almost all black." When a white clerical was assigned to Hogan Hall, he or she was "going to take one look around and say, send me somewhere else." Martin suggested that the preferences and actions of black workers were similar. He said he personally felt more comfortable "being a minority, in a minority department, than being in a department where you're just one or two ... personally, I wouldn't be comfortable, I mean I could *handle* it, but I wouldn't *choose* it." Luke agreed that tracking occurs partly when people of color don't apply for jobs "because they heard it was an all-white department and [they] don't want to be there." Another local leader made the same point: "People don't go where they're not wanted. So they don't file grievances. Maybe they don't even apply."

The inevitable calls for further research find their place on the agenda here, as well. As one of the top leaders of the local suggested, there is a need for a documented analysis of institutional racism, of institutional barriers, in the workplace, in the tradition of the death penalty studies, which document the effects of race at each step along the institutional path. Such research could be a contribution of supportive academics and would greatly add to workplace organizing movements.[12] Obtaining access would, of course, be very challenging.

The Union as Vehicle for Race Change?

The debate over personal or systemic racism aside, did clerical workers feel that the union was a vehicle for fighting the kinds of racial discrimination they had described? "Oh definitely," said Pauline, who is African American. "No doubt, I'd be fired already." "I think if it had not been for the union, these instances may have happened, but we might not have been here to tell you about them," said Aiesha. "Oh, absolutely," said Gabriella, "the union is what enables us to continue to exist at Columbia." Says Earline, "If it wasn't for the union, they would've gotten rid of us. . . . I don't know what the union's doing [about racism], I never mention it." Earline's comments well captured the common reaction: a sense of the union as a critical protection, but little inclination to actually use it.

Maxine, an African American union leader, credited the union with addressing the pay discrepancy between black and white workers: "It has gotten better since the union has tried to even up the scale." Martin adds, "For minorities it's important because we have those in our society that treat one another unjustly... they have those prejudices, and they bring them to the workforce. Having a union to keep them in check, and having a grievance procedure is important."

But that was only the beginning of the story. Although we've heard from many clerical workers of color that for them racism had a powerful presence on the job, and though several workers voiced their appreciation of the union's efforts to address discrimination, many others had a much more sober assessment. Why, then, did so many workers speak in such a qualified way about the union as a vehicle for race change? Their responses suggested a cluster of reasons as to why workers see a more qualified and complex relationship between the union and the fight for racial justice.

For many workers of color, the question of whether the union was a vehicle for race change was more an assessment about the nature of racism than the nature of the union. My question about the union as a vehicle of race change was seen as a subset of the question "How much could racism successfully be challenged?" The overall answer was: not that much.

Pointless, Risky Business

The overwhelming majority of members of color whom I interviewed felt that fighting racism at work was futile and dangerous. Lily captured the predominant sentiment when she said, "No, people in my office don't believe that the union is a vehicle to challenge it [racism]. They are afraid to cause waves . . . I think they think it is pervasive and they can't really do anything about it." Rosa concurred that "crying racism doesn't work out well": "I'd be blackballed; considered a troublemaker. My life would be hell. They'll watch me closely, wait for me to trip up. I don't want to be the target." Andrea agreed that naming racism was a personally and professionally risky tack to take. "They make you feel like you're a traitor. They give you the cold shoulder. It's very uncomfortable. They kind of push you out."

It is also important to note that as hard as the union had to fight over the bottom grades, these specific contract demands left unaddressed the issues many workers of color reported in interviews as their experience of racism in the institution. The union had a grievance procedure for discrimination claims, but Maxine, a steward, said that people did not file them because they "think there is no use. It is hard to win something on prejudice. . . . Most people just don't want the hassle of it. So they just don't say anything." Lily added, "The only recourse you have is legal. . . . You have to have it where all the elements are in place. I was hired at the same time that so and so was hired. So and so got promoted. And then you are up against a whole tidal wave of counterarguments. . . . I mean there are so many escape routes for that, that I think people don't challenge it anymore."

One white union leader's description of the realities of grievance procedures shows these fears not to be unfounded. "They may be discriminating against you, but basically that is superseded by your own fault . . . that's the operating view. It's a mix; people are not perfect; that's a reality . . . the major fights are around laid-off people who have no choice." Furthermore, said Carole, a long-term white union leader, people would rather have "someone inside who would take up the battle for them. . . . It's much less threatening to people than having to go up against who just didn't hire you and say, 'You should have hired me.'" Another problem, Lily pointed out, was that for many members, the union only has a real presence among the clerical workers every three years at contract time. The union is not much of a "physical presence," so people didn't "see it as an option."

Here Cheryl Gilkes's observation about the twinned efforts of fighting racism and of community uplift seems relevant. Gilkes points out that the struggle against racism has been "inextricably linked to concerted efforts to foster social uplift" (1988, 53). While, given the intractable nature of workplace racism, many black members haven't seen the union as a vehicle of changing racism, they do appreciate it as a vehicle of concrete betterment and survival at Columbia.

Sparse Job Options

Hard calculations about the stark realities of a "closed"—race- and sex-segregated—labor market make action all the more risky (see Stafford 1985; Rodríguez 1989). As Lily says, "Lots of black and Hispanic people I know here feel these are the best jobs they've been able to get. . . . They are afraid they will not be able to find anything else." The university uses this fear, Calvin argued, "banking on people of color kind of laying back and being really just so happy to be at Columbia, and this just being the end all for them. And this *is* the end all for a lot of people in our department. . . . Because with some people this *is* the best thing that has ever happened to them."

Compartmentalization and Low Expectations

Others suggested that there is an issue of compartmentalization: members have circumscribed expectations about what a union is all about and in what context people of color might deal with these issues. "I think that people see the union as a vehicle for getting more money. Period," said Suzanne, who earlier described the profound changes she had experienced from union activism. James described the same dynamic in trying to get folks involved in the original organizing: "Many felt 'it's just a job thing.'" He added that most people see the union as a tool for making economic gains, not for "actualiz[ing] themselves as minorities. Maybe for the stewards this is true. . . . Maybe we *wish* it were more this way." Believing that "racism and sexism are an ever present part of their lives," many members feel that they should focus instead on practical goals—things "they can actually do something about."

This sentiment echoes the work of scholars who note that compartmentalization is a critical survival strategy for workers negotiating racism in the workplace. Patricia Hill Collins quotes Ella Surrey, an elderly black woman domestic: "We've always had to live two lives—one for them and one for ourselves."[13] Management professor Ella Bell's study of how black professional women travel between the white cultures in the workplace and black cultures at home and in the community found that black women employ compartmentalization as an alternative strategy to assimilation (1990, 471–72).

Compartmentalization may also be evident in the context of the distance many workers experience between themselves and the union. This is quite visible in the recurrent "they" in members' talk when referring to the union, rather than "we," even on the part of members actively participating in the negotiating or strike committees. Jennifer pointed out, "It's one thing if the union is your primary expression of who you are." "For most people, the union may be important," but people have "church, community groups, and other ways to participate." Members aren't necessarily expecting the union to be their way to deal with racism, Jennifer was saying, and they may have other organizations that fulfill this purpose. Whether and how and the degree to which union members decompartmentalize and use the union more as an "expression of who [they] are" is of course up to the workers themselves.

Compartmentalization has often served as a necessary and successful strategy for many activists. Gilkes's study of black women community workers finds they structure their efforts at "survival" and "transformation" by working in many different organizations on many different issues. "There are lots of small pieces" of change work in a "web of affiliations" (1988, 68). Thus rather than a negative compartmentalization, circumscribed expectations can be seen as part of a more positive strategic division of labor in maintaining communities and making change. As unions are understood as being willing to undertake multi-identity struggles, activists will have increased options in how they think about dividing the "small pieces."

Race Silence

There is plenty of reason in America to be wary of talking about racism. As Patricia Hill Collins reminds us, around issues of oppression, silence is often the only viable option (1990, 92). But this was a movement two-thirds of color, and one for which demands of racial discrimination were important priorities. So why, as Aiesha told me, was talking about race considered out of bounds?

> I think that's one of those taboos, so to speak. That's like parents talking to their children about sex. Because some people think if they do, they're going to open up a can of worms. And I mean things here at Columbia are not that bad. But they're not that great either. So, I don't know, maybe

it's just not a thought in a person's head when they go to the union meetings. You don't think about bringing up incidents of racism. You don't
think about those kinds of things.

Her answer confirmed the silence I had long puzzled over. It dawned
on me slowly, but I eventually became aware of a curious incongruity. While
the union's long-standing commitment to fighting racial injustice avidly
put key demands at the center of their agenda, there was a remarkable lack
of conversation about these issues in union meetings.

I don't assume that constant, explicit discussion of race is the goal, the
ideal. My own experience in hospital organizing with white leftists who
inflicted race-primacy analysis in the most obsessed, insensitive manner, if
anything, makes me quite cautious. But the eerie silence, once I acknowledged it to myself, was hard to ignore. Why was race so rarely directly discussed? On one occasion, one of the top white women leaders brought up
Mullinix's letter at a meeting for open discussion. This was the administration letter that talked about black workers having less education, on average, than whites as a justification for the wage gap. Why when it was brought
up at a meeting of the strike committee did so very few folks respond? This
quiet seemed critical to understanding the role of race in this movement
mobilization.

After Aiesha named the taboo, I started asking about silence in other
interviews. "No, you're right, it's not something people talk about in union
meetings," said Lana, another African American activist, "but they do say it
to me, and to each other." As psychologist Beverly Tatum (1997) argues,
across race, most of us learn early that talk about race in mixed-race settings
is out of bounds. In its place reigns silence, so powerfully in command that
we rarely question it. Silence, of course, often represents correct and careful
calculations about the risks of speaking truth. "Breaking silence," writes
Collins, "represents . . . saying in public what had been said many times before to each other around the kitchen table, in church, at the hairdresser, or
at those all Black women's tables in student dining halls" (1998, 50). Breaking silence can be risky, bring retaliation, and may yield no significant change.

Few expected the union to do much about racism. This is particularly
the case given the relative newness of Columbia workers to unions. As two
union women leaders—one African American, one white—pointed out in
response to workers' quotes in this book, "It takes a while—sometimes
quite a while—until members understand what the union's all about." The
popular perception of unions is that they have the single mission of fighting
for wages and benefits rather than being an agent of broad social justice.

This is certainly what is visible in most union contract repertoires of action, how most unions generally frame their contract struggles, and how unions are generally covered by the media (see Fine 1998; Ryan 1991). White labor educator Cheryl Gooding relayed the dominant perspective: "People think if you want to deal with discrimination, you go join the NAACP, or some other organization in the Black or Latino communities. You don't look to the union" (interview, April 1994).

Valuing Color Blindness

Others believe that racist workplace practices are best fixed through color-blind attention to fairness and equality for all. They see the union as a vehicle for all workers—one that de facto addresses workplace racism, not by calling special attention to race, but by insisting on color-blind standards across the board.

This argument for color-blind fairness draws on a cherished American value of equality and justice: evaluating and treating all people as individuals, without regard to their social group categories. As Luke said, "I hate when people push you on color. . . . I hate for people to approach me on race. I know lots of people who think about it and talk about it a lot. Myself, I prefer not to go down that road. I don't like to dwell on it. . . . Anything you say that's offensive to me, I will argue with you based on that. Not because you are white or black." This discussion drops us into the broader debate over our vision of racial justice and how we get to it. This debate underlies social controversies like affirmative action, multicultural curriculum, and transracial adoption. As I will explore in chapter 8, is our goal of a nonracist, nonsexist society found in color and gender blindness, which considers individuals without regard to their race, gender, or other group characteristics? Or is it found in a multicultural or diversity-conscious approach that considers individuals in the context of their group characteristics, including that group's location in enduring social systems of inequality?

Ted, a longtime white union leader, summarized a color-blind approach:

> The thing is if you do your job and protect everybody at what you're supposed to, you know wages, hours, working conditions, and you do that equally and everyone realizes that you're defending everybody, everyone's rights equally, that you're not showing any favoritism. That's another way to sort of bolster antiracist presence here.

Especially for folks who favor a color-blind approach, the union's efforts at countering racism were largely taken for granted, seen as a regular part of union business. "We are a union that fights for *all*," argued Tory.

"Otherwise it would be kind of exclusive." I will turn to this debate in greater depth in chapter 8. In the meantime, it is clear that some members' racial ideology—valuing color blindness—constituted another factor in members' reticence to describe the union as a vehicle of race change.

Racial Composition of the Leadership

Four times in my interviews, all with activists of color, the question of the race composition of the leadership emerged spontaneously.[14] All who spoke about leadership were clear that they considered these white women fierce antiracists. But they disagreed about whether the lack of racial diversity at the top level had an impact on members' perceptions and expectations of the union as a vehicle for fighting workplace racism. Lana thought that "if one of [the leaders] were black, it may have made it easier to draw in more people. I think it's natural, it is just . . . there's this sense of automatic trust, of the other person knowing what you're talking about."

Cheryl Gooding was the founding director of the Women's Institute for Leadership Development (WILD) in Massachusetts. WILD went through a conscious process of changing from an originally white, middle-class or-ganization to one that was very diverse in race, class, and sexual orientation in both membership and leadership. Gooding's lessons from this work con-cur with Lana. "If the leadership is white (or male, or whatever—monocul-tural), then [multicultural] identity practices will be much less organic and will be present only to the extent that the white or male leaders have the consciousness and skill to allow and encourage the space for those practices to be incorporated" (1999).

Lana believed that an all-white leadership may have caused the relative silence about racism in the union meetings. But other black activists disagreed strongly. Doris said that black and Latina/o members "feel real comfort-able" with how top white women leaders handled the union. When another black member asked Doris, "Don't you think it should be a black person up there?" she replied, "That would be fine with me, if they're going to do the job that these two do. I don't care if they're green, as long as they work as hard as they do, put as much into it, get as much done. To me that would just be icing on the cake. I think others feel this way, too." Luke agreed that color was not an issue when it came to leadership. "I'm saying there is no color thing. It is more a leadership thing [being able to let go, to delegate tasks]. That's the way I see it."

In analyzing the elements of the union's success in maintaining white solidarity for racial justice, Nina, one of the white leaders, explained the ef-fectiveness of white leadership. "We were able to develop an understanding that it was unacceptable for this situation to exist. It took consistent leadership and mutual trust. Coming from a white leader and a leadership committee which was [racially] mixed, the respect was deep enough. Members felt if you tell us this is the way it is, we'll believe you. We backed it up with facts."

Representation in leadership does not necessarily guarantee anything. For a variety of reasons (including concerns about not alienating the TWU and the race/gender intersection), two white women in leadership, each a feminist, did not wrap this movement in an antisexist identity. As 1199 in its nadir period well exemplifies, focusing solely on the race composition of leadership can have calamitous effects for an organization (see chapter 3). Also, as Luke's comments suggest, the question of power—to shape agendas, set priorities, and invoke identities—resides not only in who occupies top positions but also in how much power active members have in initiating, planning, and deciding on strategy, along with top leaders. Without this dispersion of strategic power, most identity practices are determined solely by top leaders, however unconsciously. Certainly there is no essential guarantee of a black or Hispanic leader successfully raising racism issues. Yet it may well increase the potential of members so seeing the union.

The Union's Practices: "Was It a Slogan or Was It a Campaign?"

Deborah King, Audre Lorde, Bonnie Thorton Dill, and others argue that it is the members of any oppressed group, themselves, who must decide what identities to make salient, or primary, in any particular situation. Whether and how to use identity is not solely in the purview of the leadership. Organizations and strong leaders, though, do play a significant role in socially constructing the problems that they and their memberships face. Problems, argues Herbert Blumer, are not recognized as important, valid, changeable injustices until someone sets out to construct them as such (1971).

Martin acknowledged the power of the union, earlier in its history, to name and legitimize racial injustice. Before unionization, he recounted, black workers were acutely aware of differences from "whites in the salary structure... and in the hiring and promotion patterns. It was obvious, because people talked about it. But there wasn't any means to do anything about it, and people were reluctant to say it, to call it, to make allegations about it." Thus "discrimination wasn't a major issue before the union came in and ... all the information was made public and it was then that the pattern was revealed."

What role did the union play in naming the problem of racism and pointing the power of collective action toward countering it? We've seen that the union prioritized demands confronting the race wage gap and classification—two demands that confronted elements of racism. We've also seen that the union was more likely to use race-explicit framings for external audiences and was more uneven in its framing for members. Some high-profile leaflets analyzed and discussed the issue for members, but most often "inequities" and "discrimination" were a part of the long list of contract issues rather than substantially developed and explained. Often the union elected to speak in a-racial trade union language about "bringing up the bottom," "the 3s and 4s," which could be seen as racially coded. How was this read by members?

Antonietta, a Latina activist new to Columbia, said that even though she was trying to stay informed about the campaign, she did not have a full picture of the role of racial discrimination.

> It wasn't until months into this thing, until the action heated up, that I had any idea discrimination issues were an important part of what the union was fighting about in this contract. I think that the idea of putting up the [grade] 3s and the 4s was a way of dealing with discrimination. But it was a *long* time before I understood this. It was a long time into the campaign until this was articulated.

Maxine, an African American activist, said that although the union worked on developing contract demands that would address racial injustice, its actual discussion about racism was "hit and miss."

For Calvin, a young African American, the role of the union with regard to racism was largely unrealized. "I'm not down on the union...I think personally the union is more a defensive mechanism, at least at this stage of this particular union, because it is young, [rather] than offensive." He went on to explain that "forcing Columbia to really change its business practices" would happen only through an offensive campaign, not a case-by-case defensive action.

Julian, an active white member and critic of the union, expressed concern that the union was not realizing its potential. Speaking about the union's charge that "Columbia discriminates," Julian pointedly asked, "*Was it a slogan or was it a campaign?*" He went on to argue that countering racism could not just be done in union demands. "The contract, alone, is not going to do it."

Carmella regretted the union's lost opportunity of hooking the struggle up with black and Latino organizations. She searched for ways of broadening the scope of struggle, bringing more support and more public attention to the campaign. "A lot of black organizations...would be interested in what's going on here."[15]

What these members, some active, some not, underscored about the 1991 campaign is that for issues of racism to come alive, for members to be mobilized around them, the union had to actively organize a mass campaign that was widely and clearly understood to be about racism. This is another important clue of what would be necessary to more fully shape this union as a vehicle of racial justice in people's consciousness.

The Challenge and Success of Solidarity: White Responses to Union Efforts at Countering Discrimination

Given the risks of fracture associated with identity politics, it is critical to know how white members experienced the union's race-based contract demands. Not surprisingly, white members expressed a range of responses to the contract efforts challenging racial injustice. Jean, a white leader with a history of 1960s activism, spoke with deep pride about being part of a union that has always been committed to fighting for racial justice. Lawrence expressed his disappointment that the union had not been more aggressive, explicit, and broad in its challenge of racism and sexism: "We're a group of black women mostly, and we're not getting any respect. We just haven't gotten on top of that one." He and several others felt they needed more information about how racism worked at Columbia. Hank, a young white member who in the last months became supportive despite himself, said, "When you're a white, a white man, you're not gonna see it. It could be surrounding me. I'm somewhat shielded from it. At least I leave open the possibility it exists. . . . It hasn't been confirmed with proof. I know stats can be interpreted in different ways. . . . I'd like to see more information."

Cindy, a young white worker new to the union, sometimes felt isolated and defensive.

> Sometimes [tackling discrimination] was a little hard. Because I would feel, when comparisons were made, let's say, between what the average white person's salary was in comparison to what the average minority person's salary, I almost felt there were two unions. Like I was the privileged part of the union. . . . I mean, that felt just a little bit alienating sometimes.

Meghan raised a similar discomfort. "Do these people think I am making three times as much as they are?"[16] She wondered whether she should show her pay stub to clarify it. For Cindy, in the end, the union's attention to race had a "positive" effect on her. "It made me more concerned, I guess, about racial issues, and race relations. . . . [It] made me want to do something about that feeling of separation." She went on to call for more union discussion and education around the issue of racism, to enable her to know more and deal better with the issue. Cindy was new to such racial discussion—to the realities of race segmentation in this workplace, and to her own "whiteness," which is often left out of discussion on race, inevitably reproducing the white "norm," and people of color as "others."[17]

Although Cindy's reactions were positive overall, the difficulties that she discussed were voiced in a very small number of other interviews, but more negatively. These were *never* articulated in any union meeting that I attended or heard of. Yet the seedlings of race, class, and gender resentment could be found when I went looking for them. Eileen expressed concern about low-ranking workers making disproportionate gains and called for those at the bottom to use their own resources to move up.

> The people at the bottom have always profited most. . . . In the meeting, someone asked why don't we get an across-the-board increase? Julie says, it's unfair, if we get a percentage increase, you white workers at the top, it's unfair you get more. TWU, 1199, they get a straight across-the-board [increase] . . . I think we are developing divisions. . . . Donna is black, a grade 8, she earns $5,000 more than me. Why could Donna do it? If you don't strive, you don't get anywhere. No one keeps you in a grade 3.

Frank, a white clerical at the top of the grade scale, said that the money was the only thing that affected him.

> I am not really affected by much else in the contract. I think that was probably one of the problems I had with it. I felt that this contract didn't really speak to people in my sort of strata, whatever you want to call it, at the university. I really felt that turned me off at the end. . . . And then the people I was out there for weren't coming, or were very apathetic. So that started to bother me. I became very annoyed with the union, I felt they weren't really speaking to me. I guess to put it bluntly, they were speaking to black single mothers, is who they were speaking to. Or minority single mothers. . . . People in my office . . . they are not the single-parent type.

Frank's discussion uses the same category "single-parent type" that several African American women suggested is a stereotype through which management evaluates them and their work.[18]

These were the only resentments I heard in all the interviews with a range of union members. It is interesting, however, to note that there were several white folks who, despite the difficulties that the lengthy campaign posed for some of them, initially responded with a desire to fight as a matter of principle, a matter of justice. This is what propelled some white folks and people of color, who themselves were not getting great gains from the contract, to participate. Allison, a young single white member who was putting herself through graduate school, found only limited gains for herself in the contract. Yet she believed that it was important to fight for other people, "the person with four kids" and few options.[19] Even though Calvin knew he would not be at Columbia long, he "wanted to fight really hard" for the people who would be and the "people coming after him." Although it could be argued that more explicit discussions and education about workplace racism would have been "like opening Pandora's box," there is also evidence here to suggest that for some workers of all races, such explicitness could have created more support for dealing with these issues and may have helped with the mobilization and sustained solidarity.

We'll explore these risks and benefits of different identity practices in chapter 8, after considering the way this movement incorporated oppositional gender politics into the campaign.

Gender Talk/Gender Silence

Gender, too, had political meaning to participants in this campaign. Very rarely did members spontaneously mention "women," "sex," "black women," or "Hispanic women" as categories, yet gender was significant in members' thoughts. For example, members frequently argued that being a majority female union meant being taken less seriously and being severely tested by management in the negotiations. Janet, an active white member in her thirties, summed it up by saying that the university looks "at us like we're a joke." Maxine, an African American union steward, concurred:

> I think they see [the union] as a bunch of women. They don't have to [listen to us] as much as they would if we were men who would go out and break some windows, or no telling what kind of things they will do to get what they want. And they think we are softer. That we will just stand by and let it happen.

Beyond not being taken seriously, some suggested that gender was the source of extra trial or abuse by management. Doris, a black activist in her forties, said, "I've never seen a struggle like what they put us through. . . . You don't see them put the TWU through all this."

For some, the vulnerability that gender had meant in the struggle was decidedly race and class specific. Calvin, a black activist in his twenties, agreed that the university had singled this union out. "They are banking on it being primarily minority, people of color, primarily female, as this union won't fight back.... I just feel like it's a vendetta on their part." "Weak," said Carmella, a Latina in her twenties. With so many single mothers in the union, Carmella conjectured that the university thought of the union as vulnerable. They think "we can't stay out long.... There's two others [single moms] besides me on my floor. The university knows there's lots of single mothers. I'm only a paycheck away from being homeless." Outside of the interviews, this was the primary way that the femaleness of the union appeared in members' talk during union meetings. As Carmella captured, the "needs of single parents"—a gender, class, and somewhat racialized concept—was a frequently used category in negotiation and strike strategy debates, pointing to the difficulty of a long strike and the inability to go without pay.

Although the vulnerability of single parents greatly predominated, the needs of single parents were also prominent in the struggles for increased health benefits. Thus the vulnerability had also become a basis of a struggle around which many members committed themselves to the mobilization. While not always articulated, for many members the battle over health care was particularly a battle for members' children. Nina, one of the union leaders, described the campaign as "a campaign for women's health." In the interviews, negotiating committee members also pointed proudly to earlier specific union-won gains around child care, personal work, and sexual harassment protection, all of which disproportionately affected women. Martin, an African American union leader, pointed out that District 65 was the first union on the Heights to get child care. "It was a $40,000 fund for each year for three years. So that definitely is a women's issue, a family issue, or whatever. Child care affects the female population, especially single mothers." Janet pointed to the union's demand in this contract for sick leave and for "sick pay.... A woman's the one, whether she's single or married, she's the one that will end up having to stay home." "Women have different concerns," said Jennifer, a new activist, "child care, health care, I guess those issues are more important to a union with a large number of women."

The strong women's leadership of the local was the other recurrent gendered meaning of the union campaign. This included not only the paid leaders but also the many women members of the negotiating and strike committees. "The most powerful people in this union are women," said Allison, a young white union member. "It's hard to miss.... The most powerful people in this union are women, it's evident... there's some pretty mighty women out there.... It's inspirational." Danielle, a young black member who did not honor this strike, but who had participated in the 1985 strike as a work-study student, was also "very impressed with the women in terms of their strength."

Janet said, "Sitting there at the [negotiating] table listening to Maida and Julie has give me a great admiration . . . I'm just in awe of them . . . to see that capacity." She also added, "It's not just Julie and Maida, though, there are a lot of women on the negotiating committee that are very much their own person, and I admire them for that. It's nice to see there are so many strong women that are also really decent people. It shows that strength in a woman does not mean that she becomes less of a woman." Many women made such statements. Many had been truly inspired by the women's leadership and found that it had encouraged their own activism, tying them to the campaign.

For a small minority of interviewees, however, this strong women's leadership was a negative. "If they'd have men leaders, we could have gotten this whole thing over with a long time ago," said Rosa, an older Latina. Calvin also recounted a female coworker telling him that "if they had a male at the top, maybe there would be more involvement from the members." Doris's point of view was much more representative of the sentiment I heard in the interviews:

> I have a lot of respect for these women [the two top white women leaders of the local]. . . . They definitely go across the lines of color. They're really strong, really progressive. The types of issues they've fought for have always been issues of principle. They're stars. They're really special. . . . Some of the most special women in the country fighting for women in the workplace. They have a special place.

To Jean, a white union leader, the realities of sexism in the workplace and the larger society constituted an imperative for organizing. "Of course we need a union. Of course we need representation. Women need to be organized and women need to be together. That's all there is to it. And we are 80 percent women at Columbia."[20] Franny agreed that women were "under siege," but she described the difficulties that stemmed from the fact that "the image of the union is still for a lot of working women not anything they can identify with." For Ilene, one of the enduring pleasures of the early organizing and the 1985 strike was feeling that "these women had the guts to say, 'We won't take this.'"

Yet these responses of seeing the union as a vehicle of gender justice and change were a decided minority—even including those who identified themselves as feminist sympathizers. This, as we will hear, is in part a comment on the taken-for-granted nature of sexism in the labor market, and for some a reflection of attitudes toward feminism. The union's identity practices—particularly framing and use of outside resources—were also important in muting gender identity.

Many activists defined the campaign and their own participation in keeping with the tradition of black women's activism for family and community uplift. An additional factor, which I came to see later in the conversation about gender, was the manner in which I had posed the question, asking about gender meaning and gender justice separately from race meanings and justice.[21] As it was, many participants spoke from an intersectional space, placing gender identity in the context of, and far secondary to, race identity. To the degree that workers perceived this campaign as a struggle for more than "union" justice, race preempted gender.

This question of consciousness—how women workers, and especially clerical workers, draw on and develop class, gender, and race consciousness in the course of their resistance efforts—has been considered by a number of scholars and in the context of many different labor campaigns. Many of these studies consider the interaction of gender and class consciousness in mobilization, such as Blum's study of two comparable worth campaigns in California, Costello's study of women insurance workers in Wisconsin, and Goldberg's study of clerical workers in Baltimore.[22] The Columbia campaign differs significantly from these other studies in that the participants were a majority of women and men of color.[23] Across race, members saw race as more politically significant than gender, although both to a limited extent. Given the demands and the union's framing of those demands, given the history of black women's activism defining "political identities" largely "around issues of race" (Dill 1987, 205), and given the salience of race to many white workers, it is not surprising that across race, if most participants considered their union struggle to be about any other kind of justice, it was about race, not gender or gender and race. The fight for women's workplace rights, the fight against sexism, had little meaning in how the majority of participants defined this movement. At Columbia, despite the sentiments of outside commentators and some union leaders and members, I found mostly silence around gender injustice.

This is not to argue that the battle against sexism is or should be made primary. In fighting class issues in a female-dominated occupation, in fighting for a revaluation of clerical work, this union was combating sexism. There are also a multitude of practices by which antisexist politics may become significant. However, because sexism was a significant structuring factor in this situation, it is helpful to understand how union members did—and didn't—define the fight against sexism in their movement.

The Invisibility of Institutional Sexism

Gender, as we have heard, was meaningful to the participants in terms of women's leadership, vulnerability in the struggle, and demands of particular interest to working women. It's always significant to note what's absent. People who spoke at length, rapid-fire, and movingly about class injustice, racism, and capitalism paused when considering the impact of the female-ness of the union and said, "I really don't know." Only three members (one of whom was steeped in job reclassification efforts) ever mentioned the fact that this union was a group of clerical workers, and that most clerical workers are women—a significant reason why they are so poorly paid. Or differently stated, almost no one mentioned the lack of comparable worth between the clerical union and the mostly male maintenance union. Nor did any member interviewed mention the gender factor in the lack of health care parity: the mostly male maintenance unit had a number of free HMOs, but the mostly female clerical unit had none. Although one of the union leaders, Nina, described this campaign as a "fight for women's health," no worker so described it.

The invisibility of institutional sexism is one important reason for these silences. As with racism, sexism in the workplace is often understood as existing primarily on the interpersonal level. The increase in the number of women managers ("officers" in Columbia lingo) over recent years since unionization had made sexism less obvious. Ted spoke of the changing pattern of institutional sexism at the university. When the union began, "It was mostly female workers, and mostly male officers.... The university's gone far in integrating low-level managers over the last six years.... Today, the distinctions are less apparent. There's generally been a leveling effect. More women are doing officer jobs."

As we heard earlier in the chapter, for Lily, the subtleties of institutional racism at Columbia were a priority. She elaborated the intricate mechanisms she had seen at work, less directed at herself as an Asian woman than at black and Hispanic coworkers. But sexism was less tangible. "Sexism is a tough one, because both my bosses are female. I can't say that I have ever experienced sexism. It might be, certainly not with management. It might be with coworkers, like 'come in the corner' remarks." Given the race segmentation of the labor force, clericals in academic offices were disproportionately white. For the majority workers of color in the less-prestigious nonacademic offices, the lack of respect was pervasive and amply explained by class and race dynamics.

Certainly, this invisibility of institutional sexism was my own experience as a clerical worker and union leader in a major Boston hospital organizing drive. I had chosen to work at the hospital and participate in the organizing campaign explicitly because of the largely multiracial female nature of the workforce. The organizing committee emphasized child care as an important women's issue. We struggled with the overtly racist and sexist attitudes of many white skilled trades workers, who didn't want to be in a union with "those people" (black women and men service workers), and who thought we (mostly white) secretaries "sat around all day reading magazines." As a frantic, overworked clinic secretary, having such comments directed at me made me laugh and made me angry. Nor did the interpersonal sexism and classism between the parade of male cardiologists and myself fail to annoy me. Yet in the sea of so many women workers, the institutional sexism of clerical and health care industries was hard to see. It was just the way things were.

The union's own practices contributed to this invisibility. Recall that in one academic department, union members had pulled comparable worth statistics from the official union pamphlet and made a leaflet of their own (an unusual event), which highlighted gender pay discrimination. The union leadership never picked up on this initiative. Nor did the union offer any analysis of Vice President Mullinix's attack on comparable worth. In this he defended the pay gap between maintenance workers and clericals as being due to the former's "highly specialized skills" that "command a higher salary in the marketplace."[24] Mullinix also pointed out that women in the clerical unit made higher average wages than did men. It was only the Graduate Student Support Committee and Women's Faculty Caucus that addressed this in writing, and the latter in a letter to their own membership.[25] Classification discussions were not framed by the union in gender (or race) terms. Nor were discussions of the health care gap, even though, as graduate student supporters pointed out, "Health benefits and salary minimums are issues of discrimination by gender against the entire bargaining unit."[26] Unlike the frequent media discussions of comparable worth during the 1985 campaign, this time, there were few. During the 1985 campaign, the *Columbia Spectator* had an extensive article entitled "The Pink Collar Ghetto," which explained comparable worth, citing the Yale and Washington State cases. It analyzed the lack of comparable worth at Columbia.[27] Six years later, an analysis of comparable worth was no longer a hot issue. The news, like the union, was not offering any in-depth explanation of the policy.

The Union as a Vehicle for Gender Change?

After asking members about the meanings of the union's composition, I asked them about the union as a means of bringing change. Ilene, an active white member in her fifties, agreed that the union had made inroads into improving "women's condition." Doris, a leading black activist, agreed, "Yeah, we're women . . . it would be befitting. There are men in our union who recognize it." "I think we fight for the things that the women need the most," added Earline, a black member who supported the strike but was never active. "I think 65 does a great job. The union is the only thing we women have going for us. It's about time we get a change. I believe in equal rights, I believe in being liberated to a certain extent."

As Earline's comments illustrate, talking about "bringing a change for working women" often cascaded into a discussion about "the women's movement," "women's libbers," and "feminism." It seemed important to use a follow-up question about whether members saw connections between their union campaign and larger women's movement(s). Sometimes I relayed that reporters writing about the clerical unions at Harvard and Yale talked about them as "feminist," and I asked what members thought about that for their union at Columbia. Of the union women and men who I interviewed, about a third considered their union effort at Columbia to be connected to, or a part of, (the) women's movement(s). They were glad, proud of it. Luke, an African American union leader in his thirties, believed that District 65 was at "the forefront of women's rights," and that there was a "close connection between women's rights and District 65."

That these responses were a decided minority is hardly a news flash. What's considered to be the women's movement is not a widely honored American collectivity. Feminism is, for many women today, not a revered mantle in which they want to cloak themselves.[28] High-profile discussions of feminism's faltering future occurred in the winter of 1991 to 1992, in response to Susan Faludi's *Backlash,* just as this campaign took place, and were referred to by several members.[29] A century and a half of classist and racist practices by white feminist organizations made this an irrelevant, if not a spoiled, collectivity and identity for many women of color and white working-class women. What was most stunning in the 1991–1992 campaign, though, was the large number of women union members—across race—who *did* self-identify as feminists or supporters of the women's movement but did not see the union as a vehicle for gender change.

The majority of interviewees rejected "women," "sexism," and "gender" as the right category. There were many reasons. As we've heard, institutional sexism was largely taken for granted, never made a focus of the struggle. One reason for the low salience of gender for members in this campaign was that the union simply rarely made the connection in a public way. Interview comments exactly paralleled my analysis of the union's framing practices. "It's never been presented in that light." "I've never heard it put that way." "I've never heard or thought about it in that framework before," said many of the women interviewed, including self-declared feminists. Cindy noted, "During this contract issues of race were made much more prominent than issues of gender, I thought."

Another important reason I later came to understand had to do with the way I'd posed the question, asking about gender separately from other identities. Given the lack of gender framing and greater (though still limited) race framing by the union, given the legacy of injury by single-identity feminism, and given the ways black women have historically constructed their activism, members' negative responses to my questions about "change for working women" were likely. Some members—across gender and race—did speak proudly and passionately about gender justice and women's organizing. But many told me I had asked the wrong question.

Several expressed a sense that their union was not limited *solely* to dealing with women, but dealt with *all* people. These were "human issues."[30] "It's a union that deals with the protection of people, not just the protection of women," Janet told me. "The needs that are being addressed are for everybody." Others said they did not see the union campaign as a "women's issue," but more "like a survival issue." A young white single mother, Laura, said:

> If you don't have enough money to pay your rent, you could now be part of the homeless. A lot of people in Columbia aren't that far from being homeless. . . . Sometimes I really hate them [women libbers]. It's like excuse me, but before you people put your noses in here, people could survive on one paycheck. Or maybe a husband made more. Sometimes I wouldn't mind being able to stay home like the mommies did in the fifties and sixties . . . sometimes I think women's lib did that, you know. It was better pay. [pause] But I know in actuality it's just that the economy has gone to shit.

At Columbia in the initial organizing, the workforce was more predominantly young, white female. One union activist explained, "The profile, even though it has consistently been female because clerical workers are female, it has changed. It is not the white college student who happened to get their first job out of college here. It is people who plan to stay here and who have so many problems... there's a lot more at stake.... There are a lot of families involved, as opposed to just single white women [in the earlier organizing]."

Aiesha, an African American activist, said she did not look at the contract struggle from a "woman's point of view." Rather, she thought of the campaign in terms of community and family uplift. She noted the importance of the 25 percent of the union's members who were male.[31] Men were cherished coworkers active at every level of the union organization.

> I look at it from an overall point of view, because we had a lot of males, as well. I think it was more a family issue for me. It wasn't so much that I was trying to do for myself, as it was what I was trying to do for my family. And to help other people achieve for their families. So that was the way I looked at it. I think it's only fair for us to fight for the things that we want because it seems like the rich are getting richer. Everyone's catering to the rich, they're not catering to us, the ones out here breaking our necks, getting broken fingernails.... Who is it that's gone to the Gulf War?

Both Laura and Aiesha rejected terming the union's struggle a "women's" issue, but both clearly spoke of class injustice from their positions as white and African American working-class women: (mostly white) "mommies being able to stay home" and "helping people achieve for their families."

As Cheryl Gilkes points out, black women are particularly aware of the "consequences of racism not only in their own lives as Black women but in the lives of their husbands and other male relatives, of their friends and of their children" (1998, 53–54). The individualism that has characterized much of (the white) feminist movement, Dill notes, runs counter to the understanding of many black women that their progress needs to be as part of an entire community advancement (1987, 205).

Clearly, in some ways, I had asked the wrong question. In the case of Laura and Aeisha, querying them about a single aspect of their identity, in this case gender, evoked a rejection of that single category and brought on an eloquent articulation of their intersectional identities. My mistakenly asking about separate identity categories (race and gender) yielded an interesting and predictable pattern, given the pattern of race and gender in American society. It was usually gender, not race, that tended to get rejected.

I asked Allison, who considered herself a supporter of feminism, what she thought about the union's largely female membership. "If I were a black female or a Hispanic female, then I'd have something to say," she responded, "but where I'm a minority in this union, I can't really say." That the majority of women working as clericals at Columbia are of color is one factor that makes it tricky for this young white feminist to claim this campaign's gendered identity.[32] The race, class, and parental status differences among Columbia women workers mean a much greater diversity of "women's experience" is brought to the workplace. Allison didn't see herself as sharing a gender identity with the women of color; she saw herself as being racially separate. As we will see in the next chapter, the contrast to Harvard and Yale was striking.

A young white male union activist responded similarly in defining the contract battle as an issue of race, not gender. Frank had earlier in the interview criticized the union's fight for child care funding (which was actually never given much focus) and its emphasis on "minority single mothers." He felt that the union acted only for advancing their interests. Yet he said, "This was not a sex thing. It's a black and white, or a minority and white, thing, but not a man/woman thing. . . . I never felt they [top white women union leadership] were speaking to women as a minority, but just minorities as a condition of race as opposed to a condition of sex."

The dominant either/or conceptions of gender and race in our culture were also significant in members' meanings. For many white union members, the union was a very unusual experience of participating in a predominantly black and Latina/o organization. Race was a highly visible part of the daily life in this workplace. As the title *All the Women Are White, All the Blacks Are Men, But Some of Us Are Brave* adeptly captures, popular, academic, and often social movement discourses construct gender and race as two mutually exclusive categories (Hull et al. 1982). In such a world, the salience of race obliterates gender.

While there were black and Latina/o men and women among those who spoke proudly about the antisexism as well as antiracism components of their struggle, there were many women of color for whom race greatly overshadowed gender in the union struggle. In response to my question about the impact of the large number of women in the union, Rosa responded, "No, I don't see it. They [the union leadership] push it more for minorities. I think the race issue is bigger. I think it's more a color issue." As we have seen, the union's framing practices did not much claim the fight against sexism; gender framing mostly occurred in high-visibility events. This predominance of race over gender was in part, as Rosa suggests, the product of the union's practices, which gave greater meaning to antiracism than to antisexism as part of the movement's identity.

Whereas many workers spoke with extensive qualifications about the racial justice elements of this campaign, the category of race identity experienced a major surge in market share when in the interviews I asked about the significance of gender. Lily, a young Asian union activist who spoke at length about institutional racism and identified herself as interested in the women's movement, at least its beginning goals, was taken aback by my question about whether she saw the union as a vehicle for advocating for women in the workforce. "*The union?*" she asked in a loud, incredulous voice. "No!" It was the "race factor" that dominated in the union, Lily argued. The "real dichotomy working here," she said, is "between black and white."

The priority of the fight against conditions of racism is something that many women themselves brought to the campaign, in part as a continuation of black women's history of activism. Over the past year, Lana had come to see herself as what Cheryl Gilkes refers to as a "community worker" (1980, 1988). Lana took great pride in her own development during this year's struggle as a person who helped others selflessly. In just the way Lana described her friend's contribution to the black community in his work in various organizations, for her the union was a way to contribute to change in the black community as a black woman. She saw herself in the tradition of "race women" and "race men" who have long taken on such tasks.

Working-class women's activism, as we've earlier reviewed, has a long history, often located in workplace, union, community, health, education, housing, local toxic, and antiracism struggles, and is alive and well. So too is the activism of women of color—poor, working class, and professional class—in a plethora of sites in communities, schools, churches, workplaces, and academia, in addition to what are explicitly "feminist" or "womanist" organizations. Many of these efforts are identified by their participants as class and/or race movements. A few are self-identified around gender or gender/race.

As Dill and others have argued, "Sisterhood is not new to black women. It has been institutionalized in churches . . . also a basis for organization in the club movements that began in the late 1800s . . . it is clearly exemplified in black extended family groupings that frequently place great importance on female kinship ties" (Dill 1987, 205). Black women's organizations, she points out, have long been "decidedly feminist" in their "values" and "concerns," yet "focused upon issues which resulted from the racial oppression affecting *all* black people" (206). Dill goes on to say that "while black women have fostered and encouraged sisterhood, we have not used it as the anvil to forge our political identities.... The political identities of Afro-American women have largely been formed around issues of race" (205).

The Clarence Thomas/Anita Hill hearings occurring in the middle of the campaign were a powerful illustration of the either/or nature of race and gender in popular culture. These high-profile hearings were noticeably little discussed in union events.[33] The painful enactment for all the nation to see of the "calamitous uses to which the Right can turn the opposition between 'blacks' and 'women'" certainly offered no good advertisement for the possibility of simultaneous gender and race justice politics in a struggle like that of Columbia (Stansell 1992, 266). Particularly in the context of the union's scant discussion of the issue of comparable worth, which would have highlighted the role of labor market sexism (and racism), it was quite likely that race and class would have predominated over gender identity.

Many black feminist writers have argued that in addition to feminism's frequent racist practices, black freedom movements, particularly black nationalism, have often advocated race primacy analyses in which gender politics are defined not only as secondary but as abandonment and betrayal,[34] as was frequently the case in discussions of the Hill/Thomas hearings. Cornel West terms this a black "closing-ranks" mentality, which includes "black male subordination of black women in the interests of the black community in a hostile white-racist country.... Closing of ranks is usually done at the expense of black women" (1992a, 392–95). This "ideology of put-down" (Stansell 1992, 255) of black women has been amplified by white conservatism, often citing the Moynihan report of 1965 that advocated diminishing the "pathology" of black women's "unnatural" wage-earning role within the family.

In the end, though, it is activists who decide the relevance of their identities to their activism. Deborah King emphasizes this point, "As Black women, we decide for ourselves the relative salience of any and all identities and oppressions, and how and the extent to which those features inform our politics" (1990, 295).

What's Feminism Got to Do with It?

Because activists' comments about change for "working women" so often slid into discussions of "feminism" or "women's liberation," it seemed important to understand their thoughts in greater depth. As we have already seen, whether individuals identify themselves as feminists is a different, although decidedly related, question than whether they considered their movement campaign to be connected to feminism.[35]

More importantly, the question of labeling their movement "feminist" is only one element of a larger question of the ways in which gender (along with race and class) become politically meaningful in any campaign (Bookman and Morgen 1988). Feminist scholars have examined the question of how gender and race and class are drawn on in the fomenting of resistance struggles and reshaped as a product of these struggles. Activist scholars Anne Bookman and Sandra Morgen note that in different struggles of working-class women, "a distinctive political consciousness emerges in which gender becomes politically meaningful, but this does not always happen in the same way."[36] Within this enlarged context—the distinctive ways gender along with race and class had and had not "become politically significant" to the participants—I found that members' comments cascaded into discussions of feminism often enough that I began to ask how the diverse female and male clerical workers at Columbia thought about the connection between feminism and their union.

When I asked members about the connections others had drawn between clerical unions at Harvard and Yale and feminism, not surprisingly many had a negative response—but for quite different reasons: there were those who found such a label insulting or diminishing and rejected it. Interestingly, there were those who admired a feminist identity and wished that the union had made it more a part of their experience in the Columbia clerical struggle. And there were those, including feminists, who had never considered such a definition of their struggle and were attracted to the idea.

Several members took such a labeling as slanderous. Mavis, an African American member, was quite offended.

> To me, that's sexism on the outside, because what you're saying is because they want to stand up for their rights, they have to be "feminist," they have to be "sexist" [antimale], because they don't want to be trampled on, they don't want to be quiet, timid, submissive person. . . . That we've got to be an idea, a category, a stereotype, because we want to stand up for our rights.

While less passionate, Janet, a white activist, had a similar response. She considered it "an obscure kind of word" and pointed out that "people use it in many different ways." She too considered feminism a negative labeling of the movement. "In a way, that takes away from it. It's a union that deals with the protection of people, not just the protection of women." Andrea, an African American activist, concurred: "I think we're out there for *all.* . . . We're just out for equal treatment, for justice. It's our right. If something is wrong, what are we supposed to do, just sit there and let them walk in our face? Aren't we supposed to say something? I think we're supposed to be heard." Although Andrea didn't "have a problem with feminism" itself, she clearly felt such a defining of the movement was diminishing and a negative characterization.

Lana, who had newly defined herself as a "community woman" (Gilkes 1988), found such a connection to be problematic on the basis of the union's black and Hispanic composition, the priority of racial solidarity, and the whiteness of feminism.

> Black women have always had to work by her man. Okay? So, being black, that's kind of a difficult question for me [pause] [sigh]. It's like yes and no. Yes, more in the sense of being a working woman, okay? But less in the sense concerning relationships. . . . And I think most of us, well I don't know about now, but I think most black women, especially when the movement first began, it was definitely centered around white women. There's Alice Walker and Toni Morrison, but still, it's a difficult answer.

Another group were those who across race and gender considered themselves "feminist" or admired feminists but didn't find the union's practices up to what they considered feminism to be. Some focused on what they felt was the failure of the union's organizational structure and culture to conform to what they saw as defining feminism. In her insightful typology of what makes for a "feminist organization," sociologist Patricia Yancey Martin notes that "few feminist organizations reflect a pure or ideal type," which for many has been particularly defined as having a collectivist internal structure.[37] Julian, a white critic of the contract campaign, believed that to be more feminist, the union would have had to emphasize "the form of action." He explained, "That would involve changing the form of organization into a more decentralized, democratic organization. This is a one-party union."

Gloria, who is critical of unions in a university setting, worked at her job on the strike days. She was active in a black feminist organization outside of work. She described what she believed would be different in the union culture if women's politics were more a part of this campaign: "They would care for each other better. They would disseminate information in a more caring way. . . people kind of resent this top-down attitude sometimes that comes from union organizers." They would be "more sisterly" in their approach, which is "I've got to bring you to me, rather than let's come together somewhere in here. . . . It's consensus."

Louise, a young white administrative assistant who began more actively supporting the strike and credited the union with winning her benefits, became disenchanted with the union's oppositional tactics:

> There were other ways [the organizing] could be done rather than creating more hostility. . . less confrontational and understanding where people are coming from. . . . I think the suggestions I made are typical of female responses. I admit that is one of the reasons . . . I don't feel as comfortable with confrontation as some men do.

Those with issues about the conflict inherent in strikes resonated with what some Harvard activists called "women's ways of organizing" (Oppenheim 1991). As I will discuss more in the next chapter, this features caretaking, democracy, and consensus. As Lisa, a Harvard clerical union leader, puts it:

> We're not interested in having a nasty relationship. . . . We don't want to fight. We will if we have to, but we're much more interested in getting consensus. . . . It's a softer approach. It's not as if we don't have an iron fist in a velvet glove. . . . We could just bring this place to a grinding halt. We run this place.[38]

Columbia's stance toward the union didn't offer much hope of a more cooperative, less conflictual approach by the union. It is also important to know that Gloria and Louise were also fervent advocates of individual mobility through educational credentials, which led them to an ambivalent stance to unions, at best. One union leader, upon reading Gloria's and Louise's comments in an earlier draft of this book, argued, "They're just hiding their antiunion sentiments in other, more acceptable language." They may be. Where their critique of unionism ends and their concern about feminist organizational style begins is hard to sort out.

"I Would Be Interested in That": Mobilizing Potential

Although many members found my questions about women, gender justice, and the connection to women's activism confused (on my part) and confusing (for them), there was a cluster of black and white women who were visibly intrigued and drawn to the idea. Some, although not all, of these women already considered themselves feminists.

Maxine, a black woman in her forties, was a leader within her church and community, and increasingly in the union. For her, union activism was a question of "helping people out" and of working for community uplift. But the genuine pleasure and affirmation she got from the idea of linking women's organizing with union organizing was striking.

> I have never thought of it as connected to the feminist movement. But because we are all women, it doesn't hurt... because we are strong, we are women, and we are fit to be reckoned with. That is a good thing. Thanks, I like that... I feel that women, they have been a long time in the background. But I think that women now, they are everything... they have come a long way, baby. We are still growing. I think women still have a long way to go in some areas, but I think that we have come a long way... I think women are more united now....
>
> Now I think we have our own identity. We don't need a man to take care of us. Of course that is someone's wish to be able to let their man take care of them, but to also be able to decide she doesn't want to, for her to stand up on her own. And that is the kind of women we have now... I think that for myself, *yes,* I am part of the movement. Because I have become that new woman. I *am* that new woman.

Gloria and Danielle were both African American women whose voices we've previously heard and who did not honor the strike—"scabs" to their coworkers. In the interviews, each of them expressed substantial interest in feminism and regret that women's politics had not been an aspect of the campaign. Said Gloria, who was active in a black feminist organization, "I don't see that here. I don't see that consciousness here. I really don't. If I did then I might be more attracted to it." Danielle showed similar interest: "It's definitely an interesting thought... I would be interested in that. I'm teased by my brother as being feminist. So I don't think of it negatively, I'm supportive of it idealistically." Gender framing would not automatically erase these women's negative feelings about unions, but it would create a connection—a collective identity that might have the ability to vie with their antiunion ideology in tying them to the union.

Recall the two young white women—Allison, an activist, and Cindy, a supportive member—we heard earlier speak about not feeling a part of the community (or communities) of women of color in the union. Each of them identified herself as feminist but saw that as having no relevance to the campaign. Cindy, the less involved of the two, spoke at length about the challenges the race politics had posed for her. She told me, "I consider myself feminist, but not activist... yes, I think feminist issues are really important." When I asked her about what she saw for herself now that the strike was over, she said, "This was my first experience, but I might, you know... get involved in a more feminist kind of organization... to explore issues we had to deal with, issues of race, issues of gender and labor... I'm looking for something like that." While she hoped the union would do more educational work on labor and race issues, and while she "hoped to find" an organization to meet her needs, she never saw the union as a possibility for her desire to participate in women's organizing.

Although they were a decided minority in the union, for these women, more explicit use of women's or antisexist identities might have encouraged them to feel more connected and led to further activism in the campaign. Their talk suggests an untapped source of mobilization potential for some part of the workforce. For social movements, identity can be "a powerful incentive to help compel participation" (Friedman and McAdam 1992, 170).

Summary

In 1995, in a *Detroit News* article on the future of the UAW, Maida Rosenstein, president of UAW Local 2110 (which includes the Columbia local), noted, "The UAW is a large union with status and a history of progressive stands on issues like peace, civil rights, and women's rights." Rosenstein was described as saying that what appealed to her colleagues at Columbia University was "winning members in nontraditional areas by emphasizing its social vision and its support for women's and minority rights."[39] The descriptions of Columbia clericals of their experiences of the 1991–1992 campaign suggest that for many members, this was the case. For many, the campaign had been deeply meaningful as a cross-racial meeting ground and as a site of women's leadership; these workers were drawn to the campaign and inspired on this basis. For some Columbia clericals, the campaign had proudly become a vehicle of racial justice, and for very few a vehicle of gender justice.

Yet a range of factors—from the protracted nature of workplace racism and the taken-for-granted nature of sex segregation of clerical work, to the ways gender and race intersected in their workplace, to the history of black women's activism, to the union's own identity practices and workers' own ideologies on race and gender justice—made for obstacles in more fully fulfilling Rosenstein's assessment of the mobilizing potential of creating a vehicle for all kinds of justice. The union had indeed been a trailblazer in integrating gender and race justice into its unionism. Yet the words of Columbia clericals suggest the many and complex layers involved for any union in attempting to fulfill such a vision.

District 65 provides, in some ways, an interesting model of how, using multi-identity practices, an organization can respond flexibly to the many, varied, and fluid identities that members bring. Labor sociologist Roslyn Feldberg argues, "We need unions that respect differences—that do not assume that all women have the same experiences at work, at home, or in the larger community, or that work holds the same place in their lives—while fighting for equality" (1987b, 320). There was a tremendous diversity among Columbia clericals, not only by gender, race, class, age, and parenting status, but also by ideology and areas of personal interest—family, church, school, arts, community activism, et cetera. Different people connected with different identity practices of the campaign. Some saw the union as a means toward a straightforward end, improving working conditions; others were proud to be part of an effort at social justice activism.

The meanings that participants gave to race and gender in their movement were shaped by many factors: the particular race/gender intersection of this workplace, ideology and identities that individuals brought with them into the campaign, the meanings they made of contemporary historical events (such as Crown Heights and the Hill/Thomas hearings), the union's identity practices, the media's and university's practices, and dominant cultural ideas. Understanding how members thought about race and gender in the context of this campaign provides us with many insights about how people's multiple identities can—or cannot—be brought to bear in political organizing. Such strategic decisions, as Dill, Gilkes, King, and others have reminded us, are the business of movement participants. Identity matters are often unconscious, largely determined by leaders' actions, and not often the object of collective discussion.

Overall, participants' thoughts suggest that the task of shaping a labor movement as a vehicle of race and gender as well as class change is a many-layered process extending well beyond formulating specific antiracist, antisexist demands. As much as this union held out for "bringing up the bottom" to close "the race wage gap," or at least prevent it from widening, there was still a taboo about discussing workplace racism. Many workers of color were qualified in describing the union as a vehicle for race change. And this was generally not seen as any reflection on the union. Fighting institutional and personal racism in the workplace was often seen as just futile... and dangerous. Institutional labor market sexism of this decidedly female occupation—the lack of comparable worth—was largely invisible, naturalized as a nonchangeable reality. As the data here suggest, however, and as Rosenstein has argued, these justice issues not only are morally right but also have significant organizing potential, which any campaign would do well to explicitly consider.

How have these politics contributed to other mobilizations? How have clerical unions developed antisexist as well as antiracist politics? In chapter 7, we will take a field trip to view alternative race and gender practices by two other similar (but not identical) important clerical union struggles. Then, in chapter 8, with all three of these cases in mind, I will pick up the question of the mobilizing potential and risk of identity politics.

7

Other Stories, Other Possibilities: Yale and Harvard Clerical Unions

We've developed a model of how to organize.... It comes out of the experience of working women. This is not taking anything away from men. In fact, the labor movement was built by men mostly for male workers, and its traditions, its way of doing things, and its structures all come out of masculine culture. The model worked extremely well while unions were winning by organizing mostly men, working full time, supporting families. Now the workforce has changed; how and where people work has changed. So the task is different. I think if the labor movement would listen to what women organizers are saying we could be more successful in the years ahead.

—Kris Rondeau

I'm a man that stood by Martin Luther King. In my arms Martin Luther King died on the Lorraine Motel balcony in Memphis, Tennessee.... Take it from one who's been to jail forty-four times and beaten until I thought I was dead. Nothing comes to oppressed people without suffering. Privileged classes do not give up their rights without a struggle.... Yale is a great institution. Yale is a wealthy institution. But Yale is treating certain segments of its population unjustly and Yale University ought to be ashamed.... You have the opportunity to witness for justice and equality...for a grand and noble cause.

—Rev. Ralph Abernathy

The much-celebrated clerical and technical union victories at Yale and Harvard universities offer us other important models of multi-identity labor campaigns. As part of fighting for respect, equity, and democracy at work, these clerical and technical unions employed gender- and race-based identity practices that were significant in their remarkable, hard-won victories. Each employed a different collection of identity practices. What possibilities can these movements offer us about integrating gender, race, and class in labor campaigns?

It's important to begin by recognizing that these campaigns faced conditions that were significantly different from those faced by the Columbia clericals. The demographics at Yale and Harvard were similar to Columbia in terms of gender (majority women), but quite different in terms of race. Whereas in 1991 Columbia was multiracial with a majority of workers of color, Yale and Harvard were both overwhelmingly white. It is also important to note that in both the Yale and Harvard cases, I am only considering first-contract campaigns. As was true at Columbia, first campaigns more often take on the mantle of a moral mission, of which identity politics may be a significant part. The Yale campaign occurred in an earlier period when comparable worth was more prominent in the national discourse (to which Yale then gave a tremendous boost).

Methodologically, my knowledge of these cases is quite different. My discussion of Yale is based largely on secondary sources, with a few supplemental interviews.[1] At Harvard, although my research of the union's early organizing is at a much more exploratory level than the Columbia case, it is also based on a round of six interviews, union presentations at labor forums, as well as the secondary sources. In neither case have I been present as the events unfolded, nor do I have the same level of individual participant reflection.

Yet despite the differences among the cases, these brief field trips are helpful for considering some of the alternative ways in which race and gender have been made politically significant in other university clerical labor movements. It is not my goal to rank these practices; the conditions of struggle were simply not interchangeable, and the actions of one union not directly transferable to another. Rather, it is to see some of the range of identity practices by which other university clerical movements have created multi-identity politics. This, these remarkable cases do allow us to see.

Yale: Local 34 on Strike

The ten-week strike of Yale clerical and technical workers in 1984 brought the issues of comparable worth and clerical worker unionization into the national spotlight. A four-year organizing effort was financed by Local 35,

Yale's blue-collar union, after several unsuccessful organizing attempts by other unions in the 1960s and 1970s (see Gilpin et al. 1988, 18–21). Long realizing that their own survival at Yale depended on unionizing other campus workers, Local 35 of the Federation of University Employees brought great leadership, organizing, and financial support to the clerical effort. This included substantial funding from its international, the Hotel Employees and Restaurant Employees International Union. For the first year, the UAW ran a competing drive until its final withdrawal.

It was a formidable task, organizing 2,600 workers in 250 buildings. To accomplish this, the union ran a "'positive' campaign, stressing the advantages of union organization rather than the disadvantages of working at Yale." Activists wanted workers to see "the union as a vehicle through which the C&Ts could gain respect and recognition for their work, as opposed to simply a mechanism for obtaining higher wages or better benefits" (Gilpin et al. 1988, 25). They placed great emphasis on building the organizing committee. They consciously decided against using written literature, built a committee, and "simply 'talk[ed] union'" (23). "If we were going to beat the University, we had to have a gigantic organizing committee," said chief organizer John Wilhelm (22). They did with an organizing committee of 450 people, a steering committee of 150, and a rank-and-file staff of 55 (25). Overcoming the university's tough antiunion effort, the campaign culminated in an election victory of Local 34 on May 18, 1983, two weeks following the Columbia clerical election. By thirty-nine votes, Yale's 2,600 clericals and technicals—82 percent female and 14 percent black—had obtained union recognition.

Winning a first contract, as Columbia experienced, was another mountain to climb. For more than a year, the university waged a ferocious antiunion campaign. The union ferociously battled back, finally striking on September 26, 1984. The remarkable ten-week strike completely upended normal academic and campus life. "Approximately 1,700 workers—nearly two-thirds of the University's secretaries, telephone operators, library workers, computer programmers, research assistants, laboratory technicians, and hospital aides—stayed out.... These [picket] lines were honored by roughly 95 percent of Yale's maintenance and service workers" (50). Students, faculty, and administrators reeled with the effects on classes, dorms, dining halls, libraries—virtually all areas of campus—and were divided by their positions on the union and the strike.

The unionists persevered with creativity and extraordinary blue-collar/white-collar solidarity, and they rounded up financial, moral, and political support, especially from students, community, labor, women's and civil rights movements. In mid-November, the union's call for a three-day moratorium ratcheted up the costs of the strike on the already beleaguered community.

Tremendous controversy erupted over the strategy of returning "home for the holidays." With the upcoming holiday shutdown looming, some union leaders argued for "taking the strike inside"—returning to work until the January 19 expiration date of Local 35's contract. If there was no resolution, then both unions would return to strike at that time. Was this defeat or smart strategy? "For days . . . twenty hours in a row, it was fight after fight," said one activist. "It was an amazing experience. It was democracy in action," said another (84–85). It worked. With continued organizing, by late January, both Local 34 and then Local 35 each emerged victorious with their contracts.

Several threads stand out in the remarkable tapestry woven by Yale clerical workers during their struggle: strong democratic process and structure, innovative tactics and a willingness to heretically challenge sacred trade union scripts, militancy, direct action, experienced staff, and a high level of financial and other support resources. In addition to the exemplary and critical solidarity of the blue-collar workers who honored the clerical strike for the entire ten weeks, the strike achieved difficult "solidarity between students and employees, female and male, black and white."[2] Perhaps most interesting, for the purposes of this study, was Local 34's ability to prioritize race and gender issues during their campaign. While the Yale clerical workers' "union" collective identity was rooted in their demand for "respect," it was very much textured by the multi-injustice politics they wove into their identity practices. Let's take a closer look at how race and gender emerged in the 1985 clerical workers' strike at Yale.

Identity Practices in the Yale Campaign

Demands

The first contract campaign, according to Yale activist Pat Carter, "was about gaining respect." And the union understood Yale's lack of respect as being in part rooted in racism and sexism. "We didn't get respect," said Carter, "because [the administration] discriminated against women and blacks. Blacks were in the low labor grades and white men were in the upper grades."[3] The salary scale was completely lacking in comparable worth: an average salary of $13,424 for clerical workers compared poorly to an average salary of $18,500 for truck drivers at Yale (Amott and Matthaei 1984, 21). The clerical and technical workers' salaries also compared poorly to the $16,402 *low* standard of living for a family of four in New England set by the U.S. Bureau of Labor Statistics in 1981 (Gilpin et al. 1988, 15). Other critical gender demands in the campaign included respect and benefits "that would address the family needs of women employees" (Ladd-Taylor 1985, 476). Race also affected salaries.

> According to economics professor Raymond Fair, when age, time at Yale, time in labor grade, and education were held constant, women workers earned $694 less than men, and blacks earned $1,061 less than whites. Even within the clerical and technical group, blacks and women worked in the lowest paying jobs. While the average salary of white male C&Ts was $14,324, white women earned only $13,408. (468)

Black men, a very small minority of Yale C&Ts, had less seniority than the other groups but, at $12,813, averaged a higher salary than black women, who averaged $12,603 and overall had *more* seniority than any other group (488 n. 5, 468). The twin strands of workplace racism and sexism, then, drove wages down for blacks and women at Yale. Interestingly, according to Molly Ladd-Taylor, a participant-observer in Local 34's strike, the union backed away from a "comparable worth" characterization of their struggle, fearing that "professionals conducting job evaluation studies behind closed doors" would "reproduce society's notions of worth and therefore not eliminate the discrimination experienced by the poorest among them" (477). It was outsiders, including the media, who so named their demands. In questioning such notions of worth, Local 34 was protecting black women and men—Yale's lowest-paid clerical workers.

Along with raising salaries overall, the union called for a system of step increases in salaries and for "slotting," which retroactively placed employees at their appropriate step as determined by seniority. "The slotting would help undo past discrimination against women and long-time workers; the steps would help prevent the discrimination from recurring" (Gilpin et al. 1988, 35–36).

When in January 1985 the union succeeded in winning its contract, the gains were substantial. Wage increases, averaging 35 percent over three years, pay steps, elimination of the bottom grade, and other salary changes brought significant gains for C&Ts and "increased the wages of some of the poorest workers by 80 to 90 percent" (Ladd-Taylor 1985, 485). Additionally, the union won numerous benefit improvements regarding interrupted years of service, flex-time, and medical, dental, and pension benefits. "By making pay equity a major theme of its campaign, Local 34 demonstrated that unions can make 'women's issues' fighting principles—and win" (Gilpin et al. 1988, 92–93).

Framing and Ideology

According to Toni Gilpin and her coauthors in *On Strike for Respect: The Yale Strike of 1984–85,* "Local 34's campaign became a moral struggle"— which was not just about winning pay raises but about gaining recognition, respect, and self-representation (92). Working in conjunction with community leaders, members of the clergy, and elected officials, Local 34 persuaded much of the New Haven community to join in their struggle for justice. The Greater New Haven Clergy Association helped solidify the union's moral framing when they drafted a "bold statement that portrayed the university administration as Goliath, using the full force of its economic power against two little 'David' unions" (Cole 1998, 23). Those demands for respect and representation were clearly in part about issues of gender and race. Demonstrating at a meeting of the Yale corporation, civil rights leader Bayard Rustin, who had four months earlier been awarded an honorary degree by Yale, announced, "I am here . . . because I have a moral obligation. I stand by the workers and against injustices to minorities and women" (Gilpin et al. 1988, 66).

The union, along with its other themes, also forthrightly framed its struggle as an effort to end "economic discrimination against women and minorities" (Ladd-Taylor 1985, 477). An International Women's Day rally of four thousand, a one-day strike termed "59-Cent Day," a silent three-hour protest "in the tradition of Gandhi and Martin Luther King, Jr.," and a nonviolent mass arrest of 434 workers, students, New Haven residents, and faculty all "connected" the struggle for economic equality to the civil rights movement and women's movements (482–83).

In particular, the union had a strong gender focus, as evidenced in the statement of purpose in the union's bylaws: "to advance the interests of workers generally and working women in particular" (487). Giving a gender frame to the invisible and uncompensated labor she performed, one clerical worker, Deborah Chernoff, described the university as forcing her into the role of "office-wife" or "office-mother" (Gilpin et al. 1988, 46). Another clerical worker described the gendered nature of her unfair treatment in the office. "So many times, female administrative assistants run entire departments, and yet you have got this peacock of a chairman strutting around as if *he* has done all of this, as if *he* is responsible for all of this" (46).

Culture

The cross-union and community support helped to create an empowering, upbeat culture that drew together many traditions, labor, minority, and women's.

> One could scarcely walk through campus without hearing snatches of singing from various picket lines along the way. Old labor standards such as *Union Maids, We're Gonna Roll,* and *Ain't Gonna Let Nobody Turn Me Around,* reminded strikers of their place in historical tradition. In addition to these, new twists cropped up constantly... such as *Do Negotiations* (to the tune of *Locomotion*) ... *What's Yale Got To Do With It? (What's Love Got To Do With It?) Giamatti, Look and See (Mr. Postman).* (63)

One member of the negotiating committee noticed some kids break-dancing to the tune of "Beep Beep, Yale's Cheap!" and clericals on the picket line enjoyed constant honking of car horns as local drivers "beeped" their support (Cupo et al. 1984, 9). Beverly Lett, a member of Local 34's negotiating committee, noted that support from the community and families (such as a demonstration put on by the strikers' children) "changed our family lives as well as our work lives; women standing up at the workplace are also standing up at home" (9). The participation of African American clergy helped create a culture that linked the clerical workers' struggle with civil rights movement battles against injustice.

Organizational Structure and Process

From the beginning of its organizing campaign, Local 34 relied on a strong grassroots organization-building style. Turning away from literature, leaflets, and issues organizing, they emphasized relationship and organization building, as well as democratic self-representation. This was adopted by Harvard organizers, who found it critical to their own success. Their first leaflet, "Standing Together," a statement supporting unionization signed by 450 workers, powerfully reflected this sense of self-organization.

The structure of the union was designed to ensure that every group of workers was represented in the leadership. With an organizing committee made up of more than "400 leaders drawn from most departments" and a union staff consisting of "over fifty rank and file as well as paid organizers," the union structured democratic decision making into its process and "ensure[d] that communication flowed up as well as down the organization (Ladd-Taylor 1985, 469).

Recognizing that people of color were a decided minority, the union worked to give a stronger voice to minority issues. They encouraged "black leaders to come forward [and] black C&T's organized a black caucus within the union. Minority students, faculty, and community members also participated in the black caucus. Especially during the strike, the visibility of its black members strengthened everybody's commitment to Local 34's anti-discrimination program" (478). The black caucus ensured that the needs of people of color would be met. Steve Fortes, an African American activist, noted, "The more blacks are involved, the more they could raise their specific issues." The intent was that there would also be a safe place for all members to speak up. "Sometimes minority people felt more comfortable dealing with other minorities," said Fortes in an interview.

Leadership

Local 35's John Wilhelm headed Local 34's organizing and later its negotiating. As an integral part of its democratic structure, the C&T union worked to develop women and people of color as union leaders. In the course of the campaign,

> we were encouraged step by painful step to overcome the fear and the inhibitions that held us back. That was the key to our victory. It was what led us from resistance to defiance. We had to overcome the fear of taking on the mighty institution which is Yale, and we had to learn that we could bring about meaningful change in our working lives by acting together. We learned those lessons every day. (Cole 1998, 24)

The leadership, which included only one African American, Steve Fortes, worked hard to recruit other people of color. "We just targeted people that looked like they had the potential to be leaders," said Fortes of the union's aggressive efforts to bring more people of color into the leadership.

Outside Resources

Support from a range of groups, organizations, and communities was critical throughout this struggle. Gender- and race-based organizations were quite significant. Faculty and student support was disproportionately strong among women. "Campus and community women, carrying banners that read, 'In supporting Local 34, we support ourselves,' held a 'bread and roses' vigil" (Ladd-Taylor 1985, 477–78). A community-labor rally of four thousand celebrated International Women's Day in March 1984. As one Yale senior made the connection,

Women at all levels of the University structure are chronically underpaid, overworked, and not given the recognition they deserve. I challenge the women students at Yale to ask themselves . . . where do you think you will be when you graduate: can you guarantee you won't be picketing for the same rights? (Gilpin et al. 1988, 58)

Expressing a similar sentiment, two Asian students wrote in a letter to the campus newspaper, "The closed and defensive stance which the Corporation, et al., have taken towards Local 34's grievances matches the administration's unwillingness to act on minority students' needs. . . . Whether on the student or employee level, we are striving for the same dignity and equality" (58).

During the strike, other unions, feminist leaders, and organizations offered important support. "Frequent expressions of . . . feminist sentiments by Local 34 members appealed to campus women's organizations which, in turn, provided the union with consistent support" (46). The union reached out for support from off-campus women's groups (Eleanor Smeal, personal communication, 27 October 1999). Judy Goldsmith and Eleanor Smeal of NOW, and representatives of groups such as Black Women for Wages for Housework, spoke at support events.

Similarly, civil rights organizations and leaders such as Bayard Rustin (having just received an honorary degree from Yale) and Ralph Abernathy came to Yale to add to the effort. Reverend Ralph Abernathy reminded the clericals, "You have the opportunity to witness for justice and equality . . . for a grand and noble cause." At that point, remembered one rank-and-file organizer, "it really felt like this was something that was truly history" (67).

According to Ladd-Taylor, "New Haven's minority community, especially the black clergy, also supported Local 34's fight against discrimination" (1985, 478). "We reached out to them," said Steve Fortes. "We asked union members if they were active in their churches, and if we could meet with their clergy." In his 1999 interview, Fortes said that they stressed that they wanted to build long-term, reciprocal relationships with community members, not just absorb the available resources and then move on.

Notable unionists such as Cesar Chavez and AFL-CIO president Lane Kirkland made the trip to Yale to show their support. Columbia's District 65 was among the many unions who came to walk the picket lines and who offered moral and financial support.

Practices of Outside Agents: The Media

Local 34 "remained continually attuned to the importance of press coverage" and received wide-ranging coverage from all three national television networks, many major newspapers and journals, and even spots on the *Phil Donahue Show* and the *MacNeil-Lehrer NewsHour*. The strike, according to Gilpin and her coauthors, created an image of Yale as a "crippled," deserted institution, as opposed to the put-together and enlightened site of higher education and moral leadership that the Corporation so cultivated and depended on. The university's cause was hurt by the media's depiction of the campus without clerical and technical workers. Members and sympathizers "led reporters on tours of the campus, steering them to scenes of disruption caused by the strike" (Gilpin et al. 1988, 7–12).

It was the media that brought the demand for comparable worth.

> The union never explicitly demanded "comparable worth" pay. That phrase was created by the media, which simplified Local 34's more complex demands for respect and the recognition of women workers' contribution to the university into the popular term "comparable worth." (Ladd-Taylor 1985, 477)

Organizing Harvard

Like Columbia and Yale, the 1988 election victory of Harvard's 3,500 clerical and technical workers did not come easily. The members were 83 percent female and 11 percent people of color[4] and worked in approximately four hundred sites. Two earlier District 65 organizing campaigns in the Harvard medical area in 1978 and 1981 ended in close defeat (46 percent and 47 percent respectively) (Monks 1988, 5). The third attempt, under UAW control, aimed to unionize the entire university, as the labor board had ruled in the university's favor. In the summer of 1985, a year into this third attempt, Harvard organizers and the UAW irreconcilably split, mostly over issues of local autonomy and organizing strategy. The UAW continued to actively run an oppositional organizing drive for the next two years.[5] The Harvard Union of Clerical and Technical Workers (HUCTW) organizing campaign functioned as an independent union without outside financial or institutional backing for more than a year and a half, with the staff working on a voluntary basis. In January 1987, HUCTW affiliated with the American Federation of State, County, and Municipal Employees (AFSCME Local 3650) under an arrangement that ensured substantial autonomy for the Harvard committee.

Their organizing represents another, and in some ways quite different, configuration of gender, race, and class identity politics. HUCTW organized principally around themes of "speaking for ourselves" and "democracy and respect." Gender framings were muted and comprised a decidedly secondary but supportive theme. Bypassing any direct connection to feminism, HUCTW developed and articulated a "women's way of organizing." Race politics were perhaps best expressed in general workplace justice themes that especially resonated for people of color and attracted the attention of black civil rights leaders. Especially given their conflict with the UAW, Harvard unionists tended to distance themselves from the larger labor movement, in part viewing it as the antithesis to their female model of organizing. This contributed to their "democratic participation" frame, to their emphasis on their uniqueness as an organization (level 1 identity), and to their mobilization.

Building on what had worked at Yale as well as their own organizing lessons, HUCTW emphasized democratic participation and building relationships and community. "We Believe in Ourselves" meant the emphasis was not really on Harvard but on workers' own need for having a voice in the workplace.[6] They emphasized one-on-one relationship building, and a committee where people "respected and took care of each other" and each other's issues. And they had fun. Their musical group, the Pipets, often entertained the membership with spoofs like "Unions Are a Girl's Best Friend," "You Can't Hurry Love," and "Fifty-nine Cents to Every Man's Dollar." They shunned negative campaigning. "We had to show we weren't angry militant people that just hated everyone," said one organizer. "Our organizing wasn't about Harvard, it was about us, and our right to speak for ourselves."[7] "It's not anti-Harvard to be pro-union," their posters and bumper stickers proclaimed.

They also avoided issue organizing. Tactically, any issue to which they pinned the campaign, they knew, Harvard could resolve and take from them. Rather, the point was to explain the need for self-representation. They did identify areas of concern, many of which were "women's issues." As at Yale, the fact that union staff were former Harvard employees undermined the administration's "union as outside agitator" frame and underscored the union's "democratic self-determination" message. It was a smart, successful strategy. Despite Harvard's relentless legal opposition and union-busting efforts waged by President Bok (ironically, a labor scholar earlier in his career), the union was victorious in a May 1988 election.[8]

Finally, after losing its postelection legal challenges in October 1988, the university settled into building a working relationship with the clerical and technical union. Bok's choice of John Dunlop, his earlier labor co-author, to head the administration's effort helped to facilitate this process. A set of transition meetings were set up to provide each side with critical background information and "to measure intentions and trustworthiness.

The university disclosed employment data and ... Harvard's complicated system of financial governance. The union, meanwhile, sought to fill in a gap in management's knowledge of the workforce" by using "what Harvard psychologist Robert Coles calls 'the moral power of story-telling'" (Hoerr 1997, 226). "Nearly 100 mostly female clerical and technical workers told 'stories' about their work lives to managers who had never before listened to them as equals." They hoped this "set a model for the new kind of participation and sharing of experience that they hoped would characterize the labor-management relationship" (Eaton 1996, 301).

The contract negotiations grew out of the union's emphasis on democratic participation. To maximize participation, they were conducted at eight separate tables, each focusing on specific issues such as wages, health care, family leave, and others. From this, HUCTW evolved a very unusual, innovative structure. They jettisoned the grievance procedures of the traditional labor/management contract. In its place, they developed an extensive alternative structure of joint labor/management councils, as well as joint labor/management problem-solving teams in areas throughout the university. The latter resolved "grievances" and were overseen by a university-wide labor-management problem-solving team ("the gang of four"). Arbitration was available as ultimate backup but had not been used in the first year and a half that it was in place. This structure gave the union a way to continue bargaining between contracts. They began mostly with small issues, consciously setting a gradualist strategy that would allow the joint councils to develop a track record and some trust before tackling more contentious issues.[9]

The structure put Harvard at the center of the raging debate in the labor movement about joint formations. Was this a tremendous advance in democratic workplace participation by Harvard workers and their union, or was it class collaborationism that blurred the line between union and management interests and undercut the union? HUCTW agreed this was a model dependent on a strong union with a strong identity. They argued that they fit this description, and that this was a case of "cooperation through strength." HUCTW initiated the structure and put great resources into training, organizing, and consolidating the union members of these joint bodies, so that worker/union interests would not get lost. Also, their pride in the "exceptionalism" of their structure seemed to strengthen their organization-specific union identity. This counteracted the erosion of union identity that often comes with joint structures. HUCTW saw worker participation in decision making as a central goal of their union, and such efforts as fundamentally "challenging the invisibility and devaluation of clerical work" (Eaton 1996, 292). Susan Eaton argues that these illustrate "the strengths and limits of participation as a strategy for worker empowerment and increased productivity."[10]

Identity Practices in the 1988 Harvard Election Campaign

Demands

Like sister unions at Columbia and Yale, HUCTW confronted the range of deficits that clericals experienced in pay and benefits and sought to introduce dignity and democracy on the job. Although they didn't believe in issue organizing, the child care needs of younger workers and the pension poverty confronting older workers were priorities in the organizing. Overall, their contract brought home the bacon—or, in Harvard Square terms of the time, the quiche—with great improvements in wages and benefits. "Total salary increases average[d] over 29% for three years," including across-the-board increases, merit increases, and onetime "slotting increases" for long-term workers.[11] Step increases were created, and onetime longevity bonuses were given. The pension minimum more than doubled. Work/family benefits were enhanced, including the creation of a child care scholarship fund, a thirteen-week leave for mothers (with birth mothers paid for eight weeks via the short-term disability plan), and a one-week paid leave for fathers and adoptive parents.[12]

One of HUCTW's key efforts was to demand recognition for the myriad invisible aspects of clerical work. In meetings with management, HUCTW encouraged its members to name and describe the work they did. This was a step toward addressing the ways that the division of labor is often gendered and racialized, frequently leaving the contributions of women and/or people of color invisible and undervalued. Increased clericals' participation in decision making made their contribution to the institution and their expertise more visible and valued and gave power to workers who previously had no organizational channel for being heard (Eaton 1996).

Framing and Ideology

In this sound track of self-representation and democracy at work, gender was a minor theme, and race even more so. HUCTW activists articulated a range of opinions about the ways gender and race had played out in their organizing. Kristine Rondeau, leader of the organizing and first contract campaign, staked out an explicit gender frame in the *Harvard Crimson* by saying, "The issue of child care must be seen as part of a package of women's issues which includes: parental leave, pay equity, career advancement, job flexibility and child care."[13] The union's "Dignity, Democracy, and Day Care" banner definitely signaled gender identity politics at a Labor Day child care demonstration of two hundred adults and children, many in strollers, at Harvard Square's Holyoke Center. The union was also successful in obtaining media coverage of the pension plight of older women (Shanahan 1988).

Most often in my interviews, most staff and leaders preferred to avoid gender-specific framing. My questions about the importance of gender to the mobilization were met with discomfort and distancing by union staff and leaders. I asked, "Would you say that your campaign used gender as part of the base of mobilization?" Organizers answered, "We used people's lives as the base of mobilization." Yet given that 83 percent of these people were women, they point out, there's no way that gender-based issues wouldn't emerge. They were not shy, they say, to talk about their femaleness as part of why they faced the working conditions they did. As we've seen, several of the Pipets' songs used gendered themes. One of the union's few pieces of literature from the campaign highlights gender, but in a backdoor way: "A worker is a worker regardless of her sex."[14] One HUCTW staffer said,

> "Women's empowerment" has a left jargon quality. "Women," it's a little abstract. We prefer to talk about people having confidence to speak up for themselves.... It not just about or for women... It's about respect. It's not really gender specific, men get treated like shit, too. This is about people who found a voice, who gained confidence.[15]

Rosie, one of the early organizers, explained, "We didn't want it to be seen as a women's group, we wanted men to feel welcome.... But it was never *not* seen as a women's thing. The leadership was women."[16]

HUCTW mostly avoided a feminist framing of its struggle, although members strongly identified as women. "I don't know," organizers were fond of saying, "whether or not this model of organizing is feminist, but it is feminine." Many of them avoided the "feminist" language, given the negative stereotypes. This was also part of the union's more general avoidance of anything construed as rhetorical, ideological, or explicitly political. Some of them shunned such a label: "We shudder when we hear 'feminist' used to describe our union," said one staffer.[17] But others were more willing to acknowledge the connection. "I don't understand the people that don't want to be called a feminist," said Lisa. "To me it's a compliment."[18] "One of the weaknesses of the mainstream women's movement," said one staffer, "was the empowerment of working class women."[19] Clearly, HUCTW's "women's way of organizing" was about exactly that.

Yet while they used such an approach, they often preferred not to give it a gendered label. For the most part, they preferred to draw strength from the gendered aspects of the culture they created, but avoided a gendered framing. "I don't consciously think about it [women's aspects of our union]," said Lauren, an active member, "yet it's very much bred into how we conduct our affairs, how we do our relationship building."[20]

Organizational Structure and Process

Central to its approach, HUCTW developed a women's organizing culture that many members referred to as having a "womanly" quality. HUCTW organizers found their organizing experience resonated with Carol Gilligan's now classic work *In Another Voice,* which considers a female model of moral reasoning based in connection and relationship.[21] They emphasized value organizing: "treating each other with kindness and respect" (Balzer 1993, 5). They also prioritized relationship building, and a taking-care-of-each-other style of organizing.

Emphasizing a style of communication that invited participation, Kris Rondeau said the union relied on "telling stories—real life stories. . . . Management talks in abstractions. Storytelling is the language of workers" (3). Like Yale, one way that HUCTW structured open communication into their process was to avoid using printed materials. This, said Rondeau, is "a million times better for individual leadership development. Literature gets in the way of building strong relationships, stunts growth and perception, and prevents activists from developing skills" (Heggestad 1987, 49). Like both Columbia and Yale, Harvard workers relied on small-group meetings to facilitate participation and frequently scheduled them during lunchtime to mesh with members' home, school, and other life responsibilities.

This "feminine" style extended to dealing with management, as well. Lisa explained:

> I think of a masculine way of getting along with management in the traditional masculine union is totally confrontational . . . overtly adversarial. The only time you talk with management is when there's a grievance or every three years when you negotiate a new contract. They're just put right out there as the enemy, the big bad guy trying to screw you out of another buck. We've never looked at this management like that . . . we don't see them as this big meanie you've got to face off with and topple.[22]

Critics of the universalized notions of "women's ways" in Gilligan's work will find that replicated in HUCTW's "women's way of organizing" (see Stack 1997). Unlike Columbia, the Harvard union was not centrally challenged to negotiate the different cultures emerging from substantial racial diversity. It is fair to assume that the women's culture of organizing was to some extent reflective of, and facilitated by, the whiteness of the great majority of HUCTW's members. Storytelling, for example, can be inclusive, but it can also be influenced by the dominant culture of the group. "I had finally found someone speaking the same language," says Gladys McKenzie, principal organizer at the University of Minnesota, which organized with HUCTW's leaders and ideas. Her story of an older woman who gained a feeling of empowerment in the union might well not resonate with the experience of many working-class African American clericals at Columbia: "As I was growing up my father took care of me, when I got married my husband took care of me. When I went to work I had a boss to take care of me. But when I signed my union card I did it for myself" (Oppenheim 1991, 53).

Leaders did emphasize that "treating each other with kindness and respect" included watching out and fighting for someone else's issues, even if different than one's own. This, they said, is what defines solidarity.[23] Workers listened, supported one another, and built unity across the lines of class, race, age, and sexuality that differentiate their membership. "The union," said Rondeau, "has to be a place where everyone's story matters" (Oppenheim 1991, 53).

Although most of the literature sees HUCTW's shared language as a feminine language, it is important to acknowledge the degree to which the shared ethnicity—whiteness—of most of these women may have facilitated and shaped that common language and culture.

Leadership

HUCTW gave conscious attention to nurturing new leadership. "We work with each person in a very personal way," said one organizer. Rondeau pointed out that the union had adult education, training, and confidence building at its core (Oppenheim 1991). Rosie, another organizer, noted of the early leadership, "The leadership group which was very large always had a disproportionate percentage of men. Usually we had 30–40% of men in the leadership group, so we had to be very careful and make sure we were always pushing women forward to take a role."[24]

Lisa explained her experience of becoming a leader:

> The union staff...are very sophisticated about this leadership development. They do this thing they call "shaping your experiences." So they kind of put you in situations where you're set up to succeed to some degree or another, and then they're like "Wow, you did that really well, really really well." They do a lot of positive reinforcement, and then they say

"You were great at this. Want to think about being on this committee?" ...
They flatter you into doing one thing after the next until you realize "gee,
I'm doing stuff I never thought I would do a year ago, and it's almost an
insensible process ... people are sitting down and, you know, really being
quite tough with top management. So that's how they do it.[25]

One story brought this emphasis on leadership development home to
me in a striking way. "We worked to never give anyone a step too big for
them," said Rosie. To help people take a next step at a big rally, the union
set up two nights of practice, including practice using the microphone before the rally. "Three people would go up to introduce one person. They'd
just say their name, and for many that was a big step."[26] From my experience in the labor movement, this level of care, consciousness, detail of planning, and investing resources into leadership development is quite unusual.[27]
It was a big contrast to District 65, which also considered the development
of new leaders a high priority but did not have a systematic method for doing this in the 1991 campaign—largely leaving developing activists to feel
their way on their own. It was also the product of significant resource differences between these unions.

HUCTW's success in urging women to take on some sort of public
role, including public speaking, offers an interesting contrast to Karen Sacks's
experience with the mostly black female support staff in their effort to
unionize at Duke University Medical Center. Sacks notes that the women
responded with anger when they were coaxed into taking "leadership" that
felt uncomfortable to them. At Duke, black women exercised powerful leadership as "centerwomen," activating social groupings and bringing about
workplace change in ways that are invisible if one only takes into account
conventional definitions of leadership (1988b, 79). HUCTW encountered
similar discomfort with the notion of leadership, which it dealt with by using the term "activist" for those uncomfortable with "leader" (Susan Eaton,
conversation with Cynthia Peters, November 2000). HUCTW's approach,
which valued the role of centerwomen *and* nurtured more formal leadership skills, provides a useful model of leadership development that values
the many faces of leadership in any social movement.

Outside Resources

HUCTW drew widespread and varied support for its campaign: labor, faculty, students, alumni, elected officials, community groups, noted individuals like Pete Seeger and Jesse Jackson—"almost anyone who had any public standing."[28] Some outsiders were overtly supportive; others called for

Harvard's "neutrality" to allow clerical and technical workers to decide freely about unionization. Women's organizations and leaders were one minor element of a very broad, dense collection of endorsements. HUCTW obtained a letter from Coretta Scott King that noted that "Martin Luther King, Jr. gave his life in a labor struggle for decent wages and working conditions and dignity on the job."[29] Her letter acknowledged her husband's belief in the importance of trade unions for *all* workers, particularly black workers, and underscored AFSCME's record of dedication to civil rights.

HUCTW was instrumental in bringing together the other campus unions and won support from the state AFL-CIO. The drive was eagerly supported by local labor activists who keenly understood the potential impact of a HUCTW victory (Monks 1988, 5). Yet in the early years, many labor activists would describe HUCTW's relationship with labor as distant, stemming in large measure from HUCTW's treatment by the UAW. This distancing was seen by some organizers as key in winning the support of clericals who needed to know that their union was "'not like the Teamsters with Jimmy Hoffa . . . threatening and scary.' Their initial reaction to unionization [was] based on conventional media images of male-dominated, corrupt, powerful, and distant organizations" (Eaton 1996, 301).

This disassociation was also centered in HUCTW's gendered critique of trade unionism and reinforced their organization-specific collective identity. Members' fierce loyalty to, and identification with, their specific union was based in part on a kind of exceptionalism—that is, in contrast to the rest of the labor movement. It was HUCTW that had a vibrant, exciting, innovative approach in contrast to those "men with cigars" who keep "banging on tables" (phrases that emerged repeatedly in the interviews) to protect the interests of their workers. In contrast, many other women-dominated unions, including Columbia and Yale clericals, and women's labor education programs, who also see their mission as changing the labor movement, very much identify themselves as *part* of the labor movement.[30] After the first contract, a significant part of HUCTW's connection with the labor movement was focused in the field of new organizing at other institutions.[31]

Practices of Other Agents: The Media

While primarily conveying the union's frame of participation and democracy at work, the media also tended to make note of the gender features of the campaign. The union's "Democracy, Dignity, and Day Care" Labor Day demonstration resulted in a flurry of articles about child care. "Unions Are the Key to Raising Pay for Women Office-Workers," headlined one later

Globe column.[32] A *Los Angeles Times* article opened by quoting the union's song "Union's Are a Woman's Best Friend."[33] Another column on pension issues spoke of a "Mother's Loyalty."[34] And the *Los Angeles Times* put the finishing touches on the gender picture by offering up Kris Rondeau's height and weight in comparison to her "slightly larger" adversary, Harvard's antiunion campaign director, Ann Taylor.[35] Avidly avoiding the use of union literature during the election campaign, HUCTW often reproduced press articles for distribution. This practice seemed to allow them to play it both ways: to get the message across for those who might like it, but not to have responsibility for it.

Discussion

For some members, the effect of this collection of identity practices was to make gender a significant element in how they discussed and felt committed to their union. It was also an element in how these members defined their own growth. Lisa describes:

> I was used to being a passive, female worker that just had my decisions sort of made for me, and so far they seemed to be ok . . . I've just learned that if you have a problem, you don't just have to live with it for the rest of your life because you're a woman, or because you're a certain rank in Harvard. . . . I guess it's made me feel empowered to use a word that's overused, that there's nothing I just have to take. . . . I feel now like I'm designing my own life. Like I'm the architect of my life. Before Harvard was sort of the architect.[36]

Compare Lisa's testimony to that of Suzanne (at the end of chapter 1), who at the conclusion of the Columbia campaign spoke about how profoundly her participation had transformed her life, her sense of herself. Like Suzanne, Lisa developed a new and powerful sense of herself, her capacities, her ability to change her life and the world. Lisa defined gender as one element of the power hierarchies that had previously robbed her of this sense. In contrast to Columbia's 1992 campaign, where in the interviews no new activist spontaneously included gender or race politics as a significant part of her self-transforming experience of union activism, Lisa's thinking seemed likely to be connected, at least in part, to the high salience of gender in defining this collectivity.

Mobilizing Clericals and Constructing Collective Identity

Journalist John Hoerr's words at the conclusion of his book on the Harvard organizing resonate with all three campaigns. "Ordinary women," he wrote, "could do extraordinary things. They could create something meaningful for themselves by organizing around their own values. If they stuck together, with stamina and persistence they could prevail" (1997, 265).

Each of these pioneering clerical campaigns was enhanced by multi-identity politics. Each created both union and gender/race justice politics in its campaign. The Columbia, Yale, and Harvard cases teach us that there are a variety of methods unions can use to do this. Certainly there are decided continuities in the strategies and practices used and levels of identity created by these three unions. All three of them primarily developed strong local union identities. All three used demands to fight sexism and racism in the workplace, developed significant women's leadership, and shaped organizational structures to meet the realities of working women's lives. Yet in part owing to significantly different conditions, they have integrated oppositional gender and race politics into unionism in strikingly different ways.

Sociologist William Gamson, we may recall, spoke about identity being created on three levels: (1) specific organization, (2) social movement, and (3) underlying social location (women, African Americans, clerical workers, etc.). While analytically distinct, in practice the levels are less sharply differentiated, often overlapping one another. All three unions built collective identity primarily to their specific organization: Local 34 (along with Local 35), HUCTW, and Columbia Local District 65.

At Yale, Local 34 additionally used the movement level—connecting their campaign into labor, women's, and civil rights movements. Along with "Yale workers" and "C&Ts," Local 34 wove together (third-level) collective identities of "women" and "black workers." These practices helped them mobilize individual members and bring in much-needed outside resources and support, which proved important during their lengthy, arduous mobilization.

Yale used a full range of identity practices to weave together issues of gender, race, and class justice. It is in its overt framing of gender and race justice, its organizational structure (the development of a black caucus), and its heightened use of external support resources from women's and civil rights movements that Yale's identity practices most differed from those of Harvard and Columbia. "Respect," the strike's main theme, was enhanced by its frequent direct use of gender and race justice frames. Local 34 overtly proclaimed its identity as a working women's movement: in its preamble and its International Women's Day, "59 Cents Day," and other protests. Even though the Yale clericals were more white than the surrounding city, which was one-third black, the struggle did elicit strong support from the black community, in part for addressing the racial discrimination black workers experienced and the low number of black C&Ts at Yale. Local 34 developed a black caucus to enhance black worker and community participation and give higher visibility to issues of race discrimination. The union sought and won a broad range of support from women's movement, civil rights, and black community leaders and organizations, along with other constituents. The remarkable solidarity of Local 35's blue-collar workers in organizing and later throughout the protracted strike were significant in creating not only a "Yale workers" identity but a larger labor movement identity, as well.

Above all, Harvard's practices created pride in, and identity to, their specific organization—HUCTW—as an innovative, "homegrown," "grassroots" kind of union. HUCTW's strategy emphasized culture, organizational structure, and leadership development. Their "women's way of organizing" and "feminine" approach to unionism served as a decidedly secondary framing to "democracy at work," "respect," and "speaking for ourselves." Their gendered culture of "taking care of one another" and treating everyone— even management—with "kindness and respect" fostered members' pride in their specific organization. Unlike Yale, HUCTW was more reticent to make direct connections to the women's movement and often distanced themselves from (much of) the labor movement. Yet the media coverage heightened the gendering of their struggle and their creation of a new kind of unionism. This set of practices allowed the union to draw on gender identity as a source of strength in the mobilization but avoid the backlash associated with the feminist movement and the popular negative views of much of labor. Although race-based politics were not a large part of HUCTW's identity practices, their attention to overall workplace justice provided an affinity with antiracism advocates in other movements such as Coretta Scott King and Jesse Jackson. Altogether, their practices helped to define the high moral ground to outside supporters and strongly tied many members to their movement.

Columbia, too, at a later historical moment and a later stage in its movement's history, developed a vibrant organization-specific identity: District 65. This union identity was clearly racialized and gendered. Many identity practices, especially demands, but also culture, leadership, and organizational structure, created this as a multi-identity campaign. Their practices, to some extent, invoked deeper social location (third-level) identities of "blacks and Hispanics," "minorities," and much more minimally "women," "minority women," and "single moms." On the second level, their use of allies most emphasized a labor movement identity. They little connected themselves to larger racial and gender movement identity.

Identity is constructed by both movement organizations and individual members in interaction. Given the study design, I have much greater depth of knowledge of the individual participant meanings at Columbia than at Yale and Harvard. For Columbia members, to the limited degree the movement had created identities beyond "union," it was primarily around race. The union's persistent efforts around the race wage gap, the majority black and Hispanic membership, and their shaping of the informal union culture were all significant. For many black women workers, union activism was about the work black women have long done for family and community survival and uplift. For many whites, being in a predominantly black and Hispanic setting was still quite new and remarkable. The union had succeeded in maintaining remarkable cross-race solidarity through a hard struggle. For almost all those who identified the union as a vehicle of race and/or gender justice, this enhanced their commitment to the campaign.

Gender identity at the second and third levels was most directly created at Yale and Harvard and seemed to have enhanced the mobilization. If we were studying the initial organizing campaign at Columbia, we would have found more of this as well. In 1991–1992, women's leadership and demands around family issues gendered the campaign for many. Yet constraints associated with maintaining TWU support, and greater attention to race inequities, led the campaign to having more race than gender meaning, although both were muted. At Columbia, there certainly were, across race, women and men for whom the union was a vehicle of gender as well as race justice, and those who had never heard it put that way and liked it. Yet for all the foregoing reasons, they were a minority. In contrast, "Group support and cooperation," wrote labor scholar Richard Hurd of Harvard, "was facilitated, in part, by the workers' common identity as women" (1993, 323). With 14 percent workers of color at Yale and 11 percent at Harvard, as opposed to 63 percent at Columbia, in confronting their conditions of clerical labor, Harvard and Yale unions were able to draw upon a relatively more homogeneous experience to create a "women's" identity for their campaigns.[37] I say relatively because each of these unions also needed to bridge class difference in the experience of gender, as well. The two unions created a women's collective identity differently, with Local 34 overtly connecting its struggle to larger women's movements, and HUCTW avoiding movement connections in favor of a "women's way of organizing." With very different racial composition from Columbia, Yale C&Ts were able to create both strong race and gender collective identities to their campaign, largely through the use of external resources and the caucus structure.

As the race/gender workforce composition is the foremost example, in each case, structural factors and other conditions of struggle were critical in shaping collective identity: what was possible, likely, and successful. Each of these struggles occurred in the context of different histories of struggle, with different antiunion management styles, organizational and economic contexts, and social control strategies. As we'll discuss further in the next chapter, the context of a first contract struggle significantly heightens social justice claims, including those that are gender and race based. Such was the case in Columbia's first contract campaign, as well. Yale's lengthy continuous strike, as opposed to Columbia's "in-and-out," also increased the likelihood of using identity politics to gather outside support and media attention. The remarkable cross-sector, cross-gender solidarity of Yale's blue-collar union, including support for comparable worth, was highly significant in freeing Local 34 from the substantial constraints experienced by Columbia clericals in developing gender-based justice politics.

These three trailblazers offer us powerful evidence of the diverse ways unions can profitably weave race and gender identity politics into their struggles for justice. In shaping its package of identity practices, each movement organization balances potential gains and potential risks of race- and gender-specific identity practices in its particular context. In the highly charged ideological debate between color and gender blindness and multiculturalism, each movement tries to balance the high stakes of unity and diversity. On the one side are clearly recognized risks: backlash and schism, which unions are rightfully anxious to avoid. On the other side, I will argue, there are also risks: undermobilization and lost resources. The trade-offs are difficult, the dilemmas real. In the next chapter, we will explore this difficult balancing act.

8

Adding It Up: The Risks and Benefits of Multi-Identity Politics

Sometimes, I've felt like I'm not striking for myself, I'm striking for these other people. For the person that doesn't have health care, for the person that has four kids, and not enough to support them.

—Allison

Look at who is in this room. Look at who we are: women and minorities. That's why they've given us such a hard time. And that's why we have to see this thing through to the end.

—Calvin

Social movement organizations wanting to move beyond past exclusions ponder how and how much to bring in "other" injustices. What movement practices, activists wonder, will work? What "works" is commonly understood as balancing justice claims, however right, on the one side, with avoiding schism and maintaining the unity necessary for victory, on the other. In these calculations, a more explicit multi-identity approach is usually seen as risky. Because single identity is by far the default practice, and because color and gender blindness has been so dominant an ideology in American political discourse, alternative practices to lowest-common-denominator politics seem very risky, if not wrong. Activists rightfully worry, with plenty of examples to point to, that race- and gender-conscious practices have the potential to produce lots of conflict, potentially incapacitating a movement. Contrary to popular wisdom, these cases suggest something different: evidence of solidarity across difference and inequality. They also provide indications that enhanced mobilization may be another outcome of such politics, as well.

Color/Gender Blind versus Multiculturalism

Ideologically, social movements approach these strategic choices in the context of a highly charged national debate about equality and unity. In the churning social controversies over affirmative action and multicultural education are the same two dueling paradigms present in this issue: color/gender blind versus color/gender conscious. Color blindness emerged as a liberal reform; it was a "formal rejection of ideologies of black inferiority" and the practice of segregation (Crenshaw 1997, 105). Color blindness was intended to create a social world in which blacks and whites could equally compete on an individual basis for social and economic opportunity unfettered by institutional obstacles. For some time this has been the dominant ideology in American popular thought on race.

Color blindness is often associated with a highly optimistic assessment of race(ism) in America. There is a critical gap between the ideal and the enduring although transforming realities of race in America at the millennium's turn.[1] Advocates of a color-blind approach, either by naïveté or conscious ideological effort, have pointed to the civil rights movement's defeat of segregation and the growth of the black middle class and declared racism to be erased in America.

In this perspective, "persons as individuals have rights; social groups and institutions are moved to the rear."[2] Revering people being treated on their own merit as individuals, color-blind advocates argue that any use of race categories to address continuing racism in social policy is exactly the discrimination the civil rights movement set out to abolish. Diversity, within this perspective, tends to mean recognition of different heritage, holidays, and traditions, but much less recognition of power differentials and ongoing injustice.

In contrast, a race/gender conscious perspective[3] argues that race and gender are major systems of injustice that continue to make "a difference in people's lives" and are "significant factor[s] in shaping contemporary U.S. society" (Frankenberg 1993, 157). Supporters of affirmative action, multicultural education, and other race-conscious policies note that there are "acute" gaps between the color-blind ideology and the "dynamics of racial power."[4] "Race is about *everything*—historical, political, personal—and race is about *nothing*—a social construct, an invention that has changed dramatically over time. . . . race has been and continues to be, encoded in all our lives" (Thompson and Tyagi 1996, ix). Ruth Frankenberg critiques color blindness as "color-and-power-evasive," denying "differences of power organized by racial categor[ies]" (1993, 189). Given a much more sober assessment of the pervasiveness and intractability of racism in the United States, a color-conscious approach argues social group location must explicitly be part of social policy development.

These perspectives also differ in what they mean by unity. While color/gender blindness sees unity in the essential sameness of individuals,[5] the race/gender conscious approach locates unity in the collective recognition of difference, and the shared opposition to all kinds of injustice, by which solidarity is created. While a color/gender blind approach works to avert conflict, diversity-conscious organizations see conflict as a predictable part of the mix. Navigating conflict is seen as a learnable skill necessary to the coalition work that is at the heart of multiculturalism.

For movement activists, the debate about unity and difference is similar, but slightly modified. "Common-denominator" politics are the form color/gender blindness often assumes. A common-denominator perspective recognizes one social grouping—a single identity—that everyone is (mis)-understood to experience in common. Beyond that, the consideration of other social groups is seen as violating principles of fairness and democracy. "Color/gender conscious," argued one rank-and-file Columbia leader, "is not right. It's undemocratic." This is not only a matter of principle but a matter of movement strategy as well. Activists rightfully worry about how to maintain the unity a social movement organization needs to fight the battle.

Although I present these as distinct and opposite choices, these are ideal categories. Most real-world social practice exists as a mix of these paradigms. Yet we can consider identity practices to fall along a continuum between single identity (in this case, color/gender blind) on the one end and multi-identity (race/gender conscious) on the other.

What do these clerical cases have to teach us about the costs and benefits of these different approaches to "diversity"? These could potentially include level of mobilization, level of unity or internal conflict, contract gains won, injustices addressed, development of new leaders, recruitment of new members, increased level of member activism, increased organizational capacity, or development of new allies. Thus whereas some outcomes are immediate, others are long term, which impact the movement organization's ability to fight further campaigns. The design of this study does not produce hard data on outcomes that control for other variables. Yet the clerical cases do suggest potential risks and benefits of multi-injustice identity practices.

Contrary to popular movement wisdom that more explicit identity packages carry the risk of schism, each of the cases we've explored so far provides strong evidence of solidarity across diversity. Further, these cases suggest that potential consequences also include the degree to which unions can mobilize their membership and galvanize external support. Thus as social movement organizations make their calculations about where to locate themselves between common-denominator and multi-identity politics, they must not only weigh the potential for schism but also weigh the risk of undermobilization.

In this chapter, we will look at two principal areas of benefit or risk: (1) solidarity versus schism, and (2) mobilization versus undermobilization—both internally in terms of membership and externally in support resources.

Solidarity versus Schism

To many organizers, the "multicultural" or race/gender conscious end of the spectrum is quite scary and volatile. Will these particular identities be asserted for progressive change or for reactionary politics? Will the assertion of some identities and experiences within the group lead to the counterassertion by other more privileged subgroups to defend their relative privilege (white responses to affirmative action as reverse discrimination)? Can, in the face of all this, a movement maintain the unity it needs to be effective?

That which differentiates us is scary—hot, potentially explosive. It is reasonable, therefore, to try to nurture our commonalities. We are "workers," "women," "blacks," "gays," "Latinos," "women of color." Yet none of these categories is monolithic. As we've seen, with single-identity movements, each is differently defined by various other systems of injustice (Collins 1990). How do activists affirm diversity, fight for all kinds of justice, and yet stay together as a social movement organization? Labor conflicts are often warfare. Articulations of one identity claim can yield contentious debates, counterclaims, even countermovements. Will they incapacitate a movement with internal conflict or lead to disengagement and alienation?

Cheryl Gooding suggests that we cannot underestimate the fear of conflict that labor leaders bring to thinking about this issue. Contentious debate about any strategic issue—conflict of the kind that Columbia endured about the in-and-out strike strategy, or the kind Yale encountered as they debated going "home for the holidays"—is absolutely to be avoided. "Conflict is understood as doomed to weaken the union, incapacitate it in battle. This is an unchallenged assumption," argues Gooding (1999).

These are not unfounded fears, particularly in a context where (1) materially, a good deal is being contested, (2) the movement faces a tough, well-resourced opponent, and (3) a highly developed schism exists in the surrounding community. Such was the context during the Boston hospital drives of the late 1970s and early 1980s in which I participated. Separate organizing by white tradesmen was motivated by a sense that their identity and work issues were particular to them, and that they therefore belonged in their own trade unions. However, many white tradespeople were also unwilling to be in a union with "them": black women and men service workers (housekeepers, cafeteria workers, and nursing assistants), and predominantly white women secretaries and clerical workers. Substantially different conditions of work, created by sex and race segregation of labor (in external labor markets and internally within the hospitals), set the stage for such difficulties. All of this occurred during the aftershocks of the Boston busing crisis of the early 1970s.[6] Most participant accounts of union failures in the Boston hospitals during this period list racism and racial division as the top factors in failure.[7]

Practically and strategically, movement organizations weigh the benefits and costs of responding to multiple injustices: how do they trade off addressing all injustices, avoiding fracture, and winning victories? What can we learn from these clerical cases?

Clearly, the union organizing experiences and contract campaigns at Columbia, Harvard, and Yale avoided the fracture experienced in the Boston hospital drives. In fact, each case, despite varying internal and external conditions, provides evidence of multi-injustice politics bringing forth solidarity rather than fracture.

The Columbia clerical movement fashioned a multi-injustice, multi-identity politics that won important justice victories and minimized threats to unity. Over the years, this union has gone way out to where most would be afraid to tread in challenging institutional racist practices. Columbia clericals constructed multi-injustice politics principally in demands, culture, and organizational structure. Sometimes they framed their struggle in race- and gender-explicit language, but mostly not. Against a fierce opponent, they won a full range of trade union improvements around wages, benefits, grievance procedures, and seniority protection, as well as gains in affirmative action, reclassification, child care, and protection against sexual harassment. And there's been almost no conflict.

Recall one black leader's concern before the 1985 strike: would a workforce that was half white support a struggle where the benefits would disproportionately go to workers of color? They did. When only a minority of the members used child care, and the battle for child care brought the union to the brink of a second strike, the union membership held the line and supported the demand. There has never been a struggle, a countermobilization, or visible withdrawal from movement around these demands for race and gender justice. Many would say all of this is strong evidence of the perfect balance, the perfect collection of identity practices for moving beyond lowest-common-denominator politics. As a labor organizer, I would indeed be proud to have done so well. How did this happen?

In the early organizing, the "Justice Now" slogan served as an umbrella framing—which worked well to locate issues of racism and sexism in the context of a collection of injustices the union had set out to change. The large petition and posters that plastered the campus in the earlier struggle provided a good example: "As a predominantly female workforce, nearly half of whom are minorities, we have specific needs." Thus what others call "special interests," this movement redefined as "specific needs." What are usually seen as either/or identities were redefined as both/and identity claims (Collins 1990). In 1991 the union's response to the Mullinix letter, which was blown up and displayed around campus, used a similar approach (see chapter 5).

In the interviews I conducted in 1991 and 1992, several Columbia activists, including those involved for the first time, reported being moved by the justice/equity issues. "I thought this was a just cause, and I could contribute to it," said Calvin. Anna similarly commented, "I didn't think it would help me so much, but I saw there were other people who needed things to change." Laura saw herself as having grown over the previous year to "give selflessly" because "people need someone to fight for them." Sometimes folks who had fewer constraints, and had been able to negotiate individual solutions, wanted to fight for others. Ted pointed to the key role of top union leaders. "The union is very good at bringing people together. If you have reasonably enlightened leadership, that's what people totally respond to. . . . It has a lot to do with Julie [Kushner] carrying this thing from the beginning."

Lisa, now a leader in HUCTW, described the origins of her own involvement:

> When I started hearing that other people didn't have it that good [with
> their supervisors], and that there were other people who were real jerks,
> and I started hearing about the antiunion campaign, I just started think-
> ing that if I don't need this for myself, it sounds as if other people need it.
> And I'm enough of a decent person that I feel some solidarity with them,
> so I think I initially joined because it was put to me that even if you don't
> feel some crying need in your own workplace, do it for people who don't
> have it as good as you.

Roberta Goldberg's study of clerical workers' consciousness in Baltimore in the early 1980s similarly noted, "One of the most significant findings of this research is that many members presently have satisfactory job situations, yet feel the need to help others out of a sense of solidarity" (1983, 90).

Sometimes, as Allison, a young white Columbia activist, describes, this support crossed race, gender, or class lines:

> I feel like I've not been able to establish for myself the kind of cama-
> raderie that some of the other people have...because I'm not coming
> from the same place as some of the people in the union are. I do share a
> common bond with them, and I feel good about that, and I feel that's all
> the more reason for me to support the union, basically. And sometimes,
> I've felt like I'm not striking for myself, I'm striking for these other peo-
> ple. For the person that doesn't have health care, for the person that has
> four kids, and not enough to support them.

Ben, a white clerical, felt that a central challenge for District 65 was to deal with Columbia's racism and sexism as it was evidenced in their treatment of the largely women of color membership. The administration, he said, thought of the clericals as "just a lot of black women making a lot of noise...we've never gotten on top of that one." Jennifer, who is single and has no children, let it be known that although child care was not important to her, she could see and act on its importance to the group.

One of the early Harvard organizers made the same point in almost the same words. "We made it clear to people, 'You have to hear what each other's issues are, and you'll have to support each other'—which is what differentiates these politics from opportunism.... What I found, which was delightful, you give people a chance to act in a decent fashion, they will." Nina's conclusions about dealing with racial injustice at Columbia were virtually identical. "We've found you give people a chance to do the right thing, to be their best, and they usually do."

"We were in a struggle for our lives," said Pat Carter of Yale when she described why and how Local 34 members were able to work in solidarity for people's diverse needs. "This is what I need for me. This is what you need for you. So we're going to all get together and fight for it." Thus everyone supported the effort to compensate a disproportionately low number of blacks for their chronic low pay. Older women supported younger women to get day care benefits. And younger women supported older women to get better retirement plans. "Everyone worked together" (1999). Note the contrast to universal or common-denominator politics.

Yale activists noted the solidarity between the blue- and white-collar unions changed

> their respective outlooks. The clerical and technical workers, most of whom had little if any grounding in the way of unions and strikes, drew experience and confidence from the veterans of Local 35, whereas the blue-collar workers, for their part, became sensitized to the issue of sex discrimination at the workplace. It was this shared sense of revelation, as well as collective power, that gave the strike much of its dramatic edge. (Gilpin et al. 1988, 55)

These successes begin to suggest that speaking in terms of justice can create a framework on which specific identity-based struggles against oppression can be hung. We often see the choices as a fractured, conflicted movement *or* a unified, largely undifferentiated one. Conceiving of a movement as an internal coalition facilitates a both/and approach (Collins 1990): We are all Columbia University workers and District 65 members. [And] some of us are black women, Latinas, white women, African Americans, who share distinctive cultures, as well as experience particular injustices that other members are committed to opposing.

Jesse Jackson spoke at a HUCTW rally in December 1992.[8] He located the clerical and technical workers, mostly women, in the context of other injustice struggles at that time. These included efforts at Harvard (the campaign at the Law School for more women faculty of color), across the nation (policies to assist the working poor, entry into the United States for Haitians, recognition of World War II claims of Japanese Americans), and around the globe. For activists or scholars who argue that an oppositional element is needed in the creation of collective identity, here there is a "they" to create a "we." The collective task and identity is "injustice fighter," argues David Stuart. In such a "rainbow" framing, oppression is everyone's common enemy.[9]

Yet solidarity is not necessarily stable; it is a delicate creation that needs constant nurturing. A few of the people at Columbia who spoke of "doing for others" had trouble holding onto that initial perspective as the struggle elongated, and they were disappointed with the level of participation of those for whom they perceived they were making sacrifices. To some degree, this may be due to a (paternalistic) "charity" perspective, by which members of a (race/class/gender) position of privilege see themselves as kindly helping others "in need," as opposed to a more fully developed "injustice" or "coalition" perspective, by which members see themselves as fighting oppression.

Yet to some degree, this is an inherent problem: solidarity is difficult. The Columbia interviews revealed a small number of strike participants who were at odds with the union's fight for disproportionate raises to "the bottom." "That was never my thing," said Ilene, a longtime white union activist. These few opponents termed it "giving priority" to the needs of black and Hispanic workers, rather than "fighting racial discrimination." Ilene disputed who should be held accountable for workers in the bottom grades: the university or, as she would argue, the workers themselves. "If you don't strive, you don't get anywhere. No one keeps you in a grade 3." The union's focus on pay raises for the lower grades contradicted her sense of a "color-blind" ideal for racial justice. Frank, a young white member, was quite explicit in his statement that the union only advocated for "minority single mothers," which he said was a condition of race, not gender. He raised his contention with the child care demand, as well: "You know the big issue, the big deal over child care. To me, even if I had a child, I'd rather just see more money in my paycheck. Period. Amen. And with me, I felt instead of getting a 5 percent raise, we got a 4 percent raise. . . . And if we didn't fight for child care, we would have gotten maybe 4.2 or 4.5 percent."

Janet, a longtime union member, noted she was "pleasantly surprised at how the men seem to have no problem with respecting women leaders and treating them as the legitimate holders of power in the union." Yet Allison, a young white worker, voiced concern about the potential divisiveness and exclusion that she felt could come from more explicit gender framing:

ALLISON: You know I am a sympathizer with feminist movements, and I feel it's too bad people [Columbia management] are doing what they're doing . . . I think it's evident . . . there's some pretty mighty women out there. If it would be incorporated into the rhetoric, I think a lot of the men would be [pause, small laugh] scared as hell. They would feel meek and intimidated in the meetings.

SHARON: You mean if it was labeled?

ALLISON: If it was labeled, and if all of a sudden that became part of our lingo, I think the men would feel a little bit, more than they already do, they might feel a little intimidated. And on the one hand, who cares about that? But on the other hand, if we're working for unity, and not for separatism . . . [10]

Allison's prediction might turn out to be correct in some cases if the union were to adopt more gender-explicit language. Yet it is important to note that there were times when male and/or white members felt discomfort with being in a minority or with the union's justice demands but were still able to actively reach out in solidarity. Allison herself, we recall, felt acutely aware of her race and often class difference with the black women activists at the center of this campaign. Yet she did find solidarity that made her more connected to the campaign. Cindy, a first-time activist who felt a little "alienated" at first and believed that the union's racial justice demands "went against her," ended up feeling positive about her increased awareness about the role of racism. Rather than wanting to avoid her original discomfort, she wanted to confront it. Instead of demands about the race wage gap just being put forth and not "acknowledging that it was something that might be hard for some people," she still felt that more direct discussion, more chances to learn about racism, would be beneficial. Cindy said she needed help to "contextualize these issues. Because I didn't have a lot to put it into. If I had some broader understanding of labor and inequities, it might have made me feel a little more connected to the issue." Jennifer, another first-time activist, made a similar call for discussions, speculating what the impact would be "if they could keep this up between contracts, have discussions on different issues . . . the discrimination issue, women's issues."

Union leaders expressed some skepticism. "The reality is, it's just so hard to get people to participate in between contracts," argued Jean and Doris. "We would love to be able to do so many things. Time is just such a problem. People say they'd like a meeting, but when it came down to it, how many would come?"

Also, the Columbia union, as we have seen, was careful to fold discussions of racial discrimination into a larger list of union concerns. "There's a limit. We can't go too far with any one issue, we risk losing everyone else," argued Doris. Nina added, "There is this concern that you're approaching people because they're black. Race [is] a continuing discomfort in our lives." She noted with pride that at Columbia, "that tension" didn't exist, and she celebrated the "sense of community" the union was able to create. The negotiating committee is the place in the organization that union leaders have brought explicit discussion of strategy for dealing with racism. It was the negotiating committee in 1985, for example, which, building on its trust and history of working together, debated the allocation of the "special adjustment fund." Ted, whom we have several times heard appreciate the wisdom and perseverance of the leadership in helping the local to successfully deal with racism, added, "There's always a certain uneasiness that has come up from time to time trying to discuss these things" in the membership. Ted pointed out that this is where the race- and gender-blind common-denominator strategy worked well. "Poor pay is poor pay whether you're a white, black or Hispanic. There are just a lot of things that affect everybody equally." He added, "You don't have to be necessarily overtly expounding antiracist talk to be doing the work of countering discrimination."

Race Talk and Gender Talk Can Enhance Solidarity

Beverly Tatum, a psychologist working on issues of racism, would likely disagree with Ted and argue instead that overt antiracist talk is *critical* to fighting racism. For example, a white person with a growing awareness of racism (such as Cindy) needs support to continue to be open to such thinking and to be part of antiracist action. As Tatum quotes diversity trainer and activist Andrea Ayvazia, "Allies need allies" (1997, 109). The consistent advice of those engaged in multicultural or diversity or antiracist work is to break the silence. Tatum reflects on the pervasive silencing about race: she recounts extensive conversations with her preschool son as he pondered issues of race that had been raised by another child at his day care. When she asked his teacher how she dealt with such questions, the teacher "smiled and said, 'It really hasn't come up'" (35).

> Children who have been silenced often enough learn not to talk about race publicly. Their questions don't go away, they just go unasked. I see the legacy of this silencing in my psychology of racism classes. My students have learned that there is a taboo against talking about race, especially in racially mixed settings, and creating enough safety in the class to overcome that taboo is the first challenge for me as an instructor. (36)

Tatum calls on us "to continually break the silence about racism whenever we can . . . at home, at school, in our houses of worship, in our workplaces, in our community groups. . . . But talk does not mean idle chatter. It means meaningful, productive dialogue to raise consciousness and lead to effective action and social change" (193).

Although the context is different (Tatum is talking about schoolchildren and university students), the argument seems applicable. Longtime labor activist and leader Bill Fletcher Jr. describes initiatives taken by AFL-CIO education programs around the connections between class, race, ethnicity, and gender.

> We're trying to get away from the notion that you can talk about class in an abstract way, or in a way that will inoculate people against racism or sexism. Our economics education curriculum has modules on racism,

sexism, homophobia—to help people understand the genesis of these destructive tendencies, and how to strategize in response. We don't care whether people like each other, but we want them to understand what is at stake. (1998, 26–27)

Linda Stout is a white working-class organizer. She founded North Carolina's Piedmont Peace Project, a grassroots organization that is 70 percent people of color and a majority of women, which as part of its struggles faced down the Klan. Stout passionately argues that for long-term movement success, ongoing diversity work is necessary, rather than just a one-time training. Contrary to the belief that such talk and trainings detract time and energy and decrease the number of important justice victories, Stout argues they are necessary for victories: "The time and resources spent on this kind of training are essential to building long-term organizations" (1996, 84). In his toolbox for building multicultural organizations, John Anner, in *Beyond Identity Politics,* includes "holding regular discussions, forums, 'educationals,' and workshops to enhance people's understandings of other communities and individuals," and he calls specifically for antiracism trainings (1996, 155–56).

In the interviews, members made similar suggestions. A few asked for union education in labor history and women's labor history. They asked for programs that would analyze the "race wage gap," and how racism works at Columbia, and provide workers an opportunity to discuss these issues. Certainly comparable worth would make an interesting topic for a union forum or class. "More information, more background"—"more facts," details, and analysis—"like what the faculty got," said three workers who'd seen the faculty leaflets. "More details," said Allison, "not just propaganda. . . . Not just the bottom line you want us to take," but the information to answer our own questions and come to our "own analysis." More newsletters, with more in-depth articles, they suggested.

These suggestions are actually consistent with what Nina had suggested as being critical to creating cross-race solidarity in the first contract struggle. "We were able to develop an understanding that it was unacceptable for this situation to exist. It took consistent leadership and mutual trust. Coming from a white leader and a leadership committee which was mixed, the respect was deep enough. . . . We backed it up with facts." Nina added, "The key is not to blame people. White people will support antiracism so long as they don't feel you're putting blame on them." Cindy had been working very hard on her own toward such an understanding; it was help with just such issues that she would have liked to have had from union discussions.

As important as providing people with information, notes William Gamson, is creating "situations where people can gain experiential knowledge of injustice" (1992b, 184). "It's critical," says diversity trainer Erica Bronstein, "in these trainings or forums, to help people come to recognize multiple realities. People don't know, especially in a workplace with race or sex segregation, people really don't know how other people experience the situation. Hearing other people's experience is very powerful. Setting up situations where people come to understand what's happening to others in the workplace or in the union, and getting them to hold those multiple realities, helps people be able to be better allies to one another" (1999).

Speaking in part from the experience of painstakingly creating a multicultural women's labor leadership organization in Massachusetts, Cheryl Gooding notes that "building a community of safety and trust" is critical to "risk-taking, which multicultural alliances require." A "culture of participation helps to create an atmosphere of dialogue and ownership that is an important aspect of building safety and trust" (Gooding 1997a, 65).

Many union activists, like some Columbia leaders, feel wary of such "touchy-feely" process, preferring instead to concentrate on winnable contract demands. Bronstein, who has two decades of experience in the labor movement, points out that another important part of the process is collecting data about the organization and the membership.

> It can be in small focus groups, through interviews, or surveys, or caucus discussions, but it is important to collect that data and then feed it back to the group. The data is crucial to formulating demands and changes. It is also very powerful for people to hear, and for people to know their experience was heard. It's compelling. (1999)

This, along with quantitative data, would respond to the requests for "more information, more background" that some Columbia activists requested. The process also moves toward what Gooding has called "institutionalizing organizational learning," in which the insights from "needs assessments, studies, reports from special meetings or caucuses, and structured dialogues . . . can then become operationalized as new organizational practice" (1997a, 65).

For those who worry about the time demands of such a process, Bronstein responds, "It *is* time consuming, but it brings back a lot to the group. You tap into energy in places you didn't know it existed. People on the sidelines, if they're engaged, they'll come into the center and participate in ways they might not have" (1999), again supporting the idea of the mobilizing consequences of identity construction.

The height of the battle is not the only or easiest time to develop a diversity-affirming, internal-coalition collective identity. In the noncrisis period, the union or any social movement organization can more easily undertake any number of activities in this direction.

Cultural events, especially ones that are positive celebrations of differing histories, cultures, and resistance to injustice, also begin to lay the groundwork. Events commemorating Black History Month, Martin Luther King Day, International Women's Day, and Latino and Asian Culture Month all provide good opportunities. Potlucks, holiday parties, and picnics are all opportunities for an often atomized and segregated workforce to experience its wholeness and diversity. Similarly, as members suggested in interviews, but I was slow to recognize, the simple act of more unionwide membership meetings is an important experience that contradicts the segregation experienced by members who work in predominantly white or predominantly black and Hispanic areas.

They will not, however, obviate real conflicts where they do exist. The structure of internally and externally segmented labor markets creates real material divergence, if not conflict, of interest. The decision to disproportionately allocate money to workers in the bottom pay grades, to focus on affirmative action, or to reach out to larger movements, may at times generate real conflicts, which will not be banished by potlucks, parties, and educational events. Bronstein notes:

> There are times when you come down to it. Conflicts are sometimes unavoidable, especially in social movement organizations which are in struggle. The more work you've done when the group is not in crisis, the more time you've spent in the dialogue mode, the more people feel their concerns have been voiced and acknowledged, the better you'll do in crisis. (1999)

Although solidarity at Columbia was achieved, and for the most part threats to unity avoided, it may be that more race and gender talk would have strengthened the ability of workers to maintain what can be difficult solidarity.

Trading Off Schism and Solidarity: One Example

One of the biggest concerns about unity at Columbia came from outside the clerical membership. Maintaining an alliance with TWU, which represents maintenance and security workers, constituted one of the greatest constraints on explicit antisexist politics. While the blue-collar union at Yale aggressively supported clerical workers and their struggle for comparable worth,

TWU at Columbia took offense at explicit antisexist statements that compared the wages of the two unions. Even a contained articulation of the lack
of pay equity, including the salary ranges for the two unions, in "Fair Play,
Fair Pay" (see chapter 1) was enough to bring complaints from TWU. When
campus labor solidarity is a critical resource to the struggle, such opposition
needs to be taken seriously. District 65 placed high priority on keeping
TWU's support. In an important advance in campus labor solidarity, TWU
agreed with 65 and 1199 to establish the Columbia Labor Council and to
sign collective statements. Their members attended joint rallies. Unlike 1199,
however, TWU did not honor the 65 strike with a sympathy strike of its
own. The union only raised a modest amount of money for strike support.
As one faculty supporter in the 1985 clerical strike noted, "They [District
65] always had to tread carefully about TWU. It's definitely a constraint."

The contrast to Yale is striking. Recall that the Yale clerical union was
organized by Local 35, Yale's blue-collar union. Local 35's decision was
based on its assessment that its own struggle at Yale looked bleak without
the clout of additional unionized workers. But their decision did not come
cheap. They contributed to the cost of the clerical organizing campaign,
and they went out on solidarity strike with the clerical union for the duration.

During the Columbia strike period, some members of Yale's blue-collar
union, Local 35, having heard of the recent Columbia events, were in the
city and decided to make a spontaneous visit. "What is TWU doing?" they
asked. "Coming to support rallies, collecting strike support money, and
participating in the joint labor council," we answered. "*Yeah? What else?*"
they insisted. District 65 staff and members aimed for politeness, but the
Yale unionists cut right through it. "*They didn't go out with you?*" they asked
in amazement. The unfortunate reality was that TWU never mobilized itself to any substantial degree in support of the clerical union. District 65
significantly constrained its gender framing in order to keep TWU's support, yet their support did not amount to much. It may be that Columbia
clericals paid a high price for what turned out to be a small amount of solidarity. They sacrificed a gender-explicit politics that could have yielded increased mobilization (both internal and external) in exchange for nominal
blue-collar support.[11]

Caucuses: A Sign of Internal Division or Attention to Specific Needs?

Along with the question of explicit talk is the question of explicit organizational structures around diversity. Columbia's top union leaders pointed to
the lack of a black or Latino caucus, for example, as evidence of lack of division, and the successful handling of racism.[12] Does the existence of a caucus

necessarily suggest a problem in the movement? I would argue no. While often criticized as separatist, such caucuses may well be only the "home" space that historian, scholar, and musician Bernice Johnson Reagon describes as necessary preparation and replenishment for those undertaking the critical but difficult work of forging "coalition" (1992). Ruth Needleman argues:

> *Independent space* [such as a caucus] is space away from the dominant culture and the controlled structures of the union. This self-organized space provides room for women [and workers of color, gays and lesbians, etc.] to identify what in that culture excludes them or makes them uncomfortable; it also provides room for them to create a different kind of culture or work environment, to explore more familiar styles of doing things. In this space, women [and other marginal groups] can safely articulate grievances, validate feelings, and strategize about how to engage and change the dominant culture. (1998b, 161)

Local 34 at Yale, in their 1984 organizing, used a black caucus to give added weight to the concerns of the 14 percent black membership, disproportionately low for New Haven. Steve Fortes, a Yale clerical, said the goal of the black caucus "was to get more black people involved in the union. The more blacks are involved, the more they can raise their specific concerns." It also created an organizational vehicle for black community support. Not only did the black caucus raise their own concerns, but they also looked outward to kindred political struggles. Adding "the point of view of working people" to those who were working to abolish apartheid, Local 34's black caucus wrote letters to Yale, urging them to divest, and to the South African Embassy, urging an end to apartheid. Steve Fortes thought their antiapartheid efforts showed unionists "weren't just thinking about ourselves: our paychecks, our raises, our benefit packages. We were also thinking about how things affect people globally." Making connections between local and global issues had a "mobilizing and energizing" effect, said Fortes in a 1999 interview.

Certainly other unions have experienced women's committees and black, Latina/o, and gay and lesbian caucuses as positive formations. Women's committees have traditionally developed proposals about work and family issues (child care, parental leave, flextime) and dealt with issues of sexual harassment and comparable worth. They have been a support place for developing women's leadership and helping women deal with cases of discrimination. My suspicion is that tension around these formations may remain small when the caucus remains small, and its agenda circumscribed, not too charged.

In some unions, caucuses are viewed with suspicion. Aren't caucuses merely new exclusion? In addition to fears about potential conflict, some unionists find caucuses to violate the principle of color and gender blindness that they, like many Americans, hold dear. This concern has been met by the practice of some unions establishing civil rights committees, which are multiracial. These can address many of the same issues of racism in the workplace or larger society and create an identified union forum for a cross-race discussion of racism. Yet such committees are unlikely to create the kind of safe "independent space" in which workers of color might feel able to break through "taboo" discussions or raise issues about the functioning of the union itself as often occurs in caucuses.

In the 1960s and 1970s, many progressive union reform movements were largely black based and led, but they received some support by white workers, as well.[13] Cornel West's discussion of black leadership, particularly "race transcending prophetic leadership," seems useful here because it reminds us that black activism and leadership that grows out of strong antiracist politics can powerfully mobilize justice organizing across race, class, and gender. Speaking of Malcolm X's project, after 1964, West terms it "transracial, though grounded in Black turf." He speaks similarly of civil rights activist Fannie Lou Hamer, who "led the National Welfare Rights Organization, not the Black Welfare Rights Organization" (1993, 39). To the extent that caucuses support attention to justice demands and do not ghettoize women and people of color, they can be effective organizational structures for social change movements and can, in fact, push them to more energetically mobilize around a multi-injustice politics.

Mobilization Risks: In Which Direction?

Potential Internal Undermobilization

Some organizer wisdom suggests that even if explicit identity politics don't create conflicts, they may yield alienation. Those who don't resonate with a particular identity might withdraw or disengage. Frank, whom we heard voice his discontent with the degree the union spoke to "minority single mothers," was one such example, in fact the only one I am aware of in the campaign. Frank did withdraw from activism, in part around this issue, and even more around his impatience with the union's in-and-out strike strategy. Sociologists Debra Friedman and Doug McAdam similarly argue that "a collective identity that is inclusive of a wide range of attitudes tends to make the group more rather than less exclusive. . . . Social movement organizations that attempt to construct all-purpose collective identities may therefore appeal to a narrower audience than those that stand fast to a more limited conception" (1992, 164).

However, the last decades of social movement history make quite clear that identity politics can have powerful emotional appeal. They move people both inside and outside of a campaign. They can be a significant element of movements' mobilizing appeals for social justice. Recall that union leader Maida Rosenstein, in a 1995 interview about the UAW's success with white-collar workers, reported that the clericals at Columbia found the union's emphasis of "its social vision and its support for women's and minority rights" to be appealing.[14]

We have heard from the members, a minority, whose experience matched Rosenstein's claim. They were proud of the union's justice efforts, proud to be part of an organization which so defined its mission. There were those who described their activism as part of the survival and social change work that "race women" have traditionally done.

Speckled throughout Columbia's yearlong campaign were a few occasions when the energy of identity-based justice politics did burst forth, some dramatically. The interviews also revealed some unused potential of stronger race- and gender-based appeals. The data do not provide the basis to test what would have happened if the union's practices had been more explicitly identity based. To what extent would these practices have impeded some members' mobilization, as Friedman and McAdam and some organizer wisdom argue? To what extent would they have enhanced others' mobilization? How would these have balanced against each other? The data clearly do not provide the basis to argue that if only the Columbia local had more explicitly framed gendered or racialized politics, then they would have achieved twice as much, and in half the time. Rather, the data from fieldwork and interviews are merely suggestive of untapped internal resources.[15]

In a hard battle, as this was, a more fully mobilized membership would be an important additional resource. While union leaders are right to be amazed and awed at how well a high-turnover workforce came together for the contract fights, it is still the case that mobilizing the members, often new to unions, is a difficult task.

Let me tell you some stories.

During a late-night negotiating session just before a strike day, one of the District 65 leaders made an unusual, passionate, explicit race and gender justice appeal. She responded to what negotiating committee members experienced as a cavalier attitude by the university about senior workers: "You can just go get a job somewhere else." Raising her voice, she asked just where did they think that black women in New York City would go get other jobs? Having been a union representative in the publishing industry, she knew that whole industries in the city were virtually closed to black women.[16]

The impact on some union members was striking. Doris and Lana, two African American women who had been quite even tempered and polite in negotiations, were transformed. Doris started yelling at the management negotiating team about respect—and the complete lack of it she felt from them and their manner of dealing with the union. Administrators were visibly disturbed. They knew this woman, and this had not been her usual manner. She was not one of the predictable "mouths" at these meetings. Doris found a rage that lasted for several days and took the form of impassioned (although not race- or gender-specific) speeches at the mass meetings and rallies. Lana also brought anger and much more visible leadership to the picket line for the next few days. She aggressively led chants, including chants explicitly about racism, which were quite rare in this union.

Later, in an interview, Doris recounted the rage that she had felt during that confrontation with the administration. "I couldn't believe they had no regard for senior workers. And a lot of them are black. There were black people sitting on the other side of the [negotiating] table. Here are Julie and Maida, two white women . . . going way out across race, talking to a committee that included a lot of black folks, about discrimination. I really got angry . . . Columbia really disrespects us." Breaking the silence and naming the injustices had powerfully moved these women.

In March, the day after my interview with Calvin, an African American activist, he stood up in the union membership meeting during the debate over another strike authorization—for what this time would be the final push. "Look at who is in this room," Calvin argued. "Look at who we are: women and minorities. That's why they've given us such a hard time. And that's why we have to see this thing through to the end." And he framed his call for support of the final strike based on this identity appeal.

One of the union leaders with whom I'd had episodic conversations about these issues relayed this incident to me with satisfaction: this had occurred spontaneously. Not quite, I explained. Themes of gender and race, sexism and racism, had been the subject of an hourlong interview the day before. However, we never even came close to discussing them as "mobilizing strategy." That they appeared in this manner—as a mobilizing call for activism, militancy, commitment, and justice—I believe is noteworthy.

Recall Gloria and Danielle, the two strikebreakers who expressed interest in women's issues and suggested that explicit attention to women's concerns may have increased their interest in the union. Recall Cindy, who, when the strike was over, said she wanted to find an organization that worked with women in which she could invest her energies. She had absolutely no conception of the union as such an organization. Recall Maxine, who got great pleasure from the idea of the gender element of union organizing and thanked me for the question that raised the connection.

Union leaders reading these quotes in the manuscript of this book were skeptical. "Big talk," said one. "They just found more acceptable language to explain their not supporting the union," argued Ted. Doris, another leader, pointed out that the mobilizing effect of race and gender justice isn't the case for everyone. She described her own experience: "For a long time, union people were trying to get *me* to be active. I *knew* what this was about. I *knew* it was about race justice. I *knew* it was about women. But that didn't make any difference. It didn't get me to meetings because I had other priorities, other things I had to do in my life."

Doris is right: race and gender justice appeals are not an organizing panacea. I recall the conversation between two African American women walking in front of me into a membership meeting. "I don't care about that discrimination stuff," one woman told her friend. "I'm not going to be here that long." Not all minimally active workers will be brought to a higher level of activism by identity appeals. Still, these incidents and conversations at Columbia do suggest a pattern of untapped internal mobilization that a union in a fight for survival can scarcely afford to ignore. One of the union leaders spoke about the highly emotional, sometimes explosive quality of such identity framings. She spoke positively, but with caution, about the need to shape and direct that energy. So while some union leaders saw such potential, it was never systematically tapped.

Certainly, the other cases we've considered—1199, Yale, and Harvard—would offer additional support of the empowering, mobilizing effect of gender- and race-based justice appeals. When the black caucus of Local 34 got involved in antiapartheid work, many members "saw the connection between politics and unions," said Steve Fortes, and it sparked their enthusiasm for union work. "There were a number of people who were kind of jazzed by the issue [even though they could see] it wasn't going to affect them directly." Robert similarly noted that the clericals' support for the Columbia divestment movement increased the tie many black workers felt to the union. Linda Blum's analysis of comparable worth organizing in California also offers testimony to the effects of an identity-based appeal (1991). Blum considers cases, of which Columbia is one, in which comparable worth was not the principal mobilizing issue. Even in these cases, Blum saw comparable worth as having served a critical function. "It adds an important moral basis to unions' economic demands: it becomes a tool and a symbol providing women with a greater sense of legitimacy and solidary purpose, and struggling unions with better ammunition to use in public relations battles against recalcitrant employers" (188). Recall Julianne Malveaux's argument about the racial significance of comparable worth struggles in cases of race and sex segregation (see chapter 5). These issues could help organize potential supporters. In the language of this discussion, the comparable worth issue can have significant impact on the ability to mobilize internal and external resources.

At Columbia, a full frontal assault on pay equity during this time didn't make sense. The union still needed to complete the reclassification process. But emphasizing the gender- and race-based justice issues lying underneath classification demands may well have raised the commitment to these demands. At the least, such a linkage would have set the groundwork for an eventual, tough, head-on battle. Remember the women in one department who took the initiative to make their own comparable worth leaflet from the statistics in the union flyer. Had the movement as a whole taken up this framing, other workers may well have been interested. At the very least, an active, engaged union membership needs to determine how and whether to raise identity-based claims.

Because of the nature of unions (once the union exists, membership is quasi-automatic) for most workers, the question is how engaged to be.[17] Unions struggle with the classic free-rider problem: all workers benefit regardless of their level of activism (see chapter 4). Many also see the union staff as experts with special knowledge who deal with their class counterparts in the administration. Developing mass-based negotiating committees and strike committees (such as at Columbia) helps to dispel this image. Yet the notion of unions as the business of staff "experts," despite unions' hopes to the contrary, is reinforced by the large role of a small number of union staff and officers. Although Columbia clerical leaders worked hard to increase participation, the "they" in workers' talk, even that of most active workers, indicates a chasm between them and top leaders who exercise strategic power. To create a multicultural, multi-identity organization, all groups must feel empowered (in consciousness and in the reality of organizational structures, strategic planning, and decision making) to decide whether and how much and how to take up these issues.

Given the difficulty of mobilizing workers *at all* and the obstacles in getting larger numbers to commit themselves to a movement, these issues of what mobilizes and politicizes people are not to be taken lightly. Naively, years ago, when I first considered the powers of identity politics for labor, I wondered whether using identity politics would have magic-wand effects for the problem of movement participation and engagement. Obviously, this is not the case. Blum notes that in her study, regardless of the gender and class identity a group invokes, "the most difficult problem is still how to organize a previously unorganized group and how to build a sense of solidarity that can support collective action" (1991, 188). As one Columbia activist of color who prioritizes multioppression politics pointed out to me, a preeminent struggle in the Columbia campaign was just getting people to be involved, at all. Period. In this context, that which enhances mobilization must be taken seriously.

Potentially Lost External Resources

The 1199 and Yale cases, although occurring under significantly different conditions, well illustrate the potential of explicitly antiracist and antisexist labor campaigns to draw active external support. At Yale as well as Harvard, the gender justice demands were picked up by the media, which in turn led to a heightened gender framing. At Columbia, faculty, including women, played an important support role. In contrast to Yale, however, where women students and faculty played a large support role, to my knowledge, no women's student group was approached or itself approached the union.[18] During the 1984 Yale strike, leaders of the National Organization for Women and several other diverse women's organizations made support appearances, either in response to the union's request or from their own initiative. New York City has a plethora of politically diverse women's organizations. It is hard to believe that some of them would not have been pleased to undertake some active support work with the Columbia local.

In Boston, for example, a pay equity legal case of public school cafeteria workers (members of Local 26, Hotel and Restaurant Workers) was also taken on as a project of the National Organization for Women (NOW), who helped bring support and media attention to the campaign.[19] Diane Harriford's 1989 study of the New York City chapter of CLUW (the Coalition of Labor Union Women) shows it to have been an important vehicle for African American women labor activists. Particularly with much of the Columbia campaign occurring during the tortured Anita Hill days and their aftermath, I would imagine that some women's organizations, and particularly African American women's organizations, would have welcomed this as an outlet site for the energy, resistance, and rage that the hearings had generated.[20] The *New York Times* carried the "In Defense of Ourselves" statement signed by 1,603 African American women across the nation in response to the hearings.[21] A labor struggle obviously poses class politics, which may have been problematic for some of the signers. Yet some of these women, located in New York or the Northeast, may have been willing, if not eager, to support the Columbia clericals.

One of the concerns in reaching out to external allies is the problem of building a link with a larger social movement that is in a troubled state. Feminism certainly has been so viewed. This is somewhat due to its own making (a long history of racist and classist practices). It is also due to the well-developed counterattack, as the front page of *Time* blared during the Columbia contract campaign: "The War against Feminism."[22] As recent accounts of college women have indicated, feminism is an identity from which many—although not all—attempt to disassociate themselves.[23] For many, being labeled feminist can be a terrible character assault.

Here is where the Harvard clericals' "feminine," not "feminist," came in: they invoked the benefits of gender identity without the negative association. It remains an open question to what degree such a strategy reproduces the overall negative images of the movement to which it is attempting to avoid being linked. So how does a particular movement campaign locate itself in this terrain? Will association with a larger movement code the smaller movement as "political" in a way that members find uncomfortable? Will such association turn off, demobilize potential members? Even worse, will it spawn a countermobilization?

It's useful to remember that the labor movement has been similarly in trouble and discredited in many circles. Certainly this was the case at the time of this Columbia campaign (before the 1995 election of new AFL-CIO leadership). Then (and for many, still now), labor was seen as a corrupt, undemocratic, narrow, outdated, special-interest group of selfish, overpaid industrial or public-sector workers. The contrast to a virtuous movement fighting for fairness, justice, and respect for all working people is striking. Yet the Columbia and Yale clerical unions proudly identified themselves as part of the labor movement—clearly conceiving themselves as among the "best of the labor movement."

We could say this is inevitable: Columbia clericals are structurally located in the labor movement. Yet the same was true of those Harvard clericals we heard disassociate themselves from much of the rest of labor, as a male, sexist, macho, combative, undemocratic, antiquated, blue-collar movement. To be fair, this disassociation came, in part, in response to HUCTW's high-conflict relationship with the UAW, culminating in the UAW's firing their organizing staff, which led HUCTW to organize independently for a while.[24]

I point this out to remind us that it is possible to identify with a larger troubled movement. It is possible for the campaign of a specific social movement organization to draw strength from a larger movement, and simultaneously to redefine what that movement is about. The Yale clerical and technical local, for example, in its much-publicized comparable worth campaign, identified itself much more with a larger women's movement in its framing and its support resources. Such support can also draw important resources— people power, money, technical and strategic assistance, media attention— which, in a tight struggle, can be determinative.

Initiatives here can run two ways. Women's movement organizations (multiracial, white, African American, Latino, Asian) can also make overtures to the union. This would be particularly beneficial given the history of the women's movements around race and class. Offering support could help to establish feminism as a point of reference for union members.

The same is true of racial justice movements. Local 34's outreach to the larger New Haven community offers an example of how a union can mobilize external support and in the process become part of something larger. At Yale, black ministers were active supporters and raised issues around the university's missing black clerical workforce, as well as race pay differentials for the black clericals who made up 14 percent of Local 34's membership.[25] Noted national civil rights leaders also made support appearances, which enhanced strikers' sense of "being engaged in a crusade of historical significance" (Gilpin et al. 1988, 62). In return, Yale clerical workers showed up at New Haven's community events and marches, and in one successful and innovative program, the union used its own funds to support students of color at the nearby Gateway Community College. According to Steve Fortes, students of color who maintain a certain grade point average "have the rest of their courses paid for by the union, and they'd be guaranteed a job at Yale when they graduated." Designed to bring more people of color into clerical jobs at Yale, the program has succeeded in supporting people of color to find better-paying work. Mentors smooth the way for program participants, and the union actively encourages them to continue their educations and apply for better jobs within Yale. In operation for more than ten years, Local 34's affirmative action student subsidies and support creates a mechanism by which Yale and the union give something back to the community. Local 34's presence in the community, and its embracing of community issues (New Haven was the seventh-poorest city in the country), are an example of how a union can be a vehicle for all kinds of justice.

Meanwhile, at Columbia, campus support from the black student organization and from Local 1199 helped to mark the Columbia campaign as a struggle against racial injustice, as a struggle of people of color. New York Congressman Rangel, along with other politicians and unionists, was called on to pressure the university on issues of racial discrimination. Yet District 65 did not aggressively seek to develop relationships with outside social change movements or community organizations. Columbia sits at the edge of Harlem. Over the years, black community and campus organizations have come together over a number of struggles, including calling for divestment, preserving the Audubon Ballroom, and protesting racial attacks on campus. But during the 1991–1992 contract campaign, Columbia clericals did not substantially engage with outside movements or movement representatives. Recall that in the interviews, Carmella and a few other activists mourned the lost opportunity of support from more black and Latino organizations. Said Carmella, "Al Sharpton would be interested in what's going on here. Columbia would hate Al Sharpton on campus [laughing]. He'd have all the black organizations that marched across the bridge. I can picture it. They'd do it in a heartbeat."

The mention of Sharpton, of course, may set off alarms. In fact, Reverend Al Sharpton and Congressman John Lewis (a noted civil rights activist) did both make appearances at Columbia during the strike period.[26] Much less controversial, Lewis's support could have brought a good deal of attention and legitimation to the strike. Such was the case at Yale with the support of civil rights notables Bayard Rustin and Ralph Abernathy. How possible it would have been to have Lewis speak about the clericals, I do not know; yet it was never pursued.

The ideological question of which organizations, leaders, and tendencies to seek out within an external movement is a tricky dilemma. The political and ideological diversity within the membership that we've glimpsed is testimony to the misguidedness of essentialized identity politics, as Mohanty, West, and Stansell have argued.[27] Which political and ideological perspectives would the union have accepted? While Carmella loved the idea of Sharpton's championing the clerical cause, many others at Columbia would have vehemently disagreed. Some would have opposed his presence on principle; others would have objected strategically, pointing out the negative public opinion and potential conflict such an association would generate internally. The possibility of conflict, countermobilization, or withdrawal from the struggle would be great. Here is an example of the potential negative harvest of associating with a larger movement (leader) in trouble.

Problematic though it may be, this dilemma is not impossible to negotiate. The union could almost certainly have identified other black and
Latino community leaders about whom they did not have conflict. Also, in
its early organizing, while 1199 worked closely with SCLC and the NAACP,
Malcolm X also appeared in support of the union. "That two leaders in the
black community who were usually thought of as adversaries could both
celebrate the victory at Beth El and Manhattan Eye and Ear is a valid measure of 1199's ability to transform the campaign for hospital workers' rights
into a moral crusade" (Fink and Greenberg 1989, 109). While selecting
supporters may well be a point of negotiation and debate, there is ample
precedent to suggest that a movement could find plenty of supporters about
whom it agreed. Or it may be willing to have a collection of supporters representing diverse ideological positions, within a given range. Some explicit
conversation about these issues (beyond the small circle of the negotiating
committee) would be necessary—a change from the union's present practice.[28]

For the conflicts inherent in these internal coalition politics, strong
multiracial and -gender leadership and a highly participatory democratic
union life is critical. Columbia's mobilization brought forth an unprecedented
number of new African American women and Latina leaders. But unlike
Harvard, where conscious leadership development is seen as a highest-
priority movement task, there was little systematic development of these
new leaders' skills and labor education background. The top white women
leaders of the local—Maida Rosenstein and Julie Kushner—are highly respected for their fierce commitment to challenge racism. Yet given the dominant either/or conceptualizations, the leadership of women of color may
well be critical to a union's being able to affirm itself as a vehicle for progressive gender and race politics. (In the years after the 1991 campaign, more
women of color have taken leadership roles in the union.)

As significant as the issue of who occupies the top staff leadership tier
of the organization is the question of how much strategy formulation and
decision-making power the next leadership levels actually exercise. The kinds
of strategy decisions about pursuing the lack of comparable worth and responding to members' reports (in interviews and informal conversations) of
institutional racism also require an active, vibrant, participatory membership and democratic life. In the interviews, when discussing these issues, the
use of "they" in most members' speech, even to the level of very active rank-
and-file leaders, is striking. A group needs to have history of collectively
tackling such difficult questions—and again, not only in the heat of battle.
This is particularly difficult in a high-turnover workplace such as Columbia.

Linkages to other movements—to race- and gender-specific organizations—can be begun in the noncrisis periods. At a session of the annual women's labor leadership institute in Massachusetts in the early 1990s,[29] the president of a Boston AFSCME local talked of the union's involvement with the struggle for democracy in Haiti. After investigating why Haitian members who were active in Haitian politics were not active in the union, the local leadership decided it needed to "take the union to them, to their fight." The local began support work on issues confronting the Haitian community. The same local made a decision to sponsor a program of workplace breast exams, which provided an important community service. Such programs can begin to create a multiracial and -gender identity for a union.

One of the key problems with comparing Columbia's 1991 contract campaign to Harvard's and Yale's first contract struggles, or 1199's organizing efforts, is that identity issues are often more prominent in first campaigns. Unions are aware that stressing the moral nature of the struggle is a key component of gathering support for initial campaigns. Carole, a longtime white union leader, reflects that perspective in the early Columbia organizing:

> In the first strike we were extremely attuned to reaching out to the community... we've got to let them know who we are, what our problems are. You know, they'll be appalled when they find out some of this stuff. And you know, our lowest wage earner was $9,300, full time. And so I think there was a lot of that kind of "We're mostly women, we're half minority, we make these kind of salaries... we're the typists and receptionists..." We were always saying that kind of stuff. That we would not say anymore because we expect people to know something about us. We felt like people didn't know us. We literally felt like we'd been invisible.... When you're going to get a first contract, the issues are so stark. You know that you can go out and you can galvanize... the kind of publicity we did then had a lot to do with gender and race. You know when you're trying to improve language and you're trying to get x percent or y dollars, it's not as galvanizing as when you can go out and say we have full-time people making $9,300 who can't afford health care. I had extremely high hopes when we were organizing. I think they got kind of beaten down just in the weariness of trying to manage the local.[30]

Moving beyond the "stark" issues of first contract campaigns, unions face the continuing challenge of building their movement, fostering solidarity, mobilizing both internal and external resources, and dealing with management assaults. In the context of second and third contract campaigns, "the weariness of trying to manage the local," and the pared-down demands of x-percent salary increases, as Carole says, can replace the excitement of the original justice-based campaign. Evidence from Columbia's 1991–1992 contract campaign (its third contract struggle) suggests that multi-injustice politics are one way to build solidarity, mobilize members, and galvanize outside support for the union.

As any organizer knows well, in the short run, resource gathering is resource consuming. It takes time to do outreach and establish support relationships. In 1985 at Columbia the support work focused on the campus and the labor movement. When I asked about additional community support in the 1985 campaign, one of the leaders said, "We were stretched so far, we wouldn't have known what to do with them." Later, pondering this issue in the 1991 campaign, one leader asked, "Where was the community?" wondering where community initiatives to support the union might have been. Here, Cheryl Gooding argues, locals would benefit from resource support from the AFL-CIO. It's a large task; locals are stretched thin, especially during a struggle period. For some locals, it's also a question of learning new skills. This is an area where outside support to build external coalitions would be very helpful for locals (1999).

For a union that had to fight so hard for most of a year for a contract, outside resources could have been helpful. In addition to whatever other support such civil rights, black and Latino liberation, and feminist leaders and organizations may have offered, their voices may well have helped crack the media silence that the Columbia local had such great difficulty surmounting. The benefits of such an identity-based justice framing, however, are not just in stockpiling external resources. The benefits are reaped in shoring up the movement mobilization internally, as well.

Imagine the internal mobilization impact if members were part of a task force actively pursuing—and receiving—support endorsements from community organizations and churches. Groups and leaders drawn in as support from outside can help define a movement's collective identity. These supporters serve as a mirror held up to those on the inside: "This is who we are, this is what is important about our struggle, this is why our struggle matters." In defining a struggle as a moral mission, of which identity politics are one element, outsiders suggest to those in the movement that their participation really matters. This is just what Lily noted that people at Columbia were lacking. "Overall," she said, "I would just say that part of the problem was the workers really felt that their struggle was theirs only, the members. A lot of times they don't really know that outsiders . . . were sympathetic. Had they known that, I think it would have fortified them."

Learning from These Experiences

Social movement organizations considering how to handle "diversity" issues weigh the potential risks and benefits of strong multi-identity politics. With claims of injustice, however righteous, on one side, unions and other movement organizations understandably evaluate the risk of debilitating conflict to the organization on the other.

All three of these cases present evidence of solidarity and minimal threats of schism. Columbia clericals' leadership and culture and their emphasis on demands allowed them to introduce race-based justice claims in a way that did not cause fracture within the membership. Interestingly, some Columbia clericals for whom cross-race solidarity was a new stretch called for *more* explicit discussions about the impact of race. These would have "broken the silence" and given more support and guidance to those beginning to grapple with the role of racism in their workplace. While a few articulations of budding resentment could be heard, there is also evidence from Columbia that suggests that explicit race talk might have enhanced solidarity as a number of clerical workers articulated their interest in supporting others even when their issues and experiences were not the same. In their third contract campaign, Columbia clericals emphasized a trade union framing of their demands, with their "Justice Now" framing being less prominent. This may have limited their ability to mobilize external resources and even possibly resources within their own membership.

The Harvard and Yale cases presented here are first-time organizing campaigns, so they are not parallel to Columbia, but they do suggest other ways that multi-injustice politics can inspire people to action—both within the union and without. At Yale, the use of caucuses, the explicit antiracist and antisexist framing of demands, and the use of outside social movements and their leaders for support illustrate the mobilizing power of multi-injustice politics. At Harvard, the clerical workers' receptiveness to "women's ways of organizing" shows that asserting collective identity can be powerfully mobilizing. Clearly, fracture is not the only risk in selecting practices along the color/gender blind–color/gender conscious continuum. Responses of some Columbia workers to issues of identity-based justice in the campaign—those who were inspired to act and those who felt they would have been if these politics were more visible—suggest a mobilizing potential for a number of workers. More explicit identity politics also have the potential of mobilizing external resources. One of the challenges for future organizing campaigns, particularly for those mired in the more bureaucratic struggles of contract campaigns beyond the first, may have to do with *not* leaving behind the strong justice framing that helped them create a union in the first place.

Thus, in balancing the risks and benefits of identity politics, it is important to recognize that the risks are not only stacked up on one side of the equation. There is always the possibility that more explicit race and gender justice politics might bring forth more negative reactions. A few very small seedlings were visible. Would they have grown? This is the balance that District 65's framing strategy has sought to maintain. Yet, while a real concern, it is not the only concern. Whereas fashioning multi-identity politics can carry risks of schism, not fashioning identity politics can carry risks of undermobilization.

My purpose here is to clarify the risks on both sides and to allow for more conscious strategizing. The data clearly do not establish a closed case of lost victories. But what they are suggestive of are costs on both sides of the calculation. This contradicts the common organizing wisdom that dangers exist only in diversity. Wise activists assess their specific history, structural conditions, opposition, level of organizational development, and other resources to map a strategy. Identity politics are not a master strategy, nor one that can be used in all conditions or in the same way. Yet they require conscious attention and strategizing.

As Jesse Jackson said of the Democratic Party, the harvest of inclusion and speaking to unmet need is greater engagement and power. That, as we will consider in the next chapter, is not only an issue for each specific union but a critical concern for the larger labor, women's, and antiracism movements, as well as the overall Left.

9

Can We Make a Different Kind of Identity Politics?
Challenges to Labor and the Left

The struggle for diversity and inclusion within the AFL-CIO is not only a principled and moral fight, it is a battle very much in the self-interest of the labor movement. . . . the labor movement is one of the few social forces with the capacity to advance an agenda of multiracial unity and progressive social change.

—May Chen and Kent Wong

If the gay movement ultimately wants to make a real difference, as opposed to settling for handouts, it must consider creating a multi-issue revolutionary agenda. This is not about political correctness, it's about winning.

—Barbara Smith

The Challenge to Labor

Labor remains in a critical period of revitalization. The labor movement struggles to organize the millions of unorganized workers—disproportionately workers of color, immigrants, and women—to reverse the decades of decline from deindustrialization, capitalist assault, gutted labor laws, and labor's own exclusionary practices and resistance to new organizing. Millions of workers in the United States, especially the unorganized, confront contingent work, unlivable wages, job insecurity, no health care or other working family benefits, and an absence of respect and democracy in the workplace as shaped in part by race- and sex-segregated labor markets. These are conditions the labor movement seeks to redress. Can labor reemerge, in public perception and in reality, as a righteous vehicle for social justice?

What will help labor to be seen as a vehicle not only for its specific members but for working people more broadly? Redefining unions as a vehicle for all kinds of justice is one critical part of this agenda. Unions like those at Columbia, Harvard, and Yale are exactly about such an endeavor.

In 1985, after the first Columbia strike, District 65 president David Livingston held up the Columbia struggle as an example of how fighting for race and gender justice was a regular part of what the union did. Combining race, class, and gender in one struggle is powerful, he argued. "It leads to support from broad forces in the community who now identify the normal labor struggle as a struggle for justice and equality."[1]

His words reflected a growing awareness among progressives that to be powerful, movements need to address multiple injustices, not only race, class, and sex, but sexuality, nationality (immigrant status), and disability as well. In recent years, gay and lesbian labor activists across the nation have begun organizing around issues particular to their social location: health care and other benefits of domestic partnership, access to health care for HIV-positive workers, and protected status against discrimination. Among its many achievements, Boston's Gay and Lesbian Labor Activist Network (GALLAN), in the early 1990s, pulled off an impressive alliance with the Teamsters in organizing a boycott of Miller Beer. GALLAN provided important support for the boycott, protesting Miller's health care policies, including the denial of access to HIV-positive workers. After the gay community stirred up publicity for the boycott, Burke Distributing Corporation, the area wholesaler for Miller Beer, agreed to the Teamster demand for a nondiscrimination clause based on sexual orientation, as well as domestic partner bereavement benefits. Boston's Labor Page called it "a victory for the Teamsters and for the lesbian and gay community."[2] Representatives of the Teamster local were wildly cheered as they marched in solidarity with their banner in the 1992 Gay, Lesbian, and Bisexual Pride March in Boston (Krupat and McCreery 2000).

More and more, labor leaders are recognizing the importance of embracing multi-identity politics in their organizing. In a packed-to-the-walls, multiracial meeting in New York City of gay and lesbian union members—many of whom, according to GALLAN's Susan Moir, "had never seen the inside of their union hall before"—an AFSCME labor leader told the crowd, "Make no mistake about it: We need you more than you need us" (Scagliotti et al. 1999).[3]

In waging its election campaign in 1995, labor's rising leaders articulated just such an appreciation of the critical role of multi-identity politics to labor's renewal.

Together, we are forging a common agenda to build the U.S. labor movement, to strengthen coalitions between unions and communities of color, to organize the unorganized, . . . to advance civil rights, to defend affirmative action and immigrant rights, and to build a better future for all working people.

Women and people of color are increasingly the growing majority in the workplace today. We are gathered today to pledge our support to build a labor movement that embraces diversity as its strength. Women, people of color and young people represent the future and hope of the U.S. labor movement. While we are committed to defend affirmative action in the workplace, we are also committed to promote affirmative action within the labor movement.[4]

Unfortunately, in the labor movement, multi-identity politics emerge most strongly in unionization and first-contract campaigns. Yet such a moral mission is not (and should not be considered) the unique property of initial campaigns. It can be invoked in later union struggles, and doing so, argues organizer and political scientist Janice Fine, is critical to labor's comeback:

Why is it then, that even though organized labor in America has championed broad issues of social welfare and social justice, fought consistently for the underprivileged, and often succeeded in passing laws that chiefly benefited workers not covered under collective bargaining agreements, labor is still perceived as a special interest group by many? No matter how hard labor fights for the minimum wage in Congress, or the living wage in city councils, if unions define their issues narrowly at contract time, they contradict their own broader messages. The entire labor movement, the AFL-CIO and international local unions, must frame issues in general interest or social justice terms as opposed to narrow, special interest terms—not only when organizing or doing politics but also during collective bargaining. (1998, 136)

Part of what is at stake in each union campaign is the potential for defining the labor movement. While union activists weigh the risks of different identity practices, they must consider the potential for extending the labor movement's reach into new communities and new arenas of social justice. When at Columbia, despite the demands around which the union has consistently fought, so many participants who were already committed to fighting gender and race injustice did not see their union as a vehicle for these changes, then we see the depth of the challenge of creating multi-identity politics. We also have to ask whether the movement is doing the tilling but not bringing in the harvest it might. Are victories accruing and taking on as large a meaning as they might? Are we forging the much-needed connections between movements?

Even campaigns that fail in their short-term mission can lay the groundwork for future successes, future coalitions—rooted in the trust that grows out of multi-identity politics. Veterans of the ultimately unsuccessful Hormel strike in Minnesota in 1985 created a democratic, participatory, justice-based organization that has continued to influence and support local labor struggles, including AFSCME's organizing of 2,300 clerical workers (93 percent women) at the University of Minnesota, and the strike of the Hotel Employees and Restaurant Employees Local 17 (consisting of 1,500 workers, many of them immigrants, speaking seventeen different languages).[5] Out of the "failed" Hormel strike came an annual conference called "Meeting the Challenge." It "features local union activists from different parts of the country, women and men who are transforming their local unions into models of democracy and participation, who are fighting against racism and sexism, organizing the unorganized, building community coalitions, and creating cultural expressions for the labor movement" (Rachleff 2000).

Clearly, what is also at stake in each union campaign is empowerment and movement building. Have the members been through an engaging participatory process that nurtured their activism and leadership potential? Did the union's structure and culture bridge the divide between "we" (the members) and "they" (the leaders), thus making the union something that people felt they *belonged* to and could, as much as they chose, bring multiple identities to? Did they experience their campaign as a way to work for all kinds of justice? Did they build bridges to other social movements and lay the groundwork for future political work? Recall that there were those at Columbia who defined themselves as supporters of the women's movement, some specifically as feminists, and some who described a desire to participate in women's activism. When they did not see any connection between their own union activism and women's activism, an important opportunity was lost. Nurturing this multiracial "trade union feminism" is part of the labor movement task (Milkman 1985, 309).

Labor leader Bill Fletcher Jr., writing on the electoral popularity of white supremacist David Duke in the early 1990s, argued:

> To the extent that labor progressives attempt to find issues which are not "divisive," i.e., don't touch on matters of race, gender and ethnicity, we will continue to miss the mark. . . . This is the vantage point we must take on labor's future. Trade unionism must speak to the totality of problems

facing our members and the working class as a whole. It must be the haven of the dispossessed. It must be the haven for Chicanos fighting for land and political power. It must be a home for Asian immigrants working in the new sweatshops. . . .

Most important, we must rebuild its relevance in the minds of those we seek to serve by addressing the concerns and anger which they feel. (1992, 11–12)

While social change activists have little control over the conditions shaping our struggles, we do have control over a range of our own practices. All of us stakeholders inside or outside unions hope for dramatic change in the working lives of working people, especially workers of color and/or women, not only at these specific institutions, but more broadly in this country. We want union campaigns to be vehicles of the most dramatic change they can be. We know that bringing about justice in this country requires this: fully mobilized groups, and coalitions among oppressed groups and their supporters.

Strategic Questions Facing the Left

The Left is, by most accounts, in trouble. We are a series of fragmented, isolated movements that have, for the most part, not been able to generate a common agenda. This is the context of the strategic debate on the Left about the wisdom of identity politics and whether they constitute a "political blind alley" as the basis of progressive organizing, a "politic that contains the seeds of its own limitations" (Lusane 1996, 2; Collins 1998, 52).

How do we support the identity-based struggles for justice in schools, the workplace, state policy, health care, the media, and other sites, and construct a political force strong enough to win against the corporate, right-wing, and repressive government policy? At the same time, how do we avoid the recurrent common-denominator strategy that, in the name of "unity" and the fictitious assertion that "we all have the same problem," has sacrificed the needs of the least-privileged groups (Anner 1996, 9)?

There is a constant discussion about the need to link movements and build coalitions. Identity practices offer a particularization of this task, a way to target these efforts. In any movement, developing multi-identity practices allows us to build such alliances. And it is important to remember that these alliances can be made not just out there but also in here, that is, *within* each particular campaign.

It is here, I'd argue, rather than critiquing the "energy devoted to cultivating difference," that we can change what Todd Gitlin (as well as other critics of identity politics) calls an "imbalance between the politics of group assertion and the politics of commonality" (1997, 153). Rather than calling for an end to identity politics, activist and writer John Anner suggests an alternative path for the Left: "A reinvigorated social justice Movement with a capital 'm' will have to develop mechanisms of reconnecting identity politics with class issues" (1996, 11). He looks to "community and labor organizing revitalized by identity politics, and a new politics of identity that strives for identification with other communities of interest and especially with the poor and the working class" (12).

One challenge for social movements striving for multi-identity politics is that, as Stanley Aronowitz and Todd Gitlin have argued, the labor movement is not much considered in current discussions of identity politics, and that class has often dropped out of the discourse. The middle-class myth that dominates U.S. culture profoundly obscures the realities of our class relations (Navarro 1992, cover page). As Aronowitz notes, "Class is often part of the political vocabulary of actors who, nevertheless, are impelled to use a different language" (1992, 43–44). Within the labor movement, however, the problem is inverted: race and gender are often part of the vocabulary, but activists are impelled to use the language of class or union—often to the point of invisibilizing and undercutting antiracist, antisexist agendas for which unions may even be engaged in fighting.

Class must be reinserted in a Left agenda, just as race and gender (and sexuality) justice needs to be inserted at the center of labor's agenda. Avoiding the false polarities and opposition of "new" (gender, race, sexuality, environmental) and "old" (labor) social movements, with the former labeled "cultural" or "way of life" and the latter "material" or "social justice," would be helpful. Sexism and racism are as fundamental to the restructuring and operation of capitalism as are the dynamics of globalization, corporate buyouts, deregulation, new technology, and privatization. Dealing with gender and race is a class project; it is material, and it is about social justice.

National labor leadership has acknowledged that such a perspective is critical to labor's future, and labor's future is critical to the Left's future. "Labor is probably the most fruitful area in which to test the potential of a politics beyond segmented identity," argues Gitlin (1997, 162). Chen and Wong concur: "The labor movement is one of the few social forces with the capacity to advance an agenda of multiracial [and I'd add gender] unity and progressive social change" (1998, 201). David Croteau's study of class dynamics in social movement participation points to the particularly important role of the labor movement in revitalizing a broad-based progressive agenda.

Working people cannot be expected to use "new" social movements as a base for their political activity. Middle-class efforts to diversify their groups by trying to bring working people into existing organizations are misdirected . . . the workplace continues to offer great opportunity as a site for organization and mobilization. . . . The revitalization of labor unions, therefore, must be seen as a key component of a left strategy for encouraging working-class empowerment. (1995, 218, 211)

This study of the 1991–1992 Columbia contract battle, as well as the stories of Harvard's and Yale's organizing campaigns, supports the claim that the future of the Left and labor are entwined. Each of these struggles has, although in different ways, folded into its unionism fundamental challenges to labor market and workplace sexism and racism. Each has fashioned union structures and cultures that reflect its predominantly female and, at Columbia, African American and Latino(a) membership. At the same time, contrary to popular wisdom, against fierce antiunion employers, each evidenced impressive mobilization and solidarity. Each has been strengthened by its multi-injustice politics. Each offers us important lessons of the potential of multi-injustice politics for labor, and for the broader Left, as well.

We organize in a climate not friendly to such endeavors. Critics of multiculturalism advance the right-wing project of "embrac[ing] the myth of a de-differentiated society in order better to impose it upon others" (Melucci 1989, 221). The labor movement, the women's movement(s), and black, Hispanic, and other race-based liberation movements have fallen on hard times. Each, to some extent, has experienced a backlash and has been portrayed as narrow, selfish, too demanding, ineffectual, and past its heyday. Each must broaden its base and regain status as moral champion of a group legitimately fighting for inclusion, equality, and social transformation.

The funeral for the single-identity movement is more than overdue. "How, from the multiplicity of voices," asked Spelman, "will a single one be shaped?" (1998, 15). We need to see each movement itself, internally, as a coalition, a chorus for which there is no quintessential soloist.

Such a concept also helps to move us beyond the popular "either/or," "class or race," "race or gender" conceptions that have so predominated in theoretical, policy, and popular discourse. We need to see each movement as consisting of an internal (rainbow) coalition—of particular and overlapping, and sometimes conflicting, interest groups. Only in such a way do we begin to move beyond the balkanization of a Left agenda.

The fragmentation of the Left, and the carnage of identity struggles gone berserk in Eastern Europe, Africa, and around the globe, form a big pull to say "enough" to identity politics. But the need to meet the just challenges of long-oppressed communities continues. It will not go away, and as activists committed to all kinds of social justice, we are glad of it. "Enough" is not really an option.

John Edgar Wideman's words reminded us at the outset of this journey that we must neither ignore nor focus exclusively on categories such as race, class, and gender.

> If each of us chooses solely on the basis of color or race, then we are doomed. If each of us chooses to pretend that race and gender and class don't exist, or that somehow being American and being a part of this experiment in democracy exempts us from paying attention to those very real categories, or at least the reality that they manifest, then we are also doomed. (1992)

Knitting together what are now fragmented progressive movements is a priority. But there is no vacation, no hiatus from the fight for diversity and justice. Each task is challenging, as is finding the balance between them.

Cornel West suggests in *Race Matters* that "moral reasoning," rather than "racial reasoning," should guide black activism. His model should be useful to other activists, as well, because although it embraces identity, it is not confined to it. Moral reasoning could help many of us take on Wideman's challenge to neither ignore nor uniquely embrace single identities. Rooted in "mature black identity, coalition strategy, and black cultural democracy," moral reasoning rises above an "atavistic defense of blackness that mirrors the increasing xenophobia in American life" and instead produces a vision of what is fair, just, and democratic. "Where there is no vision," West writes, "the people perish; where there is no framework of moral reasoning, the people close ranks in a war of all against all" (1993, 31). The successes of labor groups moving beyond lowest-common-denominator politics suggest that coalitions form around the scaffolding of the moral mission of fighting injustice, of fighting for "fundamental social change for all who suffer from socially induced misery" (46).

"Difference," writes Audre Lorde, "must be not merely tolerated. . . . Within the interdependence of mutual (nondominant) difference lies that security which enables us to descend into the chaos of knowledge and return with true visions of our future, along with the concomitant power to effect those changes which can bring that future into being. Difference is that raw and powerful connection from which our personal [and I would add: collective] power is forged" (1984, 111–12).

Bernice Johnson Reagon affirms how very hard, but how very necessary, this effort is. "You don't go into coalition because you just *like* it. The only reason you would consider trying to team up with somebody who could possibly kill you, is because that's the only way you can figure you can stay alive" (1992, 504). Said Barbara Smith, in a passionate argument about the future of the gay and lesbian movement, "If the gay movement ultimately wants to make a real difference, as opposed to settling for handouts, it must consider creating a multi-issue revolutionary agenda. *This is not about political correctness, it's about winning*" (1993, 16; italics mine).

To survive, the labor movement and other movements must shape themselves as vehicles for addressing multiple kinds of injustice. Conscious attention to identity practices, jettisoning our ideas of single-movement identities, and adopting an internal coalition or chorus conception of social movements will begin to move us beyond the balkanization of a progressive agenda. The revitalization, if not the survival, of the labor movement and other social movements depends on it.

Methodological Issues in Social Research

The study of a social movement in the process of unfolding makes for rich, exciting, and fulfilling research. It also makes for a particular set of methodological issues. In this closing section, I will review my data collection strategy and consider the issues and dilemmas associated with such an effort.

Study Design

Between April 1991 and May 1992, I worked with and studied the Columbia clerical union. In heated periods of activism, I lived in New York on an ongoing basis. In less intense times, I commuted back and forth from Boston, for varying intervals. In-depth interviews occurred in clusters at the less frenetic times in the campaign, and in the two months following its conclusion.

I had not expected to spend so much time at Columbia. What I had planned to be two or three quick weeks of fieldwork in October turned into the whole fall, and then into January, February, and March. Concretely, this meant I had to reshape the study design. I had intended to compare three equally developed cases—Columbia, Harvard, and Yale—which would have allowed a fuller examination of alternative identity practices, as well as the impact of differing structural conditions. Time constraints made this impossible. But of course there were gains. As David Croteau (1995) notes of the fieldwork for his study of class issues in social movement culture and participation, there is insight that comes only with extended fieldwork. I was able to pursue questions about race silence, for example, by way of pointing to specific occurrences in the campaign, about which I would have had no idea had it not been for the fieldwork. My extensive fieldwork was especially useful in crossing class and race boundaries, building trust with union members, and developing a multilayered understanding of events.

My research was quite different than my picture of those heroic textbook field-workers who went to their field sites, immersed themselves, and stayed. None of this back and forth to home—loved ones and sociology mates every two or three weeks. Maybe that's just my fantasy of their experience, those classic field-worker men. In any event, I found a usefulness to the back and forth, in and out. Each transition offered an important opportunity to regain focus: what had become naturalized in the setting that at first was striking? How had the questions shifted in this context? For me, this was a good addition to the field-worker's toolbox.

My location at the union office, the center of the campaign, was simultaneously enabling and limiting. It was the most tenable location for me: my entry to Columbia was through the union staff. It allowed me complete access to all levels of union events. I was generously afforded access few would be allowed. Yet my location had its drawbacks. I had to make sure I was not overly identified with "the union" in the eyes of members. I also didn't have access to work site cultures that I would have had if I had located myself as a participant-observer in a few offices.[1] Overall, the research location I occupied worked well to allow me to examine the issues I had identified. I consider myself quite lucky.

Issues in Studying Collective Identity

In *Cultures of Solidarity*, Rick Fantasia (1988) argues that questions of consciousness must be studied collectively, and in the context of mobilization. He points out that such practice is consistent with the Marxist notion of "consciousness in association": consciousness is not merely a property of individuals but a process that occurs in collective contexts, including labor struggles. This method is in sharp contrast to the usual static, decontextualized questionnaires or in-depth interviews by which such matters have more normally been approached. As Fantasia further notes, crisis moments (such as the height of collective action) can be particularly transforming (3–24).

Like other matters of definition, collective identity is a contest. So collective identity, too, must be studied by methods that best capture development, change, and conflict. This created two issues.

First, while hardly unique to social movements, there is the problem of the research altering the very phenomenon it is investigating. This problem assumed a particular shape in this study. Because collective identity is an interactional product, and because I conducted many of my interviews while the campaign was still in process, I became acutely aware that my interviews constituted a potential intervention in the identity construction process. The best, I concluded, that I could do was to keep good track of my conversations and actions and note any consequences. A significant portion (I'd estimate 40 percent) of each interview revolved around categories of gender and race, which were largely unused in union conversations. While some found my use of these categories a bit strange or confused, most interviewees seemed largely unaffected. On a few occasions, there was a direct impact. Recall Calvin, who on the day after our interview conversation stood up in a large membership meeting and made the case for the next strike on race and gender justice terms. There was the union leader who made a point of relaying this event to me, as part of our continuing discussion of these issues. Three other activists initiated follow-up conversations with me about the issue of racial justice, although I have no evidence that it impacted their actions during the campaign.

Second, as a sociologist, I've certainly had my exposure to the concept of "triangulation" (i.e., using multiple data sources), yet I know I never comprehended its full import. The study of participants making meaning of collective resistance, I came to understand, is critically dependent on such a data collection strategy. As we have seen, collective identity is constructed at individual and collective levels of action. Individuals draw on differing preexistent ideologies, cultural resources, and life experiences, as well as campaign events, to differently construct meaning for their activism. A movement forges its identity in a range of identity practices, and the definition of the movement may vary among identity practices. Multiple data sources provided critical entry into these differing, and often conflicting, elements of the process of identity construction. Of course, I had no idea of this when I began.

As it turned out, some of the most interesting findings of this study lie in the discrepancies between data drawn from different sources. Collective identity construction varied among formal documents, daily practices, and members' meanings accessed in interviews. Identity construction also varied within each of these data sources, as well. Documents for public consumption were more framed in a gender and race identity explicit manner than those for internal member consumption. All of this suggests that in the study of collective identity, data collection needs to come from a variety of sources: in this study, fieldwork, in-depth interviews, and document content analysis.

The sharp disparity in findings among various data sources brings home a sobering lesson about the study of social movements. Not infrequently, labor and other social movement research by academics consists of spending a short time with a movement group, interviewing leaders and perhaps a few selected rank and filers, and reviewing documents. This makes sense, as fieldwork is extremely time intensive. Standpoint theory requires we acknowledge the constructed and partial nature of all accounts. Yet the variation in identity accessed by data sources suggests that accounts based on such modest data collection are even more partial than we might have imagined. This study carries no exemption. The Harvard clericals discussion is based on such a data collection strategy, and the Yale case is based on the use of secondary sources (although each of these was produced by participant-observers) with a few supplemental interviews.

Conflicts in Activist Research

I long ago walked away from the idol of "neutral" or "detached" research, agreeing with those who argue that social movement scholarship is actually sharpened, rather than compromised, by activist engagement (Bookman and Morgan 1988, ix). There were days when the activist and academic agendas came together effortlessly and seamlessly. The Friday afternoon, traffic-stopping midtown demonstration at the offices of one of the university trustees was one such occasion. Being packed in at membership meetings, witnessing heated debates, made for others. Another was sitting at 2 A.M. in the lounge of a university building as the top-level negotiations took place. In our "negotiations hotel," with sounds of sleep breathing in the background, stories of summer fishing adventures passed among those still awake. Even later, there were conversations about the echoes of late nights at sit-ins in decades gone by, and what such activist commitments mean in a person's life. There were the times of being a knowledgeable listener while those on the front lines sorted out their thoughts and feelings about a tough social movement campaign. At all these times, the activist and the research agendas came together with ease.

Yet this participant observing, this activist scholarship, is not without its intense difficulties. Many of these are (merely) the classic issues of fieldwork particularized to a social movement context. Especially when I shifted my research agenda onto the front burner, the conflicts screeched like a kettle at rapid boil.

Limiting Participation

Establishing a role—or a fluid collection of roles on the participant-observer continuum—is a recurrent issue of fieldwork. With the research site being a social movement, these took a particular shape. Day to day, I helped out in the office, doing clerical and other support tasks. Sometimes this included phone calls to members about a particular event ("I'm helping out in the office, and x union staffer asked me to give you a call"). The majority of my time working for the union was spent working with the faculty and graduate student support committee. This task brought me access to a range of union meetings, public and private: building meetings, picket captain meetings, negotiating committee meetings, and strategy sessions of the officers and staff. It also kept my agency, that is, my union support work, largely away from members. To those who knew, I was a certified union supporter who was doing research for a "future book." Others knew me as one of the people who was coordinating the relocation of classes (450 plus) for the strike. Others just knew me to be someone who was around, helped out in the office, and was friendly with people they knew and liked in the union.

I was committed to avoiding speaking in union meetings, or "organizing," that is, selling any pitch to members. It felt important to me that in union events, I not be seen as anyone trying to move an agenda forward. I did not want to be seen as much beyond a helpful, supportive person. I was there to learn from the members' knowledge, and I wanted not to be seen in ways that would compromise my researcher identity. Mostly I just endured the uncomfortable silence and glances when volunteers were desperately needed at staff meetings and I was unable to step forward. Occasionally, I declined a specific request by the staff to take on a particular task. One unfortunate consequence of this effort to avoid speaking parts, I now realize, was that it contributed to an undercommunication to members of the faculty support committee, which was especially important in a disheartened period of the struggle. In terms of the research, however, this may have been just as well, as I would have emphasized identity themes that I knew appealed to the faculty, but that other union activists would not have emphasized.

Pronouns offer an interesting example of my conflicted status. In the interviews, after intense months of working together, was "we" too presumptuous? Wouldn't it obscure my researcher role? Was "you" too objectifying and distancing? I equivocated: I'd avoid pronouns and say "the union." It made for awkward sentences.

There were practical problems as well in balancing the movement and research tasks. Which agenda takes priority when you can't be in two places at one time? In the height of movement mobilization, the critical support work and critical research moments occur at the same time. The constant balancing act that I successfully and quietly managed in moderately crazy times became impossible at the height of the struggle.

Activist and Researcher: From Which Self Do I Speak?

In the weeks following the strike period, I shifted my time from union support work to interviewing. I found myself in heightened conflict, which my field notes from December 1991 well capture.

Sitting in the coffee shops, I'm reasonably successful creating some distance from my activist role. I explain why I'd been here all along, my background, and refer to myself as "helping out in the office" in exchange for doing this research. It's good enough, craving as folks are to thrash it out with someone. And me, I'm the closest thing they've seen in these poststrike weeks to someone at the center of the campaign. They're deep into the hot issues of the moment before I can even get out a question.

So what do I do with their criticisms with which I agree? "I'm so frustrated, they had this great opportunity with that discrimination letter—I know people in the black community, the Hispanic community would support us." "They're not capitalizing on the momentum." "We were up so high, and now..."

I am here as researcher, not staffer. Yet folks don't just want to say their piece; they want to hear a response. Besides the issue of impacting the research, it's too dangerous: any word I, recognized girl from the office, say could be repeated anywhere, everywhere. Or what about the points they raise that I don't agree with, really misperceptions, that I have the information to clear up in a snap?

What of the hard personal struggles, lives dislocated? "The boundaries got all broken down," says Allison. Personal strength and defiance discovered out on the battle lines are now inappropriate leftovers in the regular "subordinate" "class" relations in the offices, as she calls them. What of the raw relations with coworkers, once tight friends and comrades, now backbiting or icing? One picket captain speaks of the contrast between what her business school textbooks and professors describe as the individualism and competition supposedly typical of capitalism versus her lived experience of solidarity and what she terms "socialism." "The union shouldn't fill our head with those expectations," Allison says, "because when we go back to work, we see it can't be." Telling a good listener is okay, but a pale substitute for the words I can say, as friend, activist. This, too, is part of organizing—the individual support, nurturing, and leadership development that organizers do. Everyone else is too busy, keeping the negotiations, the strike benefits, the grievances, the plans for the holiday party going. It is I, now researcher, who sits here. Mostly silent.

I smile sympathetically. I acknowledge how hard it is, say I am sorry for the pain. I share small snippets of my own organizing experience. But I do not spend thirty or forty-five minutes working the issues through. I have promised confidentiality to my interviewees, which rules out my raising these points with the union staff. I suggest to these members that they talk to one of the union leaders, call them for lunch or coffee, tell them their concerns, ideas, and criticisms. It is the best compromise I can find on the spot, but it pains me.[2]

Confidentiality versus the Movement's Need to Know

I promised confidentiality and knew it was sacred. There was no messing around, for principle, and in fear of what it would do to my remaining research. I explained and I evaded when the union staff asked me questions about my interviews. As an activist, I knew how badly union leaders need to know what folks are thinking and saying, especially at this moment of conflict. And ironically, several members, like Allison, quoted earlier, would have been happier if I had said her piece for her. I tried in my way, at another time, another day, in another context, to pass the information on: in the context of a discussion of what people are feeling (not attached to any specific person), or some low-key suggestion that staff and leaders talk to a particular member, timed when that thought reasonably appeared to emerge in some other context, and I never revealed its true origin. So deflected, no one paid the comments much mind.

To Push or Not to Push: Instrumentalizing Relationships

People who aren't used to being interviewed sometimes get nervous about it. I reminded myself of my task as a reporter. The interviewer pushes gently, but she pushes past discomfort to make the interview happen. She needs the interview; time is limited. People's doubts drop away when they get started. It's its own kind of praise to know that you are important to someone's study. As the friend and coactivist, however, I had trouble when I saw someone feeling very stressed by the idea of doing an interview they had earlier agreed to do. It felt like a choice between instrumentality and the integrity of the relationship and caring about the other person. Sometimes, though, my not pushing was also about instrumentality: I didn't want to ruin the relationship. I needed to continue to interact with this person daily in the fieldwork setting.

Posing the Research Question: Whose Problem?

The question of whose definition of the problem was being pursued was one of the most significant, challenging issues. While I was formulating this project, I spent a good deal of time talking with labor and community activists. The questions at the heart of this study resonated for many of them and seemed valid and important. They helped me shape that question and look for cases. In my original discussion with Columbia union leaders, it seemed that my central research question was a shared priority. This was as I had hoped.

In my first background interview, one leader recounted a pivotal question posed by a leading black activist before the 1985 strike. Would a membership that was half white be willing to go on strike for gains that would go disproportionately to workers of color to deal with past discrimination? As she recounted, they didn't know and were delighted to find the answer was yes. This question, and the issues it sits atop, confirmed Columbia to be an important case for me.

My intent was to give voice to underrepresented experiences, as Ann Bookman and Sandra Morgen describe of their collection of working-class women's struggles:

> Let working-class women speak in their own voices about their political experiences. Like oral history, this methodology expresses a commitment to letting those who make history be directly involved in the creation of the historical record, an opportunity too often reserved for those with economic and political power. (1988, ix–x)

Yet as the campaign heated up, paths diverged. Activists would certainly list the important issues of the strike as their novel in-and-out strike strategy, winning health care demands in an unfavorable period, and strategies for fighting a tough antiunion opponent like Columbia. Some would raise the inherent tensions in democratic unionism as a key problem for investigation. But the issues of gender and race, as we've heard, were not seen as central by most members and leaders.

I considered whether my framing of the questions was wrong. As sociologist Shula Reinharz has said, "You have to be willing to hear what someone is saying, even when it violates your expectations or threatens our interests. In other words, *if you want someone to tell it like it is, you have to hear it like it is*."[3] Anthony Giddens makes a similar case, arguing, "All social actors . . . have [at least] some degree of penetration of the social forces which oppress them."[4] Listening to Columbia workers and leaders had indeed shifted my thinking on these issues in significant ways. Yet posing the question of how race and gender had become politically meaningful (or not) continued to seem valid and important. Some participants' comments about race silence and others' desires for gender framing that they had found lacking also validated the utility of the question I was pursuing. My conversations with Columbia union activists continued at the end of the project, as well, when a small group of leaders read my manuscript-in-progress and gave me their feedback. These conversations—including avid disagreements with points in my argument—provided me with additional insights and opportunities to understand the meaning participants made of their contract battle.

Part of the task of sociology is to problematize the taken-for-granted, naturalized elements of everyday life, leading to naming that which is yet nameless. But I had hoped for a common agenda. Participant action research offers many strengths to scholars and activists working together. I remain skeptical that it would work well for something as unconscious as collective identity, unless the movement were for some reason in a period of conscious attention to issues of "diversity," which would be a rich but rather atypical case.

The discrepancy between my question and the union's own discourse allowed me no choice but, as Michelle Fine puts it, "to come clean, to re-insert self-consciously my interpretive self into my writings" (1992, 218). Here her writing on methodology has been helpful. Fine offers a typology of three stances researchers can take regarding their own location in their research: ventriloquy, voices, and activism. Fine argues that voices—a stance in which the researcher allows the voices of those she studies to predominate—are a decided improvement over ventriloquy, in which the researcher "tells Truth, [and] has no gender, race, class, or stance" (212). However:

> There is often a subtle slide toward romantic, uncritical, and uneven handling and a stable refusal by researchers to explicate our own stances and relations to these voices. As such researchers mystify the ways in which we select, use, and exploit voices. That we use them, I am delighted. That we fail to articulate how, how not, and within what limits is a failure of methodology and a flight from our own political responsibilities to tell tough, critical, and confusing stories about the ideological and discursive patterns of inequitable power arrangements. (219–20)

While I had imagined myself in the "voices" stance, I came to see its limits and found my place in my research better described by what Fine calls "activism." "Activist research projects seek to unearth, interrupt, and open new frames for intellectual and political theory and change. Researchers critique what seems natural, spin images of what's possible, and engage in questions of how to move from here to there" (219–20).

Whose Story Can I Tell?

This is a question of theory, method, and epistemology at the heart of this study. Although alliances are critical, as standpoint theory suggests, rarely, if ever, does one completely escape one's social location. I was a white professional-class woman in a multiracial labor struggle, wanting to talk about issues of race, gender, class, identity, and activism. It is a well-known story. In selecting a case, on the one side, I risked replicating the omission by white professional-class colleagues who point out that their study will focus on high-paid industrial unionized white men. Sorry, no women, no people of color in what they nonetheless expect us to see as a totally adequate discussion of class consciousness. On the other side, I cringe and watch others cringe as yet another race- and class-distorted telling of someone else's story by a white professional-class researcher comes by. As Margaret Andersen poses the question, "How can White scholars study those who have been historically subordinated without further producing sociological accounts distorted by the political economy of race, class, and gender?" (1997, 71).

In interviews, talk across class and race is not neutral. At the very least it can be awkward: what will be said between an African American person (union member) and a Jewish person (interviewer asking about race at Columbia) during the Crown Heights period? Speaking can be risky (personally, collectively), and not necessarily worthwhile. Speaking, I understand, is differentially privileged in a stratified society. Silence, points out Patricia Hill Collins, is often the best option, with consciousness the only free space, the only form of resistance that is viable (1990, 92). Just as several members recounted in interviews that speaking about race at union meetings was outside the boundaries (their own, the culture of the organization), why would it be any more likely in an interview?

As time went on, I came to be more comfortable with acknowledging this issue of cross-race and cross-class talk. "I know it may be awkward" or "this may be something that you don't feel comfortable talking about with a white person," I came to say. People often responded with discussions about how it was different talking to me, how they felt comfortable, and how this wasn't an issue. These could, of course, be the obligatory disclaimers. Probably in some cases they were. Yet I believe that many months of participating in the union campaign, of having been seen as a trustworthy activist, person, friend, and of being lucky enough to be friends with their friends facilitated an openness in our interviews. My decade as a service and clerical worker activist in Boston hospitals may also have helped create an intimacy, a bond based on shared experience. This work history also attuned me to some of the finer dynamics within large, internally segmented workplaces such as hospitals and universities. In the end, though, I cannot but think, as Margaret Andersen notes of her cross-race and -class research, "I know that my understanding... will always be partial, incomplete, and distorted" (1997, 77).

In the future, team research may offer help with this and other dilemmas I've raised in this discussion. As in much "diversity" training for organizations, a multiracial/class/gender team could help in dealing with such issues. Second, a team would allow for different locations in the organization's center and periphery and may make possible a study design of several researchers intensively following a union struggle through the experience of workers in different (department, class fraction) locations in a large workforce. This would also potentially allow researchers to study the interaction among work site problems, informal work site cultures, and the formal union organization or among workers' home, work, and union experiences. In such a team design, however, researchers would have to be careful to avoid talking more to each other than to union members and would also have increased issues of shaping the social reality they had come to study.

In the meantime, with awareness of these issues and limitations, I tell this story of a social movement confronting the challenge of multi-injustice politics. Says Gloria Yamato, to "whites who want to be allies to people of color," "assume that you are needed and capable of being a good ally. Know that you'll make mistakes and commit yourself to correcting them and continuing on as an ally" (1990, 23–24). Written analyses of social movement struggles are few, as activists are always in the process of bringing the wisdom learned in one conflict to bear on the next pressing challenges. I will hope that this account brings forth others that will debate, correct, sharpen, or amplify the lessons we can take from this social movement mobilization.

The Balancing Footwork of an Activist-Scholar

For the most part, I know there is no perfect resolution to the conflicts I experienced in social movement participant observation. Just as there is an inherent tension in leadership between leading (pushing a direction) and being the facilitator of democracy, I accept that these conflicts are an inherent part of the process of activist research. It is a developing acceptance that there is no solving these dilemmas, and the goal is merely finding an acceptable balance point.

Mostly it feels like hiking along a mountain ridge, precipitous drops on either side, and needing to set one foot in front of the other, carefully, to make my way along. This is not to deny that there are times when the trail opens to beautiful meadows, where the walking requires no thought. These are the days when the activist's and the scholar's agendas are one. But the balancing footwork on the ridge is an inevitable, inescapable part of the journey.

Here the problem of methods is quite similar to the substantive problem. Like the core dilemma of identity politics, these are intractable, enduring issues. For this, full awareness of the opportunities and dangers on both sides, and a commitment to honoring both of them, seem to be the only preparation and advice.

Notes

Introduction

1. See Gitlin 1995, 154, citing Freud's "the narcissism of small differences."

2. Collins 1998; Crenshaw 1989, 1992, 1994. Also see King (1990), who uses the term "multiplicity," and Baca Zinn and Dill (1996), who use "multiracial feminism."

3. Throughout this book, I use the terms "inequality" and "injustice." I use them in their fullest sense of what activists and academics would refer to as "domination" or "oppression," including institutional, cultural (ideological), and individual levels. While "inequality" and "injustice" are often popularly understood in more narrow terms of individual, legal, or economic discrimination, they are popularly accessible in a way that the others are off-putting to a nonacademic audience.

4. See chapter 8 for discussion.

5. Rather than "difference," a multi-injustice approach speaks of domination— systemic injustice on institutional, cultural, and individual levels—and works to transform it.

6. Mantsios 1998, 65. By 1999, labor density was at 13.9 percent (37.3 percent for the public sector, and 9.4 percent for the private sector). "Union Members Summary," 19 January 2000, Washington, D.C.: Bureau of Labor Force Statistics, archived at ftp://ftp.bls.gov/pub/news.release/history/union2.0127200.news.

7. Naming, we have come to realize, is an important part of resistance struggles. In interviewing, I used the term "minority" whenever workers themselves used it. In writing this book, I have avoided the word because I strongly feel that in public debates, the term "minority" maintains the marginal, dominated position of people of color and is often associated with a minimizing of their oppression. Within

the Columbia workforce, in many American cities, in the state of California, and across the globe, the term is also factually inaccurate. I use the term "people of color" despite its awkwardness and its own problems of falsely treating a range of distinct groups as one unified, homogeneous whole. I use "Latino/a" and "Hispanic," "African American" and "black," interchangeably, although each has come to have different meanings to relevant political actors. As psychologist Beverly Tatum has pointed out, "black" is the more inclusive term, especially for Afro-Caribbeans (Tatum 1997, 15). To emphasize the intersectional nature of race and gender, I sometimes speak of women *and/or* people of color.

8. "More women work in clerical and administrative jobs than in any other kind of paid employment, including nearly 31 percent of paid women workers in 1992, part of a total of 14 million administrative workers" (Eaton 1996, 293).

9. Following a 1992 union reorganization, District 65/UAW ceased to exist as a distinct entity and was restructured within the UAW. The Columbia local is now part of TOP (Technical, Office, and Professional) Local 2110, UAW. Because the union was identified by its name, District 65, during the period of this struggle, I have continued to so address it in this study.

10. Thanks to Charlotte Ryan of the Boston College Media Research and Action Project for this understanding.

11. Thanks to Nancy Whittier for this insight.

12. Kimeldorf 1999, 153–54, 208 n. 7, drawing on Raymond Williams, as quoted by Ellen Meiksins Wood. Thanks to Charlotte Ryan, Boston College Media and Action Project, for bringing Kimeldorf's use of this concept to my attention.

13. "Union Maids" is a catchy union song, popular in the CIO organizing of the 1930s and 1940s.

14. Dill 1987, 205, speaking about political identity among black women.

15. The few discussions that occurred were in meetings of the negotiating committee.

16. Crown Heights is the Brooklyn neighborhood where in August 1991, racial tensions exploded into riots after an African American boy was killed by a car in a Hasidic rabbi's motorcade. In retaliation, a Hasidic Jewish student was slain by African Americans. In the fall of 1991, Clarence Thomas—an African American conservative appointed by George Bush to the Supreme Court—faced charges of sexual harassment during his confirmation hearings. Highly televised proceedings of the Senate Judiciary Committee considered the charges by Anita Hill, an African American woman who had previously worked for him at the Equal Employment Opportunity Commission and the Department of Education.

17. "In the loosest sense," Gitlin says, "[identity politics] applies to the assumption that members of a group should band together to pursue their common interest." Gitlin says he is addressing what he calls identity politics in "its strictest

sense," that is, the assumption that "the group's identity is the only, or the over-whelming, motivating force for political action" (1997, 153).

18. Even on campuses, the fights have been material as well, such as recruiting more diverse faculty or, as at Columbia, maintaining "need-blind admissions," as an issue of student diversity. See chapter 1.

19. See chapter 4.

20. Social movements rooted in class-based identity are commonly called union or Left politics. Sociologist Craig Calhoun notes, "In the early nineteenth century, labor movements were engaged in identity politics, presenting the case that 'worker' was an identity deserving of legitimacy, calling for solidarity among those sharing this identity, demanding their inclusion in the polity, and so forth" (1994, 22).

21. In a heated debate in the *Nation* in 1998, Eric Alterman praised the Campaign for a Living Wage at the University of Virginia as an example of social justice politics, rather than identity politics. As Nelson Lichenstein replied, "The over-whelming majority of those at the bottom of the wage hierarchy are either white women or people of color. Thus 'economistic' wage campaigns are very much about 'identity' politics, which may help explain why our efforts have been endorsed by leaders of the Black Student Alliance, La Sociedad Latina and the campus chapter of NOW." See Alterman 1998, 10; and Lichenstein 1998, 2.

22. Anner 1996, 8–9. The same phenomenon of benefits to the most privileged subgroup is also true for advances among women, as well.

23. Race, class, and gender do not exhaust what Collins (1990) calls the matrix of domination. Studying sexuality, nationality, and ethnicity among blacks, Latina/os, and Asians, as well as whites, and class fraction differences among the working class would also add other important layers to our understanding of identity politics at this workplace. They remained beyond the scope of this study and make for fascinating subjects for additional case studies.

24. I also conducted a half-dozen background interviews with previous worker activists no longer working at the university.

25. Thus the sample selection categories were largely purposive—categories were created based on my knowledge of the union and my research question. Selecting individuals into those categories was largely a matter of availability. In categories such as "Latina activist at the level of the strike and negotiating committees" (race, gender, level of activism), where several respondents were readily available, I used random sampling (selecting names from a bowl).

26. These include a documentary of the early organizing and 1985 strike (Gold and Goldfarb 1986) and eight hours of unedited footage of the 1985 strike taken by a member.

27. My work experience included ten years as a hospital clerical worker and five years as a community tenant and welfare organizer, but my childhood family

and my status as a graduate student in sociology at Boston College clearly placed me as a professional.

28. In the 1970s, after years of black parents' seeking to remedy the inferior condition of black education in a highly segregated school system, federal courts ordered busing of the Boston Public Schools. Mass mobilization by white opponents to the plan led to many episodes of racial violence at the schools and in the community. See Green and Hunter 1974; Hampton and Fayer 1990; King 1981; Lukas 1985; and Useem 1980.

29. This included the Massachusetts General Hospital, Beth Israel Hospital, the Brigham and Women's Hospital, Children's Hospital, and Tufts New England Medical Center.

30. They were, to my knowledge, all trades*men*. I never saw or heard of any woman in any of the trades at MGH.

31. Also critical was the low level of commitment of resources by the unions— in terms of staffing levels and length of sponsorship of the organizing, especially in contrast to the resources of the hospital and the Harvard Medical School.

32. "Substitutionism" refers to the dynamic, however unintended, of organizers (particularly of more privileged class or race locations) "substituting" their own activism and leadership for that of the workforce or community whose organizing they attempt to facilitate.

33. See Bodman and Bailey 1980. Thanks to Laura Foner for her account of labor education work with the local after their victory.

1. "Mo' Money"

1. Glenn and Feldberg 1995, 263. According to the *Statistical Abstract of the United States,* 1999, this figure is basically unchanged: 24.2 percent of all employed women work as clericals (Washington, D.C.: U.S. Census Bureau, tables 654 and 675).

2. See Feldberg 1983. See Glenn and Feldberg 1995 for a review of arguments about the low unionization rates of clerical workers.

3. See Feldberg 1983 for discussion of the "union fever" among clericals from 1900 to 1930, and the role of the Women's Trade Union League (WTUL). See Strom 1985 for organizing efforts among clericals in the late 1930s and the 1940s under the United Office and Professional Workers of America (UOPWA).

4. For other studies of clerical organizing, see Goldberg 1983; Costello 1984, 1988; and Sacks 1988a, 1988b. For accounts of Harvard and Yale organizing, see chapter 7. For discussions of the issues, challenges, and progress of clerical organizing, see Glenn and Feldberg 1995; Gottfried and Fasenfest 1984; and Hurd 1989a, 1989b.

5. Glenn and Feldberg 1995, 278, from *Employment and Earnings,* January 1991, table 60.

6. Early history is based on (1) interviews with then District 65 UAW vice president Julie Kushner, then District 65 general organizer Maida Rosenstein, and a dozen other early activists; (2) an analysis of union documents and newspaper articles; (3) Richard Hurd's (1989a, 1989b) thorough and vivid account; and (4) Gold and Goldfarb's 1986 video of the early organizing and first strike.

7. For further discussion of District 65 white-collar organizing, including drives at Boston University and Harvard, see Hoerr 1997.

8. By the early 1990s, District 65's financial situation reached a state of complete crisis, including the collapse of its security plan, which provided medical benefits to union members through employer contributions. District 65 locals were restructured and absorbed into the UAW. The Columbia clerical local became UAW Local 2110. For further discussion of the District 65–UAW relation, see Hoerr 1997.

9. For another account of this early organizing, see Hurd 1989a.

10. Clericals, technicians, and service workers at the Columbia Medical School had also organized in the late 1960s with an independent union, which later affiliated with SEIU (Graduate Students Organization at Columbia University 1985).

11. Hurd notes success in university organizing is also due in part to public access of campuses and to geographic stability of the workplace, which rules out job flight (Hurd 1989a, 312).

12. Faculty Strike Support Committee letter, 21 October 1985.

13. Glenn and Feldberg's study of clerical workers found the lack of backup "in case of a dispute with management," as opposed to wages, to be the main reason clerical workers gave for why they considered unionization to be a good idea (1995, 278).

14. Stafford 1985, xii. See also Clara Rodriguez's study of New York City's Puerto Rican workers whose "representation in growth sectors, such as business and related professional services, finance and insurance, and real estate, was disproportionately low" (1989, 88).

15. Roberta Goldberg's study of clerical workers in Baltimore in the 1980s similarly noted that many activists were satisfied with their own job situations but participated in the organizing out of a desire to help others (1983, 90).

16. Columbia University argued to draw the boundaries of the potential union to include low-level supervisors. In December 1981 the labor board ruling agreed, and District 65 appealed.

17. Columbia Local District 65, "A Chronology of Our Union Drive," fall 1984; William Serrin, "Office Union Confident of Victory at Columbia," *New York Times,* 9 May 1983, B10.

18. Columbia Local District 65, "A Chronology of Our Union Drive," fall 1984.

19. Columbia Local District 65, "A Chronology of Our Union Drive," fall 1984; and Julie Kushner, interview by author, 24 May 1991.

20. For discussion of this movement see Hirsch 1990 and Graduate Students Organization at Columbia University 1985.

21. Following extensive statistical analysis and political debate, the fund was divided among 181 employees (Columbia Local District 65, "The People Who Make Columbia Work," fall 1988).

22. A union work/family committee had been organized well in advance of the contract campaign and decided on the idea of a child care subsidy as a priority issue. The $40,000 was shared among the quarter of the members who had children age twelve or younger (with proof of birth and/or custody).

23. Columbia Local, District 65, "Fair Play, Fair Pay," September 1991. This case went to arbitration, and a settlement was won as part of this contract.

24. Ibid.

25. For explanations and discussions of such job evaluation systems at the core of comparable worth efforts, see Acker 1989; Amott and Matthaei 1984; Feldberg 1987a; Steinberg and Haignere 1987.

26. Statistics were provided by District 65, UAW, and calculated from university personnel data supplied to the union as part of their contractual relationship. Please note slight discrepancies due to rounding off.

27. Columbia Local District 65, "Fair Play, Fair Pay," September 1991.

28. Columbia Local District 65, UAW, "Justice Now: To Our Supervisors," 11 November 1991.

29. Columbia's formula based its health maintenance organization (HMO) rates on the Blue Cross hospitalization costs to the university for each specific union (65, TWU, 1199). The university took the clerical union's premium rate for Blue Cross hospitalization and set it as the university's allotment for all other health plans (HMOs) for the clerical workers. Ironically, because District 65 members as a group were the healthiest and cheapest of the unions to insure with Blue Cross, the university allocated fewer dollars for each worker for HMO coverage than it did for other unions.

30. These are the real names of the local leaders.

31. In April 1968, five buildings were occupied in a strike lead by Students for a Democratic Society (SDS). The action protested the university's expansion into Morningside Park, and as part of a mounting antiwar movement, the action protested university support for the Institute for Defense Analysis (IDA), a multiuniversity think tank for the Pentagon. The steps outside Low Library were the site of many large demonstrations. The occupation ended with the arrest of 120 people, which

was followed by a strike for the remainder of the semester. See *Columbia Daily Spectator,* 24 April 1968. Thanks to Laura Foner for access to her personal archives of this period.

32. Kenneth C. Crowe, "Workers Protest at Columbia Fete," *New York Newsday,* 1 November 1991, 28.

33. Benjamin Strong, "Sovern says CU does not discriminate," *Columbia Daily Spectator,* 21 October 1991, 1. Such an exchange was not new. The headline of the lead article of the 14 October 1985 *Spectator* similarly read, "Sovern denies charge of worker discrimination."

34. Columbia Local District 65, "Letter to President Michael Sovern," 25 October 1991.

35. Joseph P. Mullinix, senior vice president, Columbia University, "Dear Fellow Columbian," 8 November 1991, 1.

36. Columbia Local District 65, "Dupont Awards Special Edition," 30 January 1992.

37. Columbia Local District 65, "UAW President Responds to 'Dear Fellow Columbian' Letter," Owen Bieber, *Justice Now,* 26 November 1991.

38. Martha Howell, Caroline Bynum, et al., "To Members of the Women's Faculty Caucus," 9 December 1991.

39. Author's field notes, November 1991.

40. Anthony DePalma, "As a Deficit Looms, 26 Threaten to Quit Key Columbia Posts," *New York Times,* 27 November 1991, A1–B6.

41. In addition to issues of solidarity, many faculty also understood that their health care benefits could be impacted by the ability of the administration to impose its cutbacks on the clericals.

42. I say "crossing the strike," as opposed to "crossing the picket line," because the union did not always have a picket line going in front of campus entrances on strike days. The corporate campaign strategy of taking the strike to the offices of university trustees meant that hundreds of strikers were at visible midtown locations, rather than in front of campus gates. For some faculty and student supporters, the lack of campus pickets presented an organizing difficulty: it was hard to mount support for not crossing the line when there was no line.

43. Robert D. McFadden, "Classes at Columbia Are Moved off Campus during 2 Day Strike," *New York Times,* 15 November 1991, B3.

44. The demonstration targeted Macy's senior vice president Gertrude Michelson, chair of the Columbia Board of Trustees.

45. Under Section 8(a)(5) of the Taft-Hartley Act, an "impasse" in bargaining is reached when additional bargaining would be futile. When an impasse has been reached, an employer is legally free to unilaterally implement its last proposals in bargaining. Whether an impasse has been reached is a question of fact. If the

employer declares an impasse and unilaterally imposes its last offer, but in fact an impasse has not been reached, then the employer would have committed an unfair labor practice.

2. The Single-Identity Problem

1. Thanks to Nancy Whittier for the phrasing "use" and "misuse" of multi-identity politics. She also suggests the term "nonuse" (see chapter 3) to describe a political approach that claims to be "color-blind" or "gender-blind."

2. Thanks to Eve Spangler, Boston College, personal conversation.

3. This explosion of movements, particularly identity-based movements, is a powerful example of a "cycle of protest." Social movement political scientist Sidney Tarrow describes protest waves as characterized by "heightened conflict, broad sectoral and geographic extension, the appearance of new social movement organizations and the empowerment of old ones, the creation of new 'master frames' of meaning, and the invention of new forms of collective action" (1997, 329). As we are considering here, "new frames of meaning" are particularly significant. "Frames of meaning and ideologies that justify and dignify collective action and around which a following can be mobilized . . . typically arise among insurgent groups and spread outward, which is how the traditional concept of 'rights' expanded in the United States into the 1960s" (330). See Snow and Benford 1992 for an elaboration of the role of master frames in cycles of protest.

4. King 1990, 274, quoting Michael Albert et al., *Liberating Theory* (Boston: South End Press, 1986).

5. These theorists are writing primarily in response to conditions of daily life for their communities, and to racial liberation, women's, lesbian, and gay movements, singly and intersectionally, in the United States. For some, postcolonial, national, and women's liberation struggles around the globe are also an important point of reference. Theoretically, they have responded primarily to other work in feminist theory, and to a lesser degree Marxism and race theory. For some, poststructuralism is an important theoretical location.

6. Different theorists have used different terms to describe our multilayered identities and the multiple forms of injustice we may experience: "multiplicative" (King 1998), "multiracial feminism" (Baca Zinn and Dill 1996, 326), "matrix of domination" (Collins 1990). "Multiracial feminism," while putting greater emphasis on race and gender in its title (rather than class or sexuality), develops a similar approach to "intersectionality" or "matrix of domination."

7. Lorde 1984, 116. All quotes from *Sister Outsider*, by Audre Lorde, copyright 1984, are reprinted with permission from the Crossing Press, Santa Cruz, Calif.

8. Though the women's suffrage movement is considered "first-wave" feminism, it was not the only women's movement during the nineteenth and early twen-

tieth centuries. Karen Sacks argues that during this time there were "three movements which were consciously movements for the rights of women," including "an industrial-working-class women's movement for economic improvement and equality," a "black women's movement made up of working- and middle-class black women against racism and for both economic improvement and legal equality with whites," and a "white middle-class movement for legal equality" (Sacks 1990, 540).

9. Robnett 1996, 1667. Recent accounts by Jo Ann Robinson, Fannie Lou Hamer, Bernice McNair Barnett, and Belinda Robnett have begun to fill the gap in previous tellings of the movement and to reshape its analysis.

10. Combahee 1982, 15. For experiences of Chicanas, other Latinas, and Asian and Native American women within national liberation movements of the 1960s and 1970s, see Anzaldúa 1990; Moraga and Anzaldúa 1983.

11. See Giddings 1985 for an excellent chronicle of that lineage.

12. Spelman 1988, 80, quoting Lugones.

13. Albelda 1985; Amott and Matthaei 1991; and Malveaux 1985a, 1985b, do this well.

14. Crenshaw 1989, 166. There are noted exceptions among African Americans and other men of color and white male theorists such as Manning Marable, Cornel West, Michael Omi, and Howard Winant, who do centrally incorporate sexism, homophobia, and the particular experiences of women of color and their resistance as key elements in their conceptualization of oppression.

15. Baca Zinn and Dill 1996, 324, 326. Baca Zinn and Dill additionally note, "Multi-racial feminism is an evolving body of theory and practice informed by wide-ranging intellectual traditions. This framework does not offer a singular or unified feminism but a body of knowledge situating women and men in multiple systems of domination" (323–24).

16. Collins 1998, 205. Collins additionally uses ethnicity and nationality (225).

17. Omi and Winant 1986, 68. Omi and Winant counterpose their theory of "racial formation," which "emphasizes the social nature of race, the absence of any essential racial characteristics, the historical flexibility of racial meanings and categories, the conflictual character of race at both the 'micro-' and 'macro-social' levels, and the irreducible political aspects of racial dynamics" (4).

18. Racism takes different forms for different racial groups—African Americans, Asian Americans, and Latinos (with differences by specific national groups, as well; for example, the different histories of U.S. racial policy toward Chinese and Japanese immigrants, and later Chinese American and Japanese American residents and citizens).

19. Collins 1998. It is critical to underscore that these are not static categories but *relationships* of power between groups.

20. Collins 1995, 494. Difference theory, Collins points out, comes "with its

assumed question, difference from what?" (1998, 152). Intersectionality thus avoids what difference theory re-creates: "others" in opposition to a "traditional norm" (Baca Zinn and Dill 1996, 323).

21. "The fact that a woman is not oppressed on account of her racial identity hardly leads to the conclusion that the sexist oppression to which she is subject can be understood without reference to her racial identity" (Spelman 1988, 15).

22. Thus we see the notion of many working classes—each gender, race, and class fraction specific.

23. Collins argues that two premises are critical to domination. "First, they depend on either/or, dichotomous thinking. Persons, things and ideas are conceptualized in terms of their opposites. For example, Black/White, man/woman, thought/feeling, and fact/opinion are defined in oppositional terms. . . . A second premise of additive analyses of oppression is that these dichotomous differences must be ranked. One side of the dichotomy is typically labeled dominant and the other subordinate. Thus, Whites rule Blacks, men are deemed superior to women, and reason is seen as being preferable to emotion" (1996, 215).

24. See Collins 1998, chapter 6, for a discussion of the difference in applying intersectionality to individual and institutional levels of analysis.

25. See Seidman 1996 and West 1996 for critical discussions of cultural identity politics. Often, discussions of identity politics center on cultural identity politics, which focus on the deconstruction of cultural representations of dominated groups and perhaps attempt their reconstruction. Seidman similarly notes of the debate over identity politics, "There is a preoccupation with the self and the politics of representation. Institutional and historical analysis and an integrative political vision seem to have dropped out. . . . Locating identity in multidimensional social space features its macrosocial significance; we are compelled to relate the politics of representation to institutional dynamics" (1996, 392–93). It is such a tendency that leads to the characterization of all identity politics as culture (see chapter 4 of this volume). It is also such a tendency that is the object of critique by Gitlin 1995, 1997, and Alterman 1998. See the introduction and chapter 8 of this volume.

26. See Kennelly 1999 for empirical work on the power of this "controlling image" in hiring.

27. Speaking of a piece in which writer Minnie Bruce Pratt discusses her changing sense of home, self, and community in her life as a white Southern Christian lesbian feminist, scholars Martin and Mohanty appreciate Pratt's "unsettling of any self-evident relation between blood, skin, heart . . . without dismissing the power and appeal of those connections" (1986, 200).

28. Christine Stansell, one of many insightful commentators on the Anita Hill case, warns us of "this intellectual climate, which eschews politics for identity"

and critiques a tendency on the part of white progressives of "reverence toward an undifferentiated Afro-American experience" (1992, 254).

29. See Marable 1984; Pinkney 1976. Also see Pinkney for an examination of differing Black Power ideologies.

30. To emphasize the indeterminacy of collective identity and action, and to avoid the essentialism of previous efforts, Mohanty moves away from "the logic of identity" and suggests "imagined community" and "the logic of opposition." "The idea of imagined community is useful because it leads us away from essentialist notions of third world feminist struggles, suggesting political rather than biological or cultural bases for alliance" (1991, 4–5).

31. Mohanty 1991, 38. She thus rejects any "ahistorical notion of inherent resilience and resistance of third world peoples" (5).

32. In addition to their different historical origins, consider the different organization of race and gender in contemporary society. "For African-Americans in particular, segregated spaces of all sorts—in particular, housing segregation with its concomitant effects on educational opportunities, employment prospects, and public facilities—accentuate these oppositional relationships. In contrast, gender is organized via inclusionary strategies where, via family, neighborhood, and religious groups, women live in close proximity to or belong to common social units with men. Women are encouraged to develop a commonality of interest with men, despite the gender hierarchy operating within this category of belonging" (Collins 1998, 210).

33. Collins thus alerts us to what she calls the "new myth of equivalent oppressions" (1998, 211).

34. See Collins (1998, 146) for additional arguments about the "decreasing effectiveness" of single-axis identity politics. Collins notes that such essentialized identities are increasingly co-opted by the state. "The power of a seemingly homogenous majority remains intact" while the seemingly "small unmeltable minorities" find themselves increasingly "compet[ing] with one another to receive increasingly smaller portions of the fixed segment of societal resources reserved for them" (1998, 52–53). Collins also notes the increasing commodification of identity politics: "Even the righteous anger of the oppressed can be incorporated into a toothless identity politics in which difference becomes a hot commodity" (1998, 56).

35. Seidman 1998, 290, speaking of the work of Diana Fuss 1989.

3. Labor and Identity Politics

1. Milkman's model is designed to consider labor's relationship to women. She considers four "cohorts": AFL craft unionism beginning in the nineteenth century, women garment workers' organizing in the early twentieth century, CIO organizing in the 1930s and 1940s, and public-sector organizing in the 1950s through

the 1970s. Each of these cohorts was shaped by different economic, political, and social conditions, which defined different "goals, structures, values, and ideologies" and a central strategic logic for labor (1990, 93). Each unionization wave has had differing practices regarding women's agendas, membership, leadership, and culture, which continue to be visible in the present period (1990, 1993b). Milkman cautions regarding the "problem of treating women, racial minorities, and other forms of labor in an undifferentiated way" (1987, 5). Racism and sexism are clearly not identical or parallel phenomena. Each has been shaped by differing conditions; each is characterized by particular dynamics, including patterns of segregation. Yet the logics and central strategic practices of each cohort are helpful in understanding the labor movement's relationship with men as well as women of color. As readers will note, I have drawn upon Milkman's insightful typology in my brief journey through labor's identity politics.

2. Aronowitz 1992, 37, 42. "Social clubs, civic associations, and political organizations were frequently organized along subcultural [ethnic] rather than overtly class lines, even if their composition was delineated by class membership."

3. Capitalists certainly used exclusionary practices as well. Their "divide and conquer" strategy brought blacks and/or women into their workforce as strikebreakers. For example, white women brought into the *New York World* as scabs in 1867 were dumped as soon as the strike was over (Balser 1987, 68).

4. Foner 1974, 47. "Unless he was Chinese," adds Foner. This antiracist stand did not include Chinese workers, as the Knights refused to grant charters to assemblies of Chinese workers.

5. Balser 1987, 35–36. Women's suffragist advocate Susan B. Anthony and Frances Willard, president of the National Women's Christian Temperance Union, were initiated into the Knights.

6. According to Foner (1974, 56–57), the Knights ultimately disintegrated into white supremacist politics (including calling for blacks to be deported to Africa). See Foner 1974 for a fuller discussion of the Knights' demise.

7. See Amott and Matthaei 1991, chapter 7.

8. Kessler-Harris 1985a, 127; Feldberg 1987b, 308. The Women's Typographical Union was supported by the short-lived cross-class Working Women's Association; the "Uprising of the 20,000" by the Women's Trade Union League. The labor/feminist relation often proved difficult, with tensions between two tendencies toward single-injustice analysis and agendas. Class bias of more privileged feminists presented additional obstacles. However, the material and ideological resources of the feminist movement have been pivotal.

9. Feldberg 1987b, 308. Kessler-Harris (1985a, 110, 129) notes that this was also a time when labor leaders felt "embattled" by capitalist attack and fearful of internal fracture or disloyalty of any sort. Feldberg (1987b, 308, 310) believes the

Red scares of the time and the deportation of communist immigrants made for tense relations with the Left-leaning women leaders at Local 25.

10. Foner 1974, 333–34. Randolph made the call for the NALC in 1959.

11. Foner 1974, 231; Foner 1980, 333. Foner does not say how many of the blacks were women, nor how many of the women were black.

12. Thanks to Nancy Whittier for this term.

13. Milkman 1990, 96. She goes on to say that although guided by "gender-neutral organizational strategy," much union organizing produced "highly gender-specific results" (99).

14. Foner 1974, 322. All quotes from *Women and the American Labor Movement: From World War I to the Present,* by Philip S. Foner, copyright 1980 by The Free Press, are reprinted with permission of The Free Press, a Division of Simon and Schuster, Inc.

15. Gabin 1985, 260. Gabin looks to the continuation of women's wartime activism in the efforts of women in the UAW in the 1950s. "Evidence of their activism is found in the persistent voice and influence of women within the union, the official commitment of the UAW to antidiscriminatory principles and policies, and the concerted effort of female unionists to eliminate unequal wage rates, sex-based occupational classifications, separate seniority lists and contractual restrictions on the employment of married women."

16. Foner 1974, 431–32. Also see Foner 1978, 1981.

17. Bell 1985, 285. In 1962 President Kennedy "extended limited bargaining rights to federal employees" (Bell 1985, 283).

18. Local 1199 was begun in the 1930s organizing Jewish pharmacists and drugstore clerks (Foner 1980, 420).

19. Foner 1980, 420, quoting Dan Wakefield in *Dissent* 6 (winter 1959): 162.

20. Foner 1980, 433–34, quoting from *New York Times,* 14 July 1962.

21. Foner 1980, 436–37. The $100-a-week wage was negotiated to go into effect one year after the agreement began.

22. Foner 1980, 436, quoting from Raskin, "A Union with 'Soul.'"

23. Civil rights activist Andrew Young, quoted in Fink and Greenberg 1989, 153–54.

24. Foner 1980, 442, quoting *New York Times,* 1 May 1969.

25. Foner 1980, 443–44. Foner claims, "Ms. Moultrie was probably the first rank-and-file delegate to address a national convention of the AFL-CIO."

26. See Fink and Greenberg 1989 for a detailed account of the federal intervention and final negotiations in the case.

27. See Fink and Greenberg 1989, 156–57, for a poignant account of Mary Ann Moultrie's story in the aftermath of the collapse of the local union.

28. Fink and Greenberg 1989, 158. By the end of the 1970s, the union had grown to include "80,000 health care workers from New Jersey to California" (Hudson and Caress 1991, 70).

29. See Fink and Greenberg 1989; Freeman 1984; and Hudson and Caress 1991 for detailed accounts and analyses of this period.

30. See the excellent film *Women of Summer* and Kornbluth and Frederickson 1984.

31. Needleman 1998b, 152; Gooding 1997a.

32. For further discussion of women's trade union leadership see Eaton 1992a, 1992b; Gooding and Reeve 1993; Milkman 1990.

33. Needleman 1998b, 152. Needleman identifies principal barriers as systemic, not individual. These include "centralization of union operations and functions . . . small number of leadership openings . . . the male culture of unionism, persistence of gender and race stereotypes" (1998b, 155–60).

34. "The number of minorities on the executive council went from four out of thirty-five (11 percent) to eleven out of fifty-four (20 percent)" (Marable 1997, 209).

4. What's in a Name?

1. Thanks to Nancy Whittier for her insight and articulation of this point.

2. Klandermans 1992, 77. Social movement theorists have used a wide variety of conceptual approaches to illuminate different aspects of this terrain. In addition to identity, these include political consciousness (Morris 1992; Taylor and Whittier 1995), framing (Snow et al. 1986; Snow and Benford 1988; W. Gamson 1988, 1992b; Ryan 1991, 1993, 2001; Taylor and Whittier 1995), cognitive liberation (McAdam 1982), consensus mobilization (Klandermans 1984), social movement communities (Buechler 1990; Lichterman 1995), cultures of solidarity (Fantasia 1988), solidarity (W. Gamson 1992a), and commitment (Hirsch 1990; Klandermans 1997). Several of these will be drawn into this chapter's discussion. For helpful analytic discussions of some of these concepts and their relationships, see Klandermans 1992; Taylor and Whittier 1995.

3. Klandermans has similarly argued that the social construction of meaning, more broadly, occurs at three levels: "public discourse," "persuasive communication" by collective actors in a mobilization, and changing "consciousness" during mobilizations (1992, 82).

4. See Klandermans's 1994 study of the shifting identity of the Dutch peace movement, with a changing mix of groups in the membership. See Whittier 1995 for changing meanings of radical feminism among succeeding "microcohorts" of the movement.

5. Cerulo (1997) uses these categories, noting that "some researchers approach identity as a source of mobilization rather than a product of it" (385).

6. Friedman and McAdam 1992, 156, 169–70. See Friedman and McAdam for discussion of the different challenges of "identity incentives" as a movement passes through different stages of its life cycle.

7. For useful reviews of these perspectives see Buechler 2000 (chap. 2); Jenkins 1983; Klandermans and Tarrow 1988; Morris and Herring 1987.

8. Klandermans 1997, 203. For a helpful review of societal breakdown theories, in which he distinguishes the simpler variants from more sophisticated models, see Klandermans 1997, chap. 8.

9. Gamson and Modigliani 1974. Most often the polity was the site of struggle, occasionally the economy/workplace. Taylor notes that institutional arenas other than the polity have not been seen as the site of struggle and argues that this inattention is the result of "the ignoring of a wide range of women's collective action by mainstream social movement scholars" (1999, 26).

10. As Buechler (2000, 35–36) argues, there were different tendencies within the theory: an entrepreneurial approach that used economic modeling and rational choice cost-benefit analysis (McCarthy and Zald 1973, 1977; Olson 1965) and a political approach that emphasizes political struggle (W. Gamson 1975; Tilly 1978; McAdam 1982). Particularly following McAdam's formulation (1982), the latter has been developed as "political process theory."

11. "We are willing to assume that there is always enough discontent in any society to supply the grassroots support for a movement" (McCarthy and Zald 1977, 1215). Klandermans has pointed out that it is "not that grievances were unimportant, but the focal research question became what makes aggrieved people protest, rather than what makes people aggrieved" (1997, 203–4).

12. Ferree and Hess 1985; McAdam 1982; Morris 1984. McAdam's 1982 study of the civil rights movement pointed to "cognitive liberation" as one of the necessary preconditions of a social movement mobilization. This changed consciousness included loss of legitimacy of a social system and the belief it could be changed through collective action (48–50). Gamson and Fireman's 1979 response to Olson's free-rider problem also entered social psychological elements into the discourse. In mobilizing members or potential members, movements at times confront what is known as the "free-rider" problem. "Collective goods," whether clean air in an environmental campaign, or higher wages in a labor struggle, will be shared by all members of a group, regardless of an individual's level of sacrifice to win these goals. Based on an individual utilitarian model, Olson (1968) argued that rational individuals elect to free ride on others' efforts, thus constituting a major problem for social movements. Selective material incentives (such as member services) are offered

as a solution to the problem. As much organizer wisdom would concur, Gamson and Fireman challenged the assumptions of Olson's individual economic model and suggested "collective incentives" of solidarity and moral commitment. See Friedman and McAdam 1992 for a discussion of "identity incentives."

13. McAdam's work on the civil rights movement argued political process theory to be an alternative to resource mobilization theory. McAdam took issue with resource mobilization's emphasis of external elites, underemphasis of a movement's mass base, underdevelopment of broad structural conditions, and the view of grievances as an "invariant property of social life" (1982, 33). Aldon Morris's study of the civil rights movement similarly contested the emphasis on external elite and the view that "protest groups are dependent on outside resources because they lack organizational resources and skills" (1984, 281). He developed the "indigenous perspective" as a corrective to resource mobilization. Yet I would concur with Buechler's argument that McAdam's, and I would add Morris's, work is "best seen as another illustration of the political version of resource mobilization theory" (1990, 37).

14. See Klandermans 1992 for an overview of different social constructionist approaches.

15. Klandermans points out that this "perception of reality" applies not only to grievances but also to "resources, political opportunities, and the outcomes of collective action" (1992, 77).

16. See Snow and Benford 1992; Gamson 1988, 1992b; Gamson and Modigliani 1989; Ryan 1991; Snow et al. 1986. Framing builds off of a symbolic interactionist/social constructionist approach. Goffman's idea of framing is especially significant: "'schemata of interpretation' that enable individuals to 'locate, perceive, identify, and label' occurrences within their life space and the world at large. By rendering events or occurrences meaningful, frames function to organize experience and guide action, whether individual or collective" (Snow et al. 1986, 464). Framing also builds off of work on the social construction of social problems (Blumer 1971).

17. Melucci 1989, 185; italics mine. Melucci also speaks of "difference" as "the possibility for particular individuals or groups to affirm their specificity" (207). I am reminded of the chant "We're here; we're queer; get used to it," and of Audre Lorde's demand that we move beyond "mere tolerance of difference" (1984, 111). The assertion of difference, "otherness," by oppressed groups is a complex, varied choreography. Sometimes, as Joshua Gamson points out in his insightful analysis of ACT-UP, movements can deliberately use stigmatized or exclusionary symbols and practices to "*make them mean* differently," and thus challenge the deviant label and deviantizing process (1989, 362).

It is important to recall that the marking of people of color, women, gays, lesbians and bisexuals, and people with disabilities as "others" by dominant groups not only stigmatizes and invisibilizes but also denies access to material goods, privilege, and power. Identity movements are to a significant degree responding to such domination. Thus talk about identity in movements as desire to "individuate themselves" tends to veer, however unintendingly, toward the invisibilization of domination: structural, as well as cultural.

18. New social movement theory has argued that as state and market gobble up increasing realms of social life, this alternative culture is generally characterized by its emphasis on democracy, antihierarchical structures, and direct participation. There is an emphasis on challenging norms and changing culture both inside the movement and in the larger society. Internally, these are self-reflective movements, aiming to prefigure a new social order in their organization. The process *is* the politics, or at least an important part of it. "Their 'journey' is considered at least as important as their intended destination" (Melucci 1989, 205). Externally, the movements are antimaterialist, oppose technocratic projects, and protect civil society from encroachment by market and state. See Buechler 2000; Epstein 1990; and Klandermans and Tarrow 1988 for helpful reviews of the theory.

19. As Buechler 2000 notes, E. P. Thompson points out that "'old' class-based movements were not structurally determined as much as they were socially constructed in the mobilization process itself" (47, citing E. P. Thompson's *The Making of the English Working Class*). We have seen this in the making of the U.S. labor movement's definition of the working class on race and gender grounds (see chapter 3).

The old/new dichotomy similarly dismisses class- and workplace-based struggles as anachronistic, an artifact of a previous social and economic period. Conditions of labor and issues of scarcity and distribution continue to mobilize many to struggle. Furthermore, as intersectionality highlights, many gender and race demands are class demands. The base of many contemporary movements is, as new social movement theory points out, overwhelmingly professional managerial class. However, as Epstein has noted, rather than seeing a multiplicity of agents supplementing the working class, new social movement theory has seen them supplanting the working class (1990, 48).

20. Also, the "old" labor movements and the old Left organized millions around what was also a fusion of material and way-of-life demands, as illustrated in the "8 [hours of work]/8 [hours of family and other activities]/8 [hours of sleep]" campaign and in the "Bread and Roses" strike of 1912 (see Baxandall et al. 1976; Cameron 1985; Foner 1980).

21. Professor Eve Spangler, Boston College, personal conversation.

22. Buechler 2000, 188, citing Melucci 1989.

23. Other movement scholars have made a similar distinction (Mueller 1992, 16; Buechler 2000, 191). Buechler conceptualizes collective identity as a contin-

uum with the "structurally and historically grounded" on one end and those movements that "construct collective identities from scratch, i.e., . . . not salient features
of social organization prior to the mobilization" on the other (191).

24. In a study of multiculturalism in two grassroots environmental movements, Paul Lichterman found that what he called the "everyday group practices"
by which groups "build community" constituted important obstacles to building
multicultural alliances (1995, 514). Taylor and Whittier's analysis of women's movement culture similarly suggests that we can study collective identity "by directing
attention to the observable practices (e.g., gestures, acts, dress, and appearances)
and the discourses (talk, words, speeches, symbols and texts) through which movement participants enact their activist identities" (1995, 173, citing Hunt and Benford [unpublished]).

25. Lichterman makes a similar observation in his study of community-
building practices among environmental movements: they "did not tend to take
their particular forms of togetherness as objects of critical discussion" (1995, 515).

26. Thanks to Charlotte Ryan, Boston College Media Research and Action
Project, for this understanding.

27. Thanks to Nancy Whittier for this point and for extensive comments on
an earlier version of this case.

28. Ryan 1991, 57. For very helpful work that unpacks these issues of framing
theoretically, and as a social movement practice, see Ryan 1991; Ryan et al. 1998,
2001. Her work is additionally insightful in discussing the dilemmas of movements
identifying media as a site of struggle, and considering the relationship of media
work to larger strategic questions. For an important case of media organizing in a
labor context, see Ryan 2001. For ongoing work with social movement practitioners,
contact the Boston College Media and Action Project, Chestnut Hill, MA 02167
(617-552-8708).

29. Thanks to Charlotte Ryan for insightful conversation on this relationship.

30. Taylor and Whittier 1995, 176. Taylor and Whittier examine ritual and
identity as two of four conceptual approaches (along with emergent norms and
collective action frames and discourse) by which movement theorists have analyzed
the relationship of culture to collective action.

31. Martin 1990; Stall and Stoecker 1998; Taylor and Whittier 1998. "A large
body of scholarly and popular writing valorizes egalitarianism, collectivism, altru-
ism, pacifism, and cooperation as female traits derived from an ethic of caring. . . .
In contrast, an emphasis on hierarchy, and oppressive individualism, an ethic of individual rights, violence, and competition are denounced as male values" (Taylor
and Whittier 1995, 169). Many feminist organizations make explicit claims to an
"ethic of care" that defines collective organizational structure and consensus deci-

sion making as more "feminist" than bureaucratic structure and hierarchical decision making. What has been defined as a "feminist" organization is seen, for example, in environmental feminism, peace, and lesbian movements, in contrast to a
more masculinist style of organizing—the anti–Viet Nam War movement, the Black
Panther Party, and much of the labor movement. Stall and Stoecker (1998) also note
similar gender differences in community organizing styles, contrasting a "women-
centered" model versus the traditional Alinsky approach.

32. See the Harvard clerical case, chapter 7.

33. See Needleman 1998b. See chapters 3 and 8 for discussion of this issue.

34. Karen Sacks's (1988a, 1988b) study of the organizing of Duke University
hospital workers identified two different types or understandings of leadership:
"spokespersons" (the more conventional type of leaders who tended to be "good
public speakers, representatives, and confrontational negotiators") and "center-
people" (leaders who were mainly women, mobilized already existing social networks, and "were key actors in network formation and consciousness shaping")
(1988b, 79).

35. See Needleman 1998b for "structured opportunities." See Gooding 1997a
for a thorough case study of WILD (Women's Institute for Leadership Development), a Massachusetts women's labor leadership program that consciously addressed such issues.

36. Thanks to Bill Gamson for this conceptualization.

37. Although the exact categories differ, they do share a good deal in intent
and conceptualization with these two other important projects, of which I became
aware after inductively developing identity practices in my fieldwork.

Pat Yancey Martin in "Rethinking Feminist Organizations" (1990) suggests
ten dimensions for analyzing and evaluating feminist organizations. Martin's work
is an effort to assess what defines feminist organizations, and to consider their
range. Her work is, in part, a response to the clamor for "organizational purity" in
which an overemphasis on one dimension—organizational structure, that is, "collectivism"—singularly defines feminist organization. Her dimensions, also inductively developed, are (1) "feminist ideology," (2) "feminist values," (3) "feminist
goals," (4) "feminist outcomes," (5) "founding circumstances," (6) "structure,"
(7) "practices," (8) "members and membership," (9) "scope and scale," and (10) "external relations" (1990, 190–91). Her categories are divided and labeled differently
than the identity practices I suggest in this work, but the two schemata cover much
of the same terrain.

The second related effort is Bailey Jackson and Evangelina Holvino's insightful
work "Multicultural Organization Development" (1988). Their analysis offers a
method of pulling apart—in concept and in practice—what generally appears as a

frustrating morass of issues in the struggle to develop a multicultural organization. Their work distinguishes a number of dimensions and stages, which constitute a map of such an organizational process. Jackson and Holvino identify a series of stages in multicultural development: "monocultural," "nondiscriminating," and "multicultural." Each stage is characterized by targets of change, types of interventions, and the skills required to produce organizational transformation (7–14). My study focuses on social movements as a particular kind of social formation, whereas Jackson and Holvino's dimensions of multicultural organization cover much of the same terrain for a broad range of organizations.

38. Taylor and Whittier's study of lesbian feminism similarly challenges the "view that organizing around identity directs attention away from challenges to institutionalized power structures" (1992, 105).

39. Pinkney 1976. This distinction is helpful to understanding debates among varieties of black nationalism, for example.

40. See Cerulo 1997 for a helpful overview of social movement and other sociological work on collective identity.

41. Gamson, as other sociologists, refers to this third level as a "solidary group."

42. HUCTW's distancing from much of the traditional labor movement must be understood in the context of their conflict with the UAW, which led HUCTW to organize as an independent union for a year and a half. When they affiliated with AFSCME (American Federation of State, County, and Municipal Employees), they negotiated an agreement guaranteeing them enormous autonomy. See chapter 7, and see Hoerr 1997 for extensive discussion of this conflict.

43. Taylor and Whittier 1992, 1995. Consciousness and the politicization of everyday life are the other two key processes of identity construction.

44. I will not refer to these strategies or ongoing practices by management or other authorities as "identity practices," to maintain that as a term referring to social movement practices.

45. Meyer and Whittier's 1994 study conceptualizes social movement spillover through investigating the types and mechanisms of the influence of the women's movement on the peace movement of the 1980s.

46. As scholar Richard Edwards points out, each means by which capitalists control labor generates a particular springboard for resistance.

47. Henry Hampton, *Eyes on the Prize*, episode 1, part 1, "Awakenings" (Boston: Blackside Productions, 1987), videocassette. Available through the Public Broadcasting System.

48. See Taylor and Raeburn's 1995 study of the career consequences of identity politics for gay and lesbian activist academics.

49. See Berman 1992; Aufderheide 1992; Schlesinger 1992.

50. For example, see the *Time* magazine cover story "The War against Feminism," 9 March 1992, in response to Susan Faludi's book *Backlash.*

5. Identity Practices

1. Again in the 1988 contract, the union challenged issues of race differentials in pay and pressed for a "reclassification study with union participation" and salary progression steps, in part, as efforts at narrowing the gap.

2. Using a job classification system that the union and university would agree on, all workers and supervisors would list all the components of each job. These would then be given points. Again by agreement, differing points would be assigned to grade levels, and finally salaries would be determined.

3. The causes of this discrepancy rested in the university's health care formula (see chapter 1), and TWU's decades-longer history of unionization (which is itself, of course, the product of patriarchy in the labor movement).

4. District 65, "An Open Letter to Columbia University," 1985.

5. The special adjustment fund "compensate[d] individual employees who have suffered discrimination or lack of recognition for length of service" (District 65, "VICTORY," *Picket Lines* 1, no. 4 [October]: 1985). The union's plan distributed 80 percent of the fund to workers of color (staff interview).

6. Columbia Local District 65, *Newsletter for Columbia Support Staff,* 23 January, 21 February, and 20 March 1986.

7. Columbia Local District 65, "Know Your Neighbor: Is Michael Sovern a Good Neighbor?" November 1991.

8. Race and gender "justice" or "[anti-]discrimination" are but two possibilities of a racialized or gendered framing. For example, the union could have used a "black freedom" or "power" or "pride" framing or could have spoken about their local as a "women's organization" or "women's culture," just to mention a few.

9. District 65, "Fair Play, Fair Pay: The 1991 Campaign for Justice for the Columbian Workers," September 1991.

10. District 65, "'Bases Are Loaded' for the November 13th Deadline."

11. Benjamin Strong, "Sovern Says CU Does Not Discriminate," *Columbia Daily Spectator,* 21 October 1991, 1.

12. District 65, open letter to President Michael Sovern, 25 October 1991.

13. Joseph P. Mullinix, senior vice president, Columbia University, "Dear Fellow Columbian," 8 November 1991, 1.

14. Ibid.

15. District 65 Student Support Committee, "The Columbia Participator," 18–22 November 1991, 2–3.

16. Martha Howell, Caroline Bynum, et al., "To Members of the Women's Faculty Caucus," 9 December 1991.

17. As I was the union person working with the faculty, this is a criticism of my own organizing practice, as well. Although studying these issues, I had not yet understood the potential impact the faculty letter could have on members' framing.

18. District 65, "Negotiations Update," 17 September 1991.

19. District 65, "Rally for a Just Contract," 28 November 1991.

20. District 65, "'Bases Are Loaded' for the November 13th Deadline."

21. District 65, "Striking Columbia University Clerical Workers Tell Macy's: COUNT US OUT OF YOUR THANKSGIVING DAY PARADE," 15 November 1991.

22. District 65, "Columbia's Dirty Linens Aired at Last," *DuPont Awards Special Edition, Columbia Local District 65 Extra!* 30 January 1992.

23. District 65, "Dear Faculty," 10 February 1992.

24. Kimeldorf 1999, 153–54, 208 n. 7, Raymond Williams as quoted by Ellen Meiksins Wood.

25. Fall 1991. For more information, see chapter 1, n. 29.

26. District 65 Student Support Committee, "The Columbia Participator," 18–22 November 1991, 2.

27. Author's field notes, 18 October 1991.

28. District 65, "Phone Rap: Phone Banking Instructions," 9 November 1991, and "Strike Alert," 11 November 1991.

29. Mullinix's response to the union's claims of gender inequity may also have been intended to inflame a TWU gender backlash.

30. Kenneth C. Crowe, "Workers Protest at Columbia Fête," *New York Newsday,* 1 November 1991, 28.

31. Robert D. McFadden, "Classes at Columbia Are Moved off Campus during 2 Day Strike," *New York Times,* 15 November 1991, B3.

32. Regarding Crown Heights and the Hill/Thomas hearings, see introduction, n. 16.

6. Making Meaning of the Strike

1. *Distributive 65 Worker* 17, no. 4 (December 1985): 1–2.

2. What I hope to do, then, is to explore the ways that identity practices, among other factors, contribute to how members make meaning of their union activism. Unlike historical factors and other outside influences, identity practices are at least one aspect of movement work that participants can actively shape.

3. Labor leader Bill Fletcher describes workers' perception of unions as "insurance company and law firm" (1998a, 17).

4. Thanks to an anonymous *Gender and Society* reviewer for highlighting this point.

5. I concluded, sadly, that a full examination of how members' preexisting ideologies and identities interacted with the movement's identity practices was beyond the scope that I could execute in this study. It would have necessitated substantially lengthening interviews, or conducting a series of interviews. This presented a serious obstacle, since interviews, like union business, were most easily conducted during a member's lunch break or immediately after work. Also, most of the interviews occurred during and after the contract campaign, complicating the study of preexisting ideologies.

6. See Dill 1987; King 1990; and Gilkes 1988. Rather, as Milkman (1985), Moody (1988), and others have noted, a recurrent experience of working women's organizations and trade unions is, as sociologist Patricia Yancey Martin describes, that they tend to deny or are silent about feminist ideology yet have other feminist characteristics such as goals, values, outcomes, or founding circumstances (1990).

7. Karen Sacks (1988a, 1988b) offers a similar observation from her study of hospital workers—half black, half white—unionizing at Duke University.

8. Susan Eaton, Harvard University, Kennedy School, conversation, spring 1992.

9. Feagin and Sikes 1994, 149, citing Marcus Mabry, "An Endangered Dream," 3 December 1990, 40.

10. See Frankenberg 1993 for discussion of white people's unawareness of themselves as a distinct cultural group, that is, as anything other than "the norm."

11. Kennelly's 1999 study focused on entry-level jobs, yet one can guess that the stereotypes may well carry over to clerical and administrative jobs beyond that level.

12. Such studies could look at race differentials in applications received and solicited and in positions suggested by personnel. They could assess differentials in granting interviews, job offers, starting salaries, and acceptance, controlling for differences in applicants' education and experience. They could consider racial difference in tardiness, absences, and disciplinary actions undertaken as well as differences in outcomes, grievances, and termination. In the tradition of the glass ceiling studies, research could examine racial difference in performance evaluation, trainings and special projects, mentoring, salaries, promotions, and length of tenure.

13. Collins 1990, 91, citing Gwaltney 1980, 240.

14. It would have been important to ask about reactions to the racial composition of the top leadership. Yet knowing I was in extremely taboo terrain, and having no idea of the response I would find, for activist reasons I did not want to take the chance. Three of the four black workers who spoke spontaneously on this issue

were folks with whom I was close. My guess is that if I had asked the entire sample, I would have found a similar dispersion of opinion on this leadership question.

15. She was speaking in light of the Crown Heights mobilization.

16. The "these people" language is notable.

17. Thanks to an anonymous *Gender and Society* reviewer.

18. The "single parent type" is evocative of the "controlling images" (Collins 1989, 1990) that so pervade social policy discussions regarding poor black women.

19. There were few members with four kids. As is the case in the debate over welfare policy, "four kids" appears to be a persistent stereotype of black women and Latinas.

20. The specific statistic in 1991 was 74.5 percent women.

21. Posing these two issues together in an opening sentence would have allowed participants to respond singly or intersectionally as they perceived it.

22. See Blum 1991; Costello 1984; Goldberg 1983. In actuality, in San Jose, one of the case studies in Blum's important work on the grassroots organizing experience in California comparable worth campaigns, the membership was 30 percent black in 1984 (Blum 1991, 55 n. 2). Yet as Blum acknowledges (5–6), the study never looked at race as an analytic category in the discussion of consciousness (class and gender). Similarly, in Goldberg's study of women office workers who belonged to a working women's organization, about one-third of the organization were women of color, and about 40 percent of her respondents were women of color (41, table 3-1). Yet race did not enter as a category of the analysis.

23. Karen Sacks's study of hospital workers, including clerical workers at Duke University, examines the way in which black women's labor activism draws on interlocking, oppositional race, class, and gender consciousness. Sacks points to family-based notions of taking responsibility and family- and community-based networks as critical resources in black women's activism and leadership in their unionization campaign (1988a, 1988b). See Bookman's 1988 study of Portuguese electronics workers and Zavella's 1988 study of Chicana cannery workers for cases that capture the complexity of class, gender, race, and ethnicity of labor organizing in industrial settings.

24. Joseph P. Mullinix, senior vice president, Columbia University, "Dear Fellow Columbian," 8 November 1991, 1.

25. District 65, Student Support Committee, "The Columbia Participator," 18–22 November 1991; and Martha Howell, Caroline Bynum, et al., "To Members of the Women's Faculty Caucus," 9 December 1991.

26. District 65, Student Support Committee, "The Columbia Participator," 18–22 November 1991, 2.

27. Jacqueline Shea Murphy, "Women's Work: Unions Organize for Fair Pay," "The Pink Collar Ghetto: Women Unionize for Comparable Salaries," in *Broadway: The Magazine of the Columbia Daily Spectator*, 1985, 6, 7, 10.

28. On the dedication page of *Manifesta: Young Women, Feminism, and the Future,* Jennifer Baumgardner and Amy Richards speak to this phenomenon. "To feminists everywhere," they say, "including those of our generation who say, 'I'm not a feminist but . . .' and others who say, 'I *am* a feminist, but . . .'—with the faith that young women will transform the world in ways we haven't yet imagined."

29. For example, see the *Time* magazine cover story "The War against Feminism," 9 March 1992.

30. Sociologist Margaret Anderson responds to this point often raised by students in women's studies classes. Some "will say, 'I'm not a feminist, I'm a humanist,' reflecting their belief in the betterment of life for all persons—men and women alike. But such a view does not preclude being a feminist. In fact, if one really is in favor of the betterment of all human beings, then it is logical to call oneself a humanist, antiracist, *and* feminist" (1993, 7–8). While that may be an element in Janet's response, her reaction stems at least as much from the sense of cross-gender class politics.

31. Of all the clerical workers, 1 percent were Asian men, 6 percent were black men, 8 percent were Hispanic men, and 10 percent were white men.

32. During this period, 47.4 percent of Columbia clerical workers were women of color (28.3 African American, 15.8 Hispanic, 3.3 Asian American), and 27.1 percent were white women. (Workforce statistics from District 65 based on data supplied by Columbia University.)

33. To my knowledge, the only conversation that took place in a union meeting was once at the negotiating committee, which union leaders feel is the most appropriate site for initiating such conversations given these members' greater history with the union and knowledge of its issues (see introduction). I did not have time to pursue these complex questions in the interviews, nor did they spontaneously emerge.

34. Combahee River Collective 1982; Crenshaw 1994; King 1990; Lorde 1984; Stansell 1992; West 1992a.

35. The question of an individual woman's (or man's) relation to the label "feminist," activists and researchers have found, is in fact a cluster of issues. Previous research, although using mostly white college student samples, has identified a number of distinct elements to "feminist self-labeling." Although these are usually discussed as "predictors" of the single dependent variable "feminist self-labeling" (see Cowan et al. 1992), it is useful to consider most of these as dimensions of an individual's relationship to feminism. These include awareness of gender inequality; experience of having been discriminated against on the basis of gender; attitudes about "gender roles," about feminist ideals, about "the" women's movement, and about stereotypes of the movement (see Renzetti 1987; Cowan et al. 1992); attitudes about the value of individual versus collective action (see Cowan et al. 1992); and an individual's perception of himself or herself as an activist.

A recent study by Hunter and Sellers (1998) considers whether additional factors may be significant for facilitating feminist attitudes among African American women and men. These include institutional experience (of public agencies, church and political participation); "racial ecology," including experiences of racism and perception of white racist intent; and stage of racial identity formation.

36. Bookman and Morgen 1988, 12. Feminist self-labeling, as the sole question, is reductionist, erasing, and narrowing of the broader questions explored by feminist research such as Bookman and Morgen 1988; Blum 1991; Costello 1984; Feldberg 1987b; Martin 1990; Sacks 1988; and Zavella 1988, which I attempt to consider in this study.

37. Martin 1990, 186. Martin notes great variation in the organizational characteristics of women's movement organizations. She suggests ten dimensions for evaluating an organization's feminist qualities. See chapter 4, n. 37. Two of these, "structure" and "practices," are particularly relevant to these issues raised by some Columbia clerical activists. Martin argues "that many scholars judge feminist organizations against an ideal type that is largely unattainable and that excessive attention has been paid to the issue of bureaucracy versus collectivism" (1990, 182).

38. "Lisa," HUCTW member interview, July 1991.

39. Helen Fogel, "UAW—Not Just for Autoworkers," *Detroit News,* 6 July 1995.

7. Other Stories, Other Possibilities

1. Thanks to Cynthia Peters, who conducted these interviews for me to confirm, clarify, and deepen my understanding of the Yale case from primary sources.

2. Ladd-Taylor 1985, 466. All quotes from Molly Ladd-Taylor's "Women Workers and the Yale Strike" are reprinted from *Feminist Studies* 11, no. 3 (fall 1985): 465–90, by permission of the publisher, Feminist Studies, Inc.

3. Pat Carter, interview by Cynthia Peters, 1999.

4. HUCTW staff interview, April 1991.

5. For a fuller discussion, see Hoerr 1997.

6. This slogan was also the title of one of HUCTW's major pieces of literature before the election. The glossy booklet was filled with photos and personal statements of support by more than one hundred Harvard workers.

7. Harvard staff interview, May 1991.

8. For detailed accounts, see Becker 1990; Heggestad 1987; Hoerr 1993, 1997; Hurd 1993; *Labor Notes* 1988; Monks 1988.

9. HUCTW staff interview, May 1991. After 1991, when Bok was replaced by Neil Rudenstine as president of Harvard, the university's commitment to creating an alternate participatory structure with HUCTW began to hit serious problems, as seen in the negotiation of the 1995 contract. See Hoerr 1997, chap. 15.

10. Eaton 1996, 292. For an in-depth description and assessment of such joint structures at Harvard, see Eaton 1996.

11. HUCTW, "Speaking for Ourselves, Making a Difference: Highlights from the First Contract of the Harvard Union of Clerical and Technical Workers, AFSCME Local 3650," 1990, 6.

12. HUCTW, "Speaking for Ourselves, Making a Difference," 1990, 4.

13. Melissa R. Hart, "Child Care at Harvard," *Harvard Crimson,* 16 December 1987.

14. HUCTW, "Working Together," in "We Believe in Ourselves," 1988, 37.

15. HUCTW staff interview, May 1991.

16. HUCTW staff interview, April 1991.

17. HUCTW staff interview, May 1991.

18. "Lisa," HUCTW member interview, July 1991.

19. HUCTW staff interview, May 1991.

20. "Lauren," HUCTW member interview, July 1991.

21. For Gilligan's comments on HUCTW see Jennifer Griffin, "Gilligan Says Union Is Model of Women's Different Voice," *Harvard Crimson,* 22 February 1989.

22. "Lisa," HUCTW member interview, July 1991.

23. Rondeau and Dunlop, at the Forum of the Harvard Trade Union Program given at the Kennedy School of Government, Harvard University, Storr Auditorium, 17 March 1991.

24. HUCTW staff interview, April 1991.

25. "Lisa," HUCTW member interview, July 1991.

26. HUCTW staff interview, April 1991.

27. For further discussion of HUCTW's leadership development practices, those of other unions, and a framework for approaching leadership development, see Eaton 1992a, 1992b.

28. HUCTW staff interview, May 1991.

29. Melissa R. Hart, *Harvard Crimson,* 6 February 1988.

30. This disconnection from the larger labor movement was echoed by members in several interviews. "People here are way less aware of the labor movement than in other unions," said one HUCTW leader in 1991. They rarely came to Boston area labor events. In the second contract effort in 1992–1993, faced with the university's intransigence, HUCTW drew strength from working with other unions. HUCTW made it clear that they could play and win by the hardball rules, if needed. This included not only the power of their membership but also working in alliance with the other campus unions, including those representing trades, hotel and restaurant workers, security guards, and others.

On the other side, many Massachusetts labor activists knew very little of HUCTW after they won their election. Sadly, in 1991, at the time of my interviews, several HUCTW members felt their tremendous victory had not gotten the attention and study by other unionists it deserved. "I don't think people see the victory it is. There's an element of sexism—this was done by a group of women... some weird, flaky way. There is still a struggle to get people to acknowledge the magnitude of the Harvard victory," said one early organizer. Yet their own early distancing from the labor movement must be seen as one contributing cause, depriving other unionists of the lessons, inspiration, and debates that their presence would have offered. By the mid-1990s, though, Harvard's experience was being discussed more frequently, especially in regard to new strategies for the labor movement.

31. In the early 1990s, HUCTW staffers successfully used the "Harvard model" to organize 3,200 workers at the University of Minnesota, and 2,400 at the University of Illinois (Hoerr 1997, 262), and began other new organizing campaigns within AFSCME, as well. See Oppenheim 1991 for discussion of the use of HUCTW's organizing model in subsequent organizing.

32. Juliet F. Brudney, "Unions Are the Key to Raising Pay for Women Office-Workers," *Boston Globe,* 19 April 1988.

33. Henry Weinstein, "A Textbook Labor Union Campaign," *Los Angeles Times,* 17 May 1988.

34. Edward Shanahan, "A Mother's Loyalty to Harvard Was Not Repaid," *Quincy Patriot Ledger,* June 1988.

35. Weinstein, "A Textbook Labor Union Campaign."

36. "Lisa," HUCTW member interview, July 1991.

37. Thanks to Ruth Milkman for increasing my attention to this point in the analysis.

8. Adding It Up

1. See Omi and Winant 1986; Winant 1990; Crenshaw 1997; Collins 1998.

2. Gamson 1992a, 86–87, citing Donal Carbaugh's *Talking American* (1988). "Although the term *equal rights,* for example, could apply to the claims of a group... the discourse privileges the rights of individuals and makes the articulation of collective claims problematic."

3. What I refer to as race and gender conscious is a modification of Ruth Frankenberg's term "race-cognizant." In a study of white women's attitudes toward race, particularly whiteness, Frankenberg (1993, 14–16) offers a typology of three paradigms, what she calls "discursive repertoires of race and racism": (1) "essentialist racism" (the notion of biologically determined difference), (2) "color evasiveness" and "power evasiveness," and (3) "race cognizance." I prefer the term "conscious" over "cognizant" on the basis of accessible language, as well as its invoking of the concept "consciousness." Frankenberg's work discusses approaches to understanding racial difference and equality, but the same concepts are quite applicable to

gender, class, sexuality, or any other kind of domination. See Schwerner 1996 for elaboration and an insightful case study of these issues within a women's community organization.

4. Crenshaw 1997, 99. Although the discourse was developed around race, social policy questions such as affirmative action and multicultural education extend the discussion to gender as well. While the dynamics of race and gender oppression are far from identical, the policy discourse for the most part also refers to gender.

5. In discussing color blindness, Frankenberg argues that "viewing people in terms of universal sameness overlaid with individual difference" and "emphasis on the individual over the group either as cause or as target of racism" are associated with "the disinclination to think in terms of social or political aggregates" (1993, 148).

6. See introduction, n. 28.

7. White leftists, gone off the track with a race-primacy perspective, escalated the tension further.

8. See *Bay State Banner,* 10 December 1992, 1, 8.

9. Thanks to David Stuart, Boston College Media Research and Action Project, for this insight.

10. One small group of Latino workers, for example, were initially unhappy about being in a union with these "wimpy women." Their male union organizer pointed out that it was these "wimpy women" who had led a strong five-day strike at Columbia only six years before and had won the first contract. This organizer reports that several in the group changed their perspective over the course of the arduous struggle.

11. Case studies into other successful multi-injustice struggles would be helpful in assessing potential risks and benefits. Movement activists are rich with insight about what is making the difference in efforts at "diversity" or "multi-injustice politics," and these questions are also increasingly on the agenda of social movement theory. We need for both activists and scholars, separately or together, to find ways of capturing more of the frontline knowledge that often does not make it into formal accounts and thus remains inaccessible to others. How have they differently made race, gender, class, sexuality, and other locations of domination politically meaningful? How have they faced or averted challenges to unity that may result? Under what conditions are differing practices successful?

12. Although their members were much fewer, there could have been an Asian American caucus, as well. There could also have been a gay, lesbian, bisexual caucus, as has formed in other unions.

13. See Foner 1978, 1981; Georgakas and Surkin 1975; Haddock 1973.

14. Helen Fogel, "UAW—Not Just for Autoworkers," *Detroit News,* 6 July 1995. Quoted language is Fogel's report of her conversation with Rosenstein.

15. Further empirical work of movements in different structural conditions using differing identity practices will be critical in assessing these conflicting claims about the mobilizing impact of multi-injustice collective identities.

16. This 65 leader's claim was well supported by Walter Stafford's study "Closed Labor Markets," which noted that "black females are more concentrated than any group in the study" (1985, xi–xii).

17. In an "agency shop," workers can elect not to join the union. Because they too are covered by the benefits of a union-negotiated contract, they pay an agency fee, instead of union dues, for the benefits they derive from the union contract.

18. A union leader was asked to speak at one women's studies class. The student support committee and black students' organization, with which the union did prioritize working, were gender mixed.

19. John Laidler, "Cafeteria Workers Savor Win," *Boston Globe,* 15 August 1992, 21, 28.

20. See Morrison 1992 for an important collection of black feminist responses.

21. *New York Times,* 17 November 1991.

22. *Time,* 9 March 1992. The article was partly in response to the recent publication of Susan Faludi's book *Backlash.*

23. For discussion of this issue, see Andersen 1993, 7–8; Cowan et al. 1992; Kamen 1991.

24. See Hoerr 1997 for an in-depth account of these events.

25. New Haven's population was approximately one-third black, but the clerical workforce was only 14 percent black. This gap was later addressed by a joint union-university-community program (Fortes interview, 16 October 1999).

26. October 22 and 18, respectively. *Columbia Spectator,* 21 October 1991, 1; 23 October 1991, 1.

27. Mohanty 1991; West 1992b, 1993; Stansell 1992.

28. The concern may also be raised that the degree to which the union also articulated more explicit antisexist politics may have diminished the support available from within black communities and Latino communities, especially in the Hill/Thomas period. Black community support for labor struggles has been most avid around well-paid, traditionally male jobs with long histories of exclusion, such as the construction trades, fire, and police. These jobs are historically, symbolically, and economically important for black and Hispanic communities. Yet in terms of mass employment, clerical and service jobs are also economically important. As 1199's story and support of other service workers illustrate, these jobs can become the subject of widespread community support, as well. At Yale, Local 34 successfully cultivated support of both African American and feminist organizations and leaders (and some at the intersection).

29. WILD (Women's Institute for Leadership Development) conducts leadership training programs for women trade unionists.

30. First campaigns often have more staff resources for carrying out such work. This is a significant obstacle, although union decisions to shape themselves in an "organizing," rather than solely a "service," model can fill this gap to some extent by drawing on the members' labor power.

9. Can We Make a Different Kind of Identity Politics?

1. District 65, *Distributive 65 Worker* 17, no. 4 (December 1985): 1–2.

2. Ed Hunt and Tess Ewing, "Teamsters Reach Out to Gay Community," *Labor Page,* April–May 1992, 5.

3. See Krupat and McCreery 2000 for in-depth consideration of gay and lesbian labor politics.

4. From the Joint Statement of the AFL-CIO's "Full Participation Conference," October 1995 (Chen and Wong 1998, 185).

5. In August 1985, members of the United Food and Commercial Workers (UFCW) Local P-9 at the Austin, Minnesota, Hormel meatpacking plant went out on strike. It was a militant, creative, community-based struggle against concessions that brought it into direct conflict with its international union.

Appendix

1. This would have allowed me to study various experiences in the workplace, informal work site cultures, and their relationship to formal union organizations. However, such a location would have narrowed my view to one or two small parts of the campus.

2. Author's field notes, December 1991.

3. Fine 1992, 214, quoting Reinharz 1988, 15–16; italics Fine's.

4. Gamson 1992b, 186, quoting Giddens 1986, 72.

References

Acker, Joan. 1987. "Sex Bias in Job Evaluation: A Comparable Worth Issue." In *Ingredients for Women's Employment Policy*, ed. Christine Bose and Glenna Spitze. Albany: State University of New York Press.

———. 1989. *Doing Comparable Worth: Gender, Class, and Pay Equity.* Philadelphia: Temple University Press.

Aguilar, Margarita. 1989. "New Directions in Collective Bargaining. Clerical and Technical Unions: The Case of New York University." In *Power Relationships of the Unionized Campus,* ed. Joel M. Douglas. Proceedings of the Seventeenth Annual Conference, National Center for the Study of Collective Bargaining in Higher Education and the Professions. April.

Alarcón, Norma. 1990. "The Theoretical Subject(s) of *This Bridge Called My Back* and Anglo-American Feminism." In *Making Face, Making Soul/Haciendo Caras: Creative and Critical Perspectives by Women of Color,* ed. Gloria Anzaldúa. San Francisco: Aunt Lute Foundation Books.

Albelda, Randy. 1985. "Nice Work If You Can Get It: Segmentation of White and Black Women Workers in the Post-war Period." *Review of Radical Political Economics* 17 (3): 72–85.

Alterman, Eric. 1998. "Making One and One Equal Two." *The Nation,* 25 May 266, 10.

Amott, Teresa, and Julie Matthaei. 1984. "Comparable Worth, Incomparable Pay: The Issue at Yale." *Radical America* 18 (September–October): 21–28.

———. 1991. *Race, Gender, and Work: A Multicultural Economic History of Women in the U.S.* Boston: South End Press.

Andersen, Margaret L. 1993. *Thinking about Women: Sociological Perspectives on Sex and Gender.* 3d ed. New York: Macmillan.

———. 1997. "Studying across Difference: Race, Class, and Gender in Qualitative Research." In *Through the Prism of Difference: Readings on Sex and Gender,* ed. Maxine Baca Zinn, Pierrette Hondagneu-Sotelo, and Michael A. Messner. Needham Heights, Mass.: Allyn and Bacon.

Anner, John, ed. 1996. *Beyond Identity Politics: Emerging Social Justice Movements in Communities of Color.* Boston: South End Press.

Anzaldúa, Gloria, ed. 1990. *Making Face, Making Soul/Haciendo Caras: Creative and Critical Perspectives by Women of Color.* San Francisco: Aunt Lute Foundation Books.

Aronowitz, Stanley. 1992. *The Politics of Identity: Class, Culture, and Social Movements.* New York: Routledge.

Aufderheide, Patricia, ed. 1992. *Beyond PC: Towards a Politics of Understanding.* Saint Paul, Minn.: Greywolf Press.

Baca Zinn, Maxine. 1990. "Family, Race, and Poverty in the Eighties." In *Black Women in America: Social Science Perspectives,* ed. Micheline R. Malson, Elisabeth Mudimbe-Boyi, Jean F. O'Barr, and Mary Wyer. Chicago: University of Chicago Press.

Baca Zinn, Maxine, and Bonnie Thornton Dill. 1996. "Theorizing Difference from Multiracial Feminism." *Feminist Studies* 22, no. 2 (summer): 321–31.

Balser, Diane. 1987. *Sisterhood and Solidarity: Feminism and Labor in Modern Times.* Boston: South End Press.

Balzer, Richard. 1993. "Finding Their Voices: Kris Rondeau Discusses Organizing with Richard Balzer." *Boston Review,* October–November, 5.

Barkley Brown, Elsa. 1990. "Womanist Consciousness: Maggie Lena Walker and the Independent Order of Saint Luke." In *Black Women in America: Social Science Perspectives,* ed. Micheline R. Malson, Elisabeth Mudimbe-Boyi, Jean F. O'Barr, and Mary Wyer. Chicago: University of Chicago Press.

Barnett, Bernice McNair. 1993. "Invisible Southern Black Women Leaders in the Civil Rights Movement: The Triple Constraints of Gender, Race, and Class." *Gender and Society* 7 (2): 162–82.

Baron, Harold M. 1971. "The Demand for Black Labor: Historical Notes on the Political Economy of Racism." *Radical America* 5 (2).

———. 1985. "Racism Transformed: The Implications of the 1960s," *Review of Radical Political Economics* 17 (3): 10–33.

Bass, Carole, and Paul Bass. 1984. "Union Victory at Yale: You Can't Eat Prestige." *Dollars and Sense,* July–August, 16–18.

Baumgardner, Jennifer, and Amy Richards. 2000. *Manifesta: Young Women, Feminism, and the Future.* New York: Farrar, Straus and Giroux.

Baxandall, Rosalyn, Linda Gordon, and Susan Reverby. 1976. *America's Working Women: A Documentary History, 1600 to the Present.* New York: Vintage Books.

Becker, Craig. 1990. "Lessons of the Harvard Drive." *The Nation,* 12 February, 196–98.

Bell, Deborah E. 1985. "Unionized Women in State and Local Government." In *Women, Work, and Protest: A Century of U.S. Women's Labor History,* ed. Ruth Milkman. Boston: Routledge and Kegan Paul.

Bell, Ella Louise. 1990. "The Bicultural Life Experience of Career-Oriented Black Women." *Journal of Organizational Behavior* 11: 459–77.

Berman, Paul, ed. 1992. *Debating P.C.: The Controversy over Political Correctness on College Campuses.* New York: Dell.

Blum, Linda M. 1991. *Between Feminism and Labor: The Significance of the Comparable Worth Movement.* Berkeley: University of California Press.

Blumer, Herbert. 1971. "Social Problems as Collective Behavior." *Social Problems* 18: 298–306.

Bodman, Lisa, and Joan Bailey. 1980. "The Boston University Clerical Workers' Strike and the Women's Movement: Three Oral Histories." Unpublished paper, Boston University.

Boehmer, Ulrike. 2000. *The Personal and the Political: Women's Activism in Response to the Breast Cancer and AIDS Epidemics.* Albany: State University of New York Press.

Bookman, Ann. 1988. "Unionization in an Electronics Factory: The Interplay of Gender, Ethnicity, and Class." In *Women and the Politics of Empowerment,* ed. Ann Bookman and Sandra Morgen. Philadelphia: Temple University Press.

Bookman, Ann, and Sandra Morgen, eds. 1988. *Women and the Politics of Empowerment.* Philadelphia: Temple University Press.

Brecher, Jeremy, and Tim Costello. 1998. "A 'New Labor Movement' in the Shell of the Old?" In *A New Labor Movement for the New Century,* ed. Gregory Mantsios. New York: Monthly Review Press.

———, eds. 1990. *Building Bridges: The Emerging Grassroots Coalition of Labor and Community.* New York: Monthly Review Press.

Brenner, Johanna. 1990. "Feminist Political Discourses: Radical versus Liberal Approaches to the Feminization of Poverty and Comparable Worth." In *Women, Class, and the Feminist Imagination: A Socialist-Feminist Reader,* ed. Karen V. Hansen and Ilene J. Philipson. Philadelphia: Temple University Press.

Bronfenbrenner, Kate. 1991. "Successful Union Strategies for Winning Certification Elections and First Contracts: Report to Union Participants. Part I: Organizing Survey Results." Reprinted by ILR Extension Division, New York State School of Industrial Labor Relations, Cornell University, Ithaca, N.Y.

Bronstein, Erica. 1999. Interview with author, October.

Brooks, Thomas R. 1970. "Black Upsurge in the Unions." *Dissent,* March–April, 124–34.

Brown, Elaine. 1992. *A Taste of Power: A Black Woman's Story.* New York: Pantheon.

Brudney, Juliet F. 1988. "Unions the Key to Raising Pay for Women Office-Workers." *Boston Globe,* 19 April.

Buechler, Steven M. 2000. *Social Movements in Advanced Capitalism.* New York: Oxford University Press.

Bullard, Robert, ed. 1993. *Confronting Environmental Racism: Voices from the Grassroots.* Boston: South End Press.

Calhoun, Craig. 1994. "Social Theory and the Politics of Identity." In *Social Theory and the Politics of Identity,* ed. Craig Calhoun. Cambridge: Blackwell.

Cameron, Ardis. 1985. "Bread and Roses Revisited: Women's Culture and Working-Class Activism in the Lawrence Strike of 1912." In *Women, Work, and Protest: A Century of U.S. Women's Labor History,* ed. Ruth Milkman. Boston: Routledge and Kegan Paul.

Carmichael, Stokely, and Charles V. Hamilton. 1969. *Black Power.* Middlesex, England: Penguin.

Carson, Clayborne. 1981. *In Struggle: SNCC and the Black Awakening of the 1960s.* Cambridge: Harvard University Press.

Carter, Pat. 1999. Interview with Cynthia Peters, 6 October.

Cerulo, Karen A. 1997. "Identity Construction: New Issues, New Directions." *Annual Review of Sociology* 23: 385–409.

Chan, Sucheng. 1991. *Asian Americans: An Interpretive History.* Boston: Twayne Publishers.

Chen, May, and Kent Wong. 1998. "The Challenge of Diversity and Inclusion in the AFL-CIO." In *A New Labor Movement for the New Century,* ed. Gregory Mantsios. New York: Monthly Review Press.

Cobble, Dorothy Sue, ed. 1993. *Women and Unions: Forging a Partnership.* Ithaca, N.Y.: ILR Press.

Cohen, Jean L. 1985. "Strategy or Identity: New Theoretical Paradigms and Contemporary Social Movements." *Social Research* 52 (4): 663–716.

Cole, Andrea. 1998. "How Yale Workers Defied Union Busting." *Dollars and Sense,* September–October, 23.

Colen, Shellee. 1986. "'With Respect and Feelings': Voices of West Indian Child Care and Domestic Workers in New York City." In *All American Women,* ed. Johnnetta B. Cole. New York: Free Press.

Collins, Patricia Hill. 1989. "A Comparison of Two Works on Black-Family Life." *Signs* 14 (4): 875–84.

———. 1990. *Black Feminist Thought: Knowledge, Consciousness, and the Politics of Empowerment.* Boston: Unwin Hyman.

———. 1995. "Symposium on West and Fenstermaker's 'Doing Difference.'" *Gender and Society* 9 (4): 491–513.

————. 1996. "Toward a New Vision: Race, Class, and Gender as Categories of Analysis and Connection." In *The Meaning of Difference: American Constructions of Race, Sex and Gender, Social Class, and Sexual Orientation.* New York: McGraw Hill.

————. 1998. *Fighting Words: Black Women and the Search for Justice.* Minneapolis: University of Minnesota Press.

Combahee River Collective. 1982. "A Black Feminist Statement." In *All the Women Are White, All the Blacks Are Men, But Some of Us Are Brave,* ed. Gloria T. Hull, Patricia Bell Scott, and Barbara Smith. Old Westbury, N.Y.: Feminist Press.

Connelly, Mary Jo. 1994. "Eight Micro-processes of Learning through Collective Identity and Action: Reflections on What People Learn in Social Movements Groups." Unpublished paper, University of Massachusetts, Amherst.

Costello, Cynthia. 1984. "Working Women's Consciousness: Traditional or Oppositional?" In *To Toil the Livelong Day,* ed. Carol Groneman and Mary Beth Norton. Ithaca, N.Y.: Cornell University Press.

————. 1988. "Women Workers and Collective Action: A Case Study from the Insurance Industry." In *Women and the Politics of Empowerment,* ed. Ann Bookman and Sandra Morgen. Philadelphia: Temple University Press.

Coverman, Shelley. 1988. "Sociological Explanations of the Male-Female Wage Gap: Individualist and Structuralist Theories." In *Women Working: Theories and Facts in Perspective,* ed. Ann Helton Stromberg and Shirley Harkess. 2d ed. Mountain View, Calif.: Mayfield.

Cowan, Gloria, Monja Mestlin, and Julie Masek. 1992. "Predictors of Feminist Self-Labeling." *Sex Roles* 27 (7–8): 321–30.

Crenshaw, Kimberlé. 1989. "Demarginalizing the Intersection of Race and Sex: A Black Feminist Critique of Antidiscrimination Doctrine, Feminist Theory, and Antiracist Politics." *University of Chicago Legal Forum, 1989. Feminism in the Law: Theory, Practice, and Criticism,* 139–67.

————. 1992. "Whose Story Is It, Anyway? Feminist and Antiracist Appropriations of Anita Hill." In *Race-ing Justice, En-gendering Power: Essays on Anita Hill, Clarence Thomas, and the Construction of Social Reality,* ed. Toni Morrison. New York: Pantheon Books.

————. 1994. "Mapping the Margins: Intersectionality, Identity Politics, and Violence against Women of Color." In *The Public Nature of Private Violence,* ed. Martha Albertson Fineman and Roxanne Mykitiuk. New York: Routledge.

————. 1997. "Color-Blind Dreams and Racial Nightmares: Reconfiguring Racism in the Post–Civil Rights Era." In *Birth of a Nation'hood: Gaze, Script, and Spectacle in the O.J. Simpson Case,* ed. Toni Morrison and Claudia Brodsky Lacour. New York: Random House.

Cross, William E., Jr. 1991. *Shades of Black: Diversity in African-American Identity.* Philadelphia: Temple University Press.

Croteau, David. 1995. *Politics and the Class Divide: Working People and the Middle Class Left.* Philadelphia: Temple University Press.

Crowe, Kenneth C. 1991. "Workers Protest at Columbia Fete." *New York Newsday,* 1 November, 28.

Cupo, Aldo, Molly Ladd-Taylor, Beverly Lett, and David Montgomery. 1984. "Beep, Beep, Yale's Cheap: Looking at the Yale Strike." *Radical America* 18 (5): 7–19.

Dalton, Harlon L. 1995. *Racial Healing: Confronting the Fear between Blacks and Whites.* New York: Doubleday.

Davies, Margery. 1979. "Woman's Place Is at the Typewriter: The Feminization of the Clerical Labor Force." In *Capitalist Patriarchy and the Case for Socialist Feminism,* ed. Zillah R. Eisenstein. New York: Monthly Review Press.

Davis, Angela Y. 1983. *Women, Race, and Class.* New York: Vintage Books.

Davis, Mike. 1986. *Prisoners of the American Dream: Politics and Economy in the History of the U.S. Working Class.* London: Verso.

Derber, Charles, William A. Schwartz, and Yale Magrass. 1990. *Power in the Highest Degree: Professionals and the Rise of a New Mandarin Order.* New York: Oxford University Press.

di Leonardo, Michaela. 1985. "Women's Work, Work Culture, and Consciousness." *Feminist Studies* 11 (3): 491–96.

Dill, Bonnie Thornton. 1987. "Race, Class, and Gender: Prospects for an All-Inclusive Sisterhood." In *From Different Shores: Perspectives on Race and Ethnicity in America,* ed. Ronald Takaki. New York: Oxford University Press.

———. 1988. "Making Your Job Good Yourself: Domestic Service and the Construction of Personal Dignity." In *Women and the Politics of Empowerment,* ed. Ann Bookman and Sandra Morgen. Philadelphia: Temple University Press.

Dyson, Michael Eric. 1997. "The Labor of Whiteness, the Whiteness of Labor, and the Perils of Whitewashing." In *Audacious Democracy: Labor, Intellectuals, and the Social Reconstruction of America,* ed. Steven Fraser and Joshua B. Freeman. Boston: Houghton Mifflin.

Eaton, Susan C. 1992a. "Union Leadership Development in the 1990s and Beyond: A Report with Recommendations." Working Paper, June, 92-05, Center for Science and International Affairs, Kennedy School of Government, Harvard University.

———. 1992b. "Women Workers, Unions, and Industrial Sectors in North America." Working Paper No. 1, International Labor Organization, Geneva, Switzerland.

———. 1996. "'The Customer Is Always Interesting': Unionized Harvard

Clericals Renegotiate Work Relationships." In *Working in the Service Society,* ed. Cameron Lynne MacDonald and Carmen Sirianni. Philadelphia: Temple University Press.

Edwards, Richard. 1979. *Contested Terrain: The Transformation of the Workplace in the Twentieth Century.* New York: Basic Books.

Ehrenreich, Barbara. 1987. "The Next Wave." *Ms.* 16 (1–2): 166–68.

Epstein, Barbara. 1990. "Rethinking Social Movement Theory." *Socialist Review* 20: 35–65.

Faludi, Susan. 1991. *Backlash: The Undeclared War against American Women.* New York: Crown Publishers.

Fantasia, Rick. 1988. *Cultures of Solidarity: Consciousness, Action, and Contemporary American Workers.* Berkeley: University of California Press.

Feagin, Joe R., and Melvin P. Sikes. 1994. *Living with Racism: The Black Middle-Class Experience.* Boston: Beacon Press.

Feldberg, Roslyn L. 1983. "'Union Fever': Organizing among Clerical Workers, 1900–1930." In *Workers' Struggles, Past and Present: A "Radical America" Reader,* ed. James Green. Philadelphia: Temple University Press.

———. 1987a. "Comparable Worth: The Relationship of Method and Politics." In *Ingredients for Women's Employment Policy,* ed. Christine Bose and Glenna Spitze. Albany: State University of New York Press.

———. 1987b. "Women and Trade Unions: Are We Asking the Right Questions?" In *Hidden Aspects of Women's Work,* ed. Christine Bose, Roslyn Feldberg, and Natalie Sokoloff, with the Women and Work Research Group. New York: Praeger.

Ferree, Myra Marx, and Beth B. Hess. 1985. *Controversy and Coalition: The New Feminist Movement.* Boston: Twayne.

Ferree, Myra Marx, and Frederick D. Miller. 1985. "Mobilization and Meaning: Toward an Integration of Social Psychological and Resource Perspectives on Social Movements." *Sociological Inquiry* 55 (1): 38–51.

Fine, Janice. 1998. "Moving Innovation from the Margins to the Center." In *A New Labor Movement for the New Century,* ed. Gregory Mantsios. New York: Monthly Review Press.

Fine, Michelle. 1992. "Passion, Politics, and Power: Feminist Research Possibilities." In *Disruptive Voices: The Possibilities of Feminist Research,* ed. Michelle Fine. Ann Arbor: University of Michigan Press.

Fink, Leon, and Brian Greenberg. 1989. *Upheaval in the Quiet Zone: A History of Hospital Workers' Union, Local 1199.* Urbana: University of Illinois Press.

Fletcher, Bill, Jr. 1992. "How Labor Should Fight David Duke's Appeal." *Labor Notes* 155: 11–12.

———. 1998. "Whose Democracy? Organized Labor and Member Control." In *A New Labor Movement for the New Century,* ed. Gregory Mantsios. New York: Monthly Review Press.

Fletcher, Bill, Jr., and Richard W. Hurd. 1998. "Beyond the Organizing Model: The Transformation Process in Local Unions." In *Organizing to Win: New Research on Union Strategies,* ed. Kate Bronfenbrenner, Sheldon Friedman, Richard W. Hurd, Ronald L. Seeber, and Rudolph A. Oswald. Ithaca, N.Y.: ILR Press.

Foner, Philip S. 1974. *Organized Labor and the Black Worker, 1619–1973.* New York: International Publishers.

———. 1978. "Organized Labor and the Black Worker in the 1970's." *Insurgent Sociologist* 3 (2–3): 87–95.

———. 1980. *Women and the American Labor Movement: From World War I to the Present.* New York: Free Press.

———. 1981. *Organized Labor and the Black Worker: 1619–1981.* 2d ed. New York: International Publishers.

Fordham, Signithia. 1990. "Racelessness as a Factor in Black Students' School Success: Pragmatic Strategy or Pyrrhic Victory?" In *Facing Racism in Education,* ed. Nitza M. Hidalgo, Ceasar L. McDowell, and Emilie V. Siddle. Boston: Harvard Educational Review Reprint Series no. 21.

Frankenberg, Ruth. 1993. *White Women, Race Matters: The Social Construction of Whiteness.* Minneapolis: University of Minnesota Press.

Freeman, Joshua B. 1984. "Hospital Workers, Heal Thyselves." *The Nation,* 31 March, 379–82.

Fried, Marlene Gerber, ed. 1990. *From Abortion to Reproductive Freedom: Transforming a Movement.* Boston: South End Press.

Fried, Mindy. 1987. *Babies and Bargaining.* North Dartmouth: Arnold Dubin Labor Education Center, University of Massachusetts.

Friedman, Debra, and Doug McAdam. 1992. "Collective Identity and Activism: Networks, Choices, and the Life of a Social Movement." In *Frontiers in Social Movement Theory,* ed. Aldon D. Morris and Carol Mueller. New Haven: Yale University Press.

Gabin, Nancy. 1985. "Women and the United Automobile Workers' Union in the 1950s." In *Women, Work, and Protest,* ed. Ruth Milkman. Boston: Routledge and Kegan Paul.

Gamson, Joshua. 1989. "Silence, Death, and the Invisible Enemy: AIDS Activism and Social Movement 'Newness.'" *Social Problems* 36 (4): 351–67.

———. 1995. "Must Identity Movements Self-Destruct? A Queer Dilemma." *Social Problems* 42 (3): 390–407.

————. 1997. "Messages of Exclusion: Gender, Movements, and Symbolic Boundaries." *Gender and Society* 11 (2): 178–99.

Gamson, William A. 1975. *The Strategy of Social Protest.* Chicago: Dorsey Press.

————. 1988. "Political Discourse and Collective Action." *International Social Movement Research.* Vol. 1, *From Structure to Action: Comparing Social Movement Research across Cultures,* ed. Bert Klandermans, Hanspeter Kriesi, and Sidney Tarrow. Greenwich, Conn.: JAI Press.

————. 1992a. "The Social Psychology of Collective Action." In *Frontiers in Social Movement Theory,* ed. Aldon D. Morris and Carol Mueller. New Haven: Yale University Press.

————. 1992b. *Talking Politics.* New York: Cambridge University Press.

Gamson, William A., and Bruce Fireman. 1979. "Utilitarian Logic in the Resource Mobilization Perspective." In *The Dynamics of Social Movements: Resource Mobilization, Social Control, and Tactics,* ed. Mayer N. Zald and John D. McCarthy. Cambridge, Mass.: Winthrop Publishers.

Gamson, William A., and Andre Modigliani. 1974. *Conceptions of Social Life: A Text-Reader for Social Psychology.* Boston: Little, Brown.

————. 1989. "Media Discourse and Public Opinion on Nuclear Power." *American Journal of Sociology* 95: 1–37.

Gamson, William A., David Croteau, William Hoynes, and Theodore Sasson. 1992. "Media Images and the Social Construction of Reality." *Annual Review of Sociology* 18: 373–93.

Georgakas, Dan, and Marvin Surkin. 1975. *Detroit I Do Mind Dying: A Study in Urban Revolution.* New York: St. Martin's Press.

Geschwender, James Arthur. 1977. *Class, Race, and Worker Insurgency: The League of Revolutionary Black Workers.* New York: Cambridge University Press.

Giddens, Anthony. 1984. *The Constitution of Society: Introduction of the Theory of Structuration.* Berkeley: University of California Press.

————. 1986. *Central Problems in Social Theory.* Berkeley: University of California Press.

Giddings, Paula. 1985. *When and Where I Enter: The Impact of Black Women on Race and Sex in America.* New York: Bantam Books.

Gilkes, Cheryl Townsend. 1980. "'Holding Back the Ocean with a Broom': Black Women and Community Work." In *The Black Woman,* ed. La Frances Rodgers-Rose. Beverly Hills, Calif.: Sage.

————. 1988. "Building in Many Places: Multiple Commitments and Ideologies in Black Women's Community Work." In *Women and the Politics of Empowerment,* ed. Ann Bookman and Sandra Morgen. Philadelphia: Temple University Press.

Gilpin, Toni, Gary Isaac, Dan Letwin, and Jack McKivigan. 1988. *On Strike for Respect: The Yale Strike of 1984–85.* Chicago: Charles H. Kerr.

Gitlin, Todd. 1995. *The Twilight of Common Dreams: Why America Is Wracked by Culture Wars.* New York: Henry Holt.

———. 1997. "Beyond Identity Politics: A Modest Precedent." In *Audacious Democracy: Labor, Intellectuals, and the Social Reconstruction of America,* ed. Steven Fraser and Joshua B. Freeman. Boston: Houghton Mifflin.

Glenn, Evelyn Nakano, and Roslyn L. Feldberg. 1995. "Clerical Work: The Female Occupation." In *Women: A Feminist Perspective,* ed. Jo Freeman. 5th ed. Mountain View, Calif.: Mayfield.

Gold, Tami, and Lyn Goldfarb. 1986. *With One Voice: Organizing for Change at Columbia.* Kitty Krupat, executive producer. Videocassette. New York: District 65, UAW.

Goldberg, Roberta. 1983. *Organizing Women Office Workers: Dissatisfaction, Consciousness, and Action.* New York: Praeger.

———. 1996. "Women Office Workers." In *Women and Work: A Reader,* ed. Paula J. Dubeck and Kathryn Borman. New Brunswick: Rutgers University Press.

Gooding, Cheryl. 1997a. "Building a Multicultural Union Women's Organization: Lessons from the WILD Experience." *New Solutions* (spring): 62–75.

———. 1997b. "Women and the Labor Movement in Massachusetts: Analysis of Issues and Proposed Solutions." Report of the Center for Labor Research, College of Public and Community Service, January.

———. 1999. Interview with author, August.

Gooding, Cheryl, and Patricia Reeve. 1993. "The Fruits of Our Labor: Women in the Labor Movement." *Social Policy* (summer): 56–64.

Gordon, David M., Richard Edwards, and Michael Reich. 1982. *Segmented Work, Divided Workers: The Historical Transformation of Labor in the United States.* New York: Cambridge University Press.

Gottfried, Heidi, and David Fasenfest. 1984. "Gender and Class Formation: Female Clerical Workers." *Review of Radical Political Economics* 16 (1): 89–103.

Graduate Students Organization at Columbia University. 1985. *Columbia: An Unofficial Portrait.* New York City: Graduate Students Organization at Columbia University. Summer–fall.

Green, James. 2000. "Historians as Allies of the Labor Movement." *Chronicle of Higher Education,* 28 July, B4–5.

Green, Jim, and Allen Hunter. 1974. "Racism and Busing in Boston." *Radical America* 8 (6): 1–32.

Haddock, Wilbur. 1973. "Black Workers Lead the Way." *Black Scholar* (November): 43–48.

Hall, Stuart. 1990. "The Meaning of New Times." In *New Times: The Changing Face of Politics in the 1990s,* ed. Stuart Hall and Martin Jacques. New York: Verso.

———. 1991. "Ethnicity: Identity and Difference." *Radical America* 23 (4): 9–20.

———. 1995. "Fantasy, Identity, Politics." In *Cultural Remix: Theories of Politics and the Popular,* ed. Erica Carter, James Donald, and Judith Squires. London: Lawrence and Wishart.

Halle, David. 1984. *America's Working Man: Work, Home, and Politics among Blue-Collar Property Owners.* Chicago: University of Chicago Press.

Hampton, Henry, and Steve Fayer. 1990. *Voices of Freedom: An Oral History of the Civil Rights Movement from the 1950s through the 1980s.* New York: Bantam Books.

Harley, Sharon. 1997. "Speaking Up: The Politics of Black Women's Labor History." In *Women and Work: Exploring Race, Ethnicity, and Class,* ed. Elizabeth Higginbotham and Mary Romero. Beverly Hills, Calif.: Sage.

Harriford, Diane. 1989. "Leadership and Participation Styles of Black Union Activists: New York City CLUW." Unpublished paper, Vassar College.

Hartmann, Heidi. 1979. "Capitalism, Patriarchy, and Job Segregation by Sex." In *Capitalist Patriarchy and the Case for Socialist Feminism,* ed. Zillah R. Eisenstein. New York: Monthly Review Press.

———. 1981. "The Unhappy Marriage of Marxism and Feminism: Towards a More Progressive Union." In *Women and Revolution: A Discussion of the Unhappy Marriage of Marxism and Feminism,* ed. Lydia Sargent. Boston: South End Press.

Hartsock, Nancy C. M. 1996. "Theoretical Bases for Coalition Building: An Assessment of Postmodernism." In *Feminism and Social Change: Bridging Theory and Practice,* ed. Heidi Gottfried. Chicago: University of Illinois Press.

Heckscher, Charles. 1989. "The Harvard Technical and Clerical Workers' Union: Implications for Higher Education." Lecture at Harvard Education School, 12 December.

Heggestad, Martin. 1987. "State of the Art: Defeating Harvard's Anti-union Campaign." *Radical America* 21 (5): 43–51.

Higginbotham, Elizabeth. 1997. "Black Professional Women: Job Ceilings and Employment Sectors." In *Workplace/Women's Place: An Anthology,* ed. Dana Dunn. Los Angeles: Roxbury.

Hill, Herbert. 1982. "The AFL-CIO and the Black Worker: Twenty-Five Years after the Merger." *Journal of Intergroup Relations* 10 (1): 5–78.

———. 1987. "Race, Ethnicity, and Organized Labor: The Opposition to Affirmative Action." *New Politics* 1 (2): 31–82.

Hirsch, Eric L. 1990. "Sacrifice for the Cause: Group Processes, Recruitment, and Commitment in a Student Social Movement." *American Sociological Review* 55 (April): 243–54.

———. 1991. "Columbia University: Individual and Institutional Racism." In *The Racial Crisis in American Higher Education,* ed. Philip G. Altbach and Kofi Lomotey. Albany: State University of New York Press.

Hoerr, John. 1993. "Solidaritas at Harvard: Organizing in a Different Voice." *American Prospect* (summer).

———. 1997. *We Can't Eat Prestige: The Women Who Organized Harvard.* Philadelphia: Temple University Press.

hooks, bell. 1981. *Ain't I a Woman: Black Women and Feminism.* Boston: South End Press.

———. 1984. *Feminist Theory: From Margin to Center.* Boston: South End Press.

Hudson, Gerald, and Barbara Caress. 1991. "New York's 1199 in 1989: Rebuilding a Troubled Union." *Labor Research Review* 17: 69–80.

Hull, Gloria T., Patricia Bell Scott, and Barbara Smith. 1982. *All the Women Are White, All the Blacks Are Men, But Some of Us Are Brave.* Old Westbury, N.Y.: Feminist Press.

Hunt, Scott, and Robert Benford. n.d. "Constructing Personal and Collective Identities." Unpublished paper.

Hunt, Scott A., Robert D. Benford, and David A. Snow. 1994. "Identity Fields: Framing Processes and the Social Construction of Movement Identities." In *New Social Movements: From Ideology to Identity,* ed. Enrique Laraña, Hank Johnston, and Joseph R. Gusfield. Philadelphia: Temple University Press.

Hunter, Andrea G., and Sherrill L. Sellers. 1998. "Feminist Attitudes among African American Women and Men." *Gender and Society* 12 (1): 81–100.

Hurd, Richard W. 1989a. "Learning Lessons from Clerical Unions: Two Cases of Organizing Success." *Labor Studies Journal* 14 (1): 30–51.

———. 1989b. "New Directions in Collective Bargaining. The Unionization of Clerical Workers in Colleges and Universities: A Status Report." In *Power Relationships of the Unionized Campus,* ed. Joel M. Douglas. Proceedings of the Seventeenth Annual Conference, National Center for the Study of Collective Bargaining in Higher Education and the Professions. April.

———. 1993. "Organizing and Representing Clerical Workers: The Harvard Model." In *Women and Unions: Forging a Partnership,* ed. Dorothy Sue Cobble. Ithaca, N.Y.: ILR Press.

Irons, Jenny. 1998. "The Shaping of Activist Recruitment and Participation: A Study of Women in the Mississippi Civil Rights Movement." *Gender and Society* 12 (6): 692–709.

Jackson, Bailey, and Evangelina Holvino. 1988. "Multicultural Organization Development." Working Paper 356, Center for Research on Social Organization, University of Michigan, Ann Arbor.

Jenkins, J. Craig. 1983. "Resource Mobilization Theory and the Study of Social Movements." *Annual Review of Sociology* 9: 527–53.

Johnston, Hank, and Bert Klandermans, eds. 1995. *Social Movements and Culture: Movements, Protest, and Contention.* Minneapolis: University of Minnesota Press.

Johnston, Hank, Enrique Laraña, and Joseph R. Gusfield. 1994. "Identities, Grievances, and New Social Movements." In *New Social Movements: From Ideology to Identity,* ed. Enrique Laraña, Hank Johnston, and Joseph R. Gusfield. Philadelphia: Temple University Press.

Juravich, Tom, and Kate Bronfenbrenner. 1998. "It Takes More than House Calls: Organizing to Win with a Comprehensive Union-Building Strategy." In *Organizing to Win: New Research on Union Strategies,* ed. Kate Bronfenbrenner, Sheldon Friedman, Richard W. Hurd, Ronald L. Seeber, and Rudolph A. Oswald. Ithaca, N.Y.: ILR Press.

Kadetsky, Elizabeth. 1992. "Minority Hard Hats: Muscling In on Construction Jobs." *The Nation,* 13 July, 45–48.

Kamen, Paula. 1991. *Feminist Fatale.* New York: Donald I. Fine.

Kennelly, Ivy. 1999. "'That Single Mother Element': How White Employers Typify Black Women." *Gender and Society* 13 (2): 168–92.

Kessler-Harris, Alice. 1985a. "Problems of Coalition-Building: Women and Trade Unions in the 1920s." In *Women, Work, and Protest: A Century of U.S. Women's Labor History,* ed. Ruth Milkman. Boston: Routledge and Kegan Paul.

———. 1985b. "The Debate over Equality for Women in the Work Place: Recognizing Differences." In *Women and Work: An Annual Review,* ed. Laurie Larwood. Vol. 1. Beverly Hills, Calif.: Sage.

Kimeldorf, Howard. 1999. *Battling for American Labor.* Berkeley and Los Angeles: University of California Press.

King, Deborah K. 1990. "Multiple Jeopardy, Multiple Consciousness: The Context of a Black Feminist Ideology." In *Black Women in America: Social Science Perspectives,* ed. Micheline R. Malson, Elisabeth Mudimbe-Boyi, Jean F. O'Barr, and Mary Wyer. Chicago: University of Chicago Press.

King, Mel. 1981. *Chain of Change.* Boston: South End Press.

Klandermans, Bert. 1984. "Mobilization and Participation: Social-Psychological Expansions of Resource Mobilization Theory." *American Sociological Review* 52: 519–31.

———. 1992. "The Social Construction of Protest and Multiorganizational Fields." In *Frontiers in Social Movement Theory,* ed. Aldon D. Morris and Carol Mueller. New Haven: Yale University Press.

———. 1994. "Transient Identities? Membership Patterns in the Dutch Peace Movement." In *New Social Movements: From Ideology to Identity,* ed. Enrique Laraña, Hank Johnston, and Joseph R. Gusfield. Philadelphia: Temple University Press.

———. 1997. *The Social Psychology of Protest.* Cambridge, Mass.: Blackwell Publishers.

Klandermans, Bert, and Dirk Oegema. 1987. "Potentials, Networks, Motivations, and Barriers: Steps towards Participation in Social Movements." *American Sociological Review* 52 (August): 519–31.

Klandermans, Bert, and Sidney Tarrow. 1988. "Mobilization into Social Movements: Synthesizing European and American Approaches." In *International Social Movement Research,* vol. 1, *From Structure to Action: Comparing Social Movement Research across Cultures,* ed. Bert Klandermans, Hanspeter Kriesi, and Sidney Tarrow. Greenwich, Conn.: JAI Press.

Kornbluth, Joyce L., and Mary Frederickson, eds. 1984. *Sisterhood and Solidarity: Workers' Education for Women, 1914–1984.* Philadelphia: Temple University Press.

Krupat, Kitty, and Patrick McCreery, eds. 2000. *Out at Work: Building a Gay-Labor Alliance.* Minneapolis: University of Minnesota Press.

Labor Notes. 1988. "Union Teaches Harvard a Lesson: Clerical Workers Win with Unorthodox Campaign." *Labor Notes* 112 (July): 1.

Ladd-Taylor, Molly. 1985. "Women Workers and the Yale Strike." *Feminist Studies* 11 (3): 465–89.

Ladner, Joyce A. 1993. "Black Women as Do-ers: The Social Responsibility of Black Women." In *Feminist Frontiers III,* ed. Laurel W. Richardson and Verta A. Taylor. New York: McGraw-Hill.

La Luz, José, and Paula Finn. 1998. "Getting Serious about Inclusion: A Comprehensive Approach." In *A New Labor Movement for the New Century,* ed. Gregory Mantsios. New York: Monthly Review Press.

Laraña, Enrique, Hank Johnston, and Joseph R. Gusfield, eds. 1994. *New Social Movements: From Ideology to Identity.* Philadelphia: Temple University Press.

Lichenstein, Nelson. 1998. "Are '2 Left Poles' like 2 Left Feet?" *The Nation,* 20 July, 2.

Lichterman, Paul. 1995. "Piecing Together Multicultural Community: Cultural Differences in Community Building among Grass-Roots Environmentalists." *Social Problems* 42 (4): 513–34.

Lin, Margaretta Wan Ling, and Cheng Imm Tan. 1994. "Holding Up More than Half the Heavens: Domestic Violence in Our Communities, a Call for Justice." In *The State of Asian America: Activism and Resistance in the 1990s,* ed. Karin Aguilar–San Juan. Boston: South End Press.

Lorde, Audre. 1984. *Sister Outsider.* Freedom, Calif.: Crossing Press.

Lukas, J. Anthony. 1985. *Common Ground: A Turbulent Decade in the Lives of Three American Families.* New York: Alfred A. Knopf.

Lusane, Clarence. 1996. Foreword to *Beyond Identity Politics: Emerging Social Justice Movements in Communities of Color,* ed. John Anner. Boston: South End Press.

Malveaux, Julianne. 1985a. "The Economic Interests of Black and White Women: Are They Similar?" *Review of Black Political Economy* 14 (1): 5–27.

———. 1985b. "Comparable Worth and Its Impact on Black Women." *Review of Black Political Economy* 14 (2–3): 47–62.

Mantsios, Gregory, ed. 1998. *A New Labor Movement for the New Century.* New York: Monthly Review Press.

Marable, Manning. 1983. "A. Philip Randolph and the Foundations of Black American Socialism." In *Workers' Struggles, Past and Present: A "Radical America" Reader,* ed. James R. Green. Philadelphia: Temple University Press.

———. 1984. *Race, Reform, and Rebellion: The Second Reconstruction in Black America, 1945–1982.* Jackson: University Press of Mississippi.

———. 1997. "Black Leadership and the Labor Movement." In *Audacious Democracy: Labor, Intellectuals, and the Social Reconstruction of America,* ed. Steven Fraser and Joshua B. Freeman. Boston: Houghton Mifflin.

Martin, Biddy, and Chandra Talpade Mohanty. 1986. "Feminist Politics: What's Home Got to Do with It?" In *Feminist Studies–Critical Studies,* ed. Teresa de Lauretis. Bloomington: Indiana University Press.

Martin, Patricia Yancey. 1990. "Rethinking Feminist Organizations." *Gender and Society* 4 (2): 182–206.

May, Martha. 1985. "Bread before Roses: American Workingmen, Labor Unions, and the Family Wage." In *Women, Work, and Protest: A Century of U.S. Women's Labor History,* ed. Ruth Milkman. Boston: Routledge and Kegan Paul.

McAdam, Doug. 1982. *Political Process and the Development of Black Insurgency, 1930–1970.* Chicago: University of Chicago Press.

McAdam, Doug, John D. McCarthy, and Mayer N. Zald. 1996. "Introduction: Opportunities, Mobilizing Structures, and Framing Processes—toward a Synthetic, Comparative Perspective on Social Movements." In *Comparative Perspectives on Social Movements,* ed. Doug McAdam, John D. McCarthy, and Mayer N. Zald. New York: Cambridge University Press.

McCarthy, John D., and Mayer N. Zald. 1973. *The Trend of Social Movements in America: Professionalization and Resource Mobilization.* Morristown, N.J.: General Learning Press.

————. 1977. "Resource Mobilization and Social Movements: A Partial Theory." *American Journal of Sociology* 82: 1212–41.

McKay, Nellie Y. 1992. "Remembering Anita Hill and Clarence Thomas: What Really Happened When One Black Woman Spoke Out." In *Race-ing Justice, En-gendering Power: Essays on Anita Hill, Clarence Thomas, and the Construction of Social Reality,* ed. Toni Morrison. New York: Pantheon Books.

Melucci, Alberto. 1988. "Getting Involved: Identity and Mobilization in Social Movements." In *International Social Movement Research,* vol. 1, *From Structure to Action: Comparing Social Movement Research across Cultures,* ed. Bert Klandermans, Hanspeter Kriesi, and Sidney Tarrow. Greenwich, Conn.: JAI Press.

————. 1989. *Nomads of the Present: Social Movements and Individual Needs in Contemporary Society.* Philadelphia: Temple University Press.

————. 1994. "A Strange Kind of Newness: What's 'New' in New Social Movements?" In *New Social Movements: From Ideology to Identity,* ed. Enrique Laraña, Hank Johnston, and Joseph R. Gusfield. Philadelphia: Temple University Press.

————. 1995. "The Process of Collective Identity." In *Social Movements, Protest, and Contention,* ed. Hank Johnston and Bert Klandermans. Minneapolis: University of Minnesota Press.

Meyer, David S. 1999. "Tending the Vineyard: Cultivating Political Process Research." *Sociological Forum* 14 (1): 79–92.

Meyer, David S., and Sidney Tarrow, eds. 1998. *The Social Movement Society.* Lanham, Md.: Rowman and Littlefield.

Meyer, David S., and Nancy Whittier. 1994. "Social Movement Spillover." *Social Problems* 41: 277–98.

Midwest Center for Labor Research. 1993. "Building on Diversity: The New Unionism." *Labor Research Review* 20. Chicago: Midwest Center for Labor Research.

Milkman, Ruth. 1980. "Organizing the Sexual Division of Labor: Historical Perspectives on 'Women's Work' and the American Labor Movement." *Socialist Review* 49 (January–February): 95–147.

————. 1985. "Women Workers, Feminism, and the Labor Movement since the 1960s." In *Women, Work, and Protest: A Century of U.S. Women's Labor History,* ed. Ruth Milkman. Boston: Routledge and Kegan Paul.

————. 1987. *Gender at Work: The Dynamics of Job Segregation by Sex during World War II.* Chicago: University of Illinois Press.

———. 1990. "Gender and Trade Unionism in Historical Perspective." In
Women, Politics, and Change, ed. Louise A. Tilly and Patricia Gurin. New
York: Russell Sage Foundation.

———. 1993a. "New Research in Women's Labor History." *Signs* 18 (2): 376–88.

———. 1993b. "Organizing Immigrant Women in New York's Chinatown: An
Interview with Katie Quan." In *Women and Unions,* ed. Dorothy Sue Cobble.
Ithaca, N.Y.: ILR Press.

———. 1993c. "Union Responses to Workforce Feminization in the U.S." In
The Challenge of Restructuring: North American Labor Movements Respond, ed.
Jane Jenson and Rianne Mahon. Philadelphia: Temple University Press.

———. 1998. "The New Labor Movement: Possibilities and Limits."
Contemporary Sociology 27 (2).

Mink, Gwendolyn. 1999. *Whose Welfare?* Ithaca, N.Y.: Cornell University Press.

Mishel, Lawrence, Jared Bernstein, and John Schmitt. 1997. *The State of Working
America, 1996–97.* Economic Policy Institute. New York: M. E. Sharpe.

Moberg, David. 1997. "The Resurgence of American Unions: Small Steps, Long
Journey." *Working USA,* May–June, 20–31.

Mohanty, Chandra Talpade. 1991. "Cartographies of Struggle: Third World
Women and the Politics of Feminism." In *Third World Women and the Politics
of Feminism,* ed. Chandra Talpade Mohanty, Ann Russo, and Lourdes Torres.
Bloomington: Indiana University Press.

Monks, Dick. 1988. "Never Say Never," and "HUCTW Campaign Built on
Broad Support," *Labor Page,* May–June, 5.

Moody, Kim. 1988. *An Injury to All: The Decline of American Unionism.* New
York: Verso.

Moraga, Cherríe, and Gloria Anzaldúa, eds. 1983. *This Bridge Called My Back:
Writings by Radical Women of Color.* 2d ed. New York: Kitchen Table, Women
of Color Press.

Morris, Aldon D. 1984. *The Origins of the Civil Rights Movement: Black Communities Organizing for Change.* New York: Free Press.

———. 1992. "Political Consciousness and Collective Action." In *Frontiers in
Social Movement Theory,* ed. Aldon D. Morris and Carol McClurg Mueller.
New Haven: Yale University Press.

Morris, Aldon D., and Cedric Herring. 1987. "Theory and Research in Social
Movements: A Critical Review." *Annual Review of Political Science* 2: 137–98.

Morris, Aldon D., and Carol McClurg Mueller, eds. 1992. *Frontiers in Social
Movement Theory.* New Haven: Yale University Press.

Morrison, Toni, ed. 1992. *Race-ing Justice, En-gendering Power: Essays on Anita
Hill, Clarence Thomas, and the Construction of Social Reality.* New York:
Pantheon Books.

Moynihan, Daniel P. 1965. *The Negro Family: The Case for National Action.* Washington, D.C.: United States Department of Labor, Office of Policy Planning and Research.

Mueller, Carol McClurg. 1992. "Building Social Movement Theory." In *Frontiers in Social Movement Theory,* ed. Aldon D. Morris and Carol McClurg Mueller. New Haven: Yale University Press.

———. 1994. "Conflict Networks and the Origins of Women's Liberation." In *New Social Movements: From Ideology to Identity,* ed. Enrique Laraña, Hank Johnston, and Joseph R. Gusfield. Philadelphia: Temple University Press.

Murray, Pauli. 1972. "Jim Crow and Jane Crow." In *Black Women in White America: A Documentary History,* ed. Gerda Lerner. New York: Vintage Books.

Navarro, Vicente. 1992. "The Middle Class—a Useful Myth." *The Nation,* 23 March.

Needleman, Ruth. 1997. "Organizing Low-Wage Workers." *Working USA,* May–June, 45–59.

———. 1998a. "Building Relationships for the Long Haul: Unions and Community-Based Groups Working Together to Organize Low-Wage Workers." In *Organizing to Win: New Research on Union Strategies,* ed. Kate Bronfenbrenner, Sheldon Friedman, Richard W. Hurd, Ronald L. Seeber, and Rudolph A. Oswald. Ithaca, N.Y.: ILR Press.

———. 1998b. "Women Workers: Strategies for Inclusion and Rebuilding Unionism." In *A New Labor Movement for the New Century,* ed. Gregory Mantsios. New York: Monthly Review Press.

Ness, Immanuel. 1998. "Organizing Immigrant Communities: UNITE's Workers Center Strategy." In *Organizing to Win: New Research on Union Strategies,* ed. Kate Bronfenbrenner, Sheldon Friedman, Richard W. Hurd, Ronald L. Seeber, and Rudolph A. Oswald. Ithaca, N.Y.: ILR Press.

Ngai, Mae M. 1997. "Who Is an American Worker? Asian Immigrants, Race, and the National Boundaries of Class." In *Audacious Democracy: Labor, Intellectuals, and the Social Reconstruction of America,* ed. Steven Fraser and Joshua B. Freeman. Boston: Houghton Mifflin.

Olson, Mancur. 1965. *The Logic of Collective Action.* Cambridge: Harvard University Press.

Omi, Michael, and Howard Winant. 1986. *Racial Formation in the United States from the 1960s to the 1980s.* New York: Routledge and Kegan Paul.

Oppenheim, Lisa. 1991. "Women's Ways of Organizing: A Conversation with AFSCME Organizers Kris Rondeau and Gladys McKenzie." *Labor Research Review* 18: 45–59.

Parker, Pat. 1990. "For the white person who wants to know how to be my friend." In *Making Face, Making Soul/Haciendo Caras: Creative and Critical Perspectives by Feminists of Color,* ed. Gloria Anzaldúa. San Francisco: Aunt Lute Foundation Books.

Pichardo, Nelson A. 1997. "New Social Movements: A Critical Review." *Annual Review of Sociology* 23: 411–30.

Pinkney, Alphonso. 1976. *Red, Black, and Green: Black Nationalism in the United States.* New York: Cambridge University Press.

Polletta, Francesca. 1997. "Culture and Its Discontents: Recent Theorizing on the Cultural Dimensions of Protest." *Sociological Inquiry* 67 (4): 431–50.

Pollitt, Katha. 1998a. "Race and Gender and Class, Oh My!" *The Nation,* 8 June, 9.

———. 1998b. "Far from Chile?" *The Nation,* 27 July–3 August, 9.

Poore, Grace. 1995. *Voices Heard, Sisters Unseen.* New York: Women Make Movies.

Pratt, Minnie Bruce. 1984. "Identity: Skin Blood Heart." In *Yours in Struggle: Three Feminist Perspectives on Anti-Semitism and Racism,* ed. Elly Bulkin, Minnie Bruce Pratt, and Barbara Smith. Ithaca, N.Y.: Firebrand Books.

Puga, Ana. 1993. "Guinier Hints That Clinton Erred in Withdrawing Nomination." *Boston Globe,* 5 June, 3.

Rachleff, Peter. 2000. "They Say Give Back; We Say Fight Back." *Dollars and Sense,* September–October, 20.

Reagon, Bernice Johnson. 1992. "Coalition Politics: Turning the Century." In *Race, Class, and Gender: An Anthology,* ed. Margaret L. Andersen and Patricia Hill Collins. Belmont, Calif.: Wadsworth.

Reskin, Barbara, and Patricia Roos. 1990. *Job Queues, Gender Queues.* Philadelphia: Temple University Press.

Rich, Adrienne. 1984. "Heroines." In *The Fact of a Doorframe.* New York: W. W. Norton.

———. 1986. "Compulsory Heterosexuality and Lesbian Existence." In *Blood, Bread, and Poetry: Selected Prose, 1979–1985.* New York: W. W. Norton.

Robinson, Jo Ann Gibson. 1987. *The Montgomery Bus Boycott and the Women Who Started It.* Knoxville: University of Tennessee Press.

Robnett, Belinda. 1996. "African-American Women in the Civil Rights Movement, 1954–1965: Gender, Leadership, and Micromobilization." *American Journal of Sociology* 101 (6): 1661–93.

Rodríguez, Clara E. 1989. *Puerto Ricans: Born in the U.S.A.* Boston: Unwin Hyman.

Ruffin, Josephine St. Pierre. [1895] 1972. "Address to the First National Conference of Colored Women." In *Black Women in White America: A Documentary History,* ed. Gerda Lerner. New York: Vintage Books.

Ryan, Charlotte. 1991. *Prime Time Activism: Media Strategies for Grassroots Organizing.* Boston: South End Press.

———. 1992. "Finding HOME in the Media: How Print Media Covered Cuts in the Human Service Budget." Report for the HOME Coalition, Boston.

———. 1993. "A Study of National Public Radio." *Extra!* April–May, 18–26.

———. 2001. "The 1997 UPS Strike: Movement Building in the Media Arena." *Labor at the Crossroads Series.* University of Massachusetts Boston Labor Resource Center.

Ryan, Charlotte, Kevin Carragee, and William Meinhofer. 2001. "Framing, the News Media, and Collective Action." *Journal of Broadcast and Electronic Media* (spring).

Ryan, Charlotte, Kevin Carragee, and Cassie Schwerner. 1998. "Media, Movements, and the Quest for Social Justice." *Journal of Applied Communication Research* 26: 165–81.

Sacks, Karen. 1988a. *Caring by the Hour.* Urbana: University of Illinois Press.

———. 1988b. "Gender and Grassroots Leadership." In *Women and the Politics of Empowerment,* ed. Ann Bookman and Sandra Morgen. Philadelphia: Temple University Press.

———. 1990. "The Class Roots of Feminism." In *Issues in Feminism: An Introduction to Women's Studies,* ed. Sheila Ruth. 4th ed. Mountain View, Calif.: Mayfield.

Scagliotti, John, Janet Baus, and Dan Hunt. 1999. *After Stonewall.* Videocassette. New York: First Run Features.

Schlesinger, Arthur M., Jr. 1992. *The Disuniting of America.* New York: W. W. Norton.

Schwerner, Cassie. 1996. "Sing a Song of Justice: Identity Politics and the Struggle of Multicultural Organizing." Ph.D. diss., Boston College, Sociology Department.

Scott, Ellen K. 1998. "Creating Partnerships for Change: Alliances and Betrayals in the Racial Politics of Two Feminist Organizations." *Gender and Society* 12 (4): 400–423.

Seidman, Steven. 1996. "The Politics of Subverting Identity and Foregrounding the Social." In *Multicultural Experiences, Multicultural Theories,* ed. Mary F. Rogers. New York: McGraw-Hill.

———. 1998. *Contested Knowledge: Social Theory in the Postmodern Era.* 2d ed. Malden, Mass.: Blackwell.

Shanahan, Edward. 1988. "A Mother's Loyalty to Harvard Was Not Repaid." *Quincy Patriot Ledger,* June.

Smith, Barbara. 1993. "Where's the Revolution?" *The Nation,* 5 July, 12–16.

Snow, David A., and Robert D. Benford. 1988. "Ideology, Frame Resonance, and Participant Mobilization." In *International Social Movement Research,* vol. 1, *From Structure to Action: Comparing Social Movement Research across Cultures,* ed. Bert Klandermans, Hanspeter Kriesi, and Sidney Tarrow. Greenwich, Conn.: JAI Press.

———. 1992. "Master Frames and Cycles of Protest." In *Frontiers in Social Movement Theory,* ed. Aldon D. Morris and Carol Mueller. New Haven: Yale University Press.

Snow, David A., E. Burke Rochford Jr., Steven K. Worden, and Robert D. Benford. 1986. "Frame Alignment Processes, Micromobilization, and Movement Participation." *American Sociological Review* 51: 464–81.

Sotirin, Patricia, and Heidi Gottfried. 1996. "Resistance in the Workplace." In *Women and Work: A Reader,* ed. Paula J. Dubeck and Kathryn Borman. New Brunswick, N.J.: Rutgers University Press.

Spalter-Roth, Roberta, Heidi Hartmann, and Nancy Collins. 1994. "What Do Unions Do for Women?" In *Restoring the Promise of American Labor Law,* ed. Sheldon Friedman, Richard W. Hurd, Rudolph A. Oswald, and Ronald L. Seeber. Ithaca, N.Y.: ILR Press.

Spangler, Eve. 1986. *Lawyers for Hire: Salaried Professionals at Work.* New Haven: Yale University Press.

Spelman, Elizabeth V. 1988. *Inessential Woman: Problems of Exclusion in Feminist Thought.* Boston: Beacon Press.

Stack, Carol B. 1997. "Different Voices, Different Visions: Gender, Culture, and Moral Reasoning." In *Through the Prism of Difference: Readings on Sex and Gender,* ed. Maxine Baca Zinn, Pierrette Hondagneu-Sotelo, and Michael A. Messner. Needham Heights, Mass.: Allyn and Bacon.

Stafford, Walter W. 1985. *Closed Labor Markets: Underrepresentation of Blacks, Hispanics, and Women in New York City's Core Industries and Jobs.* New York: Community Service Society of New York.

Stall, Susan, and Randy Stoecker. 1998. "Community Organizing or Organizing Community? Gender and the Crafts of Empowerment." *Gender and Society* 12 (6): 729–56.

Stansell, Christine. 1992. "White Feminists and Black Realities: The Politics of Authenticity." In *Race-ing Justice, En-gendering Power: Essays on Anita Hill, Clarence Thomas, and the Construction of Social Reality,* ed. Toni Morrison. New York: Pantheon Books.

Steinberg, Ronnie J. 1990. "Radical Challenges in a Liberal World: The Mixed Success of Comparable Worth." In *Women, Class, and the Feminist Imagination: A Socialist-Feminist Reader,* ed. Karen V. Hansen and Ilene J. Philipson. Philadelphia: Temple University Press.

Steinberg, Ronnie J., and Lois Haignere. 1987. "Equitable Compensation: Methodological Criteria for Comparable Worth." In *Ingredients for Women's Employment Policy,* ed. Christine Bose and Glenna Spitze. Albany: State University of New York Press.

Stolzman, James, and Herbert Gamberg. 1973–1974. "Marxist Class Analysis versus Stratification Analysis as General Approaches to Social Inequality." *Berkeley Journal of Sociology* 18: 105–25.

Stout, Linda. 1996. *Bridging the Class Divide, and Other Lessons for Grassroots Organizing.* Boston: Beacon Press.

Strom, Sharon Hartman. 1985. "'We're No Kitty Foyles': Organizing Office Workers for the Congress of Industrial Organizations, 1937–1950." In *Women, Work, and Protest: A Century of U.S. Women's Labor History,* ed. Ruth Milkman. Boston: Routledge and Kegan Paul.

Tarrow, Sidney. 1992. "Mentalities, Political Cultures, and Collective Action Frames: Constructing Meanings through Action." In *Frontiers in Social Movement Theory,* ed. Aldon D. Morris and Carol Mueller. New Haven: Yale University Press.

———. 1997. "Cycles of Collective Action: Between Moments of Madness and the Repertoire of Contention." In *Social Movements: Readings on Their Emergence, Mobilization, and Dynamics,* ed. Doug McAdam and David A. Snow. Los Angeles: Roxbury.

Tatum, Beverly Daniel. 1997. *"Why Are All the Black Kids Sitting Together in the Cafeteria?" and Other Conversations about Race.* New York: Basic Books.

Taylor, Dorceta E. 1996. "Environmentalism and the Politics of Inclusion." In *Multicultural Experiences, Multicultural Theories,* ed. Mary F. Rogers. New York: McGraw-Hill.

Taylor, Verta. 1997. "Social Movement Continuity: The Women's Movement in Abeyance." In *Social Movements: Readings on Their Emergence, Mobilization, and Dynamics,* ed. Doug McAdam and David A. Snow. Los Angeles: Roxbury.

———. 1999. "Gender and Social Movements: Gender Processes in Women's Self-Help Movements." *Gender and Society* 13 (1): 8–33.

Taylor, Verta, and Nicole C. Raeburn. 1995. "Identity Politics as High-Risk Activism: Career Consequences for Lesbian, Gay, and Bisexual Sociologists." *Social Problems* 42 (2): 252–73.

Taylor, Verta, and Nancy E. Whittier. 1992. "Collective Identity in Social Movement Communities: Lesbian Feminist Mobilization." In *Frontiers in Social Movement Theory,* ed. Aldon D. Morris and Carol McClurg Mueller. New Haven: Yale University Press.

————. 1995. "Analytical Approaches to Social Movement Culture: The Culture of the Women's Movement." In *Social Movements and Culture*, ed. Hank Johnston and Bert Klandermans. Minneapolis: University of Minnesota Press.

————. 1998. "Guest Editors' Introduction: Special Issue on Gender and Social Movements, Part 1." *Gender and Society* 12 (6): 622–25.

————. 1999. "Guest Editors' Introduction: Special Issue on Gender and Social Movements, Part 2." *Gender and Society* 13 (1): 5–7.

Terborg-Penn, Rosalyn. 1985. "Survival Strategies among African-American Women Workers: A Continuing Process." In *Women, Work, and Protest: A Century of U.S. Women's Labor History*, ed. Ruth Milkman. Boston: Routledge and Kegan Paul.

Thompson, Becky W. 1997. "'A Way outa No Way': Eating Problems among African-American, Latina, and White Women." In *Through the Prism of Difference: Readings on Sex and Gender*, ed. Maxine Baca Zinn, Pierrette Hondagneau-Sotelo, and Michael A. Messner. Needham Heights, Mass.: Allyn and Bacon.

Thompson, Becky, and Sangeeta Tyagi. 1996. "Storytelling as Social Conscience: The Power of Autobiography." In *Names We Call Home: Autobiography of Racial Identity*, ed. Becky Thompson and Sangeeta Tyagi. New York: Routledge.

Tilly, Charles. 1978. *From Mobilization to Revolution*. Reading, Mass.: Addison-Wesley.

Useem, Bert. 1980. "Solidarity Model, Breakdown Model, and the Boston Anti-busing Movement." *American Sociological Review* 45: 357–69.

Vellela, Tony. 1988. *New Voices: Student Activism in the '80s and '90s*. Boston: South End Press.

Waters, Mary C. 1990. *Ethnic Options*. Berkeley: University of California Press.

Weinstein, Henry. 1988. "A Textbook Labor Union Campaign." *Los Angeles Times*, 17 May.

Weber, Lynn. 1995. "Symposium: On West and Fenstermaker's 'Doing Difference.'" *Gender and Society* 9 (4): 499–503.

West, Candace, and Sarah Fenstermaker. 1995. "Doing Difference." *Gender and Society* 9 (1): 8–37.

West, Cornel. 1988. *Prophetic Fragments*. Grand Rapids, Mich.: William B. Eerdmans.

————. 1992a. "Black Leadership and the Pitfalls of Racial Reasoning." In *Racing Justice, En-gendering Power: Essays on Anita Hill, Clarence Thomas, and the Construction of Social Reality*, ed. Toni Morrison. New York: Pantheon Books.

———. 1992b. "Diverse New World." In *Debating P.C.: The Controversy over Political Correctness on College Campuses,* ed. Paul Berman. New York: Dell.

———. 1993. *Race Matters.* Boston: Beacon Press.

———. 1996. "The New Cultural Politics of Difference." In *Multicultural Experiences, Multicultural Theories,* ed. Mary F. Rogers. New York: McGraw-Hill.

Whittier, Nancy. 1995. *Feminist Generations: The Persistence of the Radical Women's Movement.* Philadelphia: Temple University Press.

Wideman, John Edgar. 1992. "Writing in a Racialized Society." Address to PEN American Center Forum, New York, 14 May.

Willis, Paul. 1977. *Learning to Labor: How Working Class Kids Get Working Class Jobs.* New York: Columbia University Press.

Wilson, William Julius. 1978. *The Declining Significance of Race.* Chicago: University of Chicago Press.

———. 1987. *The Truly Disadvantaged: The Inner City, the Underclass, and Public Policy.* Chicago: University of Chicago Press.

Winant, Howard. 1990. "Postmodern Racial Politics in the United States: Difference and Inequality." *Socialist Review* 90 (1): 121–47.

———. 1994. *Racial Conditions.* Minneapolis: University of Minnesota Press.

Wright, Erik Olin. 1980a. "Class and Occupation." *Theory and Society* 9 (3): 177–214.

———. 1980b. "Varieties of Marxist Conceptions of Class Structure." *Politics and Society* 9 (3): 299–322.

Wright, Erik Olin, and Joel Rogers. 1987. "Marxist Social Science." Syllabus, University of California–Berkeley.

Wright, Erik Olin, and Joachim Singelmann. 1982. "Proletarianization in the American Class Structure." Supplement to the *American Journal of Sociology* 88: 177–209.

Yamato, Gloria. 1990. "Something about the Subject Makes It Hard to Name." In *Making Face, Making Soul/Haciendo Caras,* ed. Gloria Anzaldúa. San Francisco: Aunt Lute Foundation Books.

Yates, Michael D. 1998. *Why Unions Matter.* New York: Monthly Review Press.

Zavella, Patricia. 1988. "The Politics of Race and Gender: Organizing Chicana Cannery Workers in Northern California." In *Women and the Politics of Empowerment,* ed. Ann Bookman and Sandra Morgen. Philadelphia: Temple University Press.

Index

Abernathy, Rev. Ralph, 149, 157, 196
Affirmative Action Committee (at
  Columbia), 88
AFL. *See* American Federation of Labor
AFL-CIO (American Federation of
  Labor/Congress of Industrial
  Organizations), 44, 63, 182; merger
  (1955), 53
African American clergy, 155, 157
African American women: autonomous
  organizations of, 31, 50–51; in
  CLUW, 63, 193; in Columbia
  clerical union, 178, 181; and
  comparable worth, 97; defining
  identity, 111–12; at Duke
  University, 246n. 23; erasing
  experience of, 32; establish own
  organizations, 48; and feminism,
  111–12, 138–41; hospital workers,
  57; in ILGWU, 51; in labor
  market, 5–6, 189–90; as leaders in
  Columbia clerical union, 101, 197;
  organizing washerwomen, domestics, and cooks (Atlanta), 48; in

public-sector organizing, 54–55;
  subordination in race-based
  movements, 31; tobacco workers,
  51; at Yale, 153. *See also* women of
  color
African American workers: and the
  AFL, 48; AFSCME sanitation
  workers, 54; challenge labor's
  exclusionary practices, 48; in CIO,
  52–53; and Columbia clerical
  workers' demands, 87–90; on
  Columbia University's negotiating
  committee, 104; community
  responses to racist exclusion, 53;
  culture of Columbia clerical union,
  99; in hospitals, 56–57; in
  industrial unions, 52; in labor
  movement, 45, 252n. 28; men as
  clerical workers, 34; naming, 224n.
  7; segregated work areas of (at
  Columbia), 117–19; in trade union
  caucuses, 53; at Yale, 152–53, 156,
  168–69. *See also* African American
  women

Sharon Kurtz is associate professor of sociology at Suffolk University in Boston. She worked for many years as a union organizer in Boston area hospitals, where she was a clerical worker, and also as a community organizer for housing, welfare, and antiracist issues.